Hamlin Garland
● OSAGE

WAUKON

● Marjorie Medary

~N CITY
~dith Willson
~ Yoseloff

● NASHUA
Charlton Laird

Bess Streeter Aldrich
R. V. Cassill
James Hearst
● CEDAR FALLS   Mona Van Duyn
● WATERLOO

● STEAMBOAT ROCK
Herbert Quick

DUBUQUE
Richard Bissell ●
Rt. Rev. Mathias M. Hoffman
Karlton Kelm

Margaret Wilson
TRAER

Jay G. Sigmund ●
WAUBEEK ●

Paul Engle
Alice Ilgenfritz Jones
(Ferris Jerome)   Elizabeth Ford
CEDAR RAPIDS ●   Clyde Tull
Steven Dow Mossman   ● MOUNT VERNON
Carl Van Vechten
Grant Wood

John Scholl
● MAQUOKETA

George Cram Cook
Floyd Dell
Arthur Davison Ficke
Alice French (Octave Thanet)
Susan Glaspell
Hiram Alvin Reid
● DAVENPORT

● NEWTON
Emerson Hough

IOWA CITY
Edwin Ford Piper
Roger S. Sergel
Carroll Coleman

Cyrenus Cole
● PELLA   ● WHAT CHEER

Samuel Hawkins Marshall Byers
● OSKALOOSA

MUSCATINE
Ellis Parker Butler

~OXVILLE
~arles Tenney Jackson

SIGOURNEY
● Dale Kramer

● ALBIA
James F. Stevens

Phil Stong
KEOSAUQUA

Robert Jones Burdette
BURLINGTON ●

"PITTSVILLE"●

KEOKUK
Calvin Kentfield

N

A Literary History of Iowa

Clarence A. Andrews

A
LITERARY
HISTORY
of
IOWA

 UNIVERSITY OF IOWA PRESS
IOWA CITY 1972

PS 283
I8 A8

Library of Congress Catalog Card Number: 72–76304
University of Iowa Press, Iowa City 52240
© *1972 by The University of Iowa. All rights reserved*
Printed in the United States of America
ISBN 87745–032–3

This Book is Dedicated To

JOHN TOWNER FREDERICK

Iowan, editor, author, teacher,

scholar, critic, and gentle man

Contents

Introduction

THIS is a history of Iowa novels, short stories, poetry, and plays; it is also about the men and women who wrote them, and the degree of critical esteem which they received. The criteria which have been applied to the selection of materials discussed in this history are:

They must have an Iowa setting; the author must have lived in Iowa long enough to know the subject about which he was writing; the material must be primarily of interest to those of high school age and beyond; the material must have been published in book form or contained in an anthology, or have some other major production format. If the author were born in Iowa, then he must have lived in the state until maturity. If he came to Iowa in later life, then he must have been in the state long enough to write with authority about his subject. There are some exceptions to these criteria, but the reader will understand why they were made when he comes to them.

As much as possible, the literary materials and the authors have been put in an historical and social context. For the reader who wishes to become an expert, the sources on which this history is based have been carefully identified—the literary works themselves, the biographies and autobiographies, the critical reviews, the newspaper and magazine accounts.

What is the value of Iowa literature? Frank Luther Mott, a native of What Cheer, Iowa, and a Pulitzer Prize winner, wrote that in Iowa literature, one finds the Iowa pioneer

. . . arrived with all his train in the realm of Romance. His prairie schooner drawn by oxen, his log-cabin, his claim, his prairie of a thousand variable charms, his founding of government and schools and churches, his "bees," his hunting—all these, because we are proud of the courage and hardihood of our grandfathers and grandmothers, and a little proud of ourselves for having descended from them . . . .[1]

To which John Towner Frederick, native of Corning, Iowa, adds this second:

From the days of Hamlin Garland and Octave Thanet to those of Martin Yoseloff [and Julie McDonald] stretch more than fifty years of effort, by a score of competent writers, to record the life of Iowa [farms], towns and cities in fiction. Major aspects of our Iowa life—the relation between town and farm, between rich and poor, between tradition and innovation—have been explored sensitively and illuminated thoughtfully. The significant tensions resulting from economic changes have been faithfully reflected in the dramatic terms of family fortunes and personal problems. It is clear that this body of fiction has unique and lasting value as social history to the people of the state. In its variety, its concreteness, its insight, it can never be matched by formal chronicle or scholarly history. Without it our cultural heritage, our understanding of the present, and our appreciation of the past would be immeasurably impoverished.[2]

I hope this history will be used and enjoyed, for I have enjoyed producing it. I was born and reared in Iowa, educated in its public schools, and in its University of Iowa, where since I have taught. More than that, I know its every corner, and many of the writers discussed here. I have lived in the twin cities of Waterloo and Cedar Falls, in Mason City, Cedar Rapids, Iowa City, Ottumwa, and in the northwestern cities of Sioux City and Sheldon. A long time ago, I learned to love this state's native literature, and if I have any regret it is that I have not contributed to it.

For all that, this book could not have been written without the advice or help of John C. Gerber, who first showed me the possibilities, and of John T. Frederick who exemplified them; of Francis Paluka in the Special Collections area of The University of Iowa Libraries who did me an infinite number of kindnesses with equal patience; of Ada Stoflet, Reference Librarian at the University Library (whose mother was my fifth-grade teacher at old Taylor School in Cedar Rapids); of Dale Bentz and Frank Hanlin of The University of Iowa Library; of all those other fine people at the University Library who answered questions, located materials, made Xerox copies, checked out books, and in other ways put up with me; of the numerous students on whom I have tried out much of

---

1   Frank Luther Mott, "Exponents of the Pioneers," *Palimpsest* 11 (February 1930):62.
2   John T. Frederick, "Town and City in Iowa Fiction," *Palimpsest* 35 (February 1954):95.

this material; of my wife Ollie and my daughter Terry, who not only put up with me and my endless demands, but also assisted in the numerous chores which accompany the production of a book such as this one.

Bibliography

PERTINENT source materials for each chapter are given at the back of the book. Additional items are given in footnotes; others are cross-referenced in the text. The following is a general bibliography of source materials:

Brigham, Johnson, ed. *A Book of Iowa Authors by Iowa Authors*. Des Moines, Iowa: Iowa State Teachers Association, 1930. (Cited as *Iowa Authors* in the text.) Essays by Iowa authors about Iowa writers of the period 1890–1930. Informative but by no means definitive.

The Midland Monthly. Des Moines, Iowa: 1894–99. This first serious attempt to publish the poetry and prose of Iowa authors contains much information about Iowa writers of the 1890s. (It is not to be confused with *The Midland*, published under the editorship of John T. Frederick at Iowa City and Chicago from 1915 through the early 1930s.) For an account of this monthly periodical, see Luella M. Wright, "The Midland Monthly," *Iowa Journal of History and Politics*, 45 (January 1947).

Earley, Jane F. "Iowa Authors: A Bibliography of Published Works 1917–1940." Honors thesis, Coe College, Cedar Rapids, Iowa, 1961. An extensive but not exhaustive bibliography of books, articles, and stories by Iowa writers. Copies are available for inspection at the Coe College Library and the University of Iowa Library.

Gohdes, C. L. F. *Literature and Theater of the United States and Regions of the United States*. Durham, N. C.: Duke University Press, 1967.

Longmire, Rowena. *Dictionary Catalogue of the Short Stories of Arkansas, Missouri, and Iowa from 1869 to 1900*. Ph.D. dissertation, University of Chicago, 1932. Contains some inaccuracies. The Longmire and Gohdes volumes are useful in helping to place Iowa literature in larger contexts, but neither covers the Iowa field well for our purposes. There is room for many doctoral, master's, and honors essays in the area of Iowa literature—bibliography, criticism, biography, history—and a great deal remains to be done.

Marple, Alice. *Iowa Authors and Their Works: A Contribution Toward a Bibliography*. Des Moines, Iowa: Historical Department of Iowa, 1918. An extensive bibliography from the beginnings of Iowa history to date of publication, and goes far beyond mere interest in *belles-lettres*.

Palimpsest. Iowa City, Iowa: State Historical Society of Iowa, 1920 to date. Although primarily a popular journal of all phases of Iowa history, it has published some scholarly articles by and about Iowa authors. See particularly these essays by John T. Frederick: "The Farm in Iowa Fiction" 32 (March 1951); "Town and City in Iowa Fiction" 35 (February 1954); "Early Iowa in Fiction" 36 (October 1955).

Paluka, Frank. *Iowa Authors: A Bio-Bibliography of Sixty Native Writers*. Iowa City, Iowa; Friends of The University of Iowa Libraries, 1967. This volume updates Marple and Earley, and, within its limits, is a most useful volume. Paluka defines the Iowa Author as one who was born in Iowa, and does not limit his list to authors of *belles-lettres*. He also requires substantial publication. (Cited as *Paluka* in the text.)

Parvin, T. S. "List of Iowa Authors." Cedar Rapids, Iowa: Iowa Masonic Library (April 10, 1890). This list (which includes Mark Twain!) refers to another list published "early in March," and suggests the possibility of further information in "Annual Reports."

Petersen, William J. *Iowa History Reference Guide*. Iowa City, Iowa: State Historical Society of Iowa, 1952. (Cited as *Petersen* in the text.) On pages 126–31 and page 133 there are references to authors and literary materials. The "Printing and Publishing" section, pages 140–43, may also be of interest.

Prairie Gold. Chicago: Reilly & Britton Co., 1917. This volume owes its existence to the patriotic fervor of World War I. It contains a few good things: an essay by Johnson Brigham, "Iowa as a Literary Field," and a story "Bread," by Ellis Parker Butler. It is most interesting as a catalog of Iowa literary people of that period.

Books at Iowa. Iowa City, Iowa: Friends of The University of Iowa Libraries, 1964 to date. Published semiannually. Contains a number of essays about Iowa authors and allied subjects.

The Iowan. Shenandoah, Iowa, 1952 to date. A periodical which has published a number of essays about Iowa writers, and a great deal of useful background material.

Tanselle, G. Thomas. *Guide to the Study of United States Imprints*. 2 vols. Cambridge: Harvard University Press, Belknap Press, 1971. Contains a listing of all known bibliographies of Iowa authors to date, and a listing of bibliographical information about Iowa private and public presses.

In addition, there is a wealth of materials in the several public and private libraries in the state—letters, newspaper clippings, locally-published brochures, catalogs, pamphlets, booklets, books, etc. There is also material in private collections. The literary remains of many Iowa authors are in depositories outside of Iowa. Iowa depositories include The University of Iowa Library's Iowa Authors Collection, the Iowa Masonic Library at Cedar Rapids, The Davenport Public Museum, the State Historical Society Library in Iowa City, and the State Department of History and Archives in Des Moines. The Phil Stong papers are at Drake University. There are also materials in other college and university libraries in the state, and at many city and county libraries and museums.

Acknowledgments

The author gratefully acknowledges permission from the following persons and publishers to quote from copyrighted material (additional credits may be found in specific citations):

Constance Garland Doyle and Isabel Garland Lord: Hamlin Garland's *My Friendly Contemporaries* and *Roadside Meetings*. The Macmillan Company: *A Son of the Middle Border*, copyright 1917 by Hamlin Garland, renewed 1945 by Mary I. Lord and Constance G. Williams. Excerpt, "Sacrifice of the Old Gentlemen," copyright 1959 by Joseph Langland, from the book, *Wheel of Summer*, by Joseph Langland, The Dial Press; originally appeared in *Poetry Northwest*. Harold Matson Company, Inc.: Phil Stong, *Hawkeyes*, copyright 1940 by Dodd, Mead & Company, Inc., renewed 1968; *Buckskin Breeches*, copyright 1937 by Phil Stong, renewed 1964; *State Fair*, copyright 1932 by Phil Stong, renewed 1959; *The Long Lane*, copyright 1939 by Phil Stong, renewed 1966; *The Rebellion of Lennie Barlow*, copyright 1937 by Phil Stong, renewed 1965. *If School Keeps*, copyright 1940 by Phil Stong, renewed 1967 by Virginia Stong; reprinted by permission of Harold Matson Co., Inc. Excerpt, *Ivanhoe Keeler*, by Phil Stong, Holt, Rinehart and Winston, Inc., copyright 1939, renewed 1967. *The Middle Western Farm Novel in the Twentieth Century*, by Roy W. Meyer, copyright 1965 by the University of Nebraska Press. "Oh Dear God, Oh Dear All," by Stanley Kauffman, *The New Republic*, copyright 1961, Harrison-Blaine of New Jersey, Inc. "Christmas in Iowa," by Phil Stong, special permission of *Holiday*, copyright 1952 by the Curtis Publishing Company. Excerpt, letters of Alice French to Richard Watson Gilder, July 15, 1888, and August 23, 1888, by permission of the Manuscript Division, The New York Public Library, Astor, Lenox and Tilden Foundations. Excerpt, Frederick Feikema Manfred's Letter to the Editor, May 3, 1952, *Publishers' Weekly*, R. R. Bowker Company, a Xerox Company, copyright 1952 by Xerox Corporation. The Bobbs-Merrill Company, Inc.: *Vandemark's Folly*, copyright 1922 by Herbert Quick; *The Hawkeye*, copyright 1923 by Herbert Quick. Excerpt, letter from Carl Van Vechten to Arthur Davison Ficke, August 19, 1937, by permission of Donald Gallup, Literary Trustee for the late Carl Van Vechten, and Curator, Collection of American Literature, Yale University Library, and by permission of Mrs. Arthur Davison Ficke. "Farm Life Fiction Reaches Maturity," by Caroline Sherman, first printed by The University of the South in *The Sewanee Review*, XXXIX, October-December 1931. Excerpts, *Sacred and Profane Memories*, copyright 1918 by Carl Van Vechten, reprinted 1971 by arrangement with Alfred A. Knopf, Inc. Allan G. Bogue, *From Prairie to Corn Belt*, copyright 1963 by the University of Chicago Press. Excerpt, *To See, To Take*, Atheneum, 1970, copyright Mona Van Duyn.

Poet on the Prairie

IOWA became a territory in 1838 and a state in 1846. But Iowa's first newspaper, the *Dubuque Visitor*, had begun in 1836, and by the following year there were presses at Burlington and Davenport. These early newspapers published occasional fiction and verse, some of it, written by Eastern writers, showing up in the "boilerplate" which was a staple of many newspapers of those times. The first issue of the *Iowa City Argus* on Saturday, July 31, 1841, for instance, "featured a sentimental poem and a romantic story."[1]

The first Iowa literary work was *The Heart Lace and Other Poems*, published on or after October 10, 1856, by A. P. Luse and Company of Davenport. Its author, Hiram Alvin Reid, claimed then and later that the ninety-six pages, three by five inches, constituted "the first volume of poems ever published in the State of Iowa."[2] He was as brash a young man as his volume demonstrates, but so far no one has refuted his claim.

Reid's brashness led him to include a "Personal Narrative" of ten pages. This "Narrative" has more of the quality of an apologia than of a biography. Reid does report, however, that he was born in a log cabin near New-Lisbon, Ohio, in 1834; he was orphaned by the death of his father and his mother when he was one year old; thereafter, he eked out a rather precarious existence as a "jour. printer." He wandered from Ohio to Boston to New Orleans, working at his trade as he might, and publishing three "miniatures" or small volumes of verse, none of which seem to be extant. He describes his method of publication in an 1854 diary. In exchange for the labor of redistributing pages of pi'd type (type accidentally spilled) at night in his room, he was allowed to use the type

---

1 *Iowa*, A Catalog of the Iowa Centennial Exhibition at the Library of Congress, December 28, 1946–April 27, 1947, item 405, p. 61. This catalog lists many of the Iowa imprints and artifacts held by the Library of Congress at that time. There is a facsimile page from Hiram Alvin Reid's *The Heart Lace and Other Poems*. A copy of the book is in the Library of Congress and another at the Davenport Public Museum. Special Collections of the University of Iowa Library has facsimiles.
2 *The Heart Lace and Other Poems*, "Preface" (n.p.n.); *History of Pasadena* (Pasadena, Calif.: 1895), p. 225.

in printing pages of his verse. In spite of the fact that one employer told him he was on a wild goose chase, he continued the arduous labor of publishing his verse:

> I am a Poet because I can't help it. I have several times tried to stop up the spring with plugs of mammon; but the stoppage caused a benumbing pressure within my mind for a while, and then burst forth again with added violence, till finally I gave it full vent and I was happy. Its impulsive flow has swept me into the great sea of letters, and thus I launched this paper boat to ride to glory in—or rather to send word that I am coming. [P. 11]

In 1855, after completing a poetic drama on Benedict Arnold, he moved to Davenport to work for the *Davenport Courier*. During the winter he wrote verse and read some of it to the "Young Men's Literary Association"; he "studied out the origin, history and 'language' of upwards of three hundred names of women"; and he gave a lecture on this subject on Wednesday evening, March 26 "at the Congregational Church, to a very slim audience."

In 1856, aside from his duties on a "Twin Cities Directory" and in a "Museum Ice Cream Saloon" (the latter in partnership with a brother), he printed a "smutty little sheet" (the description comes from his detractors), called the *Chip Basket*. The September 13 issue announced his forthcoming volume of verse, with all profits accruing to "the Library Fund of the Young Men's Literary Association," according to the preface of the work.

Reid's volume is indeed a slight vessel to launch Iowa literature on the sea of English letters. Its sole merit today lies in its primacy and in its pictures of Davenport and the Mississippi. The verse is, despite the obvious Romantic leanings of the author, in the tradition of eighteenth century neo-classical verse; rhymes, meters, images, and style are weak imitations of the earlier period. The images are the worn-out clichés of poetic diction. Despite Reid's penchant for the direct statement in prose, the lines are tortured and often vague, and the rhymes are frequently forced. None of the verse would indicate that Reid had any great future as a poet.

Heart Lace is dedicated to "Davenport, Queen of the Beautiful Land" and "all her Sons and Daughters." Following an over-sentimentalized title poem which is dedicated to a foster mother, there are several "Songs of Nature," including "Mississippi":

> Mississippi, Father of Waters!
> Itasca, rice-crowned Naiad of the North
> Makes errant pilgrimage to the far Belize —
> That gate where freshness goeth out forever.

It must have taken a mighty leap of Reid's fancy to conceive that the Mississippi, by whatever "errant pilgrimage" might reach Belize, on the far side of the Gulf of Mexico!

Here is a sample of "Davenport":

. . . .

> The prairie mantle of the Western World . . .
> In state of moving majesty sublime,
> A caravan of waters, yielding grace
> To the curt and waspish usages of trade;—
> Let pedantry declare the storied Nile,
> But humbler song may kiss thee, and drink in
> Profounder inspiration from thy purer spring.
> — Channel of wealth, no less than water course,
> Where floweth millions, — walking up and down,
> In all their pride of bearing and huge tread,
> Giants, heavy-breathing with their freighted toil —
> Or palaces that beggar Babylon
> Glide life-like, queenly ministers of travel.

Occasionally, a moral note is embedded in this bombast:

> Davenport, queen of the 'beautiful land!'
> Ignorance looketh unto thee for light, —
> And Misery, that haggard child of Rum,
> Stretches out her arms to thee, crying "Save!"
> . . . Rural grace
> So apt adorning thy commercial pride,
> Gives thee queenly state imperial; and thou,
> Queen City of the West of future years,
> Drawest tribute from all the Eastern land.

Some fifty lines describe "The Mississippi Railroad Bridge":

> Thou newest wonder of constructive skill,
> Mortal tongue hath scarcely words profound
> Of depth and big meaning to speak thy state;
> Least not sublime the Red Man's solemn "ugh!"
> Spake of thee, whiles wrapped in dumb amaze
> His keen eye traced thy parts. . . .

A raft of logs from the forests of the north finds the bridge in its way:

> —Like coarse artillery in platoons ranked,
> Creeping 'gainst a stronghold, rafts slide down

> The errant current of their stealth, and strike!
> Now log on log in wild upheave convolves,
> Crashing as embattled ships—whiles disrupt
> Each headlong plunges furiously, to retreat
> Th' unwont encounter! and thy quick bones shake
> With laughing at o'erwhelmed temerity.

An "Unfinished Poem," labeled "Iowa," is the first poetic tribute to the state:

> . . . And IOWA, full robed in queenly grace,
> Majestic mantled in her pride of place,
> Stoops to smile on cultivated thought: —
> Where prairie maids have a garden spot.

Two years later (1858), Reid published his final book of verse—this small volume was the second book of verse published in Iowa. The "Author's Preface" to *Harp of the West; A Poem, in Five Parts* supplies data on his four earlier volumes. One had been published in Ohio, and one in Boston during a stay there. He notes that he was given the privilege (like Hamlin Garland a few years later) of reading in the Boston Public Library. Half of the fifty-odd pages contain the title poem's five parts:

> Presumptuous pride in our own parent East
> Holds us in kindred but of man the beast;
> 'Tis false! the West's o'erteeming tilth of mind
> Already leaves the worn-out East behind:
> We number men of learning most profound —
> Science and letters all-brain-volumed, bound;
> We number men, devotional and brave
> To search out sin, its victim souls to save!
> We number Artists, in each various line,
> Worthy the laurels of the Classic Nine:
> We number minds that star out from their slough,
> And hosts of genius in the native rough . . . .

The pride in the developing city is obvious but not supported by fact. In the five years just before these lines were written, the "worn-out East" had produced five of the major literary works of America. On the other hand, a history of early Davenport (which fails to mention Reid, though it notes the *Chip Basket*) is able to point to only a few clerics as its representative writers.

It is unfortunate, perhaps, that Reid tried to pour the new wine of the Middle West into the old bottles of genre and style which the "worn-out

East" had already forsaken. Yet there is nothing in the range of talent exhibited to suggest that he might have done better had he followed Emerson's advice and looked for new metres.

Thus apparently ended Reid's poetic career. He seems to have found the waters of poesy too rough and his ship too fragile. But he did continue writing. In 1895 he published a well-known *History of Pasadena*. In this volume (in a section labeled "Brains"), he reports that he had written histories of Missouri; Johnson County, Iowa; and Montgomery County, Iowa. (The 1883 history of Johnson County contains no reference to its author.) By this time, Reid had acquired the titles "A.M." and "M.D.," and a wife who he notes was "among the first twelve women ever graduated from medical college in the United States."

POSTSCRIPT

In that same year of 1856, Rebecca Harrington Smith, who had recently moved to Farmington, Iowa, from Louisville, Kentucky, published a novel *Emma Bartlett, or Prejudice and Fanaticism*. Miss Smith, who sometimes used the name "R. H. Smith," and who signed her "Letters from a Prairie Cottage" as "Kate Harrington," was born in Alleghany City, Pennsylvania, on September 20, 1831. Her "Letters" were contributed to the Louisville *Journal* while she lived in Kentucky.

Although the editor of the Keokuk *Des Moines Valley Whig* called it "an Iowa book . . . the first of a purely literary character, of any particular pretensions," *Emma Bartlett* is an Iowa book only in the sense that its author was living in Iowa at the time of publication. The book is a response to Harriet Beecher Stowe's *Uncle Tom's Cabin*, exposing "the hypocrisy of Know-Nothingism and the dogmatism of Abolitionism," and its subject is not expressly related to Iowa.[3]

---

3 Marie Haefner, "Kate Harrington: An American Lady," *Palimpsest* 38 (April 1957):159-65.

Indians and Pioneers

THE first settlers in Iowa seem to have had little time for fiction and verse. Almost all of the *belles-lettristic* material concerned with Indian and pioneer life has been written by Iowans who lived after the pioneer era had passed into history.

The criteria used for the selection of literature for this period of Iowa history were set up by John T. Frederick:

The writers who have sought to recreate for their readers the Iowa frontier and the experience of the men and women who knew and lived it . . . faced problems different from those encountered by [other Iowa] writers. The fiction of Iowa farm life and of the life of Iowa towns and cities has been built for the most part on the personal experience of the writers — as in Ruth Suckow's *New Hope* and Ellis Parker Butler's *Dominie Dean;* or on family background and tradition, as in Wilson's *The Able McLaughlins* and Quick's *Vandemark's Folly.* Such substance, intimately and immediately known, is not available to the novelist who wishes to portray the fur trade or the Black Hawk War, the explorations of Zebulon Pike or the founding of Fort Des Moines. He must turn to documentary and secondary sources: the journals and letters of travelers, old newspaper files, the few remaining and scattered records of the fur trade and of military operations. His material is rich, colorful, exciting; but he must come to command it by research and study; he must be a scholar as well as a creative writer. Only when he has mastered his material, has come to know it so well that it is real and intense as imaginative experience, can he hope to share its richness with his reader in fiction that is absorbing and convincing. When such mastery of material is matched by effective storytelling, we have good fiction of earliest Iowa.

Moreover, added Professor Frederick, the writer who was to address himself to fiction of Indian life faced an additional problem:

The most stringent demand upon the writer who attempts to deal with that conflict of cultures which was a major aspect of the Westward Movement is that he shall understand the Indian mind. Without knowledge of how the Indians thought, and of the whole complex of religious belief, tradition, folklore, custom, and attitudes within which and according to which they lived, it is impossible for the writer to make of his Indians more than wooden figures, mechanically contrived and operated. A writer grows up with this necessary basic background for understanding the conduct of white men. If he fails to make the actions of his white characters convincing, the fault is usually one of technical incompetence or of sheer carelessness. It is not so for Indian characters. At best a modern writer's comprehension of the old world of the Indians can be but partial. Only by extended and patient study, by a sincere will to understand implemented by earnest effort, can he enter that world at all.[1]

It is to the credit of many Iowa writers that they have made that "extended and patient study," and with rather good results.

If we take the novels and verse about Indians and pioneers chronologically according to subject matter and *not* according to date of publication, we come first to Frederick Manfred's *Conquering Horse* (1959). The time of the book coincides with the coming of "men who are born with white paint on their faces and who come from the east" (p. 16). This reference is probably to the actual establishment of a small temporary trading post in what is now northeast Nebraska. However, no white men appear in the novel.

The setting of *Conquering Horse* is partially in what is now northwest Iowa, partially in South Dakota, Minnesota, and Nebraska. Manfred gave the name "Siouxland" to this four-state geographical area, centered on his hometown of Doon, Iowa.

Conquering Horse is the story of the initiation rite of a Sioux Indian boy, No Name, of his love for the girl, Leaf, of his rivalry with Circling Hawk for Leaf's hand, of his trials in enemy (Pawnee) country as he seeks to recover Leaf (who has been kidnapped by the Pawnees), and of his efforts to achieve the vision which will make it possible for him to replace his father as chief of the tribe.

Critics liked Manfred's ability to capture the essence of the open land and the vagaries of wind and weather. They praised his use of the "Sioux folklore and folkways." They especially felt that Conquering Horse was presented as a "real Indian youth" whose vision enabled him to see the life around him and in him as "one huge flow, with himself a streaming part of it."[2]

Paul Engle wondered whether any white writer would ever penetrate the Indian mind, although he stated that Manfred had achieved a credible "image" of it. He quoted as evidence this passage describing the end

1 John T. Frederick, "An Introductory Note," "Black Hawk and the White Men," and "Infant Iowa," *Palimpsest* 36 (October 1955):389–90, 393.
2 Walter Havighurst, *New York Herald Tribune Book Review*, July 5, 1959, p. 5.

of No Name's sun dance in the course of which thongs tied through bleeding slits on his chest have been jerked out:

No Name lay unconscious. The bleeding slits on his chest lay open and swollen as if they had just given birth to puppies. Sweat coursing down his chest caused the painted red sun to run. But the painted mare on his right cheek and the painted stallion on his left cheek remained as vividly white as when first put on. As his face convulsed, the two painted horses struggled to be released so that they might strike each other. [P. 122]

Yet Engle did not think the book had been entirely successful. It did have some "overromantic moments."[3]

Of the somewhat later period when the men with "white paint on their faces" came from the East into the Wisconsin and Iowa territories, there are a dozen or so novels by Iowa writers, based on the conflicts between white and red men and the problems of the first white settlers on the Indian lands. The Iowa writer is at some disadvantage here; there are no heroic or colorful types in Iowa history, no Davy Crocketts, Daniel Boones, Paul Bunyans. There were relatively few battles with the Indians, and, other than the Mormon trek across southern Iowa (of which as yet no Iowa writer has made fictional use), there were no major cross-country movements through Iowa; most of the great westward movements began further south to take advantage of the earlier spring season and the westward direction of the Missouri and Platte rivers.

Two Indian names stand out in this period. One was Keokuk whose memory remains in the names of an Iowa city and county. The other was Black Hawk. In the former there has been very little fictional interest. The latter has attracted one Iowa novelist. Charlton Laird has written clearly, completely and objectively about the man whose capitulation opened Iowa to settlement.

Professor Laird was born in Nashua in 1901, and spent his boyhood among the bluffs of the Mississippi near McGregor, where his father, who was a lumberman, owned a large tract of timberland. Thus he early became familiar with the territory which he was to use as the setting for his novels.

Laird graduated from McGregor High School, taught for a time in rural Iowa schools, then enrolled at the University of Iowa where he earned both bachelor's and master's degrees. His master's thesis, *Legends of Iowa Treasure*, was written under the direction of Edwin Ford Piper. After graduation he taught at Drake University and wrote several feature articles for Des Moines periodicals. The Doctor of Philosophy de-

---

3. Paul Engle, *New York Times Book Review*, June 28, 1959, p. 4.

gree, based on his study in the early 1930s of Anglo-Norman manuscripts in Europe, was awarded by Stanford University in 1940. Since that time Professor Laird has taught at universities in the west; his most recent appointment is at the University of Nevada.

Laird was well qualified for the "extended and patient study" which Frederick specified. One result of his diligence, and of his interest in language as well, is seen in *Thunder on the River* (1949)—Laird's novel about Black Hawk. Captain Brevaut, the trader, is attempting to educate Mark Eldridge on the complexities of Sauk "grammaire":

"You have these word, *u-sawa*. So. You have him, Monsieur. He mean, *peutetre* — slowly going." He started to hobble. "So now I am *u-sawa*." Then he started faster, stumping back and forth across the floor. "But now, Monsieur, I am *pai-ya-tu-sawa*." He stopped and started again. "And now, Monsieur, I am *ah-pemi-wa-pu-sawach*. . . ." Mark learned eventually that his tutor was trying to distinguish *he moves, he is walking along*, and *now he is walking along though before he was not*. [Pp. 76–77]

The larger result of Laird's study is the novel itself. *Thunder on the River* is based on actual events in the later life of Black Hawk, culminating in the massacre at the confluence of Bad Axe Creek and the Mississippi. The story is focused on a fictional character, Mark Eldridge, and his life among the Indians. The time of the story is from 1813 to 1832. The place (as shown in a map reproduced on the frontispiece of the first edition) is the Mississippi River valley from Goshen (East St. Louis, Illinois) to the Bad Axe mouth. Settings for various incidents are Burlington, Campbell's Island (near Davenport), Rock Island, Fever River (Galena), and Prairie Du Chien.

The novel details Mark Eldridge's adventures with various persons, including Colonel George Davenport, the founder of Davenport, Iowa. Midway through the novel, Mark is captured by Black Hawk. He marries Little Turtle, an Indian's widow, and from that point on we see the Black Hawk War from the Indian viewpoint. Mark comes to learn the Indian character and culture, and to reject the white man's way of life, which is seen as mean and ugly. When the Indians are massacred at Bad Axe, our sympathies are entirely with them. Still, Laird does not romanticize the Indian way of life, and he avoids propagandizing either for the Indian or against the whites.

Laird's second novel in what was described in 1953 as part of a "projected series" is *West of the River*. Mark Eldridge, his wife Little Turtle, and their daughter Dolly are important characters, but the central character is Paul Boudreau, a young French-Canadian fur trader whose nameless birth causes him some internal conflict. The setting is primarily in and around "Foxtown" (Prairie Du Chien) in the late 1830s. The story begins, however, with the burning of Boudreau's Jack Knife Trading Post in northeastern Nebraska (probably the site of that trading post referred to in the discussion of *Conquering Horse*), and with his escape (though with the loss of two fingers) from an ordeal in a blizzard on the open Nebraska prairie.

West of the River is about Paul Boudreau's change of heart about the Indians. At the beginning of the novel, Paul is able to rationalize his part in the thievery of the "Half-Breed Steal" and his seduction of the wife of the man who built the Villa Louis at Prairie Du Chien. At the end he has rejected his mistress for Little Turtle's daughter, Dolly, and he has repented his own earlier moral corruption. Finally he has redeemed himself by his actions, and can accept himself as a person of integrity.

Laird has not completed his envisioned series of novels about the Indians and the early white men, although he has begun a third book. His work has taken him in other, perhaps greater directions, and has earned him a reputation as a teacher and a scholar. His later career is documented briefly by Paluka.

In point of time, the next story about the Indians and the whites is Frederick Manfred's long story, "Arrow of Love" (*Arrow of Love*, 1961). This story is set near Fort Snelling, Minnesota, in Manfred's "Siouxland." It is about a blood feud between Chippewas and Sioux, and the love affair between a Sioux brave and a Chippewa maiden, with the inevitable tragic consequences. The whites, appearing only briefly early in the story, are seen as morally corrupt, debauching both themselves and the Indians.

The story, slightly reminiscent of one of William Faulkner's, is one of Manfred's best, and its theme, that humane values must replace tribal loyalties, is well worth adopting for our own times. Manfred has written the story with restraint and feeling, and he has involved our emotions and feelings through a fairly straightforward account. Even his symbol, the arrow which destroys Raven and thus brings Opening Rose and Raven together in death (thus becoming an "arrow of love" rather than an arrow of vengeance), is worked into the story as both literal and symbolic device. The tragic ironies developed in the story are revealed through action rather than statement.

If "Arrow of Love" is Manfred's best short story, then *Lord Grizzly* (1954) is, by all odds, the best of Manfred's full-length works. The time is the 1820s; the setting is Siouxland and the territory beyond—the Dakotas, Montana, and Wyoming. Though the setting ranges beyond the Middle West, the book does describe in detail events, scenes, and settings characteristic of a broad region which at the time had no sharply defined political boundaries.

Lord Grizzly is based on an actual event. Hugh Glass, a hunter and trapper, was attacked by a huge white grizzly and severely mauled. He survived, even though he was deserted by companions who had been detailed to watch over him until he recovered from the wounds received in the "wrestle." A major portion of Manfred's novel relates Glass's "fabulous crawl" as, with revenge in his mind and heart, he crawls back to Fort Kiowa and Fort Atkinson (in Nebraska at the confluence of the Platte and Missouri). Glass crawls on his stomach because he is unable to walk. The book is a remarkable tour de force—Manfred is able to make every mile of the crawl live with action:

The bronze quartermoon had just set when he ran into the remains of a Sioux warrior. Sewed up in a skin bundle, lying out full length, some six foot above ground on a scaffold of dry saplings, it swayed slack and lonely on four upright posts, black against the star-pricked sky. The tattered edge of a skin snapped in the slow night breeze. Little rawhide memento bags tolled in the slow breeze too. [Pp. 141-42]

Two pairs of furred slanted yellow eyes glittered down at him out of a very bright blue sky. One pair of narrowed eyes glittered very close. Dogs. Indian dogs gone wild. Strays from the Rees who'd passed by the day before. Or the advance guard dogs of a second Ree village on the move. [P. 152]

Moreover, *Lord Grizzly* is a successful book because Manfred is able to develop a powerful theme from its events. Hugh Glass, in his crawl, is forced to live with himself. When he finally meets his cowardly companions, he must make decisions which are based on larger considerations than mere desire for revenge. John R. Milton sees the structure of the book ("The Wrestle," "The Crawl," "The Showdown") as demonstrating a symbolic rise of man from the animal level to the spiritual.[4] (But John Williams argues that Manfred has "failed to recognize . . . that [his] subject is mythical.")[5] Milton and Williams also disagree about the quality of the novel's style. Milton says that the novel "is told in an almost Biblical style—forceful, simple, poetic, rhythmic—which is also surprisingly similar to the natural style of the old Indian story tellers." But Williams believes otherwise: "Manfred has chosen a rhetoric derived from the Homeric epic, the Old Testament and folk speech which tends

4 John R. Milton, "Frederick Feikema Manfred," *Western Review* 22 (Spring 1958):181–99. See also his "Voice from Siouxland; Frederick Feikema Manfred," *College English* 19 (December 1957):104–11, where similar material is presented.
5 John Williams, "The 'Western': Definition of the Myth," *Nation* 193 (November 18, 1961):400–04.

to inflate the subject where it needs constriction and to deflate it where it needs elevation—a rhetoric, in short, which falsifies the subject."

Glass's story has a long literary history. He first told it upon his arrival at Fort Atkinson in June 1824. Someone who heard it there retold it to James Hall, one of the new west's first literary people, then living in Shawneetown, Illinois. Hall published the account in his *Letters from the West* (1828), and in his *Port Folio* (1825). Washington Irving reported the incident in *A Tour on the Prairies* (1835). The *Missouri Intelligencer* carried an account in 1825; this account was retold in Hugh Chittenden's *The American Fur Trade of the Far West* (reprinted 1954). In 1915, John G. Neihardt, the Nebraska poet laureate, used the theme in his narrative poem, *The Song of Hugh Glass*. Verne Bright used the theme in his poem *Mountain Man* (1948). Manfred has said that while writing *The Golden Bowl* he came across a reference to Hugh Glass in the *South Dakota Guide Book* which "instantly caught my eye— this man fighting the bear alone—it struck me that here was the first real contact of the white man with the raw west."[6]

Manfred's novels and short stories about the Indians and the pioneers were written after his first autobiographical novels and farm novels which have their settings in the twentieth century (Chapters 8 and 9). In a 1959 interview with four editors of *Critique*, he explained why he had turned to the earlier period for source material:

. . . I began to feel a thinness in my own heroes. No matter how hard I worked, how much I thought about them, somehow they did not have all the dimensions for me. They lacked something; they lacked a . . . "usable past" within themselves; there wasn't enough history or country or culture for me to throw it up to use as a background, for me to throw my characters against, to deepen them in *that* sense. Some of the novels that we think are great take on an added greatness because we're acquainted with the culture from which they come so that the least little gesture of the author or the hero inside that book instantly evokes part of the whole background and if that background isn't there and the author is busy pushing the front part of the book with not much background, there's always an empty hole. So I went out — I was interested then to find the heroes or the ancestors of my men like Pier and Maury, Elof and Eric. I thought, well, maybe I should look a little more to find, not just who were their fathers and mothers, but who the people were before them on the land — furtrappers, the first mountain men, and so on. Perhaps these people left some residue in the air, not only left their marks on the soil but left them in the air and the way they handled the new thing they hit first which transmitted itself down, say, to my grandfather and so on.[7]

---

6 "West of the Mississippi: An Interview with Frederick Manfred," *Critique* 2 (Winter 1959):39–40.
7 "West of the Mississippi: An Interview with Frederick Manfred."

Johnson Brigham's *The Sinclairs of Old Fort Des Moines* is set in the period 1843–46. Although it was published in 1927, its author (then about 81) had been born about the time of the novel, and had lived in Iowa since 1881. Moreover he had been an historian, a writer, an editor, a publisher of a literary monthly, and a friend of many nineteenth century pioneers.

Considering the age of its author, the book is remarkable. But from the reader's point of view, the book, while interesting in its recreation of scenes, events, and characters, is not a very good novel. It is not well-paced, it leaps somewhat frantically from place to place and time to time. Some scenes which have a great deal of potential are all too briefly reported. The book is at best a series of anecdotes told by a garrulous old man, all loosely strung together by a purported romance and a series of rather incredible melodramatic scenes.

Still the novel is not hopeless. It does deal with steamboat traffic on the Des Moines River, and with the founding and operation of old Fort Des Moines at the junction of the Raccoon and the Des Moines. Some Indians famous in Iowa history are depicted, but there is no real understanding of them. The other characters are presented in stereotyped phrases for the most part, but they are historical characters or have their basis in history. There is some of the flavor of frontier social life.

Phil Stong's *Buckskin Breeches* (1937) is a much better novel of a group of settlers in the "mid-wave of settlement" who leave their Ohio homes (in "the United States") in the year 1837, and "come on" to the Iowa territory where they settle in the Big Bend country near Keosauqua. The county was later named for the man who was President of the United States that year—Martin Van Buren—but Phil Stong, following the lines laid down by Hamlin Garland and Frederick Manfred, took literary possession of the area and called it Pittsville. *Buckskin Breeches* relates the first settling of the Pittsville area, describes the Indians who were already there, the settlers who came, and tells us why they came.

The factual parts of the novel are in large part based upon the history of Stong's own family (Stong was born in Keosauqua), and upon "Memories of Frontier Iowa,"[8] whose author was Stong's grandfather, George Crawford Duffield. Duffield came to the Big Bend country in the period 1836–38, a time when a large part of America's eastern seaboard was undergoing a business depression, and a large share of the population, thrown out of work in the mills and factories, or dispossessed by bank failures and mortgage foreclosures, was looking westward to the opportunities on the middle border.

---

8 George C. Duffield, "Coming Into Iowa in 1837," *Annals of Iowa*, series 3, vol. 6 (April 1903), pp. 1–8.

The central characters of *Buckskin Breeches* are the family of Jesse and Margaret Ellison. Jesse is one of those typical Stong heroic figures— he has "never wounded game," he doesn't care for the menial work of bartending, and he is opposed to all injustice. Margaret is as typically a Stong heroine—a cultured woman who discusses Sir Walter Scott with a minister who tries to persuade her to leave her husband. But Margaret, for all the minister's culture, sticks to her husband—"anyone can capture a tame sheep," and in Stong's world it takes a real woman to hold a man like Jesse.

The novel demonstrates what the settlers must have felt about their migrations:

"But—" It was almost on his lips that he would shortly turn around and go back. He smothered the speech and for a moment tried to realize the feeling of one who had come to this fantastic wilderness to live forever. For the first time he got the full meaning that his father and mother and Sue and Ted and Hi meant to stay here and exercise whatever force their lives might have against these untracked lands and stubborn forests. Next year they would be here—in twenty years—in fifty they would be here, dead or living.

It was then that the whole journey quickly became uncompromisingly actual for David for the first time. None of these people would return—the voyage ended at its western limit. [P. 231]

In the new land, the settlers come in contact with the agricultural Indians of the Des Moines River valley:

In the lodge the men were holding what they called a council, but any white man would have recognized it as plain loafing. The women had no similar social resort in the winter; besides they were busy for now while the hides were finely furred all the curing and sewing for a year had to be done. There was no leisure in a woman's life. Clothes and moccasins must be made, baskets woven, children reared. [P. 268]

Two other contacts with the Indians occur, whose handling by Stong, Paul Engle called "superb." On one occasion, one of the Ellison boys, misunderstanding an Indian boy's intentions, calls the boy a "nigger sonofabitch," thus demonstrating one of the invidious influences of his former life on the Ohio frontier. On another, old Eli, the book's "comic relief," shows his long-treasured scalps to the Iowa Indians:

Eli spat majestically into the fire and flung his moldy bundle at River Heron's feet. "There, God damn ye—count them!" [P. 311]

The Ellison children, naturally enough for a Stong novel, get themselves romantically involved with mates. One of the Ellison girls has a romantic affair with a character named Ivanhoe Keeler. But Stong apparently decided to save Keeler for a later novel, and so Sue Ellison passes over "the butterfly" to marry the less alive but thewed and admirable Caesar Crawford.

The Ellisons go west to escape civilization, but soon civilization catches up with them in the form of a school, a church, a store, more neighbors—and eventually Martin Van Buren's government which insists that the settlers acquire formal titles to their land. On that fateful day in Burlington when it appears that speculators and profiteers may gobble up the settlers' homes, the Ellisons and their neighbors cooperate to eliminate the threat (just as Iowa farmers did at "penny sales" in the 1930s), and once more they become a part of the expanding nation they had come west to escape.

John Frederick said that *"Buckskin Breeches* is a genuinely worthy literary interpretation of the founding of Iowa and of the people who achieved it. . . . The richness of vivid detail and the robust humor which are always characteristic of Stong's work mark this book in especially generous measure."[9] Paul Engle, looking back on his own pioneer ancestry, found it a "pleasant" novel but an "unreal . . . account of frontier life":

> where the author has used his original sources the book is accurate and convincing, one of the best frontier novels, but where he has linked them together with a romantic plot, it becomes over-written and artificial.[10]

Stephen Vincent Benét thought it was "a sincere and highly readable story" with "now and then . . . a certain Swiss Family Robinson quality about the Ellisons."[11]

Two of Stong's other novels are related to this period, but have only a part of their setting in Iowa. *Forty Pounds of Gold* (1951) is the story of James Warwick who leaves Iowa and travels to California by the Panama route with the other gold seekers. Eventually he gets his forty pounds of gold which is his goal, but he gets it by raising onions, and by building "cradles" for the other gold seekers. At the end of the novel he returns to Iowa and uses his gold to build a home in the Pittsville area— an incident modeled on Stong family history.

Ivanhoe Keeler (1939), written the year after *Buckskin Breeches*, and while Stong's mind was still taken with his hero and the frontier, relates

---

9 Frederick, "An Introductory Note," "Black Hawk and the White Men," and "Infant Iowa," p. 420.
10 Paul Engle, "The Gemütlich Frontier," *Saturday Review of Literature* 15 (April 17, 1937):11.
11 Stephen Vincent Benét, *New York Herald Tribune Book Review*, April 11, 1937, p. 5.

the further adventures of the young fiddler who says of himself: "I'm not only a parasite—I'm a damn fool. Every time I see a tasty girl I believe my own music." Ivanhoe had hoped to marry Sue Ellison but like James Warwick, who learns that his sweetheart has married a preacher, he also loses his girl. The crowning blow to Keeler's pride is his discovery that Sue has had twins.

Ivanhoe, in his wanderings up and down the Mississippi Valley, is accompanied by Charlie Hoskin—who reminds us somewhat of the towering Pier in Manfred's *This is the Year*—and a person whom John Frederick called "an Admirable Crichton of a Negro body-servant named Samaliel"—but nicknamed Sammy.[12] We see Sammy, Ivanhoe, and Governor Briggs of Iowa in a passage which is vintage Stong—what John Frederick called "Stong's lusty humor and power of phrase,"[13] and what Roy Meyer termed "gay inconsequence":

He went into the dining room gaily. It would have been a reflection on Sammy's various skills if he had not been the best-dressed and groomed man in the room. The governor and the intimates who were traveling with him were still working through an enormous Iowa breakfast—buckwheat cakes, sausages and bacon with eggs, porkchops or steaks and potato cakes with hominy, lots of coffee and open-face apple pie made from tart dried apples. A duty of the good politician in the time and place was to be a hearty eater and Briggs, with a platter of breakfast steaks in plain view, was taking a second helping of sausages, eggs, potatoes and gravy.

Evelyn, the weak vessel, was toying with a reasonable slice of pie on which she had poured thick cream. [P. 304]

Ultimately, Ivanhoe wins Evelyn, whose father is a business leader in the new state, and comes to an understanding of himself.

In the late 1850s and early 1860s there were Sioux Indian uprisings in northwest Iowa and Southwest Minnesota, out of which came Iowa's only Indian "massacre"—although the Spirit Lake Massacre did not result from the activities of a war party, but rather from the actions of a group of renegades searching for "*wis-kee*" and loot. MacKinlay Kantor used the incident as the basis for his very long novel *Spirit Lake* (1961).

Although Kantor says that "I cannot swear that I formed a recognizable ambition to tell my own kind of tale then and there," he recalls in his autobiography of his boyhood *But Look the Morn* (1947) that his

---

12 Frederick, "An Introductory Note," "Black Hawk and the White Men," and "Infant Iowa," p. 412.
13 Frederick, "An Introductory Note," "Black Hawk and the White Men," and "Infant Iowa," p. 413.

mother read the account of the raid to him from Jesse W. Lee's 1912 *History of Hamilton County*:

On or about the 8th of March, 1857, Ink-pa-du-tah, a Sioux renegade, with about forty followers, made an attack upon the settlements at Spirit Lake, and killed or captured everyone found there.

Kantor remembers vividly that he listened on past the curfew while

Mother's voice read on, thrilling with the epic account of morbid terror, of bloodshed, of rescuers who fought their way through frozen sloughs and swirling drifts. . . . [P. 146]

John N. Maxwell, one of the rescue party, had "sat in that very chair where Grandma was now leaning forward—I had seen him sitting there," and Frank R. Mason, another, was the grandfather of one of his school-mates. As he listened to "Mother's voice, alive with compulsion of the drama," it seemed to the young Kantor that

. . . back beyond our age and our house was the whole racking, icy chronicle of the pioneers. Branches swayed beyond the window; some dry leaves blew past and touched the glass, like ghostly fingers of Dakotahs come to remind us that they, too, had camped upon that soil for a little while. [P. 146]

It was this sense of the continuing existence of the past that Manfred sought for in writing his novels of Indians and pioneers. As for Kantor, he felt himself "torn, and still grown noble in this recounting of ancient sufferings. The sponge of [his] brain soaked up the dark juices . . . exhausted, sleepy in body but not in spirit, [he] listened" (p. 147).

Kantor first used the theme of the Spirit Lake raid in a narrative poem, "The Snow of the Okoboji," in his *Turkey in the Straw* (1935). But before he began to write *Spirit Lake*, he read and researched extensively; his raw materials are listed in the "notes and Bibliography" appended to the novel. Two of his sources were Thomas Teakle's *The Spirit Lake Massacre* (1918) and Abbie Gardner-Sharp's *History of the Spirit Lake Massacre* (1885); the latter is a first-hand account by one of the survivors, who had been a fourteen or fifteen-year-old girl at the time of the event.

Kantor's technique in *Spirit Lake* is essentially that of Thornton Wilder's *The Bridge of San Luis Rey* (1927), which is to ask who were these Indians and whites, and what were they doing in this place at the time when the disaster struck. Brother Juniper conducts his investigation to determine whether the collapse of the Peruvian bridge was an accident or part of Divine Plan; Kantor's investigation into the Spirit Lake raid apparently has a more mundane purpose.

The novel probes into the past of those who were involved in the massacre: the Gardner family, Dr. Isaac Harriott, the Markans, Mrs. Atta Rush (the widow of Sergeant Rush), the Rev. Harvey Luce and his family, Bert Snyder, a Frenchman who had been born Robert Didier, the Mattock family, the Marble family, Charles Flandrau, the Howe family, Inkpaduta, a Wahpekute ("about as miserable a bastard as fiction has seen recently"), his wife, Corn Sucker, and others. *Spirit Lake* "is extended by a cast of more than four dozen characters cursed with total recall and the folksiest dialect since Mr. Dooley," said *Time* magazine.

Critical reaction to *Spirit Lake* varied. Paul Engle thought that "Kantor's imaginative construction of the settlers' backgrounds is one of the finest things he has ever done," and that "he has also done a remarkable thing in going down inside the Sioux Indian mind and offering what seems an absolutely valid account of events, attitudes, emotions and beliefs found there."[14] Stanley Kauffman, writing in *The New Republic* was lengthily caustic, particularly about the length of the book.[15] William Van O'Connor, on the other hand, saw a relationship between the "expansiveness of the land between the two great mountain ranges" and the expansiveness of the novel.[16] As well, the critics were of mixed feelings about the style, some finding items to praise, Kauffman damning the "carbonated lyric gush" of the prose. And the *Christian Science Monitor* critic commented: "The irony is that the net effect of Mr. Kantor's research is likely to leave the American Indian with misapprehensions about him exaggerated, not clarified."[17]

Frederick Manfred's *Scarlet Plume* (1964) is a much better book than *Spirit Lake*, if only because it is shorter. It is set in southwestern Minnesota during the Sioux uprisings of 1862–64. A band of Indians attacks a small white settlement and brutally destroys most of the whites; Manfred's narrative of the event is not for the squeamish reader (neither are some portions of *Spirit Lake*, for that matter). The story then focuses on Judith Raveling, one of the survivors. Although cruelly ravished and mistreated by the Indians, she eventually comes to love one of them, Scarlet Plume. Later, soldiers under General H. H. Sibley round up the Indians and execute many of them. Scarlet Plume, although innocent of any activity against the whites, is among those executed. Judith leaves her

---

14 Paul Engle, "At the End of the Trail a Massacre," *New York Times Book Review*, October 22, 1961, pp. 4–5.
15 Stanley Kauffman, "O dear God, O dear All," *New Republic* 145 (October 30, 1961):23.
16 William Van O'Connor, "Go West Young Man . . . to the Massacre," *Saturday Review* 44 (October 21, 1961):23.
17 *Christian Science Monitor*, October 26, 1961, p. 7.

white husband and casts her lot with the Indians; she has come to accept them as a finer social group than the whites:

> She had suffered cruelly at the hands of the Indians. Yet the sheen of an idyll lay upon the harrowing times she had had with them. . . . Yankton life was devoted to the sheer joy of living, not to getting.
> The Yanktons had no property, no gold stored in temples. Yet their sense of wealth was profound. . . .
> They had no records. Yet their sense of history was profound. They not only loved their own children . . . but all children.
> They had no clocks. Yet their sense of time was profound. They lived spontaneous from moment to moment, a wandering across a flowering prairie. . . .
> She thought, "How stupid of the white man. When he came upon this Eden prairie, why did he take by force what he could have had by love?" [Pp. 240–41]

This is one of Manfred's better books, but suffers from his obvious delight in describing rape, sexual intercourse, and acts of brutality. The author has argued that that is the way it was—or even worse. Nevertheless, many readers will find these accounts to be revolting.

Two long narrative poems by Iowa authors use the pioneer period for their subject matter. The first, Leonard Brown's 1865 poem, *Iowa,* has a scene describing the meeting of Indian and white:

> Thus having said, again he sate
> Him down among these men of state,
> And there awaited calm his fate.
> Did they arise with furious yell,
> Bend over him like fiends of hell,
> Bury the tom'hawk in his brain,
> And bid him sleep, nor wake again?
> Ah, no, full glad I am to say
> How well they welcomed him that day!

The Pioneers (1896) by Samuel Hawkins Marshall Byers looked back to an earlier day which Byers, born in 1838, had known:

> Ah! that log house, with its plain puncheon floor,
>   Its clapboard roof, and papered window-screen,
> Could it but speak and tell the tales once more
>   Of the old days that it and they have seen!
> The simple fire-place, built of sticks and clay,
>   The unbolted door, on wooden-hinges swung;
> *"Come in,"* was writ on every heart that day,
>   The welcoming latch string to the stranger hung.

Byers's poem narrates the day-to-day events of pioneer life—"the spelling school," the "weekly mail," the "circuit preacher," the "first green grave," the "old-time weddings," the animal and bird life of the prairie, the prairie fire:

> In bounds and darts the lighted grasses go;
>   Leaps to its start the dreaded *prairie fire,*
> In long, long, lines the burning billows glow,
>   Roars the night wind, the flames are leaping higher....
> One sweep, one roar, and flowers and grass are gone;
>   The moon goes out; there is not any star.
> Wild, fierce, devouring, o'er the waste they come,
>   The very ground burns 'neath them as they pass,
> As if the world were hurrying to its doom,
>   And earth and sky had turned to molten brass.

This is much better poetry than we saw in Hiram Reid's efforts, and much better than Brown's *Iowa;* the description of the prairie fire, although hampered by too much reliance on "poetic diction" (not noticeable in this excerpt) is not at all bad.

It was in such pale imitations of better poets that Iowa poetry had its beginnings. But while the style and form was imitative, the material was drawn from the actual observations of the writer—although too often the reporting of those observations was inhibited by too heavy a dependence on archaic style. In general it can be said that all Iowa literature, poetry and prose alike, has continued in this tradition, almost always relying on traditional forms and techniques, rarely improvising or inventing, but reporting observations of the state's life.

Supporting this generalization, Phil Stong in his "biography of Iowa," *Hawkeyes,* says:

Education came too quickly and too generally to permit any primitive foundation for a native art. Mt. Pleasant College, . . . was founded in 1844 [seven years after the events reported in *Buckskin Breeches*] . . . Iowa College . . . followed in 1848, and the State University in 1855 [sic], from which point colleges followed thick and fast.

This hardly gave the wildland birds a chance to start singing, before they were subjected to the indignities of voice culture. . . . rhetoric was taught in the heroic manner, with dissertations on the character of the trochaic, introduction to the iambic verse, notes on the pathetic fallacy—and daily composition in all manners. Unfortunate little sophomore farmers were stuffed with anapests and dactyls; classics were discussed in terms of phrase form and rhythm, and definitions were demanded for words . . . that the youngsters would certainly never hear again in field or farmhouse. . . . It is not at all difficult to trace this pedantic method which governed elementary teaching in the use of English back to Boston, via Ohio and all the western trails. [Stong's own Jesse Ellison, based on an actual person, had quoted Vergil in the original Latin.] The texts . . . were as unsuitable for young Iowans as bottom-wigs or ruffled cuffs. . . .

William Cullen Bryant was a fatal influence . . . and the number of times "Thanatopsis," in a more or less altered form, appeared in the early journals of the state, composed by children anywhere from fifteen to senile desuetude, was a state and probably a national scandal.[18]

Emerson Hough's *The Covered Wagon* (1922) is not an "Iowa" book, although its author was born in Newton. It treats of an aspect of pioneer life which became familiar to many who stopped in Iowa for a while—the continuing migration westward over the land. *The Covered Wagon* attempts to be epic in its scope as it presents its panorama of the westward movement to the Pacific. At times it succeeds very well, but it suffers from a badly conceived plot. Moreover, in some places it is so badly written as to draw snickers from a modern reader. Nevertheless, in 1967 it was reprinted as a paperback, and a motion picture made in the early twenties based on the novel (*The Covered Wagon*, 1923) became one of the classics of the American film.

In 1857, the year after the publication of Reid's first volume, a poem was written which was to achieve a reputation and posterity denied to the Davenport writer. The writer was Dr. W. S. Pitts, a teacher and student of music; the title was "The Little Brown Church in the Vale":

> There's a church in the valley by the wildwood,
> No lovelier place in the dale;
> No spot is so dear to my childhood
> As the little brown church in the vale.

The poem was "inspired by a small church in Bradford, Chickasaw County [a few miles northeast of Nashua], where an academy existed for a time. It is said that the church was painted brown because that happened to be the least expensive color, then, but it has such a quaint charm and is so typical of pioneer days, that it has become a literary and historical shrine." It has also become a very popular place for weddings.

Tacitus Hussey, a well-known nineteenth-century Iowa poet and author of "a collection of poems of humor and sentiment," *The River Bend and Other Poems*, wrote one verse which earned a kind of fame because of its subject:

> The corn-fields of billowy gold,
> In Iowa, "Beautiful Land,"

---

18   Phil Stong, *Hawkeyes* (New York: Dodd, Mead & Co., 1940), pp. 39–41.

Are smiling with treasure untold,
In Iowa, "Beautiful Land."

It was put to music (by a Congressman!) and sung for a while, but it soon gave way to the more robust "Iowa Corn Song."

Leonard Brown wrote other poems about pioneer life in the mid-nineteenth century. Abel Beach, an early pioneer of Iowa City, published his *Western Airs*, a small volume of verse on the same general subject. The first poem, "Iowa," was dedicated to the early settlers of Johnson County. These men produced some good scenes, but the verse, although generally better than Hiram Alvin Reid's, is still sentimental and ordinary.

MacKinlay Kantor, in his *Turkey in the Straw*, has given us a much better set of verses on the pioneer theme than any of the nineteenth-century versifiers. "Granny" is a dirge in memory of a pioneer woman, "Sarah Brewer Bonbright, Webster City, Iowa, 1837–1930." In "Lyman Dillon and His Plow," there is a sense of the historical and cultural impact in the order to "plow a furrow from Dubuque to Iowa City . . . as a guide for the surveyors who would open this new territory with a military road." In "Miller Adam," the contributions of one man to the flow of events are reported from the vantage point of one looking back over the years. "The Pale White Rose" tells of a farmer who holds a prairie flower in his hand and recalls for his son, in his colloquial voice, what the rose has seen through the years of westward migration. In "Hallowed Be Thy Name," Kantor memorializes his grandfather who "strode in the fours of infantry" as a "Lincoln soldier," and who "died in the Richmond soldiers' home in nineteen-thirty three." The poem is another of the indications of Kantor's lifelong interest in the Civil War, an interest which has informed much of his verse and prose.

Eight of the poems in the book are on the subject of the Civil War and ten are on the subject of the pioneers. The other seventeen treat topical subjects; most of these have little reference to Iowa. Whatever shortcomings Kantor's verse may have as poetry, it is still honest stuff, rooted in events he knew about, and written in a language appropriate to his themes. While he sometimes uses rhyme and even a formal stanzaic pattern, he ranges far beyond archaic form and stereotyped diction; his verse, while expressing a nostalgic lament for the past, have an individual quality.

Other later Iowa poets also wrote about pioneer life in Iowa. In "Ancestral Iowa," Paul Engle remembered the "tough old countrymen" who had been on the land before him, and from whose loins he sprung.[19] Raymond Kresensky's "The Old Families" looked back at the "Calls, the

---

19 Paul Engle, "Ancestral Iowa," *West of Midnight* (New York: Random House, 1941), pp. 61–70.

Blackfords, the Inghams, the Daltons, the Smiths, the Hendersons, the Lessings, Heckerts, Hudsons, McGetchies and the Kings," whose "blood runs purple through generations."[20]

Edwin Ford Piper's *Barbed Wire and Other Poems*, first published in *The Midland* in 1917, and republished as *Barbed Wire and Wayfarers* by the Macmillan Company in 1924, contains many poems on the prairie world. Piper wrote much of this verse after he had moved to Iowa, and it is true to the Iowa pioneer scene, but Piper was in many cases recalling his Nebraska background. Whatever the situation, the volume contains what is probably the best poetry ever written about the prairie and the pioneer days.[21]

Two of Frederick Manfred's short stories from his *Apples of Paradise* (1968) are set in the transitional period during which the prairie was settled. "Blood Will Tell" is a story of a love triangle involving Ira Barber, a trapper, Dr. Cyrenius Chalmers of "Wodan," and Dawn Breaking, a half-breed and Ira's common-law wife. Ira beats Dawn, breaking her leg on one occasion, and she comes to live with the doctor. Then Ira shows up, repentant, admits he is half Negro, half Indian, and agrees to marry Dawn Breaking both the white man's and the Indian's way. The story's theme seems to be the loose class relationships that existed on the frontier.

"Wild Land" is the story of Jasper Dollarhide who homesteads on the southwest Minnesota prairie near the Iowa line. He marries Lucy and keeps her sister Delphine in their sod hut as well. Eventually he builds a frame building. No children result from the wedding (barrenness is a theme in several of the stories in *Apples of Paradise*); after Lucy dies of pneumonia, Jasper marries Delphine and in the ensuing years they have six children. The early part of the story describes Jasper's "sodbusting" of ten or twenty acres at a time, until he has his land almost completely under the plow. The title refers to one four-acre piece of creek bottom land which is supposed to be cursed because the Indians once fought a battle there. Although Delphine warns Jasper against plowing the land because of the curse, she is the one who eventually breaks it to the plow while Jasper lies ill.

In these two stories, Manfred seems to be trying to establish a relationship, through land and through people, between the historical past of his Siouxland and the present of his later novels.

Julie McDonald's *Amalie's Story* (1970) repeats a theme seen in Marjorie Medary's *Prairie Anchorage*—the coming of a family from the old country to Iowa. Mrs. McDonald's people are seen in their Danish home

20 Raymond Kresensky, "The Old Families," *The North American Mentor Anthology of Poems* (Conesville, Iowa: John Westburg & Associates, 1965), p. 16.
21 Edwin Ford Piper, "Breaking Sod" from *Barbed Wire and Other Poems*, in *The Midland* 3 (February 1917):58. Also published as *Barbed Wire and Wayfarers* (New York: MacMillan Co.) 1924.

in the first part of the novel, and in their Harlan, Iowa, home for the second part. Both parts of the novel are steeped in Danish culture; the latter half dramatizes some of the problems faced by members of a foreign culture, speaking a foreign language, in adapting to a new land.

The story is told through Amalie Ibsen's eyes from her childhood through marriage and childbirth and the eventual death of her husband. Although it is possible that the novel may hold more interest for women than for men, it is a "superbly done novel" as Murray Hickey Ley has said.[22]

Mrs. McDonald (of Davenport) was raised in the Harlan community which is part of her setting. She is herself of Danish descent, and for her novel did research in Denmark, and in Iowa archives which contain relevant material. Born in a farmhouse near Fiscus (near Audubon), she is a Phi Beta Kappa graduate of the University of Iowa and has worked as a newspaper reporter.

At the turn of the century, eight books of the frontier, intended for boys, were written by Franklin Welles Calkins. He came to Iowa as a boy after the Civil War (as did Hamlin Garland), and attended school in Ames and Spencer, where he lived for a number of years. The story titles usually suggest the subject matter: *Boy's Life on the Frontier* (n.d.), *The Cougar-Tamer and Other Stories of Adventure* (1898), *Frontier Sketches* (1893), *Indian Tales* (1893), *My Host the Enemy* (1901), *The Young Homesteaders* (serialized in Johnson Brigham's *Midland Monthly*, 1897), *Hunting Stories* (1893), and *Two Wilderness Voyages* (1902). The last book and stories in the other collections are set in Iowa.

Professor Luella M. Wright says about Calkins:

... in his "Young Homesteaders" ... [he] presented a prototype of ... Bess Streeter Aldrich's *A Lantern in Her Hand*. His story combines the realistic details and hardships of pioneering—prairie fires, blizzards, and drought—with the philosophy of *Poor Richard's Almanac* that hard work, thrift, and determination will, in the final outcome, work out propitiously.

Calkins had two assets: he knew how to write effectively and he knew the Middle and Far West intimately. Moreover, he had steeped himself in western history, legends, and folklore. ... What is more, he could see how "a flat stretch of weather-beaten prairie" could turn itself into literary material.[23]

A more recent writer of stories of the prairie for young people is Marjorie Medary, who was born in Waukon and reared with the smell of printer's ink in her nostrils, for her father was a Waukon newspaper publisher. She was educated at Cornell College. *Prairie Anchorage* (1934)

22 Murray Hickey Ley, *Sunday Times-Democrat*, Davenport, Iowa, September 20, 1970. See also article by Shirley Davis in the same newspaper, August 2, 1970.
23 Luella M. Wright, "The Midland Monthly," *Iowa Journal of History and Politics* 45 (January 1947):45–48.

is a novel about the coming of the Jameson family from Yarmouth in England to northeast Iowa by schooner, river steamboat, and rail. One incident involves Amelia Jenks Bloomer. On the prairie (the year is 1855) the family encounter wolves, a prairie fire, and a great deal of advice as to their future plans.

Marjorie Medary also wrote two books about Tom Kenyon, a young boy who wants to become a printer. The second of these is *Prairie Printer* (1949).

Two Iowa poets, Edwin Ford Piper and Jay Sigmund, wrote short poetic dramas about the Indians. Piper's play, *Masque of the Aiowas*, set in the time of the coming of Marquette and Joliet to Iowa, was performed at the Diamond Jubilee Celebration of the University of Iowa, February 24 and 25, 1925. The music for the masque, which featured animals, fruits and allegorical figures, as well as Indians and historical persons, was written by Philip Greeley Clapp. It was directed by Edward C. Mabie.

Sigmund's unpublished play (the typescript is at the University of Iowa) is based on a familiar Indian legend, for which Sigmund's setting is the "black-rock" bluffs along the Wapsipinicon River near Waubeek. *The Wapsipinicon* relates how Wapsie, an Indian maiden, daughter of the chief of the Foxes, and Pinicon, son of the chief of the Iowas, throw themselves from the bluffs into the river when the two chiefs refuse to permit the marriage of the couple. Tradition has it that the river received its name from this sacrifice.

Cornelia Lynde Meigs was born in Rock Island, grew up in Keokuk, matriculated at Bryn Mawr, and then came to Davenport to teach. From about 1915 on she was writing literature for children; three of her books about the Indian-white transitional period are written well enough so that adults can enjoy them, and moreover are accurate accounts of the period. *As the Crow Flies* (1927) is the story of Natzoon, an Indian boy who becomes a protege of Black Hawk. Zebulon Pike is a character in the story. *The New Moon* (1924) begins in Ireland, moves on to Pennsylvania, and ends in Keokuk County in southeast Iowa. *Swift Rivers* (1937) is a story of the log-rafting days on the Mississippi.[24]

Although Iowa authors may not have completely plumbed the depths of the Indian psyche (as their critics have thought), they have been understanding in their treatment of the Indian; and although they have not been sentimental or maudlin, they have been compassionate. From Garland to Kantor and Manfred, Iowa authors have been ahead of their fellows in their attempts to comprehend the Indian and be fair to him.

---

24 See John T. Frederick's account in "Early Iowa in Fiction," *Palimpsest* 36 (October 1955):395 ff. There is a partial bibliography of Cornelia Meigs' children's books in *Books at Iowa* no. 9 (November 1968):17–18.

The Prairie Becomes the Farmbelt — The Cabin Becomes the Town

IN what now seems like a handful of years . . . on the prairies of . . . Iowa . . . a mobile energetic population made the Corn Belt [wrote Allan Bogue]. *Spurred by technological achievements and expanding markets, commercial farmers built one of the most prosperous agricultural economies the world had ever seen, in this land where each year the rains, the summer heat, and productive soils produced broad-leafed fields of dark green.*[1]

But apparently most of those nineteenth-century Iowans were too busy building the Corn Belt, for with the exception of Hamlin Garland (Chapter 4) and one or two others, most of the writing about the farm-builders and town-builders of that time has been done by writers in this century.

Two novels by Bess Streeter Aldrich (1881–1954), *A Lantern in Her Hand* (1928) and *Song of Years* (1939), like those poems of MacKinlay Kantor discussed in the last chapter, are written from the viewpoint of a person living in the writer's present and looking back at the life of the pioneers. However, Mrs. Aldrich's books usually focus on a woman.

The two novels begin after the death of their protagonists, and then, in long flashbacks, reconstruct their lives. Both books imply that the era of our pioneer past was a better era in that it brought out the sterling qualities of its people. Life was more rugged and difficult, but the pioneers are shown as equal to the conditions facing them, and there is always an atmosphere of optimism. Both books exhibit a sentimental closeness to their chief characters on the part of the narrator. Both utilize actual experiences of Mrs. Aldrich's family.

Mrs. Aldrich was born Bess Genevra Streeter in Cedar Falls, Iowa, February 17, 1881, the last of eight children. Her parents were already middle-aged; the three oldest children were already in their twenties. The Streeters were old New England stock, one of their ancestors a "Captain Remember Eaker, one of the Green Mountain boys and a cousin of Ethan

---

1 Allan G. Bogue, *From Prairie to Corn Belt* (Chicago: University of Chicago Press, 1963), p. 287.

Allen, who was shot by an Indian, his head cut off, and buried by a British officer."[2]

Her grandfather was "the honorable Zimri Streeter," who once owned the land which is now the site of the Waterloo–Cedar Falls airport. He was "one of the Iowa signers for the new Republican party when it split from the Whigs," and a member of the first Iowa legislature which met in Des Moines. He was known as "Old Black Hawk" for the county he represented, and as "the wag of the House" for his "dry Yankee wit." He had come to Iowa in 1852, bringing with him the author's father and nine other children, taking three weeks to travel from Dubuque to the site of his farm. On the way they had passed one building—a tavern where Independence now stands.

Her mother had also come from Illinois to Iowa, in 1854, driving one of the family's wagons all the way from Lockport. Once it had upset, dumping eight sacks of flour and some goose feather pillows in a stream. Before she married the author's father, she taught school.

The Streeter family had no meetings with Indians, although on the occasion of the Spirit Lake Massacre (1857) there were reports that the "Indians were on the warpath," and Zimri Streeter's cabin became the gathering place for all the nearby families.

In 1864, old Zimri was appointed by Governor Kirkwood to go to Atlanta, Georgia, to bring back the votes of the Iowa men serving with Logan's Fifteenth Army Corps. He arrived on the scene just as Atlanta fell, and he accompanied Sherman's Army to the sea.

Mrs. Aldrich thought that her Grandmother Anderson had a more romantic background. At sixteen, living with "her parents in a humble cottage on the moors of Scotland," she had been wooed and won by Basil Anderson of "the gentry," and had gone to live "in the large ancestral home," where Mrs. Aldrich's aunts and uncles were born. Then he brought his family to Quebec, where Mrs. Aldrich's mother, Mary, was born. Later, when the family moved to "the farming lands of Illinois," Grandmother Anderson had managed to bring along "a basket containing her lovely Chelseaware china."[3]

The transition from raw prairie to urban life, from the wagon which brought Mary Anderson to Iowa to the high-speed automobile and transcontinental airplane, all occurring during the lifetime of Mary Anderson's daughter, made it possible for Mrs. Aldrich to present the whole panorama of growth and development of the prairie in the life of a single

---

2 *National Cyclopedia of American Biography*, vol. H, p. 242; Robert Streeter Aldrich, "Introduction," *A Bess Streeter Aldrich Treasury* (New York: Appleton-Century Crofts, 1959).
3 *National Cyclopedia of American Biography*; Robert Streeter Aldrich, "Introduction," *A Bess Streeter Aldrich Treasury*.

character. The use of her family's experiences, as she had heard the stories "many times," gives her work validity, even though she wrote in the 1920s and 1930s, and even though, as Professor Roy W. Meyer says, they "contribute nothing essentially new to the story of pioneering in Iowa and Nebraska."[4]

A Lantern in Her Hand is the story of Abbie Mackenzie Deal from her pioneer childhood near Cedar Falls and Waterloo to her death in her farm home near Cedartown (Elmwood), Nebraska, at the age of eighty. Abbie's experiences as a child and through her marriage are those of Mary Anderson; the Deal and Mackenzie families are modeled after the Anderson and Streeter families. There is no plot to the novel as such—there is simply the slow roll of years, the cycles of crop failures and successes, the growth of towns and cities, the proliferation of families, the forestation of the bare land, the coming of the railroad, the building of schools and colleges. These are the background against which Abbie Deal constructs her life and the lives of her children. There is the building of the "soddy," (a cabin built of turf, in layers), death by rattlesnake, the inevitable blizzard and prairie fire, the grasshopper invasion. One of the novel's themes is the paradox of Nature—as provider, as giver of pleasant sensations, as destroyer—a theme which informs almost every novel of life on the Iowa prairie. A second theme is the conflict between the values of life on the prairie and life in the growing towns. A third theme is that of sacrifice for love—and this one is present in several Aldrich novels.

Though the townspeople seem to do better, it is Abbie Deal whom Mrs. Aldrich admires: "And those who think she was not cheerful through it all, do not know the Abbie Deals of pioneer stock."

When her mother was a very old lady, Mrs. Aldrich once remarked to her "how sorry I was that she had endured such a hard life when she was young. She looked at me with an odd sort of expression and said . . . 'Save your pity. We had the best time in the world.' "[5]

Song of Years presents a greatly detailed picture of that life around Sturgis Falls (Cedar Falls) and Prairie Rapids (Waterloo) which Abbie Deal left behind when she moved to Nebraska. There are many echoes in this book of the earlier one. Perhaps the most notable echo is that both heroines choose a country boy over a city boy (who is presented in less favorable light in both cases), and the rugged rural life over a comfortable city life. Both heroines sometimes wonder if they have made the right choice. (Mrs. Aldrich herself chose the comfortable town life!)

Song of Years, however, focuses on the Martin family, and again the

---

4 Roy W. Meyer, *The Middle Western Farm Novel in the Twentieth Century* (Lincoln: University of Nebraska Press, 1965), pp. 68–69.
5 *Wilson [Library] Bulletin* 3 (April 1929):608.

passage of time is the major theme. The Spirit Lake Massacre is glanced at, and the impact of the Civil War is felt. Sturgis Falls and Prairie Rapids grow and nature takes its inevitable toll. And there is the same admiration for the settler with his sturdy qualities and his puritan ethic of work and struggle:

One other gift remains, one other thing handed down. . . . You cannot sit in it as you can in the old rocker, nor pick it up . . . nor point to it. . . . It is immaterial, but nevertheless existent. It is something typically and sturdily America which has not been entirely extinguished—a bit of the old pioneers' independence, practical philosophy, ingenuity, and propensity to *pull on through*.

A White Bird Flying (1931) is a sequel to *A Lantern in Her Hand*. It begins with the death of Abbie Deal and focuses on Abbie's granddaughter and her stereotyped romance which is brought to a typical Aldrich happy ending. The novel is superficial and badly written; the treatment of Laura Deal's college days will not stand up to Ruth Suckow's description of the college life of *her* characters. Yet (probably because of their romanticism) Mrs. Aldrich's books were more widely read. Taken together, her books passed through twenty-seven foreign editions in several languages; there were also numerous American editions.

Two later novels, *Spring Came on Forever* (1935) and her last book *The Lieutenant's Lady* (1942), also treat slightly of the pioneer theme, but the burden of both is romance, and the last is incredibly bad for a writer of Mrs. Aldrich's caliber.

The work of two Iowans who wrote about the Civil War lies somewhat outside of the scope of this work. In 1896, Samuel Hawkins Marshall Byers attained wide fame with his narrative poem, *The March to the Sea*, which he based on his own experiences with Sherman's army. Byers (1838–1933) was born in Pennsylvania but came to Iowa with his parents in 1851. Settling in Oskaloosa, he became a lawyer. As a commissioned officer in the Fifth Iowa Volunteers, he was captured by the Confederates at the Battle of Missionary Ridge, Chattanooga, Tennessee, and held prisoner for sixteen months, part of the time in the notorious Libby Prison. He escaped three times, but was recaptured, and his poem was written while in prison. Escaping for the fourth time at Columbia, South Carolina, he soon joined General Sherman's staff.

"We had a poet, Major Byers, still alive in my lifetime," wrote Phil Stong:

who sat around a Southern prison camp scratching out patriotic ballads. He sent one of them up north in the wooden leg of an exchanged prisoner—

"Sherman Marched Down to the Sea." It was no good at all—none of his verse was—but on the little stir he had made as a distinguished, and captured, military officer he eked out what must have been a moderately satisfactory literary life.

Of course, if the South Carolinians had ever caught that prisoner with the wretched piece of doggerel in his wooden stump they would have hanged him offhand. I would have hanged him myself for a different reason.[6]

John Frederick was more sympathetic. Writing in 1930, when Byers was in his ninety-second year, he commented that "in very few cases do we find literary interpretation of the Civil War by the men who fought in it," and he praised the poem as a "solid and valuable contribution to the literature of the Civil War as viewed by those who fought it."[7]

MacKinlay Kantor (1904–) has written the novels which represent the greatest Iowa literary efforts on the subject of the Civil War: *Long Remember* (1934) and *Andersonville* (1955), the latter winning the 1956 Pulitzer Prize.

Kantor's interest in the Civil War began, he tells us in *But Look the Morn* (1947), when he played, as a boy in Webster City, with his great-grandfather's Civil War uniform's buttons. It was reinforced by his grandmother and mother, and by visits of the "survivors of the Northern Border Brigade" to his home: "Amid their nasal reminiscences, I heard again the swift scream of fifes which had sounded when I was three years old and played with the buttonbag" (pp. 138–39).

But between those boyhood days with their Decoration Day parades and *Long Remember* was an apprenticeship during which he wrote some fifty short stories about the Civil War, read voluminously, and did on-the-site research, making himself the "historical expert" which he thought the historical novelist must be. The setting for *Long Remember* is brief in time and tiny in space but almost cosmic in its scope: the three-day battle which took place in and around Gettysburg, Pennsylvania, near the Fourth of July 1863.

Kantor, fascinated by the potential of the vast canvas of the battle, has elected to write about it by focusing only incidentally on the military forces (though the armies and soldiers are on most of the pages) and mainly on Daniel Bale, a civilian, who doesn't "intend to go to war." Bale has fallen in love with Irene Fanning, the wife of a soldier, and he searches through the holocaust of Gettysburg for Tyler Fanning as a point of personal honor. The device permits Kantor to reconstruct every aspect of the battle.

---

6 Phil Stong, *Hawkeyes* (New York: Dodd, Mead & Co., 1940), p. 45.

7 John T. Frederick, "Samuel H. M. Byers," in *A Book of Iowa Authors by Iowa Authors*, ed. Johnson Brigham (Des Moines, Iowa: Iowa State Teachers Assn., 1930), pp. 46, 52.

Why did Kantor write a historical novel rather than history?

> It was my great desire to make the Gettysburg battle as contemporaneous, as much a part of the reader's life, as if the wounded were still having their bandages renewed in the hospitals—as if the wheel-ruts of the Whitworth rifles were still creased across the nasturtium beds. . . . I was imbued deeply with the notion that I must make the lesson and the tragedy of Gettysburg a part of the lives of all readers. . . . I held to the notion that . . . factual history is accepted more completely if presented through the roundabout approach of a story, than on the pages of a scholarly tome intended primarily for the intelligence of fellow historians.

The term "historical novel," Kantor said in a lecture (quoted above) given at the Library of Congress in January 1957, "should be applied only to those works wherein a deliberate attempt has been made to recreate the past."[8]

Kantor added that in terms of popular success, *Long Remember* was a book club selection; in terms of military success, the novel "was to be used as a supplementary textbook at the United States Military Academy at West Point." And he quoted the critic Allen Tate: "It would be a distinct addition to American fiction if a school of historical novelists should pattern themselves upon this model."[9]

Andersonville is based on the notorious Southern prison of the same name; like *Spirit Lake* and *Long Remember*, it is lengthy, detailed, and grim. Kantor has argued that historical fiction which did not present the seamy side of an event was not an "historical novel" but rather a "romance": "The hard flat board of prudishness was strapped across the brow of our infant literature, and thus the cranium was distorted and misshapen, as surely as were the skulls of unfortunate papooses in the Columbia Valley long ago."[10]

Apparently the first Iowa novel is a story of life in a prairie town, *High-Water Mark* (1879). The author was Alice Ilgenfritz of Cedar Rapids who used the pseudonym Ferris Jerome. She was born in Shanesville, Ohio, January 9, 1846, to Henry and Ann Ilgenfritz; members of her family later settled in Clarksville, Iowa. In 1884 she married Hiram Edward Jones, long-time Cedar Rapids furniture merchant (1849–1929).

---

8   MacKinlay Kantor, "The Historical Novel," in *Three Views of the Novel* (Washington: The Library of Congress, Reference Dept., 1957), pp. 36–37. Originally a Gertrude Clarke Whittall Poetry and Literature Fund lecture.
9   Kantor, "The Historical Novel," pp. 36–37.
10   Kantor, "The Historical Novel," pp. 36–37.

According to an obituary in the *Cedar Rapids Gazette* of March 5, 1906, she

> . . . lived the greater part of her life in Iowa. . . . Before her marriage she had achieved a reputation as a writer and besides had been a regular contributor to *Lippincott's Magazine* . . . . Mrs. Jones has written *Unveiling a Parallel* (in collaboration . . .), *Beatrice of Bayou Teche* [serialized in *The Midland Monthly*, beginning with the first issue] and *The Chevalier de St. Denis.*

The title of *High-Water Mark* is taken from the name of the prairie town in and around which most of the action takes place. It is located just above the high water stages of a nearby river. High-Water Mark seems to be a typical nineteenth-century prairie town with its lawyers, politicians, ministers, newspaper man, and its quota of those who will become wealthy by speculating in land. The two protagonists of the novel are law partners who seem to prefer long philosophical discussions, and readings of their own badly-conceived and badly-written romantic verse instead of affairs with young ladies. The story drags, there is too much dull talk, too little action, and little character development. A prairie blizzard is described only to serve as a means of bringing about poetic justice.

High-Water Mark is much more akin to the Gothic romances which were written in such profusion for the female readers of the nineteenth century than it is to the genre of the novel of Midwest pioneer life. It continues that tendency of nineteenth-century Iowa literature to follow the stereotypes of another time and place, and this figurative pouring of new wine into old bottles produced little that was good.

Young and Fair is Iowa (1946) by the Right Reverend Mathias Martin Hoffman is an attempt to create an historical novel out of the beginnings of Dubuque and Iowa. Actual historical figures, among whom are Dr. Mathias Loras, first Iowa bishop for the Roman Catholic Church and the man for whom Loras College is named; the Reverend Samuel Mazzucheli, O.P., an early missionary and a reputed architect of Old Capitol at Iowa City; Augustus Caesar Dodge (a character also in *Buckskin Breeches*) and George Wallace Jones, both of whom were generals in the Black Hawk War and later United States Senators, are mixed with imaginary characters. Among these, the central character is Eliphalet Foster; his love for a French girl, Julie De L'Isle, forms part of the story line. The other part is concerned with a false charge of murder against Foster. The story begins in 1834 and runs for a quarter of a century before the couple settle their religious differences, the love affair reaches a satisfactory conclusion, and the charge of murder is disproved. There is a Mexican War sequence and a "California" interlude. The most interesting characters are Captain Hiram Kimbell and his unscrupulous daughter, Cora. Their introduction gives the reader a look at the growing Mississippi River steamboat traffic. At the novel's end, the abolition issue is becoming a factor in the city's growth.

The Right Reverend Hoffman was born in Dubuque on January 7, 1889, and was educated at Loras Academy, St. Paul's Seminary, the University of America, and Oxford University. He died January 10, 1961.

Josephine Donovan's *Black Soil* (1930) is set in the Mill Creek area of O'Brien County in northwest Iowa. The novel begins with the settlement on the bare prairie of an Irish Catholic family, Tim and Nell Connor and their children, plus an orphan girl, Sheila. Around them the land is taken up by High and Low Germans and Holland Dutch, and cultural frictions arise. "The chief distinction of *Black Soil*," says Roy Meyer, "is that it, almost alone among farm novels, deals with a group that consists chiefly of Catholics, the Irish and German settlers of northwestern Iowa."[11]

Aside from the standard catalog of prairie tribulations, the book presents two new themes. A German immigrant boy becomes despondent over his failures and, unwilling to return to his native land, hangs himself. The suicide is a familiar figure in Iowa farm fiction. The second theme is that of miscegenation (the only other instance in an Iowa novel is in Manfred's *Scarlet Plume*, written several decades later). In *Black Soil* (as in *Scarlet Plume*) the instance is that of the love of a white woman for an Indian. But there is a significant difference. In *Black Soil* we are told at once that Wild Goose had had an Anglo-Saxon grandmother, but it is only near the end of the novel that we learn that Sheila Connor had an Indian mother. Of this situation a critic said: "It is difficult to take seriously a novel in which a girl named Sheila Connor is discovered to be part Indian and in the last chapter rides off into the sunset with her Indian lover." (The description is not factually accurate—in any case, Sheila and Wild Goose have been married by a priest in a formal ceremony.)[12]

The novel ends on a happy note with Tim and Nell Connor "on the door-step of the old house" watching "the summer sunshine flood their stubble with a maze of golden light." The coming of the railroad through the Connor land has brought prosperity to the settlers at last. It has also brought a new town to the prairie—Casvales (like Primghar, the county seat of O'Brien county) named by combining the initial letters of the founders' names into an acronym.

Although this description of farming on the prairies in the 1880s had

---

11 Meyer, *The Middle Western Farm Novel in the Twentieth Century*, pp. 68–69.
12 Charles T. Dougherty, "Novels of the Middle-Border: A Critical Bibliography for Historians," *Historical Bulletin* 25 (May 1947):87.

been written a half century later than the incidents it describes, Mrs. Donovan had a solid basis for the novel. She had been born in Granville, Iowa (in Sioux County, close to the novel's setting), on August 18, 1888, the daughter of Thomas Barry, whose reminiscences of a prairie fire and a grasshopper plague she reported in the *Palimpsest* of 1923. Mrs. Donovan graduated from the University of Iowa in 1909, and in that same year she married Dr. William H. Donovan of Iowa City. In 1929 she entered the University's School of Letters, where, according to Wallace Stegner, she

. . . offered her novel *Black Earth* [sic] as a Master's Thesis. . . . It was accepted [although no copy of it reposes in the University's library], but before she could finish the degree, the novel was bought for publication, won a two-thousand dollar prize, and was being dickered for by the movies. So Miss Donovan lost interest in the academic M.A.[13]

Despite the fact that it won a prize, and despite the fact that one critic listed it as one of "the ten best books of 1930," most critics were cool toward the book, noting its lack of stylistic distinction and Mrs. Donovan's failures to capitalize on dramatic situations.

Eastern Iowa is the setting for *The Able McLaughlins* (1923) and *The Law and the McLaughlins* (1936) by Margaret Wilson, who was born in Traer, Iowa, in 1882. She came from the same family as "Tama Jim" Wilson, U.S. Secretary of Agriculture from 1897 to 1913. Her family, like her fictional heroes, were Scotch Covenanters:

I was born in Iowa . . . the most middle western of all middle westerners. Not only [was] my mother not a Daughter of Eastern Revolutions, but my father, that unaspiring man, [was] not even eligible to membership in the Ku Klux Klan. My forebears were in no sense gentle folk. Yet they were strong and loving humans. Being farmers, they were not good at keeping up appearances. Indeed, they were too poor to have an appearance to keep up. Yet they could stare reality in the face without batting an eye. Thy were pleased with good crops, but they would have been transported with delight if their continual attempts at versification had in the generations brought forth a slight harvest of poetry. It is lamentable to consider how greatly they lacked books of etiquette. . . . Still, their creditors slept easy, knowing they scorned the lazy evasions of bankruptcy. They had, in fact, a rather interesting collection of scorns, including a Scotch abhorrence of American methods of land exhaustion. They appreciated themselves too thoroly to wonder whether the world appreciated them or not, and they plowed with long heads and high hearts. And when their crops failed, they groaned internally only, attributing their failures

---

13 Wallace Stegner, "The Trail of the Hawkeye," *Saturday Review of Literature* 18 (July 30, 1938):3–4, 16–17.

not to lack of legislation, populistic or otherwise, but to their own lack of knowledge of the resources of their soil. While some agitated and paraded, they experimented and devised better methods, and their wisdom has been justified by the children of their minds. To their lesser offspring they bequeathed a certain inclination towards the simplicities of life, so that to this day my nose prefers the fundamental and rhythmic odors of a sunny manure pile to such jazzy intricacies of incense as burns, say, in St. Mark's of the Bowery.[14]

The qualities of warm humor, of tenderness, of toughness, of thriftiness, of compassion, of common sense, of intelligence and self-reliance implied in this essay are the qualities of Miss Wilson's novels.

After moving to Chicago with her family, Miss Wilson attended Englewood High School and graduated from the University of Chicago. She spent the next half-dozen years in India, an experience she described in "The City of Taffeta Trousers." Returning to Chicago, she taught in West Pullman High School.

The Able McLaughlins was submitted to Harper & Brothers in a contest which attracted seven hundred and fifty writers. When it was announced that she had won the first prize of two thousand dollars no one knew her, for she had published her articles in *Harper's Magazine* over the signature of "An Elderly Spinster"—a pseudonym she used because "I was at that time the oldest woman in the United States."[15]

The Able McLaughlins is a novel of the Scotch settlers of eastern Iowa, "the ragged lairds of the Waupsipinnikon," self-styled not because they live near the Wapsipinicon, but because their poetic natures are appealed to by "a name so whimsical, so rollicking." The time of the story is the late years of the Civil War and the post-war years following.

The novel is two stories in one—the story of Wully and Chirstie McLaughlin, and the story of Alex McNair, Chirstie's father, "and the poor wee thing," Barbara, his second wife, who thinks she is coming from Scotland to a castle on the prairie, only to discover she is to have to live in a "pig sty" of a house. The story of Wully and Chirstie borders on tragedy—the story of Alex and Barbara is high comedy. Miss Wilson has succeeded in blending the two.

Wully, returning from the Civil War, finds his beloved Chirstie pregnant—the seducer their common cousin, Peter Keith. Wully marries Chirstie because he loves her; but he is determined to avenge himself on Keith,

---

14 "Margaret Wilson," *Wilson [Library] Bulletin* 6 (May 1932):596. Autobiographical sketch. Similar information is presented in "Margaret Wilson—A Sketch," by Katherine Scobey Putnam, *Overland Monthly and Out West Magazine* 82 (September 1924):399.
15 "Margaret Wilson," *Wilson [Library] Bulletin*, p. 600.

if Keith ever returns to the community from which Wully has driven
him. In the meantime Barbara, who loves comfort and fine things, is
determined to have a new house. Alex, who is not quite as thrifty as a
neighbor, John McKnight, "who, when he went to mill always took
with him a hen tied in a little basket, to eat the oats that fell from his
horse's mid-day feeding" (p. 92), is determined to put all his money into
land. Eventually, Barbara gets her fine home. Eventually also, Wully,
who has accepted the blame for his wife's pregnancy, forgives Peter Keith
—after finding Peter dying, and realizing his own happiness with Chirstie
and Peter's son.

One of the novel's themes is the reason why men farm:

> To John, now, a field of wheat was a field of wheat, capable of being sold
> for so many dollars. To Wully, as to his father, there was first always, to be
> sure, the promise of money in growing grain, and he needed money. But
> besides that, there was more in it than perhaps anyone can say—certainly more
> than he ever said—all that keeps farm-minded men farming. It was the perfect
> symbol of rewarded, lavished labor, of wifely faithfulness, of the flower and
> fruit of life, its beauty, ecstacy. Wully was too essentially a farmer ever to try
> to express his deep satisfaction in words. [P. 127]

The ethnic immigrant's problem with language is also a theme:

> Now that [John] had been in Chicago he had a growing contempt . . . for the
> speech of his own people. What was it they spoke, he demanded scornfully.
> . . . It wasn't Scotch no longer. It wasn't English. It wasn't American certainly.
> It was just a kind of—he tried all summer to describe it satisfactorily in a word.
> Once he called it "the gruntings of the inarticulate forthright" . . . . Wully's
> and Chirstie's articulation he supervised continually, their grammar and their
> diction. They were not allowed to say before John, "She won't can some," or
> "I used to could." [P. 129]

In 1924 *The Able McLaughlins* won the Pulitzer Prize for the novel
"that shall best present the wholesome atmosphere of American life and
the highest standards of American manners and manhood," and was pronounced the "most distinctive book of the year." Dr. Henry Seidel
Canby said:

> *The Able McLaughlins* deserved the [Harper's] prize for its literary art and
> for its sound and solid substance of rich American life. But it also possessed
> that quality rarer in fine literary work than style or penetration; it stirred the
> emotions and appealed to the universal love of a good story effectively told.[16]

---

16 "Margaret Wilson," *Wilson [Library] Bulletin*, p. 608.

On Christmas Eve of 1923, Miss Wilson was married to G. D. Turner, then a tutor at Oxford and later warden of Dartmoor Prison. A 1933 novel, *The Valiant Wife*, has its setting in the prison during the War of 1812. Then in 1936 she returned to the McLaughlins for a sequel to her first novel.

In *The Law and the McLaughlins*, we see the beginnings of town life, the coming of the railroad, and the development of a system of justice on the frontier. The novel begins six months after the end of the first with Wully (now Willy, his wife is now Kirstie) discovering the bodies of two hanged men on his uncle's farm. Investigation reveals the men were lynched by three men who live some distance away. The "lairds of the Wapsipinnicon" demand revenge for the deed committed in their demesne, but frontier justice grinds slowly and so does the story. Jean, Willy's sister, goes away to school, meets an innocent accomplice of the lynch party, and marries him. Eight years pass; Jean's husband dies of tuberculosis, and the lynchers remain free. The story is, as Roy Meyer says, an "inferior" sequel, and it does not hold our interest.

J. (John) Hyatt Downing's novels belong in this period. Downing was born in Granville, Iowa, on March 8, 1887 (just a few months before Mrs. Donovan's birth in the same small town). "Shortly after," in Downing's words, "my family moved to Hawarden, Iowa, a small town in the northwestern part of the state; the birthplace of Ruth Suckow. I remember how I sighed at the long sermons her father, who was our pastor, used to preach."[17]

When Downing was about thirteen, the family moved to Blunt, South Dakota, a small town about twenty miles east of Pierre, and the setting for his first two novels, *A Prayer for Tomorrow* (1938), and *Hope of Living* (1939). But, as Downing said, "the cheap land lured and destroyed" the settlers, and "the hot winds sucked the moisture from the land and hope from [their] hearts!"[18]

In 1902, the elder Downing began a lumber business, hoping to sell lumber to the large numbers of people then moving in. Two years later, the younger Downing began working on a geodetic survey for the Northwestern Railroad in Wyoming. But a telegram from his father sending him fifty dollars brought him home and he enrolled in the University of South Dakota.

After two years at the University, Downing began drifting through Wyoming, Nebraska, and the Black Hills, working at such jobs as herding sheep or night-clerking in hotels. Then he returned to the University,

---

17 *Collier's Magazine* 116 (December 1, 1945):89.
18 *Collier's Magazine* 116 (December 1, 1945):89.

played football on the championship team of 1912, and became literary editor of the University paper.

After graduation in 1913, Downing attempted unsuccessfully to work for newspapers and to write fiction in Sioux City and elsewhere. For a while he was a deputy collector of internal revenue at Aberdeen, South Dakota. Then, learning he had tuberculosis, he moved to Carlsbad, New Mexico, where with his new wife he managed an alfalfa farm.

Back in the Middle West, Downing began selling insurance. In 1925, *Scribner's Magazine* published his short story "Closed Roads," and in 1926 it published "Rewards," a story which Edward J. O'Brien placed on his honor roll for the year. In the next four years *Scribner's* bought four more stories, at which point the insurance company offered him a promotion on the condition that he "quit writing them damn pieces." "I didn't touch a typewriter for [the next] seven years," he later said, "and I was about as unhappy as possible."

While living in St. Paul, he had met F. Scott Fitzgerald, Sinclair Lewis, and Joseph Hergesheimer in Tom Boyd's Kilmarnoch Book Shop. No doubt, meeting these men before "the log fire in the back room where all the writers used to come to meet" stimulated Downing to turn his back on the insurance business and take up writing once more. But the insurance years had a consequence—an unpublished manuscript, *Garth*, a novel based on the insurance business.[19]

Back in Sioux City, Downing began *A Prayer for Tomorrow*, a novel set in and around Rudge (Blunt), South Dakota, in the 1880s and 1890s. The story is told through the eyes of the young Lynn McVeigh, thus, in the words of one critic "reducing the elaborate and detailed Main Street fabric to the adolescent adjustments of a sensitive boy."[20]

There is a range war between cattle ranchers and the invading farmers who are "bent on fencing off the land and breaking it to the plow"—the land which up to that time had been matted with buffalo grass but which would become the dust bowl—Manfred's *Golden Bowl*. Among the farmers who come to build "fences around the old water holes and . . . squat towns at the prairie's edge are the McVeighs, who give up ranching and make a fortune in the lumber business; Cynthia and Clarence Carr, the latter rising from bank clerk to wealthy landowner, the former becoming the "cultural ornament of the town"; the Winterslips who become landed gentry; Charlie Thyme who founds the town paper and becomes the town drunk; and "a whole phalanx of Swedish farmers" who come in search of the free land "with their pitiful households and their plump,

---

19 Anthony T. Wadden, "J. Hyatt Downing: The Chronicle of an Era," *Books at Iowa* 8 (April 1968):11–23.
20 Wadden, "J. Hyatt Downing: The Chronicle of an Era," pp. 11–23.

strapping daughters." For a while there is a boom; but the bust comes—
and then the exodus to Texas, to California, back to Iowa.

Critics found the "characters stiff, like family album photographs," and
the structure of the book "mechanical," but they praised the moments
when Downing "writes about the eternal wind, sweeping sundrenched
flatlands, about the harsh dry coughing sound of tractors, the smell of
dying crops, the contrasts of savage prairie winters and summer drought."
In such moments, they said, the novel "achieve[d] power and beauty."[21]

Hope of Living, set in the same general area, is an expansion of the
short story "Rewards." Anna Walrod, a woman of unyielding resolution,
is married to a man she has never loved, a man who by choice as well as
nature is a hired hand on a farm. In the novel, Anna falls in love with
young Dr. Michael Shea, a romance hinted at in the story. The novel
also has an unfrocked minister who is "garrulously blasphemous and per-
sistently predatory"; before the story is ended, Dr. Shea is forced to
kill him.

Anna succeeds as a farmer, both because of her own driving will and
because she accepts the advice of Gus Schultz, a German neighbor who
has the foresight to see that the Dakota country is not adaptable to farming as, for example, Iowa is. He advocates a system of combined farming
and cattle raising.

Sioux City (1940) and *Anthony Trant* (1941) are set in the northwest
Iowa metropolis from its boom days in 1884 and later, ending with the
post World War I period—a time when "young men, their heads full of
dreams and their voices full of laughter" built a cable car line up Jackson
Street, and President Cleveland "came to express astonishment at the Corn
Palace," and "the steel tentacles of an elevated railroad, the third in the
world, began to reach across the flood plain of the Missouri, ending,
rather vaguely in Morningside."

Sioux City focuses on the early career of Anthony Trant, a budding
aristocrat, who believes that "democracies are completely inept," and that
life's rewards should be bestowed upon "a select few who were, by virtue of birth and extraordinary abilities, entitled to them." "Money is the
concrete result of human endeavor," says Anthony, who as a boy loved
to play "bank" when the girl next door wanted to play house. To
Anthony, fresh out of college, rejecting the medical career his unselfish
father (an M.D.) had wanted him to have, "the stamp of wealth [is]
more to be desired than the love of angels."

So Anthony becomes an employee of Major Gavin's bank. Frank
Luther Mott once observed that the place to see the inner workings of

---

21 *New York Herald Tribune Books*, March 27, 1938, p. 8.

an Iowa town was either the newspaper office or the parsonage. He should have included the bank as well; Trant comes to meet many people whose lives and his become intertwined in *Sioux City* and its sequel.

There is Mavis Garnett, the country school teacher, daughter of Joe Garnett, a nearby farmer who doesn't do as well at farming as he does at fathering children. One of Joe's sons becomes a well-known eastern artist. When Trant first meets Joe he wonders "what was the mysterious thing that the land did to people who toiled with it? The coarsening and insensitiveness which crept into the eyes of farmers?"

There is Charlie Blessington, a lawyer, who may be "a greater scoundrel than some of the felons he defends. . . . [He] could be a big man if he didn't have weaknesses big men can't afford to have." There is Louise Ashland who runs one of the town's gambling establishments and whose banking affairs are Major Gavin's private business. She had once "killed a man, shot him through the back of the head coolly and without the slightest compunction, as he knelt twisting the dials of her large old-fashioned safe in the rear room."

There is also Cullen, a one-time river rat and scoundrel whose life is saved by Dr. Trant and who ever after is the doctor's loyal man of all work. He is cast in the same mold as Sammy of *Buckskin Breeches*, and most of Phil Stong's hired men. Like Louise Ashland, he is also cast in the Bret Harte mold; both are somewhat unbelievable.

The tangled affairs of these characters are set against the boom period which the "embryo Chicago" undergoes. At the novel's end, Anthony Trant, his romance with Mavis Garnett ended, has left the bank for what seems to be a bigger future in a bank in St. Paul.

Sioux City was a best selling book and a *Book-of-the-Month Club* selection. David Selznick, who had recently finished filming another historical romance, *Gone With the Wind*, bought the film rights. The novel achieved some critical success also. Professor Richard Cordell called it "a vigorous, interesting novel" which represented an improvement over the earlier novels, and he compared it with Hamlin Garland's work. Garland, he said, had not told "the whole story," and Downing, "with greater perspective and wider personal experience," knew it. Still he thought that Downing had "no buoyant illusions" about his subject matter.[22]

Anthony Trant picks up the life of Downing's hero three years later. Cavanagh, the man who had persuaded Trant to come to St. Paul, and Trant are both bankrupt—all that Trant has are his clothes and "the old house back in Sioux City." He is no longer self-assured—he contemplates suicide. Cavanagh tells him he has lost his nerve. He returns to Sioux City

---

22   Richard A. Cordell, "Boom City of the Eighties," *Saturday Review of Literature*
22   (July 6, 1940):13.

so depressed that he cannot consider returning to Major Gavin's bank. He has been false to himself and to those who trusted him.

From these depths, Anthony Trant begins his upward climb, for a time working for nine dollars a week, "mucking" clay in a brickyard. Soon he returns to the Major's bank, and in time takes charge of it. He marries Mavis Garnett and life seems settled. Then with the advent of World War I, the boom is on again. Trant, by now an honest conservative banker, will have no part in the speculation. It is his son, Stephen, with Trant's old lust for an easy "fast buck" who joins the speculators—a group promoting a packing plant in Sioux City. For a while with the world-wide demand for foodstuffs, affairs look rosy for Sioux City and its dishonest boomers. Then the foreign nations, no longer embroiled in war, and having learned American food producing technologies, begin to produce their own food again. The markets are satiated with grain and livestock, and there is the inevitable "bust" of the early 1920s. The novel ends with Stephen facing a prison sentence.

Anthony Trant was not received as enthusiastically as the first book, although reviewers praised it and noted there was "no romanticizing" in this "saga of business in the corn country."

Downing left Iowa for California where for a time he wrote radio scripts and motion picture publicity. After World War II, he wrote short stories and articles for *Collier's, Liberty, Holiday*, and other periodicals.

Anthony T. Wadden has summarized Downing's themes as ones of "individualism, personal responsibility, honor, prudence, industry, faith and simplicity," all operating "within an economic cycle of speculation, boom, and depression."[23]

"A writer must not start to write until he has something to say, a vivid thought to bring out," Downing once said. "If all authors would write their own individual philosophies of life, their books would be more worthwhile. As in so many other fields simplicity is the keynote to achievement, so we find it true in writing. Altogether too many authors think they must create a certain style in order to have their works read and remembered."[24]

In early 1972, Tom McHale (born in Sioux City in 1902) published *Dooley's Delusion* ·(Anderson, S.C.: Droke House-Hallux), a novel set in "Great West (Sioux City) in the 1880's and 1890's." McHale's protagonist, Gabriel Dooley, is a member of the impoverished "shanty Irish" of the town, with dreams of becoming a Catholic priest in his native Ireland. But the novel focuses more on the bitter quarrel between the Irish and the affluent "lace curtain" society on the other side of the tracks.

---

23 Wadden, "J. Hyatt Downing: The Chronicle of an Era," pp. 11–23.
24 *Collier's Magazine* 116 (December 1, 1945):89.

McHale utilizes the same "boom or bust" period as Downing, but he also intermingles Irish mythology and Catholic theology, themes not used by other Iowa writers. Moreover, there is an unusual note—a typical Irish wake with its mixture of solemnity and socializing. For these interesting additions to Iowa literary themes, McHale (in 1972 a real estate executive in Dallas, Texas) drew upon his own Irish Catholic boyhood in Sioux City, and some five years of historical research as well.[25]

Walter John Muilenburg was born in Orange City, Iowa, in 1893—and thus he was a near neighbor of Ruth Suckow, J. Hyatt Downing and Josephine Barry Donovan. After growing up in the recently-settled Dutch country town, he went to the University of Iowa in 1911. There he met John T. Frederick, Ival McPeak, Roger L. Sergel, and Raymond Durboraw, fellow undergraduates soon to be associated in *The Midland*. His writing talents were encouraged by Clark Fisher Ansley, head of the English department, and Edwin Ford Piper, author of *Barbed Wire and Other Poems*.

While still an undergraduate, he wrote "The Prairie" (*The Midland*, August 1915) a short story about the efforts of John Barrett and his wife Lizzie to establish a farm on the prairie. Newly married, Barrett, a "ne'er-do-well," and Lizzie, "only one of the Deltons," have left the "little burg" that was their home because the villagers "talk too dam' much about us. If we make good, they'd hate us; if we lose out, they'd laugh." Those notes of the effects of small town gossip and social pressures are sounded often in Iowa fiction.

The Barretts find the prairie pleasant in the spring, but as the months pass and their attempts to wrest a living from the land are rebuffed by the dry climate and a prairie fire, their early enthusiasm flags, and "the grip of the prairie seem[s] to close upon their souls." When Lizzie dies from the effects of the fire, Barrett gives up the farm to become a vagabond.

In "Heart of Youth" (*The Midland*, November 1915), Muilenburg described the frustration of a farm boy, arising from conflict between the boy and his father over the father's demands that the boy help work the farm.

Both "The Prairie" and "The Heart of Youth" attracted the notice of Edward J. O'Brien who was publishing his first "Best Short Stories" yearbook in 1915. O'Brien published "The Heart of Youth" and praised both stories highly (along with *The Midland*), predicting that greater things would come from both Muilenburg and the magazine.

Muilenburg graduated from Iowa in 1915, then spent two years in

25   William J. O'Keefe, Review of *Dooley's Delusion* by Tom McHale, *Des Moines Sunday Register*, April 2, 1972, Sec. C, p. 7.

"country weekly" journalism and high school teaching. In 1917 he returned to the University to teach in its English Department.

In 1925, following the publication of several other stories dealing with father-son conflicts, Muilenburg published *Prairie*, a novel which is both a combination and extension of the themes of the first two short stories. *Prairie* is the story of Elias Vaughn whose hard-working Bible-reading father wants the son to follow in his own steps and eventually take over the successful family farm in Iowa.

Elias quarrels with his father over the father's puritanism and the son's marriage to the daughter of a shiftless farm family. The father gives the son nine hundred dollars, telling him, "I'm through with you and I won't have that woman on my yard."

Prairie relates the grim struggle of the younger Vaughns to wrest a living from the land, despite drought, prairie fire and hail storm. Elias gradually becomes "set in his ways" like his father; Lizzie, the wife, becomes mentally unstable. Ultimately, the wheel comes full circle and Elias and his son also break off relationships.

For all its grimness, *Prairie* is a beautifully-told story which would have been better had Muilenburg supplied more detail to flesh it out. Edward J. O'Brien said that over all of Muilenburg's work there is "a sense of nature brooding over human effort with impending portent, almost as vividly as the same sense in Thomas Hardy, and very completely realized in his work."[26] Roy Meyer noted that *Prairie*, dealing with a theme of Rölvaag's *Giants in the Earth* ("the theme of a man and woman unequal in psychological stamina and in their enthusiasm for the pioneer experience together 'facing the great desolation' "), preceded the English version of the latter novel (1927), but, compared with Rölvaag's novel, seems "ineffective . . . crude but not negligible. . . ."[27]

Muilenburg left Iowa in 1926 to teach at Michigan State College at East Lansing. He and John T. Frederick purchased adjoining farms in northern Michigan and there spent their summers together. But he published no more stories or novels.

---

26 Edward J. O'Brien, *The Best Short Stories of 1916* (Boston: Small Maynard Co., 1917), p. 378.
27 Meyer, *The Middle Western Farm Novel in the Twentieth Century*, pp. 68–69.

Alice French (Octave Thanet)

ALICE French (1850–1934) came to Davenport in May 1856, the same year that Hiram Alvin Reid was publishing his two slender volumes. Her father, George Henry French, had brought his wife, two sons and Alice, and the wealth he had amassed as a young merchant in Andover, Massachusetts, to the city of sixteen thousand on the Mississippi's west bank. He left the sophistication of the East for the uncertainties of life in a raw prairie town for his health. George French had developed symptoms of tuberculosis, and Iowa's salubrious prairie air was thought to be good for a man in that condition. In the next thirty-two years he became a successful manufacturer of lumber products and farm implements, a bank and railway president, an official of the school board and the mayor, before succumbing to cancer.

Alice had been born on March 19, 1850, in a home which had belonged to her family's ancestors. Her mother was the daughter of a governor of Massachusetts, and her father's ancestry was equally good. Moreover, George French had chosen Davenport over other Iowa towns because his wife's brother-in-law was the bishop of the newly-established Episcopal diocese.

Alice found the bishop's library with its "queer old pamphlets and old reprints, and sometimes originals of the dead and buried gossip of the sixteenth century" fascinating reading which "often" later repaid her. "The sermons of that time had the pith of manners and politics in them . . . they were the mirrors of the times [written] with a style of singular simplicity and strength, the style . . . of the King James translation." Alice later credited her own "simple, direct, and . . . picturesque" style to her readings in these "old English divines."[1]

Alice attended grade and high school in Davenport. At home she played at knights and ladies with her dolls, making up stories as she

---

1 Mary J. Reid, "Octave Thanet at Home," *Midland Monthly* 3 (January 1895):36–42; "The Theories of Octave Thanet and Other Western Realists," *Midland Monthly* 9 (February 1898):99–108.

played. She read newspapers and magazines, Mrs. E. D. E. N. South-
worth's novels, a life of Napoleon, Macaulay's *History of England*. And
there was the war-time excitement generated by the army camp just outside the town, the Federal prison for "rebs" on Rock Island, and the
soldiers passing through Davenport on their way south.[2]

The family influence was strong. "My father always encouraged me
and believed in me more than I believed in myself," she once said. "His
taste in art and his high sense of honor were unconscious influences for
me but nevertheless strong."[3]

The Frenches sent Alice to Vassar, rejecting the coeducational University of Iowa because they had heard that it might not provide the most
suitable environment for their daughter. (In 1900, the University named
a literary society for her, and in 1911, it awarded her an honorary Litt.
D.) Alice did not care for Vassar, however, and came home before the
first semester ended. The following year she enrolled at Abbot Academy
in Andover, just down the street from her birthplace. Her roommate at
Abbot was Octavia Putnam. Alice remembered the name.

Abbot Academy may have influenced Alice's inclinations toward writing; Harriet Beecher Stowe lived in Andover, and the school encouraged
its young ladies to write.

But back home in Davenport, Alice chose the life of a socialite. The
family constantly entertained; Marshall Field was a friend of the family
and Alice bought her dresses at Field's Chicago department store. The
Field store was to play a part in Alice French's fiction.

In 1871, Alice published her first story in the Davenport *Gazette* under
the pseudonym of Frances Essex. On July 3, her youngest brother Robert
was born. Also that summer, Bronson Alcott stayed at the French home
while giving Davenport some of his "Conversations." He proved fascinating to Alice because he was the father of the author of *Little Women*.

Still, Alice's career as an author lagged. She read, becoming familiar
with Hegel and Kant and "all the great western writers of literature."[4]
She enjoyed Chaucer, Shakespeare, Lady Mary Wortley Montagu, Lord
Chesterfield. In 1874 she traveled to Europe with her family. In all this
time she wrote only one story and that was returned by the editor.

In the mid-1870s a series of labor agitations led to strikes and violence
across the nation. In Chicago the federal cavalry attacked a crowd of
laborers in Halstead Street and there was a strike at the John Deere plant
in Moline. But probably because George French had always practiced a

2 George McMichael, *Journey to Obscurity: The Life of Octave Thanet* (Lincoln:
University of Nebraska Press, 1965), p. 22.
3 Reid, "The Theories of Octave Thanet and Other Western Realists," p. 107.
4 Reid, p. 106.

kind of benevolent paternalism toward his workers, there was no strike in the French family plant.

Out of Alice's reading and observations of the strikes and violence came her first major story, "Communists and Capitalists: A Sketch from Life" (*Lippincott's Magazine*, October 1878). She got forty-two dollars for this, one of the earliest stories of labor strife, and she always regarded it as her favorite story. Critics agree that it is her best story.

There are four characters in the story: the Countess Von Arno, an investor and clerk in the Seleigman's plow works; her schoolday friend, Therese Greymer; Mrs. Greymer's friend, Mrs. William Bailey; and William Bailey, the "Communist." Bailey, unemployed because of his political sympathies, lives with his wife and their six children in a squalid collection of huts along the riverbank. Their "hideous shanty" has holes in the ceiling "out of one of [which] peered the pointed nose and gleaming eyes of a great rat." We are told that the rats eat "a little of the children now and then."[5]

The story centers on the philosophical disagreements between Bailey, who "believes in the cause of Labor and will stick to it until he dies," and the Countess who argues that "Capital is brain and labor muscle," and "muscle cannot do without brain." Mrs. Greymer is on Bailey's side and tells the Countess that Labor, like Samson "may one day pull down the pillars of the temple about our heads." To which the Countess responds, "If we are wise, we shall be ready and shoot him dead."

The story ends in Chicago where Mrs. Bailey is accidentally killed in the Haymarket Riots while the Countess watches. "You and the likes of you with your smooth cant have killed her," Bailey tells the Countess. "You crush us and starve us until we turn and then you shoot us down like dogs."

The story, later anthologized as "A Communist's Wife," presents both sides of the labor-capital argument as the late nineteenth century saw it, and the ending is not distorted so as to lead to a "happy" conclusion. In many of her later stories, Alice French was to write equally realistically of equally pertinent social subjects, but she was to distort her endings with romantic conclusions. Such distortions were her reaction to the "horror of our age [which] is reflected in our art, the passionate pilgrims of the garbage can who believe in picking out horror, and disregarding any relief or hope or gaiety."[6]

Alice had sent the story off under the pseudonym "Octave Thanet," but she signed the cover letter "A. French," obviously in both cases try-

5 Octave Thanet, "A Communist's Wife," *Knitters in the Sun* (Boston: Houghton, Mifflin & Co., 1887), p. 173 ff.
6 Reid, p. 108.

ing to conceal the fact of her sex. She continued to use the pen name on her fiction, although her identity was made known by various loyal critics (among them the wife of President Schaeffer of the University of Iowa) who wrote adulatory essays about her. Alice told various stories about the derivation of the pseudonym; however, the "Octave" seems surely to have been borrowed from her Abbot roommate. She claimed that she had seen "Thanet" on a railroad boxcar in various places—in the East, in Davenport, in the South.

The *Lippincott's Magazine* story marked the beginning of her career; Alice French had found her metier in life as Octave Thanet, author. During the next thirty-five years stories, sketches, articles, essays, and novels flowed from her pen and her typewriter—she adapted very quickly to the new writing machine. Her stories and novels appeared in the major eastern magazines and were bargained for by the nation's leading publishers. Her editors included W. D. Howells (who once publicly admitted he had misread one of her stories), Thomas Bailey Aldrich, and Richard Watson Gilder. Her readers and admirers included Andrew Carnegie (who gave a library to Davenport at her request) and President Theodore Roosevelt (who invited her to the White House for dinner, and who told her on another occasion that he had carried a copy of one of her books on safari in Africa).

Among her friends was Hamlin Garland, although on occasion they had their differences. At the World's Columbian Exposition, Chicago 1893, Garland said, in a lecture attended by many writers, that "every novelist should draw his inspiration from the soil, should write of nothing but the country he was bred in and the people most familiar to him." Alice, who once said she "wrote from experience" sided with him in the resulting discussion, agreeing that art must have its basis in realism, but she added that in her opinion art required that nature must be idealized.

Garland flared at this. "What do you know of the farm realities I describe? You are the daughter of a banker in a country town riding up our lane in a covered buggy. Yet you look across the barbed-wire fence and you see two young men binding grain on a Marsh harvester. 'How picturesque,' you say. 'How poetic!' But I happen to be one of those binding the grain. I have been at it for ten hours. . . . I know western farm life. No one can tell me anything about it. . . . You city folk can't criticize my stories of farm life—I've lived them."

Many years later Garland recalled "that I spoke in opposition . . . in a measure to Alice French, whose work I admire. She was essentially on my side but like many other prosperous town dwellers, was of the opinion that I had overemphasized the dirt and toil and loneliness of the farmer's life."[7]

Her skill in writing and bargaining with editors ("my favorite people"[8]) and publishers made her a financial success; by 1891 she was setting her own terms and getting five cents a word when Garland was getting only a half-a-cent. For a time there seemed no end to her possibilities. In 1895 a critic said that in eight years she had risen to the front rank of short story writers, and in 1905 another critic listed her as one of the ten greatest American women authors.[9]

Her single life and her state of affluence enabled Alice to travel when and where she pleased, and she began writing "local color" stories about her travels. Much of her local color came from Davenport and helped produce the broad range of characters to appear in her fiction. Someone once noted that she wrote about cathedrals and jails, about factories and the homes of the very well-to-do.

To Alice French, the short story was "an incident . . . a single glimpse into life" which had to be "typical and significant":

The people we picture we must understand and make intelligible. We must look at life from their point of view, or we cannot show them coherently as human beings.[10]

As for the local color, she wanted "atmosphere" but not so "thick that it will be a fog." Nevertheless, some of her local color dialogues had to be footnoted.

A major part of Alice's local color came from Thanford, her plantation at Clover Bend in northeastern Arkansas, on the Black River, eight miles from the railroad. Here she and a life-long friend, Jane Allen Crawford, passed their winters from 1883 to 1909. "Away off in the land of nowhere, she lived an idyllic life and at the same time engaged in useful pursuits," one guest wrote. When not busy overseeing the black labor force and the chickens, she wrote the first short stories about Arkansas plantation life. Those guests who could find their way inland over the corduroy roads were entertained lavishly. William Allen White and Marie Therese Blanc, the latter an admirer from France, came away from

---

7 Hamlin Garland, *Roadside Meetings* (New York: Macmillan Co., 1930), pp. 252–56; *Critic* 22 (July 22, 1893):6; Donald Pizer, *Hamlin Garland's Early Work and Career* (Berkeley: University of California Press, 1960), pp. 115–18; George McMichael, *Journey to Obscurity*, pp. 133–38.
8 "Alice French," *Reader Magazine* 4 (October 1904):586–88.
9 Hamilton Wright Mabie, "Mr. Mabie Answers Some Questions," *Ladies Home Journal* 23 (March 1906):20.
10 Reid, "The Theories of Octave Thanet and Other Western Realists," p. 100.

Thanford disagreeing with their host's political beliefs, but praising the gourmet-type meals and rare French wines chilled with ice shipped by steamboat from St. Louis.[11]

One of her Arkansas stories described the brutalities of Arkansas prison camps, but the "horror and squalor and *brutality*" of the story had to be "softened a good deal" before the readers of the Genteel Age could be trusted with it. Alice agreed easily to the softening; "some-things are too ugly for art."[12]

Out of the Arkansas years came the 1910 novel, *By Inheritance*, whose themes were the relationships between white and black, and the readiness of the black for higher education. The heroine was a sixty-year-old single lady who could have been mistaken for Alice French (she had a New England background and drove an electric car like the one Alice drove in Davenport). Agatha Danforth (undoubtedly an anagram of *Thanford*) was a philanthropist who wanted to help a black graduate of Harvard College and its law school found a southern university for blacks. Agatha had the notion that education could serve to unite blacks and whites.

A family crisis brought Agatha to an Arkansas plantation and into closer contact with blacks. She began to accept the white position that "agriculture is the work for the niggro," because the black would find factory work too monotonous, that the black graduate of Harvard Law School would undoubtedly find happiness waiting on table in a good white family home or else chauffeuring for them. A member of Agatha's family asserted the "brutal scientific facts" that through evolution the black's skull "ossified," became "stiff as iron."

Eventually Agatha agrees that the black should not risk civil war with the white—he should accept happiness in a menial position rather than enlightenment. She began to see that "it is an awful thing . . . to run your theories into facts." And she concluded with a statement that must also have been true for Alice French: "I only know the problem is too vast for me."

The novel achieved something of a success. Alice was compared to Harriet Beecher Stowe, and the novel was rated second only to *Uncle Tom's Cabin* as a story about the blacks. Some went so far as to call her the Harriet Beecher Stowe of the Twentieth Century. But in 1926 a black critic, Benjamin Brawley, writing about the "Negro in American Literature" did not mention the book or its author.

Alice French was capable of a moderate viewpoint. In her story "Sist'

---

11 Evelyn S. Schaeffer, "In Arkansas Apropos of Octave Thanet's Romances," *Midland Monthly* 6 (July and August 1896):37–47, 136–45. Translation of "Dans l'Arkansas: A Propos des Romans d' Octave Thanet," Th. Bentzon (Marie Therese Blanc), *Revue des Deux Mondes* 134 (February 1, 1896):542–72.
12 Alice French to Richard Watson Gilder, July 15, 1888, Century Collection, New York Public Library. Quoted with permission.

Chaney's Black Silk," one of the characters says: "You Northern people all allowed that the Niggers were angels during the war, and ayfter the war when you came down here and found out they weren't, you turned plum round and think they're all trash. Fact is, they're just middlin' like the rest of us."[13]

Alice French had other talents. She edited an edition of *The Best Letters of Lady Mary Wortley Montagu* (1890), and wrote a factual book, *An Adventure in Photography* (1893). She used her Arkansas experiences as a basis for a juvenile novel, *We All* (1891), and began anthologizing her short stories. Ten are in *Otto the Knight and Other Trans-Mississippi Stories* (1891): one of these was based on the disastrous Grinnell cyclone; and others are in *A Book of True Lovers* (1897).

The untimely death in Canada in 1897 of her favorite brother, Robert, may have served as the catalyst for her most thorough study of the labor-capital struggle at the end of the century, *The Man of the Hour* (1905). Although Robert had gone to Andover and Harvard, he had decided to begin his industrial career laboring in the family plant, and in the Carnegie Mills in Homestead, Pennsylvania. While he was working in the Bettendorf Wheel factory, a wave of strikes spread across the country and this time the French employees struck. Alice and Robert, who daily engaged in discussions of political and economic theories, decided to go to Pullman, Illinois (the model town on the south side of Chicago built by the inventor of the Pullman car for his workers) to study the strike there at first hand. In Pullman, they both talked with strikers and on one occasion were accosted by a mob. But Alice called them a bunch of "bad boys" and sent them on their way.

Alice used her experience as a basis for "The Contented Masses" in which she reported the good news that revolution could never take place in Iowa because of the large numbers of Europeans in the state. But the article makes it plain that Alice was unable to see clearly what was happening in the labor movement; she still believed too strongly in a philosophy of benevolent paternalism: "If I am a believer in the obligations of employers to those employed, it is because I was reared in such principles, just as I was reared in a hatred of socialism, anarchy, and all efforts to alter the laws of nature by legislative folly."[14]

The hero of *The Man of the Hour* is obviously modeled on Robert French. The novel concerns the struggle which takes place within John-Ivan Winslow as he attempts to cope with the changing labor situation in America and in his father's plant in Fairport (Davenport). At first, John-Ivan follows the idealistic and nihilistic philosophies of his mother, a Rus-

---

13 Octave Thanet, "Sist' Chaney's Black Silk," in *Otto the Knight and Other Trans-Mississippi Stories* (New York: Houghton, Mifflin & Co., 1891).
14 Reid, "The Theories of Octave Thanet and Other Western Realists," p. 107.

sian princess who had once given a "priceless sable coat to a beggar." He leaves the family plant and engages in labor activities, using his share of an inheritance. But he comes into conflict with other labor leaders, who are shown in the novel as conniving, criminal types, willing to sell out their unions for their own private profit. After a series of melodramatic adventures, John-Ivan undergoes a change of mind, and begins to accept the philosophies of his father, Josiah Winslow, descendant of a long line of New England ancestors, who has long before exiled his wife to Switzerland. The novel ends with John-Ivan breaking the strike at the Old Colony Plow Works by smuggling Negro strikebreakers into the plant at three o'clock in the morning, and then leading a Harvard-type football rush against the pickets. (He is cheered on by a child who sings Harvard pep songs during the struggle!)

Alice's career continued to be marked with evidences of success. She continued to publish her short stories and to anthologize them: *A Slave to Duty and Other Women* (1898); *The Heart of Toil* (1898); *The Captured Dream and Other Stories* (1899); and *Stories That End Well* (1911). A 1907 potboiler, *The Lion's Share*, which brought negative criticism from even her friend, Sarah Orne Jewett, indicated that her powers were beginning to fail; *A Step on the Stair* (1913), and *And the Captain Answered* (1917) were further indications that her career as a writer was ending. She began to direct her energies toward such movements as Russian Relief; she opposed both the Prohibition and the suffragette movements.

She was an influence on many of the younger Davenport writers. Susan Glaspell began her career writing local color stories set in "Freeport"— an undoubted nod toward Alice French. Arthur Ficke paid tribute to her in his poem "My Princess." William J. Petersen says she was an influence on George Cram Cook, and Harry Hansen recalls winning two prizes created in her honor by the Colonial Dames of America. But Floyd Dell found her patrician attitudes irritating.

Although she was Iowa's first major literary figure, her reputation gradually faded. When she died in January 1934, she was old, ill, impoverished by the depression, no longer the grand dame. The Octave Thanet literary society at the University of Iowa had passed out of existence the year before; the day of college literary societies was past. At the University an Octave Thanet literary prize of $50 lasted into the mid-fifties, but the winners were not reading her stories. Her books remain in the libraries gathering dust.

But in her lifetime the faint promise in Hiram Alvin Reid's poetry of a literary Iowa had been brought to full fruition, and she was largely responsible. She had looked carefully at the growth of city and industry in Iowa, and she had used the novel and the short story as well as she knew how to interpret that growth.

Hamlin Garland: The Prairie Realist

THE life of (Hannibal) Hamlin Garland reads like one of those "rags-to-riches" accounts so familiar and so popular in the nineteenth and early twentieth centuries. Born in 1860 on a Wisconsin coulee farm to a union of sturdy pioneer stock which had come from New England, he became an internationally known writer, the friend of many literary giants—Whitman, Howells, James, Conrad, Twain, Crane, and Kipling, among others. He was long-lived—he was born during the lifetimes of Melville, Hawthorne, Emerson and Thoreau, and he outlived Thomas Wolfe and died the same year (1940) as F. Scott Fitzgerald. In an age which saw the rise of a truly great American literature, he was not only a transition figure but one of the major persons in its development. At his birth the technological age was beginning to have its first real effects on the prairie land on which he lived; at his death his "middle border" had become a major part of America's industrial, commercial, and economic state.

His best books, the ones which brought him fame and success, and on which his claim to be an Iowa author is based, are set primarily on the northeast Iowa prairie—in Winneshiek and Mitchell counties—where he lived from his ninth until his twenty-first year, and where he got almost all of his formal education. They are: *Main-Travelled Roads* (1891); *Boy Life on the Prairie* (1899); *A Son of the Middle Border* (1917); and *A Daughter of the Middle Border* (1921). The latter book won the Pulitzer Prize. Actually, he had been considered for the prize in 1917 (for *A Son of the Middle Border*, a much better book), but he had been passed over in that first year of the award, probably because he was a member of the selections committee.

Many details of Garland's life in Iowa can be surmised, at least, from the stories and narratives in these books which (along with another related work, *Trail Makers of the Middle Border* [1920]) straddle the line between fiction and biography: "I lived substantially the life of the boys herein depicted. . . . All of the incidents . . . were experiences of other boys and might have been mine. . . . I plowed and sowed, bound grain on a station, herded cattle, speared fish, hunted prairie chickens, and killed rattlesnakes."[1]

Garland was born on a farm near West Salem, Wisconsin. Most of his Iowa years were spent either on a farm near Osage, or in Osage, where his father manged the Grange elevator briefly. For five years, from 1876 to 1881, he attended the Cedar Valley Seminary at Osage.

Out of school, he tramped through the eastern states with a brother, working as a carpenter in Illinois and in Massachusetts to earn the money he needed. In the meanwhile, his wanderlust father had taken the family on to North Dakota, and Garland joined them there, but this time home-steading on his own. Unable to endure the deadly routine of farm life "in the land of the straddlebugs," he returned east to Boston. There, barely eking out an existence, he continued his education by reading in the Boston Public Library, and by attending the Boston School of Oratory. He began to attract the attention of influential people and, with their help, to write reviews for the *Boston Transcript*, and to give public lectures on the subjects he had read up on in the library. The writers and artists he met encouraged his interest in literary matters and social problems.

In 1887, Garland visited in Wisconsin, Iowa, and South Dakota where he was especially struck by the apparent willingness of old friends to settle into a drab routine of existence, and by the effects of the severity of hard work, harsh climate, and poverty on those he had known when he was a boy—and particularly on his mother.

From his mother he heard an account of a neighbor, and, sitting on the doorstep of the Dakota home, he converted it into his first short story, "Mrs. Ripley's Trip." He got seventy dollars for the story and promptly sent half of the money to his mother so that she might buy a new dress.

The description of the Ripley home probably fit the Garland home at the time—a "poor little shanty . . . set like a chicken trap on the vast Iowa prairie" with the only light from "a tallow candle" because the Ripleys "couldn't afford 'none of them new-fangled lamps.'" Their home is a place "where poverty was a never-absent guest."

The setting for this story, the choice of incident and character and theme were not casual. Earlier that year Garland had reviewed Joseph Kirkland's *Zury* for an eastern magazine, and had praised it as "the most realistic novel of American interior life."[2] On his way west, Garland had

---

1   Hamlin Garland, "Preface," *Boy Life on the Prairie* (New York: Macmillan Co., 1899).
2   Hamlin Garland, *Boston Transcript*, May 16, 1887. Review of *Zury: The Meanest Man in Spring County*. Reprinted as an advertisement in Joseph Kirkland's *Chicago Massacre*.

stopped off in Chicago to meet Kirkland, and Kirkland asked, "Why don't you write fiction?" Garland answered, "I can't manage the dialogue," and Kirkland said: ". . . Buckle to it—you can write stories as well as I can—but you must sweat. . . . You can go far if you'll only work . . . you must bend to your desk like a man. You must grind!"[3]

Garland's life was becoming oriented toward the eastern world of artists and writers but still he was to ask: "Is it not time that we of the [rural] west should depict our own distinctive life? The middle border has its own poetry, its beauty, if we can only see it."[4]

Encouraged by Kirkland and his first check for a story, he began writing more stories of the "middle border . . . a vaguely defined region . . . the line drawn by the plow, and broadly speaking, [running] parallel to the upper Mississippi . . . between the land of the hunter and the harvester."[5] Some of these stories were so realistic that the eastern magazine editors of the genteel tradition refused them. But public acceptance of realistic fiction was increasing in the 1890s, and eventually Garland's stories found their way into magazines and books.

Nevertheless, Garland found himself the center of a conflict over his choice of subjects and point of view. "It is a mistake for you to be associated with cranks like Henry George and writers like [Walt] Whitman," he was told. "It is a mistake to be published by the *Arena*. . . . If you will fling away your radical notions and consent to amuse the governing classes, you will succeed." He was warned not to preach but rather to exemplify—"Don't let your stories degenerate into tracts." William Dean Howells advised him to "be fine, be fine—but not too fine!" And Richard Watson Gilder, who was also one of Alice French's editors, warned Garland "not to leave Beauty out of the picture."[6]

Garland knew Henry George and had been reading his arguments for the "single tax"—an economic instrument which George argued would alleviate the farmer's situation. The *Arena* was a Boston magazine with a reputation for radicalism, and its editor, O. B. Flower, was Garland's "most loyal supporter." Flower was insistent that Garland be a reformer—"he was essentially ethical rather than esthetic," said Garland, who realized that he had to "keep a certain balance between Significance and Beauty."[7]

But Garland knew that he had struck a new vein in writing about the middle border. Only Edward Eggleston's *Hoosier Schoolmaster* (1871),

---

3 Hamlin Garland, *A Son of the Middle Border* (New York: Macmillan Co., 1917), p. 354.
4 Hamlin Garland, *Crumbling Idols* (Chicago & Cambridge, 1894), p. 14.
5 Hamlin Garland, *My Friendly Contemporaries* (New York: Macmillan Co., 1932), p. 519.
6 Garland, *A Son of the Middle Border*, pp. 414–16.
7 Garland, *A Son of the Middle Border*, pp. 414–16.

Howe's *Story of a Country Town,* Joseph Kirkland's *Zury,* and Alice French's first book of stories had used this material. Moreover, those American authors already writing in the realist tradition welcomed Garland to their fold—Edward Everett Hale, Mary E. Wilkins, Thomas Wentworth Higginson, Charles Dudley Warner, and others.

In 1891, Garland combined a number of his stories in *Main-Travelled Roads* (republished in varying editions in 1893, 1899, 1909, 1922, 1930, and 1956). The settings for these stories are northeast Iowa, southwest Wisconsin and the eastern Dakotas—the places where Garland had lived. Most of his best stories are in this collection—"A Branch Road," "Up the Coolly [or Coulee]," "Among the Corn Rows," "The Return of a Private," "A Day's Pleasure," and "Under the Lion's Paw."

Garland dedicated his book to his "Father and Mother, whose half-century pilgrimage on the main-travelled road of life has brought them only toil and deprivation." Later he wrote that at the time his parents were faced with deep personal sorrow because of the death of Garland's sister, and because they "were alone on the bleak plain, seventeen hundred miles from their sons," his mother "hopelessly crippled."[8] It is probably true, as some critics have insisted, that Garland's view of the farmer's situation was conditioned by his sentimental attitude toward his parents.

Garland's stories reflect every aspect of pioneer farm life—work in the fields plowing, sowing and harvesting, life in the home, the plight of the rural woman, visits to town, the rural religious experiences, social events, the rural funeral. His themes are many: the moral problem in breaking up an unhappy wedding; the enervating effects of farm life, often leading to mental depression or suicide; the romantic and realistic views of nature; contrast between farm and city life, leading to what came to be called "the revolt against the farm," and "the revolt against the village"; the role of wheat in the farm economy; the role of Henry George's "unearned increment" in farm economy; the conflict between landlord and tenant; the possibilities for individual realization on the self-operated farm; the conflicts resulting from the family demands on farm youth; the role of man as a spoiler of nature; the conflict between man and nature; the casual treatment of romantic love affairs on the prairie; the passing of the West and nostalgia for the past; class distinctions on the prairie and in town; and the cleverness of the townsman as contrasted with the farmer.

Garland's characters cover an equally broad range: the rural "gang"; the isolated black man; the tin-peddler and the creamery man; the rural evangelist; the town banker and lawyer; the well-to-do and the poor; the

8   Garland, *A Son of the Middle Border,* pp. 414–16.

old, middle-aged and young of both sexes; farmers who think they are socially better than their neighbors; the "old-timer" whose roots go back to the east coast and pre-Revolutionary days; the village cronies; the returned Civil War soldier and the expatriate to the East; the greedy landlord; and many more.

Main-Travelled Roads brought both outcries of protest and words of praise. One critic, outraged by the "devil-take-the-farm attitude" expressed in the stories, argued that "tilling the soil was the noblest vocation in the world, not in the least like the picture this eastern[!] author has drawn of it." In Garland's words, "statistics were employed [by his critics] to show that pianos and Brussels carpets adorned almost every farmhouse"; Garland said he had been determined "once for all" to show a "proper proportion of the sweat, flies, heat, dirt and drudgery" of farm life.[9]

William Dean Howells, the "Dean of American letters," praised the book in a *Harper's* essay: "If anyone is still at a loss to account for that uprising of the farmers in the West which is the translation of the Peasants' War into modern and republican terms, let him read Main-Travelled Roads," he wrote. "It is a work of art, first of all, and we think of fine art."[10]

The book was a literary and social success, if not a financial one. Garland got a royalty of five cents on the fifty-cent paperback, and ten cents on the one-dollar cloth bound edition. "My readers were poor," Garland said. "The sale was mainly in the fifty-cent edition."

In 1892, Garland combined a dozen verses and eleven more stories in *Prairie Folks*. In his preface Garland said that the plan of the first book had "brought together stories peculiarly sombre in effect"; the second volume contained tales which were "nearly all of the prairie lands of the West. . . . Both books refer to conditions that have already passed or are passing away. . . . all are descriptive of life as I saw it."

Some of the verse is written in the same "local color" dialect that Alice French had used in some of her fiction:

> Made me think of a clock run down,
> Sure's y're born, that woman did;
> A-workin' away for old Ben Brown
> Patient as a Job an' meek as a kid,
> Till she sort o' stopped one day—
> Heart quitt tickin', a feller'd say.

---

9   Garland, *A Son of the Middle Border*, pp. 414–16.
10   William Dean Howells, "The Study," *Harper's* 87 (September 1893):639–40. Reprinted in Harper & Brothers' 1956 edition of *Main-Travelled Roads*.

All but two of the stories are set in Garland's imaginary Cedar County and Rock River—the town and county are based on Osage and Mitchell County. A number of characters appear in several of the stories—William Bacon, Lyman Gilman, John Jennings and his wife and their son Milton who is a student at the seminary, Bettie Moss, Shephard Watson, William Councill.

The two best stories are "Lucretia Burns" and "Daddy Deering"—the one the story of a despondent farm woman, the other the story of a lively old man. Two other stories deal with the enthusiasms created by religious evangelism, and there is one humorous story, an account of a crucial checkers match. The final story, "Drifting Crane," is the one Garland story in which an Indian appears as the central character. There is an oblique reference in the story to the "massa-*cree*" at New Ulm which Manfred describes in one of his books. At the end of the story a white man tells Drifting Crane that "this is all wrong. . . . There's land enough for us all, or ought to be."

In 1894, Garland explicated his literary theories in *Crumbling Idols*, the only book of this type ever produced by an Iowa writer. Garland's theories were derived from his reading of two French theorists, Hippolyte Adolphe Taine and Eugen Veron, and from his own reflections on American literature as it was. He called his theory of art "veritism."

His book called for the same revolt against European art theories that had already been made in politics; Americans were "still provincial in literary and religious things. . . . American poets and artists were merely shadows or doubles successively of [British poets]. . . . American poets reflected the American taste fairly well, but the spirit and form of their work (with a few notable exceptions) was imitative."

It was time, Garland wrote, for "the great Western middle states,— . . . Wisconsin, Illinois, and Iowa" to turn away from the "pirated exotics" which the middle border journals offered as literature and to write about the "infinite drama . . . going on in those wide spaces of the West,—a drama that is as thrilling, as full of heart and hope and battle, as any that ever surrounded any man; a life that was unlike any ever seen on earth" (pp. 14, 4–5).

Meanwhile, Garland had turned to longer works as media for his "reforming side." *Jason Edwards* (1892) is a novel of a family's failure in the Boston slums and on the western prairies; the story is propaganda for Henry George's single-tax theories and not much more, though it contains some fine scenes, including one of a disastrous prairie hail storm. He dramatized the book with the title *Under the Wheel*, but the play was not successful. Also in 1892 he published *A Spoil of Office*, a novel relating the rise of a farm hand to the Congress of the United States. It is also propagandistic and marred by its too-idealistic, do-nothing-much hero, by a poorly-conceived love affair (Garland was never too sure of himself in describing such matters), and by Garland's obvious ignorance of the ways of legislatures. He had violated, in this book, his own precept that one should write about what one knew.

But his next novel, *Rose of Dutcher's Coolly* (1895), is a fine story of a farm girl who faces the often-fictionalized dilemma of life on the farm versus an education. For its time the book was a strong dose of medicine; it didn't seem to condemn premarital sexual relations and it seemed to support trial marriage. The protests against it were similar to those made against Dreiser's *Sister Carrie*, with which it needs to be compared, though Rose and Carrie are cut from unlike bolts of cloth. As a result of the protests, Garland made some slight revisions in later editions.

When John Frederick's *Druida* appeared in 1923, readers and critics were quick to note the similarities between Frederick's novel and Garland's. There are some differences, however. Rose leaves the farm for an education (both girls are discovered and encouraged by teachers), and in college acquires a taste for arts and culture. She marries a city man and moves on to big-city-life at a rather high social level. Druida is in college only a short time and soon decides to marry a farm man and move to the prairies of Montana. Rose sometimes returns to her father's farm; Druida would never return. Rose's father cares for his daughter; Druida's real father has been gone for years and her stepfather is a drunken lout.

Garland carries his argument for city life so far, however, that the cultural life of the city becomes mere dilettantism. The fault is in Garland himself, as his friend H. B. Fuller's satirical sketch *Under the Skylights* (1901) implies.[11] From a reading of Garland's works and his biography, one can only conclude that Garland himself was a dilettante who never truly comprehended the problems of the artist or of art.

After *Rose of Dutcher's Coolly*, Garland did not write again about the farm life of the Middle Border until 1917. Perhaps the reason was that ascribed to his writer-hero in the novel: "I don't admire the country people unreservedly . . . my experience with them has not been such as to make them heroic sufferers, as the new school of fiction sets 'em forth." More likely the reason was an economic one. Garland discovered that he could do far better lecturing and writing the kind of romances the public would buy and read.

Nevertheless, in 1899 and again in 1910, Garland produced two new anthologies of prairie literature, using stories and verse he had written earlier. *Boy Life on the Prairie* looks back to 1887, a time when Garland thought that he "was too young to begin to write reminiscences." Already

---

11   Henry Blake Fuller, "The Downfall of Abner Joyce," *Under the Skylights* (New York: D. Appleton Co., 1901). "Abner Joyce" is a satirical sketch of Garland.

in 1887, the life he intended to depict was passing; the "machinery of that day" was already gone; the methods of haying, harvesting, threshing . . . quite changed."[12]

The time of the book is 1869–70 (the years of the coming of the Garland family to Iowa), and the setting is "The Big Prairie" of Mitchell County in northeast Iowa. The protagonists are the members of the Duncan Stewart family, including the boys Lincoln and Owen, who have just come onto the prairie from the "coolly" country of Wisconsin, Milton Jennings, and Rance Knapp, who "is the hero of the book, as far as any character can by courtesy be called."[13]

Boy Life on the Prairie is a classic of prairie life. It is much more than the mine from which Garland drew the later *A Son of the Middle Border*, and it is a far better book than Jean Holloway, Garland's biographer, thinks it is.

Garland's description, through a boy's eyes, of this land of strong contrasts, a land which is at once friend and foe to man as he attempts to wrest a living from earth which has never felt man's implements before, is much fresher and clearer than the later book, which is seen through the scrim of nostalgia and golden age. Garland is much closer to the days of his boyhood; he is more a man of the prairie, less a literary man. He remembers more vividly the animal life which was unique to the prairie, he is closer to the possibility of sudden death, and he can still feel the ache of cold in his bones.

Boy Life on the Prairie contains many delightful chapters—"The Coming of the Circus" and "The Battle of the Bulls" among them. These two chapters contain scenes only slightly touched upon in *A Son of the Middle Border*. Moreover, in the earlier book the passages are more concrete, and there are other significant differences. Here, for example, are the two passages describing the horse herd seen by young Lincoln Stewart on his first day on "The Big Prairie," and by young Hamlin Garland on his first day in Mitchell County:

Sitting astride the roof board, he gazed away into the northwest, where no house broke the horizon line, wondering what lay beyond that high ridge.

While seated thus, he heard a distant roar and trample, and saw a cloud of dust rising along the fence which bounded the farm to the west. It was like the rush of a whirlwind, and, before he could call to his father, out on the smooth sod to the south burst a platoon of wild horses, led by a beautiful roan mare. The boy's heart leaped with excitement as the shaggy colts swept round to the east, racing like wolves at play. Their long tails and abundant manes streamed in the wind, and their imperious bugling voiced their contempt for man.

---

12   Garland, "Preface," *Boy Life on the Prairie.*
13   Garland, "Preface," *Boy Life on the Prairie.*

Lincoln clapped his hands with joy, and all of the family ran to the fence to enjoy the sight. A boy, splendidly mounted on a fleet roan, the mate of the leader, was riding at a slashing pace, with intent to turn the troop to the south. He was a superb rider, and the little Morgan strove gallantly without need of whip or spur. He laid out like a hare. He seemed to float like a hawk, skimming the weeds, and his rider sat him like one born to the saddle, erect and supple, and of little hindrance to the beast.

On swept the herd, circling to the left, heading for the wild lands to the east. Gallantly strove the roan with his resolute rider, disdaining to be beaten by his own mate, his breath roaring like a furnace, his nostrils blown like trumpets, his hoofs pounding the resounding sod.

All in vain; even with the inside track he was no match for his wild, free mate. The herd drew ahead, and plunging through a short lane, vanished over a big swell to the east, and their drumming rush died rapidly into silence.

This was a glorious introduction to the life of the prairies, and Lincoln's heart filled with boundless joy, and longing to know it—all of it, east, west, north, and south. He had no further wish to return to his coolly home. The horseman had become his ideal, the prairie his domain. [Pp. 6–7]

A few hours later, while my brother and I were on the roof of the house with intent to peer "over the edge of the prairie" something grandly significant happened. Upon a low hill to the west a herd of horses suddenly appeared running swiftly, led by a beautiful sorrel pony with shining white mane. On they came, like a platoon of cavalry rushing down across the open sod which lay before our door. The leader moved with lofty and graceful action, easily out-stretching all his fellows. Forward they swept, their long tails floating in the wind like banners,—on in a great curve as if scenting danger in the smoke of our fire. Surely, next to a herd of buffalo this squadron of wild horses was the most satisfactory evidence of the wilderness into which we had been thrust.

Riding as if to intercept the leader, a solitary herder now appeared, mounted upon a horse which very evidently was the mate of the leader. He rode magnificently, and under him the lithe mare strove resolutely to overtake and head off the leader.—All to no purpose! The halterless steeds of the prairie snorted derisively at their former companion, bridled and saddled, and carrying the weight of a master. Swiftly they thundered across the sod, dropped into a ravine, and disappeared in a cloud of dust.

Silently we watched the rider turn and ride slowly homeward. The plain had become our new domain, the horseman our ideal. [P. 84]

The language of the first passage is fresh and youthful, recapturing the excitement of the young boy over the strenuous contest; the second is adult and literary, the excitement of the contest has gone, and we are conscious of the mature view in the references to the cavalry charge and the buffalo herd—products of Garland's western years, not of the early Iowa prairie life. Finally, the boy rider in the first passage disappears from view still in full pursuit of his goal; the boy rider in the second turns off in defeat. That significant difference in symbolism may say quite a bit about the sixty-year-old man who was writing *A Son of the Middle Border*.

In 1910, Garland took six of the stories and three of the verses in *Prairie Folks*, and added five other stories to make up a volume he titled *Other Main-Travelled Roads*. The *Main-Travelled Roads* books, he said, contained all of the stories he had written from 1887 to 1889. And, although conditions had changed from 1889 to 1910, "yet for the hired man and the renter life in the West is still a stern round of drudgery." His books presented that life, "not as the summer boarder or the young lady novelist sees it—but as the working farmer endures it." But, he added, "youth and love are able to transmit a bleak prairie town into a poem, and to make of a barbed-wire lane a highway of romance."

For all that, three of the stories in the 1910 collection are the sort of romances that lady novelists were writing, and one is not much more than a temperance tract. If these have any asset at all, it is simply that they were written by a writer who had far more craftsmanship at his command than many of his now long-forgotten peers.

Some of these stories raise the question: Had Garland always been honest in his fictional accounts of rural love, had he always practiced the "veritism" he had advocated? No, he said:

Even my youthful zeal faltered in the midst of a revelation of the lives led by the women on the farms of the middle border. Before the tragic futility of their suffering, my pen refused to shed its ink. Over the hidden chamber of their maternal agonies I drew the veil.[14]

Was Garland presenting the truth of the Iowa farmer's situation in his stories? As far as some of his characters and situations are concerned, there probably was some truth. A Lucretia Burns, isolated in her prairie home day after day with no one around—no telephone, no radio, no television to bring in the sound of a human voice—could become depressed and mentally ill. At least, as Professor Bartholow Crawford once remarked, the man in the field had his animals to talk to!

Nevertheless there is probably some overemphasis on the seamy side in passages such as this from "Lucretia Burns":

"I hate farm life," she went on with a bitter inflection. "It's nothing but fret, fret, and work the whole time, never going any place, never seeing anybody but a lot of neighbors, just as big fools as you are. I spend my time fighting flies and washing dishes and churning. I'm sick of it all."

Moreover, the hero of "Under the Lion's Paw" is not actually victimized by land laws or the unearned increment; he is rather the victim of his

---

14   Garland, *A Son of the Middle Border*, pp. 414–16.

failure to obtain a written contract, and of his trust in handshakes and the word of another. (Such trust became one of the West's myths.) Too late he learns that he is dealing with a rascal and a scoundrel. Still one doesn't feel too sorry for the Haskins. A family that can "put a farm on its feet" in three years will end up owning half the township.

When one turns from Garland's fiction to Allan G. Bogue's *From Prairie to Corn Belt* (1963), one can only conclude that Garland's understanding of the farmer's situation was superficial, limited, and prejudiced. There were land speculators, but the farmers dealt with them by forming clubs and entering into private agreements (as we see in Stong's *Buckskin Breeches*). There were undoubtedly instances of usury although interest charges of over ten per cent were prohibited by law, and in the 1880s and 1890s the average rate of interest was closer to six per cent. There were foreclosures and farm failures, but Bogue's book systematically demonstrates that for the most part "work often brought success."[15] But Garland was right about the hard endless work—and no amount of social protest could change that. Only the oncoming technological developments were to change the situation so that human and animal energy could be replaced by energy derived from other sources and the farmer's life made easier and more comfortable.

Most critics think that Garland's masterpieces are the two books of his later years, *A Son of the Middle Border* (1917) and *A Daughter of the Middle Border* (1921). The first narrates his birth and early Wisconsin days, his coming to Iowa and his life there, and his travels through the East and the Middle Border. It also relates his life in Boston and the beginnings of his literary and lecturing careers. It terminates in 1893 at a time when Garland had fulfilled his dream of bringing his family back to a home of their own in West Salem, Wisconsin. (He did it primarily for his mother, for his father never got the plains out of his system and for many years continued to return to South Dakota to work his fields there.)

The second book takes up Garland's career in 1893, and relates his life in Chicago (which became his home in 1899), his marriage to Zulime Taft, the sister of Lorado Taft, the famous American sculptor, the birth of his two daughters, his continuing travels to Europe and Colorado and the Far West, his lectures, his friendships with famous literary men, and so forth. It is not as good a book for a number of reasons; the life of a boy on the Iowa prairie makes a more interesting subject than the self-lionizing of a successful literary man. The earlier book is more tightly structured by its central settings and themes, and there is more vigor and less sentimentalizing in it.

Trail Makers of the Middle Border is the third volume in the series of

---

15 Allan G. Bogue, *From Prairie to Farm Belt* (Chicago: University of Chicago Press, 1963), p. 287.

Garland's efforts to mine his memories. It recounts the history of the Garland and McClintock families from their New England days until the return of Richard Garland from the Civil War—an incident which was the basis for Garland's best short story, "The Return of a Private." The reader who would like to see how Garland used and reused this material over a period of thirty-five years might compare Garland's treatment of the final incident in *Trail Makers* with the corresponding passages in the short story and in *A Son of the Middle Border*, noticing the change in viewpoints, and in the kind and amount of details furnished.

From the late 1890s on, Garland had been writing books and essays about the land west of the Middle Border. *A Captain of the Gray Horse Troop* treats of the Indian, and *Cavanagh, Forest Ranger* relates to the theme of conservation of the great western spaces. Some of the attitudes expressed in these books and in *Her Mountain Lover* reflect the same kind of protesting viewpoint Garland had used in his prairie stories; some of them reflect his warm admiration for Theodore Roosevelt's philosophy of the "strenuous life" and for his conservation policies. The first book is the best, but all three are too romantic in treatment. So too is *Hesper*, a romance set in the mines of Colorado, which too often substitutes stereo-typed bookish materials for verisimilitude.

As Garland visited and revisited the West (using West Salem and Onte-ora, New York, as his bases), he became more and more interested in the culture and problems of the Indian. His *Book of the American Indian* (1923) has been highly praised as an early recognition of the Indian as literary material.

In this century too much of Garland's energy was expended on matters other than writing about his native states. He was always traveling some-where to lecture or vacation. He took an interest in spiritualism and wrote a book on that subject. He visited the Yukon during the Gold Rush of 1898 and wrote a book on that experience. He helped found the American Academy of Arts and Letters and was in due time elected to it; later he became one of its directors. He served on the first Pulitzer Prize com-mittee.

In later life honors, awards, and wealth came his way. His books were published and republished and one or two were filmed. Northwestern University and the Universities of Wisconsin and Southern California awarded him honorary degrees—the latter receiving custody of his papers as a result. President Theodore Roosevelt became a close friend and con-sulted often with Garland on problems of conservation and the Indian. After the death of William Dean Howells, in 1920, the one-time Iowa farm boy was acclaimed as the new "Dean of American letters." Even within his adopted state he was a hero; he was a leader in that movement in the period 1910–20 which began to assert the merits and presence of an Iowa literature. He came to a gathering of Iowa authors in Des

Moines in 1914, lectured at the University of Iowa, and with other Iowa authors contributed to *Prairie Gold* (1917), a volume which memorialized the role of Iowa servicemen in World War I.

Although he has been criticized in later years for his romanticism, and although he has been accused of having yielded his models to models set before him by eastern editors of the genteel tradition, his reputation still stands. Wallace Stegner said that "as a man of the gifted group that gathered in Chicago, and as a forerunner of the many writers who now profess cultural regionalism as a literary creed, Garland is of the first importance."[16] Granville Hicks, who was sometimes extremely critical of Garland, said that "he wrote some of the finest stories yet written of American farm life—direct, comprehensive, moving and savagely honest."[17] John Frederick says of his best stories that they "remain after sixty years very much alive. They have a strong characterization, rich texture of farm experience, vigorous drama. They meet the requirements of literature."[18] John T. Flanagan commented that "in one sense, . . . Garland's picture was distorted" and "it remained for later writers to present a more balanced picture of the farm," and then added:

The scenes he drew were unprecedented in the pages of American fiction. . . . A half-century has passed since his gaunt farm wives and work-harried farmers first appeared in fiction, but they have not been forgotten. No one before Garland drew with such bitter truth the hopeless struggles of the coulee dwellers or the efforts of men on the Dakota prairies to raise wheat in the face of wind and drought. His books have influenced every subsequent novelist of the farm.[19]

Garland in his Middle Border fiction used the truth as he saw it, and created art out of that truth. In the lives of homely people he found great themes: romanticism versus realism in the lives of people close to nature; town versus country; the restlessness of an age; the urge to succeed; rascality versus altruism; the human struggle to endure; and the beginnings of the movement from rural life back to the city. Garland insisted that there was a potential for art in the affairs of common folk, and he insisted on the importance of the Middle Border. Finally, by inventing and defining the Middle Border, and by using it as a thematic focus for literature, he provided a model for such later creations as Phil Stong's Pittsville and Frederick Manfred's Siouxland.

16 Wallace Stegner, "The Trail of the Hawkeye," *Saturday Review of Literature* 18 (July 30, 1938):4.
17 Granville Hicks, *The Great Tradition* (New York: Macmillan Co., 1935), p. 146.
18 John T. Frederick, "The Farm in Iowa Fiction," *Palimpsest* 32 (March 1951): 124–26.
19 John T. Flanagan, "The Middle Western Farm Novel," *Minnesota History* 23 (June 1942):115–16.

Herbert Quick:
The Social Life of the Prairie

JOHN Herbert Quick was born October 23, 1861, just thirteen months after Hamlin Garland, and so his pioneer experiences parallel those of Garland. Of those defined herein as Iowa writers, Quick was the first to be born in Iowa, his birthplace having been on a farm on the Grundy-Hardin county line near Steamboat Rock. While Garland was growing up in and near Osage, Quick was living only fifty or sixty miles away. But that was a great distance in the 1870s, just as great a distance as that which separates the literary tactics of the two men. Garland is at his best writing of the individual and the family, and he looks only rarely at the larger social scene—an occasional Grange picnic or evening get-together, or the threshing. When he does turn to the larger scene (as in *Spoil of Office* or *Rose of Dutcher's Coolly*), he is obviously uncomfortable, even unfamiliar, with his materials. Quick, on the other hand, while focusing on individuals and small groups as the novelist must, usually shows them in the larger setting: threshing, at a Grange meeting, grading a road, moving across the prairies, attending a caucus, in the county courthouse, and so on. In all fairness to our understanding of the nineteenth-century Iowa scene then, we should read the two side by side, so that we are aware that while Garland's people are working out their individual destinies "Among the Corn Rows" or "Up the Coulee," Quick's "Cow" Vandemark, Magnus Thorkelson, "Raws" Upright, and "Freem" McConkey are struggling to establish the communities of Monterey County and Monterey Center.

Moreover, Quick and Garland do not agree on the life of the pioneer woman. One needs to contrast only Garland's Lucretia Burns with the following apostrophe of Quick's to the prairie mother to see the difference:

The mothers of the frontiers! They felt the oncoming of another day for their children. No life was so laborious, no situation so unpropitious, no poverty so deep that they did not through a divine gift of prophecy see beyond the gloom a better day for their children. In the smoky over-heated kitchens, struggling to feed the "gangs" of harvesters and threshers, as they washed and

mopped and baked and brewed and spun and wove and knit and boiled soap
and mended and cut and basted and sewed and strained milk and skimmed
cream and churned and worked over butter, catching now and then an opportunity to read while rocking a child to sleep, drinking in once in a while a bit
of poetry from the sky or the cloud or the flower; they were haloed like suns
of progress for their families and for their nation, as they worked and
planned and assumed for themselves a higher and higher culture of its sort—
all for their children. We build monuments in the public square for the soldiers
of our wars; but where is the monument for the Kate McConkeys who made
possible so much of the good which is represented by the public square itself?
Unless it is a monument not made with our hands, in our hearts and souls, none
can ever exist which can be in any way adequate.[1]

In that contrast is all the difference between the points of view of Garland and Quick. Quick knew about sod huts and prairie homes made of
basswood, but his philosophy of life and art was different. He would not
align himself with that "school of writers who have set themselves to the
analysis and description of country, village and town communities" to
display to the world the rural "sordid drabness, their utter poverty of
inspiration, their lack of men and women above the plane of two-legged
hogs and cattle." Those writers were "looking for darkness," but Quick
was "looking for light."[2]

Garland came early to the literary life, but Quick was "like a setter
pup, forever smelling out something new." He seemed "to have been
'capable de tout.' He was a school teacher, lawyer, journalist, politician,
prosecutor of boodlers, mayor, organizer of the Federal Farm Bureau,
Red Cross executive in the Far East, a suasive and delightful speaker, a
country gentleman."[3]

His experiences in these various roles gave him the wealth of subject
matter on which he drew for his books when he eventually came to write.

Quick would have agreed with Garland that "all fiction is autobiographical . . . the novelist starts with what he has known." But "when his
creation begins to live in the pages of his story, it takes on an individuality
of its own and reaches heights or sinks to depths never attained by the
original, which grows dimmer and dimmer as the work of art begins to
throb with its own life."[4]

As far as the advantages and disadvantages of the Iowa scene for fiction
are concerned, Quick is sometimes a bit satirical. Fremont McConkey,

---

1 Herbert Quick, *The Hawkeye* (Indianapolis: Bobbs-Merrill Co., 1923), p. 196.
2 Herbert Quick, *One Man's Life* (Indianapolis: Bobbs-Merrill Co., 1925), p. 164.
(Elsewhere, Quick makes it clear he was referring to *Main Street* and *Winesburg,
Ohio*.)
3 "A Creator," *New York Times*, May 12, 1925, p. 22.
4 Quick, *One Man's Life*, p. 60.

his would-be writer in *The Hawkeye*, after observing some juicy bits of scandal in the county court, wishes "that the parties had been a little more foreign or ancient so that he could have made a story of it," or that the "story could be given some locale where judges wore robes, now—but he was such a funny little man, and so common with all his dignity!"[5]

In his more serious moods, Quick recognized the problems facing him in his choice of characters and subjects. They had certain limitations, these Iowa prairie people "in morals [and] in intellect . . . in spite of their impenetrability, their formidable character, their power of impressing."[6]

Quick's family (he claimed to be $15/16$th's Holland Dutch) originated in the Rondout valley of New York and came to Iowa from Wisconsin in 1857, intending to take up land in the "Fort Dodge country." But, because of high water in the Iowa River that rainy spring, they stopped at what is now Steamboat Rock. Quick attended a rural school in a building situated at the headwaters of the creek which was later dammed to form the lake in Pine Lake State Park. The school building is now a museum in Grundy Center.

As a boy he acquired a reputation for being a bookish type. His father did not read so there were not many items of reading material in the bare prairie home, but neighbors contributed discarded items, much of it the romantic trash published in the popular journals of the time. Consequently, he was probably not too unlike Fremont McConkey, who was given to flights of fancy about his environment, similar to those of Tom Sawyer.

Although he had a childhood attack of polio (the effects of which kept him from a possible West Point appointment), he was always the brightest child in his school. He attributed his excellence to the polio, maintaining that it left its victims superior to others. One can well imagine him helping the other children with their studies as Fremont McConkey once helped Bently Bushyager with "the cabalistic word 'PREFACE: . . . *Peter Rice Eats Fish, Alligators Catches Eels, Eels Catches Alligators, Fish Eats Raw Potaters.*'"[7]

Quick later claimed that at the age of ten he began to have as his object in life "success in literature." He early had a reputation among his peers for telling "fine stories . . . partly cribbed" from his reading, with forgotten details replaced by his own fertile imagination.

At sixteen he attended a summer "teacher's institute" at Grundy Center where he succeeded so well that he was soon teaching in a country school and eventually (in succeeding summers) in the institute itself—often find-

---

5 Quick, *The Hawkeye*, pp. 295–96.
6 Quick, *The Hawkeye*, p. 171.
7 Quick, *The Hawkeye*, p. 30.

ing among his students men who had far better educations and far more experience. On one occasion, the eminent feminist, Carrie Lane Chapman Catt, then head of the Mason City school system, complained that the standards of education were being lowered because Quick, "a country school teacher," had been appointed to teach in an institute.

Later Quick taught at Wesley, Iowa, for a year, and then he moved to Mason City where he taught in the old South Ward (later Garfield) school, while at the same time reading law in a local law office—thus acquiring the background for a good many incidents in his novels. He also sang in a church choir and in local Gilbert and Sullivan musicals.

Eventually he passed the Iowa bar examination, thus compensating at least partially for his inability to attend a college. But on one occasion when a fellow lawyer asked for the name of his *"alma mater"* he "shocked the learned brother . . . by [saying], 'Not to have attended some schools is in itself a liberal education.' "[8]

Quick's life up to this point (about 1890) is narrated at length in *One Man's Life* (1925), an autobiography which is often fascinating, sometimes humorous, and too often merely garrulous.

Quick was mayor of Sioux City from 1898 to 1900. The election was a form of reward for his having led "a forlorn hope against a corrupt ring in the county and city," and, according to Quick was not what he had wanted—he had hoped to become the county attorney as a means of building his law business.

In 1901 he published "a book of fables . . . a tale of the Puk Wudjies (*In the Fairy Land of America*)." He wanted to create "the household American fairy." A year later, he used a lunch period to write "A Whiff of Smoke," a poem which the editor of the *Century Magazine* accepted. To Quick, this "accolade in the form of a nice letter from a real poet was what counted."[9] But he was already forty-one years old, married and a father, and this piece of verse had been written in that eighteenth-century English style against which Garland had protested a decade earlier.

Encouraged, Quick began to write (while supporting himself by practicing law) and in 1904 published *Aladdin and Company*, a novel based on the boom theme which always appealed to him. The "Lattimore" of the novel seems to be a combination of Sioux City and Mason City, but many of the incidents are based on his Sioux City experiences with the "corrupt ring" he had prosecuted, and with the boom which J. Hyatt Downing was later to write about. But compared with *Sioux City*, Quick's novel comes off a poor second. For one thing, in Downing's

8 Herbert Quick, "I Picked My Goal at Ten—Reached It at Sixty," *American Magazine* 94 (October 1922):162.
9 Quick, "I Picked My Goal at Ten," p. 164.

novel we feel we are in a recognizable city. (Except for his scenes along the Erie Canal and on the Monterey prairie, Quick does not establish locale well.) Also, Downing's characters seem much more real and believable.

Quick's success in getting this book published led him to write others. He learned "the game of serialization,"[10] offering his stories first to a magazine for serial publication, then bringing the work out in book form. *Double Trouble* (1906), serialized as *The Occultation of Florian Amidon*, is the story of an Iowa business man living two lives (a theme handled much better in *Three Faces of Eve*). It and *The Broken Lance* (1907), categorized by Quick as "the best and most searching sociological novel" he ever wrote, need not concern us.

He had given up his law practice to write. But his books did not make him any money, so he took over the associate editorship of *LaFollette's Weekly*, and, subsequently, the editorship of *Farm and Fireside*. His success as an editor in the days when Iowa farmers were becoming "book farmers" (much to Quick's dismay) is recounted in W. E. Ogilvie's *Pioneer Agricultural Journalists*.

During these years he published several short stories of Iowa farm life which were later collected (1911) with other non-farm stories in *Yellowstone Nights*—a book in the *Canterbury Tales* tradition. Members of a Yellowstone National Park stage tour recount stories around the campfire each night, some of them the farm stories. The stories were modeled too much along the lines of current popular magazine fiction, and they reveal a continuing romantic bent.

One of Quick's literary faults is a tendency to moralize or to propagandize. The tendency appears in his 1915 novel, *The Brown Mouse*, a story with a conventional love affair built around a farm hand who becomes a rural school teacher at the same time his girl becomes county superintendent of schools. The hero sets out to reform rural education by developing a curriculum based on the practical needs of rural youngsters: "the work of the school should be correlated with the life of the home and farm—a school which would be in the highest degree cultural by being consciously useful and obviously practical." Ironically, for Quick, the farm mothers object to this program—they want their children to have the same cultural advantages as city children! But Quick seems to miss their point. The novel is marred by its didactic purposes, by its wooden dialogue, and by its stereotyped romance. Still it shows a stage in the development of rural life; the automobile and the telephone make their appearance in the farm scene, and the hero argues for cooperative farm enterprises and the consolidated school.

---

10 Quick, "I Picked My Goal at Ten," p. 163.

During World War I Quick resigned his editorship to accept President Wilson's offer of a position on the Federal Farm Loan Board (at a reduced salary). Quick welcomed the opportunity "to be engaged in building up a great financial system for the farmers."[11] Out of this experience came his plea for farm reform, including the county agent system, *The Fairview Idea* (1919). He noted in this book that "the world has always despised and contemned the farmer." The word *farmer* itself is used by city people to denote a second-class citizen:

. . . it follows a tendency which inheres in the language . . . "boor" meant farmer before it meant cad; "carle" . . . once took in all peasants and then came to mean a low fellow; "churl" . . . goes from the soil to bad manners, like "boor;" "villain" . . . was once a man who belonged to a farm or villa, but is now any bad man; "yokel," once a farmer, but now a "hick;" "pagan," from "paganus," a country-man; "heathen," a dweller among the heaths.

Quick concluded that "it is no accident that any term which signifies a farmer or farm laborer in one century is likely to mean something despicable or ignorant or criminal the next."[12]

The war over, he resigned from the Board because *Vandemark's Folly* "lay partly written on [his] desk," and he hoped "to make it really 'literature'." Long before, he had envisioned the book as "The Tewksbury Tribe," but his original scheme had changed "in the light of a few decades of development of the Mid-West situation with which it deals."[13]

But he "was not through following squirrel tracks off into the woods," and soon he was heading "a commission for the American Red Cross to wind up their affairs in Siberia." He became dangerously ill in Vladivostok and, "given up to die by the doctors" he sent a "last message . . . to a friend . . . to finish 'Vandemark's Folly'" for him.[14] But he recovered and returned to America.

Quick was now sixty, an age when most writers have long since done their best work. Only five years of his life remained, but in those five years he wrote his two best works (*Vandemark's Folly* and *The Hawkeye*) and *The Invisible Woman, The Real Trouble with Farmers,* and *One Man's Life.* His vitality and energy were waning, as one can see if the books are read in the order written, but his literary skill, now at its peak, lasted long enough for him to produce the two best novels ever

---

11 Quick, "I Picked My Goal at Ten," p. 164.
12 Herbert Quick, "Restoring Our Rural Morale," *The Fairview Idea* (Indianapolis: Bobbs-Merrill Co., 1919). See seventh page of this unnumbered prefatory essay.
13 Quick, "I Picked My Goal at Ten," p. 164.
14 Quick, "I Picked My Goal at Ten," p. 164.

written about the Iowa farm and town scene of the nineteenth century—
books which earned him an international reputation.

Vandemark's Folly (1922), *The Hawkeye* (1923), and *The Invisible
Woman* (1924) constitute a trilogy set in Monterey County (based on
Grundy County), Lithopolis (which resembles Steamboat Rock), and
Monterey Center (which resembles Mason City, even to its initial letters). The first novel begins on the Erie Canal in 1838 and continues past
the Civil War; the second book begins before the Civil War and continues
until the 1890s; the third book is limited to the early 1890s.

In these three novels, we are given the story of the men, women, and
children who came out to Iowa from the East, who took up land on the
prairie and broke it to their use, and who in a generation brought about
a sociological and economic revolution, "the first great experiment in the
building of a democracy based on ponderous production . . . of keeping
a people economically free while living an industrial and agricultural
life and dependent on highways made by man instead of those created by
nature."[15] Quick's novels present a view of the "agricultural revolution
felt all over the world" which is never seen in Garland's books.

Vandemark's Folly begins with "the west . . . on the road," with "Iowa
on the road"; it shows the social classes who settled the new state; the
"speculators, missionaries, land-hunters, merchants; criminals escaping
from justice; couples fleeing from the law; families seeking homes; the
wrecks of homes seeking secrecy; gold-seekers . . . politicians . . . editors
. . . adventurers . . . lawyers . . . Abolitionists . . . and most numerous of
all, homeseekers 'hunting country'—a nation on wheels, an empire in the
commotion and pangs of birth." *Vandemark's Folly* is narrated by Jaco-
bus Teunis Vandemark who began life as an Americanized Dutch boy in
the Rondout valley of New York, ran away from a tyrannical stepfather
and a sick mother to become a "driver" on the Erie Canal, then came
west in search of his mother. His stepfather, after telling young Jacob
that his mother is dead, persuades the boy to accept a deed to a mile-
square area of land in Monterey County, Iowa, as his share of his mother's
estate. Not knowing that the stepfather has intended to swindle him,
Jacob comes on to Iowa, trading horses for cattle, and cattle for cattle,
as he travels, thus acquiring the nickname of "Cow" Vandemark. Along
the way he has several adventures, in one of which he meets the girl he
later marries. As Jacob comes up out of the Mississippi River valley west
of Dubuque, tears come to his eyes as he views the "great green sea"
before him—"the newest, strangest, most delightful, sternest, most wonderful thing in the world—the Iowa prairie. . . ." The long passage in

---

15 Quick, *The Hawkeye*, p. 99.

which Quick describes the boy's first view of the prairie has been widely praised, particularly by the great prairie naturalist, Professor Bohumil Shimek of the University of Iowa, himself a product of the prairie lands.

The balance of the novel tells of Jacob's discovery that his mile-square of land is largely Hell Slew, his philosophical acceptance of his situation, the settling of the marsh and the land around it by Jacob, Magnus Thorkelson, the Fewkes, Buck Gowdy, and others, and the beginnings of the towns of Monterey Center and Lithopolis. In Gowdy, we see an interesting type, never described by Garland, a farmer of great wealth and huge land holdings. Quick, when he created this character, had in mind one George Wells whose "great estate" was close to Wellsburg, where Quick, a boy of sixteen, got his first teaching job. The story line of *Vandemark's Folly* concerns Jacob's romance with Virginia Royal, to whom he had been a benefactor along the ridge road west of Dubuque, and the seduction of Rowena Fewkes by Buck Gowdy, and the consequences of those two affairs. A prairie fire and a blizzard play important parts in bringing about the denouement of the novel.

The Hawkeye picks up the story line with the birth of Fremont McConkey in June 1857 in a house where his mother "could look out through a hole in the roof and see the great prairie stars serenely burning their golden lamps in the sky, while she heard the yelping of the hungry wolves outside." The narrative is related in the third person, but at the end the narrator tells us that he and Fremont McConkey are one.

Because of Quick's theories about writing novels, and because the fictitious Fremont McConkey's birthday is very close to Quick's, one might assume that the incidents in *The Hawkeye* and in *One Man's Life* would demonstrate some similarities. Such is the case; the fate of the Bushyagers is a case in point. Their real life models were the Rainsbargers—Manse and Pitt—whose lynching in Eldora was described in the *Palimpsest* of August 1923.[16]

Both Fremont and Quick have authorial ambitions, and both are iconoclasts. Like Quick, Fremont becomes a schoolteacher, a politician, and finally a lawyer. Unlike Quick, he becomes a member of the courthouse "ring," and eventually a newspaper man. Unlike Quick (who married a New York girl he met in Chicago), Fremont has three romances—marrying the first time a girl not unlike David Copperfield's first wife, then, after his wife's death, proposing to her sister to save her from marrying Fremont's political enemy, and finally, to prevent scandal, marrying his wife's other sister, who is caring for the two children of his first marriage.

Although Fremont is a well-developed character, two others in the novel are more interesting. One is Bently Bushyager, a member of the

16 Jocelyn Wallace, "An Iowa Doone Band," *Palimpsest* 4 (August 1923):267–80.

Bushyager gang of horsethieves and robbers, a companion of Fremont in his youth, and at last a victim of mob violence. The other is Quick's most fascinating creation, J. Roswell Upright, otherwise known as "Raws," a man who lives by his brashness and by his willingness to profit on the fluid county government situation and the greed of his fellow men. Among the latter is "The Non-Resident Owner," a speculator who hoped to profit on unimproved land which increased in value as the land around it was improved by hard work and thrift. "Raws's" treatment of these speculators had its basis in at least one Iowa county—O'Brien, in northwest Iowa.[17]

In *The Invisible Woman*, Quick turns to Christina Thorkelson, the daughter of Magnus Thorkelson and that Rowena Fewkes who had been betrayed by the wealthy Buck Gowdy. Christina moves to town, becomes a stenotypist in a law office, and eventually marries her employer. Her step-brother, Owen Gowdy, the illegitimate son of Buck and Rowena, ultimately acquires a major share of Buck's wealth in a lawsuit which takes up the latter part of the novel. Aside from the comic Surrajer Fewkes there are no interesting characters, and there is too much trivial dialogue, too much summary, too much moralizing. Here and there we see Quick trying to reproduce the triumphs of his other novels in the trilogy, but he does not succeed. The shift in emphasis from Christina to the Gowdy trial results in a breakdown in the structure of the novel.

Quick's accomplishment is that he has shown us the development of a pioneer society on the land with all its broader implications. He has shown us pictures of pioneer life which reflect a long lifetime of experience, and which are, as Professor Bogue and others have said, accurate.[18] If Quick is not a great artist, it may be because of the limitations of his environment:

Iowa has not always smiled on her dreamers, her poets, her children with the divine fire in their souls, whether much or little of it. . . . And yet I know if the artist in Iowa could only be allowed such a life of the soul as would impel him to respect his Iowa materials, and to ponder them long enough and deeply enough, every element of great art would be found here.[19]

Or it may be true, as Walter Van Tilburg Clark once said, that the Iowa cultural background is not rich enough to provide for the kind of

---

17 Josephine Donovan, "Old O'Brien," *Palimpsest* 5 (January 1924), p. 23 ff.
18 Allan G. Bogue, *From Prairie to Corn Belt* (Chicago: University of Chicago Press, 1963), pp. 135, 159.
19 Quick, *The Hawkeye*, p. 476.

art that a Russian background provided for Tolstoi and Dostoievski. It
lacks, in Professor Clark's word, "humus."[20] Perhaps Fremont McConkey
is right in speculating that if Iowa "were only a mountain country, or a
coast" better stories might result.

Still, in the process of reporting and interpreting the new life on the
prairie, a life which sprang into being in the nineteenth century, had an
ephemeral existence and then vanished even as the prairie vanished, Quick
(and Garland as well) caught, in Professor Bogue's words "the duality
in the impact of the prairie . . . [the] uplift and oppression, promise and
threat." "How ironic, thought Herbert Quick, that the richest of soils
would reduce rather than enhance the freedom of the men who tilled
them!"[21]

Professor Bogue undoubtedly had "Cow" Vandemark's words in mind:
"Breaking prairie was the most beautiful, the most epochal, and most
hopeful, and as I look back at it, in one way the most pathetic thing man
ever did, for in it, one of the loveliest things ever created began to come
to its predestined end."

Both Garland and Quick caught the new language that sprang up on
the prairie. Words and phrases with an earthy quality show up on their
pages for the first time:

back furrow, banger board, bear down, bedaddled, big gun, binding on a
station, bitting-rig, body, soul and britches, bog down, boiled shirt, botch job,
boughten, bulldoze, full-bite high, goose is cooked, high-toned, kick over the
hull apple cart, nepoed, nimshies, north end of a south wind, odd as Dick's
hatband, off ox—.

The list goes on and on.

Professor A. G. Kennedy found in *Vandemark's Folly* "three outstand-
ing vocabulary types worthy of consideration": the colloquial, popular
English:

So I had to knuckle under . . . I thought as much as could be that my first
name was Jacot. . . .
I who-hawed and gee-upped my way back to Monterey Center. . . .;

the dialectal matter:

"We're gwine to Canayda . . . I kess . . . it mus' have peen your team I put
in de parn lass night. Come in. Preckfuss is retty. . . . Ay know de man! So it

---

20   Clarence A. Andrews, "You've Gotta Have More Humus," *Frivol* 33 (December
1951):6, 25. (Interview with Walter Van Tilburg Clark. *Frivol* was published at the
University of Iowa. Volume 33 is wrongly identified as volume 27.)
21   Bogue, *From Prairie to Corn Belt,* p. 66.

vas in de ol' country! Rich fallar bane t'inking poor girl notting but like fresh fruit for him to eat; . . . ."

Finally, there are Quick's linguistic notes on "sitheing" and "sighing;" on the difference between "cursing" and "cussing," and, in *The Hawkeye*, the marvelous case of the St. Troplas Hotel where the coming together of a French sign painter and an unlettered Yankee produced a new saint in the hagiology![22]

Quick, like Garland, accepted the "single tax" theories of Henry George; they are mentioned in the trilogy, and as late as *One Man's Life* Quick wrote that George's ideas must be accepted "not only in America but all over the world if civilization is not to rot down into ruin." But there is this difference between Garland and Quick. Whereas Garland's farmers despair of their condition and blame it on the failure to legalize the principle of the "unearned increment," Quick's farmers do something about their situation. They set up two levels of taxes—a low one on the land which is being broken to the plow and a higher one on the speculator-held land which is increasing in value as the land around is farmed. This action of Quick's farmers is verified by Professor Allan Bogue.[23]

Vandemark's Folly and *The Hawkeye* have been widely praised by book reviewers, historians, literary critics, university professors, and a vast popular audience as well. John T. Flanagan said that they "are invaluable documents in the social history of the state. . . . they contain remarkable pictures of the immigrant farmers who developed the prairie state . . . [Quick's] scenes are vivid and real."[24] John T. Frederick said he "found positive pleasure in re-reading [*Vandemark's Folly*], . . . in its vitality, its sensitiveness, its firmness in portrayal of people, especially of the central character, "Cow" Vandemark, himself . . . the loving and precise observation of varied aspects of the pioneer experience. . . ."[25] Frank Luther Mott said that *Vandemark's Folly* was "the best literary interpretation of pioneer life in Iowa before the Civil War."[26]

Herbert Quick spent the latter years of his life on his farm, "Coolfont," near Berkeley Springs, West Virginia. He died of a heart attack on May 10, 1925, while on a lecture trip to Columbia, Missouri.

---

22 A. G. K. [A. G. Kennedy], "Bibliographical Department," *American Speech* 2 (December 1926):153–55.
23 Bogue, *From Prairie to Corn Belt*, p. 45.
24 John T. Flanagan, "The Middle Western Farm Novel," *Minnesota History* 23 (June 1942):118–19.
25 John T. Frederick, "The Farm in Iowa Fiction," *Palimpsest* 32 (March 1951): 128–29.
26 Frank Luther Mott, "Exponents of the Pioneers," *Palimpsest* 11 (February 1930): 62.

Ruth Suckow:
The Poetry of Place

RUTH Suckow was born in Hawarden, Iowa, August 6, 1892, the descendant of nineteenth-century immigrants. On her father's side, her grandfather, John Suckow, had come to America from the dukedom of Mecklenburg, Germany, without knowing a word of English. He worked in Albany in "York State" until he could send to the old country for his sweetheart, Caroline. After their marriage and the birth of their children, they came to northeast Iowa where they took a farm "in the timber." Later they moved on to the slough and prairie country of German Township (renamed "Liberty" during World War I) in Hancock County. Some years later when his son considered buying land near Mobile, Alabama, the old man remonstrated that there were only two places worth living in: York State and "Old Iowa."

Her mother was Anna Mary Kluckholn whose parents were "of a different [better] social class." They emigrated from the small city of Lippe-Detmold in the province of Lippe, coming first to Chicago, then to Michigan and Minnesota. Finally being advised (like Alice French's father) to move to Iowa for his health, the Reverend Charles Kluckholn brought his family to German Township. (Like the Suckows, the Kluckholns had been converted to Methodism by Peter Cartwright, the Illinois Methodist Episcopal preacher.) Grandfather Kluckholn died when Miss Suckow was a small child so she had little memory of the man some called a "saint," but her Grandmother Kluckholn lived long enough to become, in Miss Suckow's words, "a bitter-tongued old woman" from whom Ruth "steered clear."

Miss Suckow's father, who was always called W. J. Suckow (pronounced sook-oe), was a minister who "had the rare faculty of appealing to young and old alike—to the wise and to the simple."

His sermons, though of the intellectual order, were not coldly secular, but warmed by a deeper than intellectual order . . . these sermons had form—"did not ramble," was the way we put it. There was no padding, but a purity and economy of style and organization. His manner of preaching contained no false climaxes, singsong or sentimentalism, no play-acting, no bid to the gallery.[1]

Ruth's description of her father's sermons might be applied almost equally well to her own fiction.

The family's church in Hawarden was Congregationalist, but the Suckows had gone through several conversions. In Albany, they had been members of a Dutch Reformed Church. In Elkport, in Clayton County, Iowa, they belonged to a German Lutheran Church, which the family found to be "artificially stilted, oppressively solemn, painfully ministerial," in Mr. W. J. Suckow's words. About this time they began attending a German Methodist Church. Mr. Suckow's training, according to his daughter, consisted of a "scanty theological course" at Galena, Illinois. He first applied to the English-speaking Northwest Iowa Conference, passing over the German Conference, and was assigned to a church in Sioux Rapids, Iowa. Then, deciding that the Methodist Conference was "machine ruled," he chose to take the Congregational pulpit at Hawarden which was offered to him in 1889.

Although the Suckows moved from Hawarden by the time Ruth was six, the town and especially its newness of only ten years' existence made a strong impression on her. It became the setting for her 1942 novel *New Hope*, and there are quite a few pages about Hawarden in "A Memoir" (*Some Others and Myself*, 1952).

For one year (1894) of those first six years, W. J. Suckow preached in Le Mars, but Miss Suckow lived in Paullina with her mother, who was being treated for a thyroid condition. From 1898 to 1902 the family lived in Algona and Ruth attended Central school. From 1902 to 1905 the family was in Fort Dodge where Ruth attended Wahkonsa school and her sister Emma graduated from high school. Successively, for periods ranging from one to three years, the family lived in Manchester, Grinnell (the "Vincent Park" of some of her fiction), and Davenport. Ruth graduated from Grinnell High School and matriculated at Grinnell College. She did not finish her work there but the College awarded her an honorary degree in 1930. Emma married one of Ruth's classmates.

The pattern of mobility thus established continued to be the pattern of Miss Suckow's life and, moreover, gave her the authority for describing the settings she used in her fiction. She spent a summer as a waitress at Yellowstone Park (capitalizing on the experience in *Cora*), then became a student at the Curry School of Expression in Boston (Marjorie Schoessel attends a similar Boston school in *The Odyssey of a Nice Girl*), lived with her father at Manchester, got a Bachelor of Arts degree and a Master

---

1 Ruth Suckow, *Some Others and Myself* (New York: Rinehart & Co., 1952), p. 206.

of Arts degree from the University of Denver, then lived in Denver (the setting for some of her fiction) in 1918 and 1919, writing copy for automotive guide books and learning the apiary business. In 1919 her mother died and was buried at Garner. Later that year, Miss Suckow went with her father to Mobile, Alabama, to look at land (an experience she used in "An Investment for the Future").

When her father accepted a pastorate at Earlville about 1920, she moved to the parsonage with him and established her "Orchard Apiary" at the edge of town. The keeping of bees is introduced in many of her fictions, and Miss Suckow became known among her fellows as "the Iowa writer who raised bees."

In 1918, she published her first poem, "An Old Woman in a Garden," and in the fall of that year John T. Frederick accepted her first *Midland* contribution:

> Heart, as shiningly wear your grief
> As frost upon a lilac leaf;
> As mist along the stubble rye,
> As silver rain across the sky.

Although these lines and the lines of her other published verse demonstrate a lyrical gift of high order, Miss Suckow was fated not to be a lyrical poet.

In 1921, her father began a pastorate at Forest City, and Miss Suckow's first published short story "Uprooted" appeared in *The Midland* for February. She was receiving a great deal of encouragement from Frederick, and for six months in 1921–22 she became an editorial assistant on *The Midland*. Writing in *The Borzoi 1925*, Frederick recalled a "Literary Evening—Iowa Style" where Miss Suckow had been present:

In the old house on the side street a dozen of us were sitting in the light around a book-strewn table, while a midwestern thunderstorm roared and beat around the windows. There was a Doctor of Philosophy who has not forgotten how to laugh; there was the demoniacally clever, externally sanctimonious young editor of a student literary magazine, and the calmly brilliant girl who piloted that magazine through its first year; there were the students who represent the true *literati* and *intelligentsia* of a huge midwestern University—clear-eyed, keen, lovable young men and women; and there was Ruth Suckow. Her clear skin was browned from days out of doors. She was small and cool and comradely. She talked genuinely and generously, and what she said crackled and burned with the fire of a tremendously vigorous intellect, ruthless and fearless, and yet tempered by profound understanding and sympathy.[2]

---

2 John T. Frederick, "Literary Evening, Iowa Style," *The Borzoi 1925* (New York: Alfred A. Knopf, 1925), p. 84.

Her father remarried at Cedar Falls in 1922 and Miss Suckow spent the winter of 1922–23 with him and his wife, the former Mrs. Opal Swindle. In 1923, her sister Emma died of tuberculosis. Three years later, the Rev. W. J. Suckow took his last pastorate at Alden, Iowa.

The Midland published several more of Miss Suckow's short stories, but because the magazine had no funds for payment to its authors, and because he saw a successful literary career for her, Frederick introduced Ruth Suckow to H. L. Mencken who, with George Jean Nathan, had been a co-editor of *Smart Set* since 1914. Mencken published all of the stories which Miss Suckow sent him; their realistic qualities and their emphasis on scrutinizing a part of the American scene undoubtedly appealed to him as much as their literary qualities. When he and Nathan left *Smart Set* and founded *The American Mercury* in January 1924, he continued to publish her work. Miss Suckow's stories appealed to editors whose aims "were to tell the truth with novelty, to keep common sense as fast as they can, to belabor sham as agreeably as possible, to give a civilized entertainment."[3] Mencken said that Ruth Suckow was "unquestionably the most remarkable woman . . . writing short stories in the republic."[4]

But Mencken and Nathan would not publish the longer pieces she was beginning to write, and she sent these to *Century Magazine*—notably *Country People*, which Mencken felt was too long for him; at the same time he said that serialization would spoil its effect. Despite this last bit of advice, the *Century* published it in four parts. Immediately afterward, Knopf published it as Miss Suckow's first book (1924). The attention she was getting from eastern publishers led her to spend the winters from 1924 to 1934 in New York City; summers she operated her apiary at Earlville.

By the end of those ten years, Miss Suckow had published all her major work and most of what she was to write: *The Odyssey of a Nice Girl* (1925), *Iowa Interiors*, a collection of her short stories (1926), *The Bonney Family* (1928), *The Kramer Girls* (1930), *Children and Older People*, another collection of short stories (1931), and *The Folks* (1934). She had also published three short novels in *Smart Set:* "The Best of the Lot" (1922), "Other People's Ambitions" (1923), and "A Part of the Institution" (1923).

On March 11, 1929, in San Diego, Miss Suckow married Ferner Nuhn of Cedar Falls, himself a writer of short fiction, a book reviewer, and a literary critic. The Nuhns lived for a short period in McGregor, Iowa, in 1931, then moved to Cedar Falls where Ruth served as a "guest instruc-

---

3 "Editorial," *American Mercury* 1 (January 1924):27.
4 H. L. Mencken, "The Library," *American Mercury* 9 (November 1926):382.

tor" at Iowa State Teachers College; she also lectured on the art of the short story at the University of Iowa and at Indiana University. For a while she lived in the Washington, D.C., area; her husband had a government writing job and she served on the Farm Tenancy Committee. She lived at Robert Frost's home in Vermont. In Cedar Falls, where (in Professor Kissane's words) she "occupied an honored place in the Cedar Falls community . . . Miss Suckow was virtually writer in residence in her relationship with the Iowa State English staff who loved and respected her profoundly."[5]

In 1939, she travelled with her husband in the Scandinavian countries and England. During World War II she visited young men in service (for the Society of Friends, an organization which attracted her more and more as the years passed). In 1952, she established her home at Claremont, California, where she died on January 23, 1960.

In those last two and one-half decades of her life she published *Carry-Over* (1936), a volume which reprinted *Country People, The Bonney Family*, and a number of her short stories; *New Hope*, an autobiographical novel based on her childhood in Hawarden; *Some Others and Myself* (1952), a collection of seven stories about women and the "A Memoir," the nearest thing to an autobiography she ever wrote; a number of essays and reviews, including two which presented her theories of the short story; and *The John Wood Case* (1959), a novel based on several incidents of embezzlement of which she had learned during her father's pastorates.

In all of her fiction (there were some three dozen short stories), Miss Suckow relied on her Iowa experiences, as she observed them and remembered them, for most of her materials. Aside from her use of Hawarden in *New Hope*, her town and country settings are usually composites. Her father said that *Country People* was based on descriptions of the grandfather's farm in Hancock County, but some of the settings seem more like northeastern Iowa. Her towns, for the most part, are given names of Iowa communities, but there is usually no direct connection between the fictive town and the real town. Onawa, for example, is the name of a western Iowa town, but Miss Suckow's "Onawa" in *Cora* is an old industrial city which seems more like the Davenport and Moline of Alice French's fiction. Where she seems to be describing an actual town (the college town in *The Bonney Family*, for example) she invents a name. Sometimes she refers to an actual place by name: Dubuque, for instance, in *Country People*. Sometimes she uses a thinly veiled allusion: "The Rapids," in *Cora*, an eastern Iowa shortening of Cedar Rapids. For the most part her towns

5 Leedice McAnnelly Kissane, *Ruth Suckow* (New York: Twayne Publishers, 1969), p. 115.

are the small rural towns of 1920 Iowa—closely connected to the country-side around them.

Her stories are always told from the woman's point of view, and as some critics have noted, from the viewpoint of a daughter of German immigrants, or the daughter of an Iowa parson. With respect to this point, Frank Luther Mott commented that "probably the three best vantage points from which one [might] observe life in . . . midwestern small towns are the office of the local newspaper, the doctor's office, and the parsonage; and so Miss Suckow (who must have had very sharp eyes from childhood) was advantageously placed."[6]

But other critics have noted that this advantage was also a disadvantage, and that her fiction might have been improved had broader viewpoints been used. One British critic went so far as to wish that her work might have included a bit of the "meretricious," which so narrow a point of view prevented.

Her use of familiar small town material led to the charge that she was a "regionalist." To this she replied that she had "always believed that the matter of locality [had] been over-emphasized in estimations of her fiction. . . . If the stories did not throw a shadow beyond locality, she would never have gone to the trouble of writing them."[7]

In a letter to a Cornell College student, Miss Suckow said that "my own deepest interest lies in people and situations rather than settings as such. That is, I don't write about section so much as of people in situations somewhere, not nowhere—or anyway, I love the 'poetry of place.'"[8]

Her fiction looks at all the classes she found in Iowa, the "best people . . . our ex-patriots . . . the mild idealism of the colleges, very milk-and-watery," the "good prosperous Babbitry that judges life in terms of houses, automobiles and radios, and lets its womenfolk go in for books and frills in the Woman's Club; the Main Street element of small town hardness, dreariness and tense material ambitions." Contrasted with these "is the retired farmer element in the towns . . . whose women still apologize if caught spending good time . . . over a book," and "the working farmers, the folk element" which is "still the very soil and bedrock" of Iowa culture. The latter "give a saving rudeness, vigor and individuality to the too mild brew which . . . would be the spirit of Iowa without them."[9]

From her Iowa characters and her pictures of Iowa rural and small-

6 Frank Luther Mott, "Ruth Suckow," *A Book of Iowa Authors by Iowa Authors*, ed. Johnson Brigham (Des Moines: Iowa State Teachers Assn., 1930), p. 215.

7 Ruth Suckow, "Comment and Addenda," *Carry-Over* (New York: Farrar & Rinehart, 1936), pp. vii–ix.

8 Abigail Ann Hamblen, "The Poetry of Place," Cornell College *Husk* 40 (March 1961):75.

9 Ruth Suckow, "Iowa," *American Mercury* 9 (September 1926):44–45.

town life, Miss Suckow draws her themes: the uprooting of family and social relationships; the interrelationships among children and adults; disillusionment and innocence; alienation; the necessity to compromise to exist; attitudes of women toward each other; social and family situations which have reached an impasse; the problems of the retired person; character studies of women; mobility; old age; family differences; the life of the renter (the theme used by Garland in "Under the Lion's Paw"); the life of the rural minister; the return of the expatriate (the theme used by Garland in "Up the Coolly"); the role of the warmhearted person; old age and death; and the woman who sacrifices her own life to care for her mother and family (for instance in "The Best of the Lot"[10]).

Miss Suckow liked to use details of personal description, place and thing to reinforce her themes. But these details—testifying to Miss Suckow's "sharp eyes"—were not used merely to reinforce theme, nor to establish setting or mood alone. There is a very real relationship between Miss Suckow's characters and the details in their lives. "I don't want to leave here," says Grandma Shafer in "Uprooted." "I've always lived here —all my things is here—." And Grandpa Shafer says, "Why I'd hate awful to leave the place . . . I don't know, we been here so long, it'd be awful hard to break away. I don't know what'd become of the beasts—they've got used to me. . . ." And Grandma Shafer concludes, "I'm gona have my own things. I ain't gona use Hat's."[11]

In addition to her sharp eyes for detail, Miss Suckow had sharp ears for the sounds of the colloquial Iowa voice—its rhythms, its vocabulary, its pronunciations, its usages and grammar.

As no other writer (whether or not from Iowa) Miss Suckow has caught the life of the small town and the farm in many of its aspects. John Frederick's estimate of her "A Start in Life," "Retired," "Four Generations," and "A Rural Community" is true of many of her other stories:

[They] perform the miracle of which the short story at its very best is capable: their revelation is at once extended and profound. Within the space of a few pages, they open for the reader the significant outward circumstances and the inner tensions, the quality and the meaning of experience, for a family, a community, a whole way of life.[12]

Miss Suckow's critics agree that she reached her artistic peak in her short stories. H. L. Mencken said that although her people were "simple Iowa peasants," they did not become in Miss Suckow's stories "stock

10   Ruth Suckow, "The Best of the Lot," *Smart Set* 69 (November 1922), p. 30.
11   Ruth Suckow, *Iowa Interiors* (New York: Alfred A. Knopf, 1924), pp. 103, 105.
12   John T. Frederick, "The New Realism," *Palimpsest* 36 (March 1955):134.

types, ludicrous and artificial" as they might in the hands of other writers. "Miss Suckow differentiates them sharply," he wrote, "and into every one she breathes something of the eternal tragedy of man.

"Through her the dumb speak," he concluded.[13]

Florence Haxton Britten said that "within her field—the lives of the meagre-minded in the small towns of 'Ioway'"—Miss Suckow's work carried the "final authority of utter perfection." Her characters are "the little people, the sparrows of God." She had "an extraordinary faculty for getting inside these people and making them live." Her stories had the quality "of indicating the inevitable outcome and stopping well short of it."

And she concluded, "For a painstaking capacity to say the subtly unsayable, Miss Suckow ranks with Kathryn Mansfield."[14]

But Herbert Asbury saw Miss Suckow as portraying "the hideous darkness of existence on the farms and in the hamlets . . . the petty selfishness and the vicious currents of hatred which dominate human intercourse in the corn country."

Asbury, who admitted having grown up in the "corn country," added that her characters "die without having caught a fleeting glimpse of the beauty of living which they can neither capture or understand."[15]

Miss Suckow did not agree with this last form of criticism: "Some of this [criticism] seemed . . . peculiarly ill-judged," she wrote:

Most of these [stories] were first published in an era when American self-consciousness was highly aroused and very touchy. Their purpose was frequently taken for an "indictment" of American rural and small town life, particularly in the Middlewest, or for a sort of exposition on the general futility of human existence. Obviously, the [stories] are neither indictment or celebration.[16]

Miss Suckow's success with her short stories was not accidental. She knew what she was doing. Except in *The Folks,* she did not try to expound philosophies or illustrate theses as Garland had in many, if not all, of his stories. She did have strong moral and political philosophies—she had a major disagreement with her father over his support of World War I from the pulpit—but she did not use her short fiction to propagandize them.

Her theories of the short story are best illustrated by her stories. How-

---

13   Mencken, "The Library," p. 382.
14   Florence Haxton Britten, "Sparrows of Iowa," *New York Herald Tribune Books,* August 16, 1931, p. 7.
15   Herbert Asbury, "The American Interior," *New York Herald Tribune Books,* October 3, 1926, pp. 6–7.
16   Suckow, "Comment and Addenda."

ever, in two essays, "The Short Story," and "I Could Write, if only—," and in several critical reviews, she outlined some of her theories. America is too interested in finding a "master key" to her problems, she noted, whether the problem is one of producing goods or literature. As a result, particularly in fiction, there has been a tendency to search for formulas, for external forms to be applied to subject matter. Such techniques would not work. The story writer must find a way best suited to his own intention. That way is not through method but through "consciousness" of American life "roving, unsettled, restless, unassimilated, here and gone again—a chaos so huge, a life so varied and so multitudinous that its meaning could be caught only in fragments, perceived only by will-o-the-wisp gleams, preserved only in tiny pieces of perfection." The short story is a "running commentary upon life; fireflies in the dark; questions and answers; fragments, or small and finished bits of beauty; whatever, in fact, [the] author has the power to make of [it]."[17]

When Ruth Suckow turned to longer fiction pieces, she continued to focus for the most part on the same settings and classes of characters. She did not give up the short story as a medium but wrote in both forms concurrently. At first her longer works show a falling off in power as she experimented with expanding the compact statement (used often for understatement) of the short story into the "short novel." And, although in the longer works she never repeated the triumphs she achieved in "Uprooted," "A Start in Life," "The Little Girl from Town," "A Great Mollie," and "Eminence," yet two are at least minor classics.

"The Best of the Lot" (*Smart Set*, November 1922) has a familiar Suckow figure—the woman who sacrifices her own life to care for her mother and family. Although the theme of the short novel seems to be that "the ones that deserved the most got the least half the time in this world," the story seems to demonstrate also that total unselfishness is not altogether a virtue.

The second story "Other People's Ambitions" (*Smart Set*, March 1923) is the poorest of these three, although George Jean Nathan, co-editor of the magazine commented that it "still contains an ample measure of excellent writing." The story tells of the son of an Iowa glove manufacturer (a man who might better have been a "professor of dead languages" at some small college) who is destroyed by the driving ambitions of, first, the boy's father, and second, the young man's wife.

As Professor Kissane has noted, "the dominant note of 'The Best of the Lot' is pathos; that of 'Other People's Ambitions' is tragedy; [and] that

---

17 Ruth Suckow, "The Short Story," *Saturday Review of Literature* 4 (November 19, 1927):317–18.

of [the third short novel] 'A Part of the Institution' is satire."[18] But mild satire.

The setting for "A Part of the Institution," the best of the three short novels (*Smart Set*, October 1923) is Adams College, "the Pioneer College of the Prairies," which had been "founded some forty years ago by a little band of home missionaries from New England, dedicated to 'the interests of Christianity and of the higher learning in the West.'" Adams College is in Adamsville; the temptation to see Grinnell and Grinnell College in the fictional settings is strong. The central character is Hester Harris whose constant prayer is to be taken into "the EBB [the Elizabeth Barrett Browning society, one of Adams' prestige groups]." The story follows Hester from her childhood days in the college to a time many years later when she has become a minor member of the college staff, looking forward each year to the annual reunions of her class. The novel focuses on Hester's college years and particularly her relationships with three persons, Jay Oehrle, one of the "all-around" students who is internally corrupt, Joe Forrest, who tells Hester that her main problem is that she thinks "Prexie was the Pope," and Jinny. Joe knows well that although ostensibly the college's philosophy is to encourage the student to think for himself, in reality the administration, the faculty, and the students have joined in an educational process in which the student is told what to think and to believe. Jinny with her "round, soft-featured, dark rebellious face, her curling dusky hair and dark starry eyes" is the prototype of those bohemian girls we will meet in later Suckow novels. At the same time she reminds us of those "literary soubrettes" whom Miss Suckow described in an essay, and whom she so obviously admires.[19] "A Part of the Institution" is one of the best treatments of college life that we have.

About the time she was writing these short novels, Miss Suckow was also at work on *Country People* and *The Odyssey of a Nice Girl*. The three short novels (twenty to twenty-five thousand words each) and *Country People* (fifty thousand words) are all written in the same narrative style.

Country People is the story of three generations of German emigrants, but it focuses primarily on August Kaetterhenry and his wife Emma (nee Stille) during the years from 1859 (the year of August's birth) to some time after 1922 (the year of his death). The setting seems to be the Wapsipinicon River valley between the county seat town of Wapsie and the neighboring town of Richland. Nearby are Dubuque and Rapids City; further away is Rochester, Minnesota, with its famed hospital complex.

18   Kissane, *Ruth Suckow*, p. 115.
19   Ruth Suckow, "Literary Soubrettes," *The Bookman* 63 (July 1928):517–21.

The narrator of the story is Miss Suckow's typical omniscient narrator, in this case someone who knows the Kaetterhenrys and who lives on after August is dead. This narrator's voice produces, in Miss Suckow's words, a style which "has no particular beauty of its own. Yet it does fit the subject matter: in its careful country minutiae, its touch of dry country humor, even its hardness and tightness. It has a certain monotonous music, like the tuneless tune of the windmill in the country air."[20]

The novel seems to concentrate on the farm work and its virtues and the virtues of thrift and economy. Yet for all of its emphasis on August Kaetterhenry and his farm, *Country People* is primarily Emma's story. One can see this over and over in the emphasis given to details of housekeeping as contrasted with the details of the farm itself. For instance, we are told that August "paid for part of his stock and implements and went in debt for the rest. . . . The house—*ach*, that didn't matter so much." But, nevertheless, although we hear no more about the "stock and implements," the "gloomy, bare little house" is treated in a full page of detail!

Country People is a novel of change in the rural scene in Iowa during the period in which pioneer life gave way to a settled Iowa. The old names of Herman and August give way to "Maxine, Velda, Delight, Gwendolyn, Eugene, Dwayne. . . . All of the children lived better than their parents. . . ." The old conservatism of the rural church ruled against "the pleasure drive on Sunday," cards, dancing, and the "Sunday baseball game"; at the novel's end only the old people attend church. For those who do attend, "German church" has yielded to "English church." For August and his older children a limited rural schooling had been enough; now the youngest goes off to Rapids City for a business education course.

Country People is a novel of personal, rather than social, growth. Some social events are shown—attendance at church, the box social, the Fourth of July, the County Fair, August's funeral. But there is barely any mention of politics. Even the changing economic scene is barely touched upon—August saves his money and is opposed to improvements which lead to increases in taxes, and Carl institutes farm reforms—but that is all. Finally, *Country People* is a novel which seems to uphold the middle-class virtues of hard work, religious devotion, and thrift.

John Frederick criticized *Country People* on the grounds that it seemed "to have been limited by a convention which Miss Suckow had created for herself—a notion as to what a novel of 'country people' should be and do . . . somewhat too bare a chronicle of a German farm family," and he said that he "found it only partially satisfying."[21]

---

20 Hamblen, "The Poetry of Place."
21 Frederick, "The New Realism," p. 132.

But Sinclair Lewis praised the novel, declaring it to be a "spiritual accounting of the whole business . . . of that bright hardy country which stands at the head of the Great |Mississippi| Valley."[22] And Joseph Wood Krutch said that *Country People* "has the advantage of wide observation, absolute honesty, and the knack of selecting just those incidents calculated to picture to the imagination the life which she is describing. . . . It gives the impression of completeness without being either tedious or dull."[23]

In the depression years, some twelve years after the first publication of the novel, Josephine Herbst, the radical Iowa novelist, was less happy with *Country People*. She wrote that Ruth Suckow's

work appears to rest considerably on the delight readers feel in recognizing known things. The single daily occupations of self-respecting folk whose sensitive qualities had little time for blossom . . . are detailed with a fine degree of accuracy and insight. Within its limits this appears to be actual farm life as the more steady well fixed farmers lived it. . . . The patient struggle toward ownership is typical. . . . one wonders if sympathy, no matter how patient or intelligent, is enough to bring to the scene and the time. . . . Her attitude quite evidently is a Christian one and her selection of materials, rich as they are, was nevertheless motivated by a conscientious sense of wanting to be just to characters and scene without fully realizing the deep integration between the two. As a result there is a calmness and even tone that does not adequately hint at the incipient violence within farm life. . . . This repudiation of the idea of violence is extremely important as a clue to her basic attitude.[24]

To criticism of this sort from Miss Herbst and others, Miss Suckow replied in a 1936 edition of *Country People* that the book was not "a saga of the pioneers" nor "an epic of the soil." The novel was not intended as a typical farm novel: "There is no writer nor artist concealed among its characters who is destined to come back later . . . to write a book about . . . the farm of August Kaetterhenry. August himself never offers a soliloquy upon The Soil; he never seduces a hired girl; and he dies in bed, not overlooking his broad acres, nor clutching a handful of his own good earth."[25]

The Odyssey of a Nice Girl must have represented a major undertaking for Miss Suckow—it runs to some two hundred and twenty thousand words, the longest piece of writing she had done so far. Mrs. Alfred

---

22 Sinclair Lewis, "Introductory Remarks" to *Country People* in *Three Readers* (New York: Press of the Reader's Club, 1943), pp. 176–77.
23 Joseph Wood Krutch, "The Tragic Lift," *Nation* 119 (August 20, 1924):194.
24 Josephine Herbst, Review of *Carry-Over*, *New Republic* 88 (October 21, 1936): 318–19.
25 Suckow, "Comment and Addenda."

Knopf, wife of her publisher, wanted to know why she couldn't "get this girl between covers" in ninety thousand words—but by this time the novel was in typescript form and the author had her way. John Frederick thought the book was "unfortunately titled." And H. L. Mencken commented about the "nice girl's" name—"what a name!"—but he spelled it *Stoessel!* The "nice girl" is Marjorie Schoessel, the Iowa small-town daughter of Ed and Etta Schoessel, themselves, like the Kaetterhenrys, the offspring of German immigrant farmers. But the Schoessels, of the second generation, have moved to town and operate a furniture store with an undertaking business on the side. We see Marjorie from the summer of 1902 when she goes to visit Grandma and Grandpa Schoessel in Germantown until "she fades into nothingness, lawfully tied to a member of the American Legion," as Mencken comments.[26]

Marjorie, in her mother's word, is a "fussy" girl whose fastidiousness is encouraged by the life she lives as the daughter of comfortably-fixed parents; she is romantically inclined, and her romantic inclinations are encouraged by her various social successes and by her success as a declamatory student. But, while attending an "Academy of Expression" in the East, some of her romanticism begins to disappear; she concludes that "perhaps nothing is romantic when you knew more about it." For a while she enters into a semi-bohemian life with a girl named Emily, another of Miss Suckow's bohemian girls. Back home in Iowa, all of her romantic dreams come to an end as she finds herself living fruitlessly, frustrated by her failure to be the kind of girl that she thinks people expected a "nice girl" to be. Eventually she marries a war veteran who has disappointed his parents by not completing his law studies. The book ends with a whimper, not a bang, Marjorie's marriage not having furnished the typical romantic happy ending.

The length of the book is due partially to the use of topical details which give the book an aura of reality—of having actually happened. The realistic effect is enhanced by the authenticity of town names—Buena Vista, Leland, Shell Rock, Germantown—and by the homely names of characters such as Orpha Putz, Ray Bender, Fish Carter, Aunt Lottie. The details extend to the many small town characters: Miss Battles, "her tiny waist, held snugly by a leather belt; her pompadour, lofty, tight on the sides, and with two little curls that hung from the figure 8 at the back of her head"; Percy Franklin, "the cashier in the First National . . . the only man in Buena Vista who wore white flannel trousers and a dark coat, like the heroes in magazine illustrations"; George Rooney who, "in spite of his 'tough reputation,' held an admired position in the high school. His

---

26 H. L. Mencken, "The Library," *American Mercury* 7 (April 1926):506–07.

name was oftener upon the four o'clock [delinquency] list than that of any other pupil."

H. L. Mencken praised *The Odyssey of a Nice Girl,* saying that in this story of a "highly respectable and more than a little stupid maiden," Miss Suckow "plow[ed] deeper, and turn[ed] up stuff of far more significance" than in *Country People.* Though the story was "commonplace," it demonstrated that Miss Suckow could "discern and evoke the eternal tragedy in the life of man."[27]

John Frederick thought the novel was a better one than *Country People:* "In Marjory, Miss Suckow epitomizes a very great part of the cultural aspirations of America in the last and present generations, as well as of the attempt of American women to find lives of their own."[28]

In *The Bonney Family,* the setting is a pair of Iowa small towns—Morning Sun, where the Reverend Mr. Bonney and his family live an idyllic pastoral life, and Vincent Park, a larger town with twenty thousand people and a street car, the site of Frampton College, where the Reverend Mr. Bonney moves to become a "part of the institution." Unlike *The Odyssey of a Nice Girl* which centers its attention on the quest of one girl, in this novel an entire family becomes the protagonist.

The destinies of the Bonney family—the Reverend Mr. Bonney, his wife, Grandpa and Grandma Bonney, and the children, Warren, Sarah, and the twins Wilma and Wilfred, and even the cat "Washington Bonney, Beloved Cat of Wilfred Warren Bonney"—are worked out through the first quarter of this century. The quiet tone of frustration and pathos which marks the life of the Bonneys is contrasted with the violent tragedy of the life of the family of the "too autocratic" perfectionist Professor Satterley. All of this is presented in an even, dispassionate tone with no climactic moments—in the words of a critic, "the emphasis upon the events throughout is as great as, and no greater than, the emphasis upon life itself."[29]

In a review written just three months before his marriage to Miss Suckow, Ferner Nuhn commented that "in the career of this family are meanings which hold for all families: the inevitable isolation of one generation from the next; the effort of parents to socialize the children, and the effort—often ineffectual—of the children to retain in this socialization what essences of important individuality (which so often are the very elements the parents want to get rid of) they may possess. This is, indeed, in

---

27   Mencken, "The Library," pp. 506–07.
28   John T. Frederick, "Ruth Suckow and the Middle Western Literary Movement," *The English Journal* 20 (January 1931):32.
29   Allan Nevins, "A Painter of Iowa," *Saturday Review of Literature* 4 (March 10, 1928):666.

part, a novel of the defeat of talent (if not genius) in children through unpropitious paternalism."[30]

Josephine Herbst felt that the novel had failed to portray life as it actually existed in small towns: "the recognition of individual characteristics is somehow separate from recognition of the background and its social implications."

This divided vision weakens the force of her novels and at the same time endows her characters with a too complacent tenderness. One may compare *The Bonney Family* with a much earlier novel, also about a minister's family in Iowa, *The Damnation of Theron Ware* . . . to see the difference between the searching mind and a searching mind too saturated with the milk of human kindness.[31]

But Allan Nevins responded to criticism of this kind coming from the socialist writers of the thirties:

What we find admirable in Miss Suckow's art are just those qualities which to many spoiled readers of our overspiced and overwritten American fiction would seem defects. . . . [Miss Suckow] deals with the everyday, commonplace people of one of the most commonplace, undistinguished parts of the world. . . . By careful detail she builds up the routine of their lives, and by a multitude of delicate touches she reveals the warmth and tenacity of their small emotions, the hold which associations of place, family and custom have upon them, the complexities and the changes in their characters. . . .[32]

As for the style of the book, Ferner Nuhn felt that it had "color and a textural beauty which few realists achieve . . . to one . . . [who] likes to savor word and image, it is the sort of language that is more than language; which continually reaches out and becomes the thing itself."[33]

In *Cora* Miss Suckow returned to her theme of an interpretation of a woman's life. In *The Odyssey of a Nice Girl* her central character had engaged in a quest for personal achievement and recognition; in *Cora*, the central character strives for economic success and personal satisfaction. She achieves the former, moving upward on the economic ladder in the course of the novel, but is less successful in the latter. In the process of delineating Cora's upward climb, Miss Suckow, for the first time, showed the seamier side of life; one of her settings is Onawa, an industrial city, where Cora's father finds a place in a factory, and we smell the odor of "herded humanity." By the end of the novel, Cora has "got somewhere,"

---

30 Ferner Nuhn, *New York Herald Tribune Books*, November 22, 1928, p. 7.
31 Herbst, Review of *Carry-Over*.
32 Nevins, "A Painter of Iowa."
33 Ferner Nuhn, *New York Herald Tribune Books*, November 22, 1928, p. 7.

in the sense that she has become a fairly typical middle-class woman, but, as H. L. Mencken said, "in her heart a great emptiness" exists.

Mencken did not praise this novel as he had her earlier work. Instead, he said that although the story was "very deftly put together," Cora, in the latter parts of the book, becomes "a sort of case history in a thesis: one has an uneasy sense that she is being used to prove something." This novel was "not her best."[34]

The Kramer Girls reverts to a focus on a group—three sisters, Georgie, Anne, and Rose. There is an invalid mother also, and a father, a real estate dealer, who is barely seen. The family lives in Valley Junction but the fact is not insisted upon; in this book Miss Suckow seems to rely more on details of behavior, less on details of place and thing. Her theme is that things are not as they ought to be.

Georgie is the mannish type, a favorite Suckow type; Anne becomes a spinster; and Rose, originally a career girl, becomes the maternal woman. Georgie's efforts to direct Rose's life remind us of Mrs. Bonney's efforts to direct her family; Miss Suckow seems to be telling us it shouldn't be done this way. In Chicago during the career phase of her life, Rose has a bohemian friend, Jane. One wonders why Miss Suckow never made a full-length study of the intellectual non-conforming girl.

One of the theses presented in *The Kramer Girls* is the defense of the way of life in an Iowa small town as compared with the city:

She could enjoy having everybody she met on the street speak to her; knowing people by their names . . . She loved the way the road dipped down and then rose in the distance, with blue sky between and above thick trees. She loved the chance and unconsidered way in which little unnamed side streets petered out and dwindled into country. She loved being able to know that country was all around her and that any moment she could reach it . . . And just as much, although in a different way, she loved going along the street and knowing every step of the way.

Looking back at Miss Suckow's novels to this time, John T. Frederick wrote:

Ruth Suckow's women are not magazine-cover heroines, not romantically virtuous or interestingly unprincipled; they are not such figures as middle-aged masculine reviewers tend to fall in love with. But they are human beings of terrible veracity. And they are human beings related in their experience to the most critical social contours of our times.[35]

----

34 H. L. Mencken, "The Library," *The American Mercury* 19 (January 1930):127.
35 Frederick, "Ruth Suckow and the Middle Western Literary Movement," p. 40.

Frederick called *The Kramer Girls* a "fine novel," but other reviewers were not so happy with it. "*The Bonney Family* was by far a finer piece of literary accomplishment," said Dorothy Foster Gilman. In this novel, "in her zeal for human photography, Miss Suckow [had forgotten] to tell an interesting story. . . . The three heroines are disconcertingly ineffective. . . ."[36] And Professor Martin Mohr said that the novels from *The Odyssey of a Nice Girl* to *The Kramer Girls* "are decidedly second-rate fiction of the kind one finds serialized in the various ladies' magazines."[37]

Through these novels there had been a gradual shift in emphasis which had been hinted at in the defense of the small town in *The Kramer Girls*, and which became most pronounced in *The Folks*—written, as Professor Joseph Baker pointed out, over a four-year period to illustrate a thesis that she had set forth in "The Folk Idea of American Life."

As Professor Mohr has said, Ruth Suckow's *Country People* is based on her theory of "regionalism" which she had outlined in a 1926 essay on "Iowa":

Whatever real value the culture and art of Iowa can have is founded upon this bedrock [the working farmers, the folk element]. Other elements may influence and vary it, but this is at the bottom of them all. Our varying nationalities meet in this rich soil which has still some of the old pioneer virtue of sturdy freshness—perhaps the only virtue, genuine and clearly distinguishable from all others, which the native culture of this young country has to offer. . . . What we call culture in Iowa . . . [is] held together and strengthened by the simplicity and severity of its hard working farmer people.[38]

But in her 1930 essay on "The Folk Idea in American Life," Miss Suckow argued that "among all the varied peoples who went to make up the new nation, likeness was in fortune and aim rather than in blood. Whatever else they might be they were the people who wanted to get ahead. This was the uniting principle. These people were not a folk. They were many—they were the folks . . . the folk idea in America has become the idea of "folks."[39]

"Whereas before," said Professor Mohr, "her characters were crude primitives bound together and steeped in the mysticism of The Soil, they [were] now middle class townspeople trying to get ahead."[40]

---

36 Dorothy Foster Gilman, "Out of the Old Family Album," *New York Herald Tribune Books*, March 30, 1930, p. 5.
37 Martin Mohr, "Ruth Suckow—Regionalism and Beyond" (M.A. thesis, University of Iowa, 1955), p. 91.
38 Suckow, "Iowa."
39 Ruth Suckow, "The Folk Idea in American Life," *Scribner's* 88 (September 1930): 245–55.
40 Mohr, "Ruth Suckow—Regionalism and Beyond," p. 60.

In *The Folks*, Miss Suckow returned to a format which she had used in *The Odyssey of a Nice Girl*—a lengthy chronological account supported by a mass of detail. The book is long—at least twice as long as the *Odyssey* about which Mrs. Knopf had complained. "It seems as if nowadays a novel must run over five hundred pages to get into print," one critic lamented.

The protagonists of this "epic of middle class America" are a whole family: Fred and Annie Ferguson, the "old folks"; Carl, the "good son"; Dorothy, the next in line; Margaret, the "other girl," who changes her name to Margot (Miss Suckow's most in-depth study of the bohemian girl personality); and Bunny, the "youngest." Although the story has Belmond, a small Iowa town, as its base, its settings range from Greenwich Village to Santa Fe and Los Angeles, as Miss Suckow shifts her emphasis from Iowa to the nation. Says Professor Mohr: "*The Folks* is an attempt to bring order to that aesthetic confusion [of which, according to Miss Suckow, the nation was "hearing so much" just then], to systematize the chaos of the American scene, to reveal a pattern by which the truly American fiction might be written."[41]

The narrative is divided into six parts: Parts I and VI focus on Fred and Annie; Part II focuses on Carl and his puritanical wife Lillian; Part III on Dorothy's wedding to Jesse Woodward; Part IV on Margaret; and Part V partially on Bunny and Charlotte Corday Bukowska, the socialist girl he marries. The narrative is picked up at a time when Fred Ferguson has parted with his last horse and is contemplating buying a car; it ends with the completion of Fred and Annie's round trip in an automobile to California and back to Iowa—a span of twenty-five to thirty years. Although the story is so little concerned with the social and political upheavals of the early part of the twentieth century that it is difficult to date, it begins at approximately the beginning of the century (Carl, Margaret, and Dorothy are school children, and Bunny is not yet born) and continues to the first year or so of the depression (Carl is "middle-aged," Bunny has been married a year or so, one of the Belmond banks has failed, and there is a sense of harder times ahead). In the whole book there are scarcely a dozen references to social or political matters which do not directly impinge on the lives of the Fergusons.

The six parts of the book overlap; succeeding parts go back in time to pick up the affairs of one or the other of the Fergusons. No attempt is made to correlate or interlock one part of the book with another; Bunny, for instance, shows up in the book with no reference to his birth other than the fact that he was an unexpected child. We see Carl and Lillian at Dorothy's wedding, but we are not told at what point in Carl's life the

41 Mohr, "Ruth Suckow—Regionalism and Beyond," p. 69.

wedding takes place, nor do he and his wife play any important part in the wedding section. The "Dorothy" and the "Margaret" sections could stand by themselves as short novels.

The theme of all but one of Miss Suckow's novels up to and including *The Folks* had been one of quest. Marjorie Schoessel went to Boston seeking the training that would enable her to become what people "expected" of her; then she returned home to fulfill that expectation, but finding that fulfillment impossible, she drifted on to Denver and marriage. The Bonney family leave Morning Sun in quest of a better education for their children; the children, educated and grown up, search for tenable living situations. Cora's quest is for economic security, a better material existence; she digresses occasionally in a quest for romance. Georgie, Anne and Rose each search for fulfillment, Georgie first as *mater familias*, then as a chiropractor; Rose through education, career, and marriage; Anne in a job in "the Rapids." The Fergusons have attempted to build a home for their children and give each an education; Carl has sought marriage and a career as a school superintendent; Dorothy has sought a romantic marriage; Margaret has sought fulfillment as an independent woman, free of the restrictions placed on the women of her time; Bunny has sought companionship and marriage.

With one exception each of these quests ends in something less than satisfaction. Marjorie's marriage doesn't seem the right fate for a "nice girl" with her apparent potential; Mr. Bonney's second marriage (after his wife's death) splits the family. Warren, although a professor in Montana, seems destined for a mediocre career which belies his early promise; Wilma's marriage leads to monotony; Wilfred is dead in the war; and Sarah seems to be drifting. Georgie dies of cancer, Anne is satisfied with a very routine existence, and Rose is satisfied with a marriage which seems to everyone else at least to be unpromising. Carl's marriage and career deny his early promise; Margaret has come to terms with an arrangement with a married man which can hardly offer much hope to her; Bunny has drifted off into obscurity with a wife who surely will present some problems to him; and Dorothy doesn't face the best of futures, even in the bright golden dreamland of California. For "the folks" even, "things have changed . . . in the darkening twilight that [they] face, along with the others that were left, [they] couldn't see what was beyond" (p. 726).

The Folks is undoubtedly Miss Suckow's best novel; in particular, the narrative of Dorothy and Jesse's wedding has been widely praised for its lyrical qualities. Yet the novel was disturbing to some, who found it aimless, plotless, and even pointless. Miss Suckow's essay on the culture of the "folks" had suggested an optimistic future for the subject matter and the thematic treatments, but her novel with its atmosphere of hopelessness, despair, and pessimism for every one of the "folks" did not bear out the optimism. That this was the case is shown by the fact that neither Miss Suckow nor other writers did any more with the theme.

Writing of the degree of Miss Suckow's achievement in the novel, Joseph Warren Beach wondered about "the work of authors who fall just below the standard of distinction which we set for ourselves," and he said he "puzzled a good deal over the works of writers, like Ruth Suckow, who seem to have all the materials for significant fiction—character, background, feeling and understanding, seriousness and industry—and yet somehow just fail to ring the bell." And he concluded that while "rigorous selection of matter" might help, "it is not so much selection itself that is wanting as a principle of selection . . . some coloring of the mind (beyond mere honesty and goodwill) which would give a more special turn to all that is said."[42]

Carl Van Doren thought that Miss Suckow had "studied contemporary life with honest realism," and in *The Folks* "came nearer than any other writer has done to representing the whole of American life on farms and in small towns."[43]

Professor Joseph Baker had both praise and criticism for the novel. "It gives us an unsurpassed picture of the people of Iowa (and of Middle-Westerners in New York and California)." But he found it "lacking in suspense and drama"; it did not "show the folks' ideas," and "her characters tend[ed] to be types, studied from the outside . . . ." Still, he concluded, "her scenes live . . . they catch the group spirit, the feeling, the atmosphere of the Middle-Western farms, churches, streets, homes, band concerts, schools—presented not as if they were static, but changing, as living organisms change, with the growth of the century."[44]

Miss Suckow was now forty-two, married to Ferner Nuhn, and, with him, apparently more concerned about travel and other matters than writing; during the next eight years she published only three short stories. In 1936, she re-issued in one volume *The Bonney Family, Country People*, and a number of her short stories with an "Addenda" (*Carry-Over*). Most of the "Addenda" was concentrated in projecting the later years of the lives of the Kaetterhenrys and the Bonneys.

In her 1942 novel, *New Hope*, Miss Suckow turned back in time to the Hawarden days of her childhood—as one can plainly see if one compares this novel with her "A Memoir" in the later *Some Others and Myself*. The protagonists of *New Hope* are two children, Delight Greenwood,

---

42 Joseph Warren Beach, *American Fiction 1920–1940* (New York: Macmillan Co., 1942), pp. 7–8.

43 Carl Van Doren, *The American Novel 1789–1939* (New York: Macmillan Co., 1962), p. 361.

44 Joseph E. Baker, "Regionalism in the Middle West," *American Review* 4 (March 1935):609–10.

daughter of the Congregational minister who serves the New Hope church during the two years of the novel, and Clarence Miller, son of the town's banker and chief booster. The story is told in what is essentially a series of tableaux: "Arrival," "The Church," "The Town," "The Countryside," "The Parsonage," "Festivals," "Exodus," and so on. The children are thrust into each of these settings so that we may see their reaction—or, as Professor Kissane has put it, so that we may see "what life becomes for a small boy when Delight is part of it."[45]

In a letter to her publishers, Miss Suckow said that she hoped the book would present "a certain poetic quality of past and present mingling." Professor Kissane suggests that she succeeds and adds that furthermore it is the "quality of youth recaptured that distinguishes *New Hope*."[46] Professor Richard Cordell wished that the book had had "a more resolute narrative," but he found the children "as real and living as any pre-adolescents who ever played, dreamed, quarreled, wheedled, and strutted between the covers of a book."[47] Edith H. Walton said that *New Hope* was "a weaker novel than *The Folks* and a more sentimental one." She added that Miss Suckow, "never an inspired writer . . . but one who has a genius for detail" had in this novel "gone beyond realism and come very close to the borders of romance."[48]

Professor Mohr argued that Miss Suckow had turned "as if in admission of frustration, back to her childhood . . . [for] *New Hope* is a nostalgic idealization of a simple, happy time before the outside world intruded on the complacency of . . . Iowa." He concluded that the novel was deficient in having no story line—"plotted fiction is not her forte"—and in the inconsequential quality of many of its events. The novel lacked "concentration" because of its casualness.[49]

In the early thirties, Miss Suckow had published two short stories, "An Elegy for Alma's Aunt Amy" and "Auntie Bissell," in *Harper's Monthly* and *Scribner's Magazine* respectively. Now she combined these hitherto uncollected stories and other unpublished stories with the aforementioned "A Memoir" in *Some Others and Myself* (1952).

All of the stories are about women. In five of them, the narrator (in one story identified as a "writer" and in another as a "teacher") relates her own experiences with the women in the stories. Two of the stories are told by an omniscient narrator, and one is plainly written as an exposition of a thesis which is stated in the first paragraph. One, "Auntie Bissell," is

45   Kissane, *Ruth Suckow*, p. 115.
46   Kissane, *Ruth Suckow*, p. 115.
47   Richard Cordell, "Suckow . . . ," *Saturday Review of Literature* 25 (February 28, 1942):8.
48   Edith H. Walton, *New York Times Book Review*, February 22, 1942, p. 8.
49   Mohr, "Ruth Suckow—Regionalism and Beyond," pp. 4, 9.

as close to high comedy as Miss Suckow ever got in its satirical exposé of the lives of Auntie Bissell, an expatriate Iowan in Hollywood, the Hollywood screen hopefuls, a fantastic collection of brats, and the equally fantastic Mausoleum, the "final scene of the great American fairy tale with its resolutely happy ending."

"A Memoir" is both a spiritual and an historical biography of Miss Suckow, her father and her mother—although Miss Suckow and her father receive the major share of attention. In it she recounts what it was like to be a "minister's child, brought up in a Protestant church," what life was like in Hawarden in the 1890s, and she recalls her reading, her father's work and social habits, his philosophies of life, some of his family history, and so forth.

Most critics found the "A Memoir" of more interest than the stories. "The narrator's art has become diffuse and repetitious," said John T. Flanagan, "the stories drag." But he felt that the "A Memoir" was "one of Miss Suckow's best pieces of writing. . . . it shares the qualities of her best stories—simplicity, dignity, quiet observation, fidelity to fact, sympathy, and understanding."[50]

Miss Suckow's final published work was *The John Wood Case,* a novel which bears very little resemblance to any of her other work. It was published in 1958 when she was sixty-six, just two years before her death (January 23, 1960) in Claremont, California.

The novel is based on the reactions of the family of John Wood, the members of the Congregational Church, of which John Wood is a mainstay, of Colonel Merriam and his family, and of the entire small Iowa community to the disclosure that John Wood has embezzled money from the Merriam Title Insurance and Farm Loan Company. "I had special needs," is John Wood's only defense—he is referring to the fact that he had used the embezzled money for medical care for his invalid wife.

In reviewing this novel, Professor Willard Reninger said:

With her last two novels . . . [Miss] Suckow was . . . doing something with American life that she had not done before. Just as she had earlier moved from Midwestern life to American life as a whole, she now moved into the whole of humanity, especially in *The John Wood Case.* She now embraced humanity, using American life to dramatize her symbolic, or universal, truth. This truth must be *felt* as it is dramatized in these two novels to absorb its impact because when I state that truth as an abstraction, it sounds obvious and frightfully old-fashioned. But I am sure that Ruth Suckow would say, "precisely—that's what's so basic and eternal about it all." Her truth is that justice and social amelioration will come only from the depths of the human heart where love, not competition and hate, is the mover of mankind. *The John Wood Case* is liter-

---

50   John T. Flanagan, *American Literature* 24 (January 1953):568–69.

ally about the moral crisis in a small town, but figuratively the book is about the moral crisis in the world itself.

Ruth Suckow's recognition of this crisis and the spiritual, not materialistic, cures to be applied represent the highest point in her artistic-spiritual growth.[51]

The John Wood Case is a fitting climax to the career of the woman, who, however minor she may be as an American author, is close to being the best Iowa writer of fiction. That she was born in Iowa, educated in the state, encouraged and developed by Iowa teachers of writing, published at first in an Iowa literary publication, and widely appreciated, both in her state and in the nation, is a testament as to how far Iowa had come in literary affairs in the few short years since Hiram Alvin Reid first set his fragile vessel afloat.

The novel is also a fitting testament to a woman who, in Professor Reninger's words "leaves us as she came, an artist with incorruptible integrity whose moral and spiritual values were the foundation of her life and art."[52]

51 H. W. Reninger, "Spoken at the Memorial Service for Ruth Suckow Nuhn," *Midwest*, Iowa State Teachers College [University of Northern Iowa] (Spring 1960), pp. 13 ff.
52 Reninger, ". . . Memorial Service . . . ."

Pittsville and Siouxland Come of Age

PHILIP Duffield Stong (1889–1957) and Frederick Manfred ("Feike Feikema," 1912–) are two of the more prolific Iowa writers. Phil Stong wrote more than forty books, some of them for young readers; Manfred has already published sixteen and is still writing. Of the two, Stong was by far the more successful, both financially and in reaching larger audiences. Some of his books were book club selections, and at least one was filmed. Manfred seems to have needed subsidies from time to time, and it is doubtful that his books have as yet begun to attract the audiences that Stong's did. On the other hand Manfred's books have attracted some serious critical attention.

Phil Stong was born at Pittsburg, a hamlet just west of Keosauqua, on the west side of the "big bend" of the Des Moines River where the Chequest Creek flows into it. Readers of *Buckskin Breeches* will recognize the spot as the site where Jess Ellison settled; readers of *Village Tale* or *Stranger's Return* will associate it with the site of the village of Four Corners; readers of *State Fair* will recognize the store (once run by Stong's uncle, "Peck" Stong) as the Storekeeper's store. The farm house in which Stong was born appears in various novels as Linwood or Storrhaven. These sites are part of Stong's fictional "Pittsville" country. Pittsville, itself, is based on Keosauqua; "Brunswick" is a town about seven miles upriver from Keosauqua; Abel Frake's farm (in *State Fair*) lies midway between the latter two towns. The "long lane" of several of the novels is the reach of road leading west from Keosauqua to the Pittsburg bridge. The whole two-mile stretch between the towns is seen in the first chapter of *The Long Lane:*

The Long Lane was a measured road. The Sauk and the Fox had originally made a straight trail of something like two miles from a ford at one end of an oxbow in the river to a ford at the other end. The settlers had found a better ford up the western end of the trail and turned the road off at the edge of the river hills at the start of the oxbow.

Through passages such as this one Stong creates the sense of an historical past in his Pittsville stories.

Stong's parents were Benjamin J. Stong and Evesta Duffield Stong. His father operated the B. J. Stong Variety Goods store in Keosauqua, described by Stong in the December 1957 *Palimpsest*. Linwood Farm had been his mother's home:

> . . . the river front of Linwood . . . looks about as it always has, since Grandpa Duffield came home from the Gold Rush in 1852 with enough money to buy the land and build the house of bricks from his own clay fired in his own kiln. As we turned from the river road up the long approach to the house, I was glad I, too, had dug some gold in California twenty years ago, enough to buy this old place back into the family. My digging was done in a movie studio, but it was just as strenuous as grandpa's.[1]

Grandpa Duffield's spirit of self-reliance is a theme in many of Stong's novels.

In *If School Keeps* (1940), Stong has described his education in the Keosauqua school, at Drake University (where he got a B.A.), at Columbia University (where he did not get an M.A.), and twelve hours of correspondence courses in education from Kansas University. Following his B.A. he taught "Americans," "Bohunks," "Squareheads," "Slobs," "Norskes," "Wops," "Micks," "Suomis," and "Yids," on the iron range at Biwabik, Minnesota in 1919 and 1920—the inelegant "loose verbiage" is Stong's.[2] After his year at Columbia, he taught at the Neodesha, Kansas, high school until the spring of 1924 when he returned to Drake as an instructor in journalism.

Quite early Stong began to have an interest in a career as a writer. At Drake he studied under Lewis Worthington Smith, who encouraged him, in some directions:

> "Prof." Smith . . . had a profound distaste for my personal grooming and dress, which were terrible, and my manners, which were worse, in my earlier year with him as a freshman—this as a gentleman; as a scholar he gave attention to the fact that I must have read a great deal, spelled correctly for the most part, and had a strong ambition to be Shakespeare. . . . He gave me hours of time in conference and special reading of my literary attempts.[3]

---

1 Phil Stong, "Christmas in Iowa," *Holiday* (December 1952). Reprinted in *Palimpsest* 38 (December 1957):501–19. Gold is used in several novels by Stong. In *Forty Pounds of Gold*, John Warwick gets gold by mining and by building cradles to sell to other miners. In other novels, the farm was bought with this gold; in one or two novels the farm is bought with silver from mines in Nevada.
2 Phil Stong, *If School Keeps* (New York: Frederick A. Stokes Co., 1940), p. 173.
3 *If School Keeps*, pp. 131–33.

From Professor Smith he seems to have learned that "the teaching of writing, in three words, is 'Don't do it,' and this refers to both writing practices and personal conduct. . . . Writing must be learned by enormous reading and constant exercise; 'experience' doesn't amount to a damn."[4]

Stong seems to have been disappointed with Columbia's graduate program in English, except for his contacts with "Dorothy Scarborough, the backstop of the Short Story Course with her fine critical method and gentle soul," and with Carl Van Doren, who offered "lucid and amusing and even exciting comments on American literature."[5] He "learned a great deal more about what [he] wanted to know—writing—from Harry Stephen Keeler, the editor of Ten Story Book" who gave him "extravagantly generous critiques" and an occasional six-dollar check. (One of the stories which Keeler helped him with was sold to *Top-Notch* magazine for forty dollars!)[6]

While at Neodesha, and probably with the encouragement of Professor Smith, he sent a story, "Hymeneal," to John T. Frederick at *The Midland*, and it was accepted. "Hymeneal" shows that Stong was already thinking of "Pittsville" as a literary creation:

Pittsville was very old—almost a hundred years. Its infancy it had passed in squalling at the Indians and the Rebels; in adolescence it had courted factories, railroads, greatness; in maturity it had bred a poet and a statesman; now it had settled to the contemplative serenity of age.[7]

"Hymeneal" is also of interest because one of its characters is a Negro. Keosauqua had been a station on the Underground Railroad; in Stong's boyhood there had been a "Nigger Hill" in the town, and about fifteen per cent of the school pupils were black. Negro adults and Negro boys and girls appear in many Stong stories; we have seen Sammy in *Ivanhoe Keeler*. The most sharply delineated is the "bad little nigger," Soapy Randolph, the bootlegger in *Career*.

Stong must already have been displaying that exuberance of spirit which was a life-long characteristic and which bubbles up through his prose in nearly everything he wrote: "It was an exciting time," said Stong, "I sent sixty-odd 'poems' to one little magazine in Illinois at one burst; they published three and it was four or five years before I came to my senses enough to destroy my copies." He also sent poems to H. L. Mencken at *The American Mercury*, and for years he "treasured a note

---

4   *If School Keeps*, pp. 131–33.
5   *If School Keeps*, p. 212.
6   *If School Keeps*, pp. 214–15.
7   Phil Stong, "Hymeneal," *The Midland* 7 (June 1921):370.

from Mencken: 'I don't like your verse; we would like to see some more of your prose.'"[8]

While at Drake (where he was teaching and taking graduate courses), he took on a part-time reporting job on "the hotel run" for the *Des Moines Register*. In the meanwhile he was sending off one novel after another to publishers and getting all but one back. Harvey Ingham, one of the *Register's* great editors, helped him "peel the more florid terms and locutions" out of the stories he was writing for the newspaper, and Stong "suddenly observed that it makes one's writing more forceful if he does not indulge in words that chase the reader to the dictionary, unless it is necessary, and that figures of speech get to be a cheap trick if the trick is used too often."[9]

During that year at Drake he decided that a career as a writer and journalist was preferable to an M.A. and Ph.D., and a career as a teacher. In 1925, he became an editor for the Associated Press, then worked successively for *Liberty, Editor and Publisher*, and the *New York World*.

In 1925, he married Virginia Maude Swain; she died in 1969 at their home in Washington, Connecticut, to which they had moved in 1934, and where Stong himself died in 1957.

It was the publication of *State Fair* in 1932 which brought fame and fortune to Stong; the book became a Literary Guild Selection for May of that year, and soon everyone, it seemed, was talking about the novel which "had a hog as its hero." Many were shocked by (what seemed in 1932) the lurid scenes in the book, but they found even greater pleasure in the freshness of the Frake family, and in the skepticism of the Storekeeper. Hollywood filmed the book with Will Rogers in the role of Abel Frake, and a champion hog from a farm adjoining Linwood as the lovesick and homesick Blue Boy. Thirteen years later *State Fair* became a bright engaging musical with Vivian Blaine in the role of "the lovelier Emily," and Jeanne Crain singing "Grand Night for Singing," and "It Might as Well be Spring." In 1962, the film was again made into a musical, this time with a forgettable cast. The setting was the Texas State Fair! By popular and critical consent, the third version of Stong's delightful story was a failure, which seems to prove that poetic justice must now and then run its course.

The story line of *State Fair* is simple: Abel Frake, his wife Melissa, and their teen-age son and daughter, Wayne and Margy, take a trip to the Iowa State Fair at Des Moines. There Abel hopes that his prize boar, Blue Boy, will do better than his red ribbon of the year before, and Melissa dreams that her pickles will also garner a blue ribbon or so. Wayne wants

8 *If School Keeps,* pp. 255–57.
9 *If School Keeps,* pp. 263–65.

revenge against the carnival game which had cheated him the year before, and Margy is along for the fun and experience the State Fair offers.

But the Storekeeper, who "believed . . . that Heaven ordains all things for the worse" is gloomy about the Frake family prospects: "Don't let your hog get too good," he warns Abel, "Because if he's the best hog . . . he'll never win the sweepstakes. If a hog or man ever got what he was entitled to once, the eternal stars would quit making melody in their spheres."

Given these circumstances and the tone of the novel, events work out about as one might expect. Blue Boy wins the Sweepstakes, Melissa's pickles win the blue ribbons, and Margy and Wayne, with the help of Pat Gilbert, a Des Moines reporter who seems to have plenty of time for riding on roller coasters, and Emily, a carnival girl, learn something about boy-girl relationships they had never known in Brunswick. After a week at the Fair, the family returns to Brunswick in various emotional moods, and the Storekeeper has a final moment with "Them."

Critics were uneven in their praise of *State Fair*. Like John Frederick, they usually "prized the brilliant rendering of the state fair setting and atmosphere and the integrity of the minor characters—not forgetting Blue Boy, one of the most famous animals in American literature";[10] they granted that the novel would furnish "two hours of welcome relief from the depression";[11] but they deplored the romantic elements, arguing that they were not only "artistically and morally bad,"[12] but also that they produced characters "not only inconsistent with their character and environment . . . but out of key with the gay, richly humorous tone of the whole story, and the note on which it ends, with the all seeing storekeeper 'chuckling sardonically but not unpleasantly.' "[13]

Two of the better reviews placed the novel in the larger context of the farm novel as social statement. Garreta Busey, from the hog-and-hominy [sic] country, wrote:

With Hamlin Garland and Herbert Quick, we saw reflected in the middle border our pride in the adventures and our sympathy for the hardships of its frontiersman. To Ruth Suckow it looked dreary . . . and sordid naturalism became . . . firmly associated with the Mississippi Valley. . . . But Phil Stong,

10   John T. Frederick, "Iowa's Phil Stong," *Palimpsest* 38 (December 1957):521. Entire issue devoted to Stong; contains his "Christmas in Iowa" essay, an essay on Stong by Frederick, and a series of reminiscences by William J. Petersen; complete bibliography and photographs of Stong and Keosauqua.
11   Louis Kronenberger, "The Brighter Side of Farm Life," *New York Times Book Review*, May 8, 1932, p. 6.
12   John T. Frederick, "The Farm in Iowa Fiction," *Palimpsest* 32 (March 1951):136.
13   Arthur Ruhl, "Iowa, Old Style," *Saturday Review of Literature* 8 (May 7, 1932): 713.

looking back at Iowa, from whence he sprung, sees with artistic detachment and sympathetic humor, a group of honest and naive, but soundly intelligent, farmers having *mirabile dictu* a good time.[14]

But Robert Cantwell was critical of Stong's point of view:

There has been a great imaginative migration in American literature: our cities are peopled with heroes who left home in the final chapter. The central character of *Winesburg, Ohio,* turning his back on the small town, can serve as the most common symbol for a whole literary generation, for it is no mere change of residence that is suggested by his action, but the end of one way of living and the beginning of another. . . . Now, in *State Fair,* the emphasis is neatly reversed. The Middle West is no longer the villain, but the hero. There are no frustrated farmer's wives, no baffled philosophers, no unhappy young people longing to get to Chicago or New York or Paris. The state fair is only a brief idyll in the idyllic lives of the Frakes, and the Frakes are prosperous people, intelligent, tolerant and not too whimsical. . . .

Mr. Stong's dreamy Iowa would seem an even more appealing land if we did not have so much evidence indicating quite clearly that it does not exist.[15]

State Fair became the first novel in the Pittsville series; its time was the time of the publication of the novel. The other novels, and the periods of time they cover are: *The Princess* (1941), the years from 1900 to about 1930; *The Long Lane* (1939), from 1911 to 1914; *Career* (1936), the late 1920s; *Stranger's Return* (1933) and *Village Tale* (1934), the period 1931 to 1933; *The Rebellion of Lennie Barlow* (1937), the year 1930; *One Destiny* (1942), the years 1941 to 1942; *Return in August* (1953), a "sequel" to *State Fair,* 1952; and *Blizzard* (1955), one winter weekend in 1954. Taken together, these novels are about life in Pittsville and the surrounding villages, on and near the river, and on some of the nearby farms.

We have the social life of the towns:

The men, talking politics, crops, and local happenings in little groups, were in their working clothes, but they were conspicuously washed and brushed. The women were obviously in their Sunday best, for this was shopping afternoon—a female afternoon. They moved by twos and threes slowly past the shop windows and in and out of stores. They chose the middle of the sidewalk to meet and chat and made the men step off the curb. They enjoyed themselves quietly and magnificently. [*Stranger's Return,* pp. 73–74]

---

14 Garreta Busey, "Middle West, New Style," *New York Tribune Books,* May 8, 1932, p. 1.
15 Robert Cantwell, "This Side of Paradise," *New Republic* 71 (July 6, 1932):215.

The town's social stratifications:

There were very definite social lines between the River Rats, Courthouse Hill, Nigger Hill, the Schoolhouse Top, South Pittsville, and the center of the town. All these things in a town of less than a thousand people. [*The Rebellion of Lennie Barlow*, p. 227]

The river:

Occasionally the river would drown someone, and once or twice it had come up in the spring and threatened to take away the business street, but after a few days or weeks Pittsville always forgave it. [*Stranger's Return*, pp. 72–73]

The farm and the land:

He was looking down the sweep of lawn, across the cornfields at the bottom of the river. . . . "This where we're standing, down to the river and over to the creek is the old Storr place. Father settled that back in the 'Thirties. I can remember the little Indian devils that played in that grove down there. A squaw spanked me once. Jim . . . took up the hundred and sixty north there—where you see the trees. He liked trees. It's pretty good pasture though. All the rest of it, west and southwest, I bought with money I made in Nevada mining silver." [*Stranger's Return*, pp. 31–32]

The post office and the railroad which connect this rural area to the outer world:

This trickle in the great tide of transportation, too, made Brunswick, that little freckle of faint orange lights, feel its association with Ottumwa, and Chicago where there was the mail-order house, and all societies of men . . . there was *no end* to the iron track which ran before the Brunswick depot, short of remote cities in Canada and Mexico. [*Village Tale*, p. 8]

Against this background of rural and village scenes, Stong has set off his novels. His technique in each case is to place a group of actors in one of the settings, and then to let them work out their destinies in a series of well-plotted incidents over periods of time ranging from a weekend to some thirty years.

In *The Long Lane*, the central character, young Ken Brubaker, is seen as he faces the problem of divorce in his home and the coming of a step-mother. For a time Ken has to live in Des Moines, a situation which enables Stong to show us the world of a theatrical stock company in the early part of this century, and to give Des Moines "the only really lively and substantial portrayal it has received in our fiction." And Frederick further remarks:

Stong's best realized characters are boys and girls. He always treats childhood with insight and sympathy, and probably his finest achievement is Kenneth Brubaker . . . as Stong follows him through the ordeal of adjustment following the desertion of their home by his mother—to marry an uncle_whom the boy has especially loved.[16]

The Princess centers on the debate between Arnhold Edeson, who, as an orphan, has been raised by one of Phil Stong's miraculous hired hands, and Weldon Armbruster, a composer. Although Arnhold has had no formal education, the education she has received from the hired man and her brother, thirty-two years her senior, enables her to relate freely and easily with Armbruster. The matter of the debate is: shall she forsake the family farm and become Armbruster's city wife, or shall he forsake his musical career for a life on the farm as a farmwife's husband. An accident to his hand resolves the debate, and Armbruster comes to the farm to take up life as a gentleman farmer and composer.

Career recounts six months in the lives of Carl and Amy Krueger and their son Ray, a medical student at Johns Hopkins. The affairs of three families are interwoven in the novel: the Kruegers, Clem Bartholomew, his daughter Sylvia and his son Mellie, and Middleton "Mudcat" Katz and his daughter Merta. Over half of the story is taken up with Pittsville's Fourth of July celebration, during which Mudcat gets drunk with Soapy Randolph and nearly drowns in the river, the romance of Mellie and Merta is revealed, and Ray is attracted to Sylvia. Clem's greed (he begins the novel with two million dollars and a bank) leads in the end to the bank's failure and a convocation of the local Ku Klux Klan. When their attempts to lynch Clem are halted by Ray, they resolve their frustrations by running Soapy out of town.

Stranger's Return uses the same stereotyped theme which Bess Streeter Aldrich had used seven years earlier in *The Rim of the Prairie:* an Iowa girl dissolves an unsatisfactory marriage with an eastern husband and returns to a middle western farm home. Stong's theme is complicated by the presence of a pair of conniving women relatives who are trying to persuade Grandpa Storr that he is insane so that they can acquire possession of the family farm. A further complication has Louise Storr, the returnee, in love with Guy Crane, a neighboring farmer who is not very happily married. Guy, one of Stong's many learned farmers—he recites Whitman with all the aplomb of a specialist in nineteenth-century

---

16   John T. Frederick, "The Nineteen Thirties," *Palimpsest* 35 (February 1954):77–78.

American literature—resolves the dilemma by going to Cornell University to teach. The scheming ladies, one of whom is seduced in the haymow by the inevitable hired man, are undone by foxy Grandpa, and all ends well.

One of the highlights of the novel is the threshing dinner at which Louise wins acceptance from the farmers who up to that time have regarded her as just another "dumb" city slicker.

"To read this book is to realize that we have again an authentic novel of the soil," said Paul Allen. "We may well be grateful to Mr. Stong for such healthy examples of authentic naturalism as this book and *State Fair*. Because he has integrity and a range of sympathies beyond the merely sectional, he can give us a delineation of Iowa and the people that have in them something of the universality all good writing should share."[17]

Amy Loveman said that although at that point in the Depression we should "pity the poor farmer," there was no need to pity Phil Stong's farmer "with his bursting granaries and corncribs, his fat fields, his lavish meals of roast duck and heaped platters of vegetables." But she concluded that for all of Stong's obvious zest, the book was not as good as *State Fair*.[18]

The *New York Times* said that Stong had "brought a welcome quality to the American novel of the soil . . . he writes of Iowa farmers . . . with an evident love of life and a full sympathy for unregenerate human nature, [he] is not befogged by false sentiment, [his] blood does not sour at the thought of the human race."[19] But Ferner Nuhn said that *Stranger's Return*, although varying "the fable" somewhat, did not differ from other "idyl[s] celebrating the well-known salubrity of rural life." Moreover, he didn't think that Stong was "always happy in his details of Iowa life and idiom."[20]

In contrast with the "rural salubrity" of *Stranger's Return*, *Village Tale* is a complicated bitter story of rural illicit desire, rural cuckoldry and rural savagery, with strong overtones of Shakespeare's *Othello*. Much of the story, certainly its bitter episodes, takes place at night in the cold depths of an Iowa winter with the whistle blast of the Kaydee 6:45, "long and gravely sad," furnishing the background for "pity and passion and terror . . . —and love, which was not principally passion." But unlike Shakespeare's tragedy, in Stong's tale poetic justice triumphs all around.

Louis Kronenberger's review of the book was harsh, and, coming from an Easterner, perhaps unfair to a writer from the provinces, except that

---

17 Paul Allen, "A Tale Deeply Rooted in our Tradition," *New York Herald Tribune Books*, July 9, 1933, p. 3.
18 Amy Loveman, "Back to the Land," *Saturday Review of Literature* 9 (July 8, 1933): 685, 690.
19 J. D. A., "Phil Stong's Rib-Tickling Iowa Comedy," *New York Times Book Review*, July 9, 1933, p. 7.
20 Ferner Nuhn, "Pastoral Fable," *Nation* 137 (August 2, 1933): 135–36.

by this time Stong himself had left the Middle West for the East. Kronenberger, echoing an opinion which was to gain circulation, called Stong "slick" and accused him of trying to satisfy both the "discriminating and the undiscriminating reader alike." He charged that Stong was a "writer who scents tragedy" and yet "exploits melodrama."

Stong "is a realist who, at the decisive moment, runs away from the truth," he added. "He seems to be heading dangerously toward popular success."[21]

The Rebellion of Lennie Barlow is one of Stong's better books. Its theme is "the essential fluidity of the lines" of social stratification in a small town and their "susceptibility to modification under the impact of personality."[22] In this novel the complexities of small-town social stratification are enhanced by vestiges of the old North-South ideological conflicts. At the heart of the conflict is Lennie Barlow, another of Stong's young heroes.

The last three novels, *One Destiny*, *Return in August*, and *Blizzard*, are formula novels, about which *Time*'s 1936 comment about *Career* would seem to be true: "By last week no intelligent reader had to be told that Phil Stong's eager gaze was bent not on Parnassus but on the hills of Hollywood."[23] *One Destiny* brings the shooting war between the Nazis and the Allies to the banks of Chequest Creek; *Blizzard* assembles an unlikely group in the home of a Pittsville farm daughter (like all the rest she is a piano virtuoso, reads esoteric literature, and discusses esoteric subjects). *Return in August* reunites Pat Gilbert and Margy Frake Ware—this time, fat, middle-aged, and prosperous, they wed.

Stong wrote one other novel about Pittsville people. In *Farmer in the Dell* (1935) Pa Boyer, a Pittsville farmer, visiting in Hollywood, is picked off the street to play in a film which resembles *State Fair*. There has always been an audience for films and fiction about the film industry, and Stong, in Hollywood for the filming of *State Fair*, must have gotten the message.

Although Stong's farm novels were written during the depression years of the thirties, they ignore the problems which were facing the farmers of those years—over-production, low farm prices, farm conservation, rural electricity, and farm-to-market roads, among others. Stong implies farmers are of two types—good managers who always succeed and shiftless types who fail. Farm success seems to go with intelligence. Stong's novels belong in the "bless the farm" group—of which, more later.

A characteristic of the Stong novel is the constant use of hyperbole.

21 Louis Kronenberger, "Phil Stong's *Village Tale*," *New York Times Book Review*, March 11, 1934, p. 8.
22 Frederick, "The Nineteen Thirties."
23 *Time* 26 (January 13, 1936), p. 67.

Luigi Lafferty, the young photographer in *Return in August,* is a second Edward Steichen—farm families always eat on Haviland china, have coin-silver spoons, Steinway pianos in the parlor, and their apple cider surpasses vintage French champagnes. Nowhere is this tendency seen to better effect than in Stong's farmhands: Smokey in *Blizzard* (with his private stock of whiskey and his private library of Tom Paine, Shakespeare, Ingersoll, and Mark Twain!), old Jake Steward (a descendant of the English Stuarts!) in *The Princess,* and Lea in *The Long Lane* are the best of a long line.

Perhaps John T. Frederick's summary of Phil Stong's work, written at the end of Stong's life, is the best final word:

> Phil Stong's achievement is based on far more substantial grounds than mere productiveness. He was the first Iowan to produce a nationally popular novel built around such a typically midwestern institution as the state fair. He was the first to create adequate, colorful and memorable fictional treatment of the trek to Iowa and the beginnings of settlement. He was the first to portray in a group of novels a representative small Iowa community in its entirety—its business and professional life, its people of town and farm. He was one of the few to see that in Iowa's relatively brief history there is rich material for regiments of novelists. The whole body of his work is marked by and expressive of a personality singularly rich, frank and generous, full of love of life.
>
> ... his writing is always alive—very much alive: which is after all the cardinal virtue, is it not, if we stop to think?[24]

Phil Stong relies on familiar places, family history, and some standardized plot material in his fiction; Frederick Manfred uses personal and general history, familiar places, and an occasional standardized plot. Manfred was born on a farm near Doon, southwest of Rock Rapids in northwest Iowa, near the Minnesota and South Dakota borders (an area since named Siouxland by him). Manfred, a six-foot-nine-inch giant of a man, was the oldest of six brothers. His father, Feike Feikes Feikema VI, was of West Frisian descent; his mother, Aeltsje (Alice) von Engen, was of East Frisian and Saxon ancestry. In some of his novels, Manfred tries to work this Frisian-Saxon ancestry in as a part of the cultural background.

Doon had been settled by English farmers, but there had been an influx of Dutch as well, and Manfred was educated in the parochial Calvinistic schools in Doon and Hull. He attended Calvin College, Grand Rapids, Michigan, where he played basketball, joined various literary, philosophy, and dramatic clubs, read "avidly," wrote poetry, and helped edit the college magazine. He received a B.A. in 1934.

---

24 Frederick, "Iowa's Phil Stong," p. 524.

For the next three years, he hitchhiked around the United States and worked at all kinds of odd jobs, an experience which duplicated that of his Sioux County neighbor, J. Hyatt Downing. For two years he wrote for the Minneapolis *Journal*, losing his job in 1939, partially because he helped organize the American Newspaper Guild, partially because he actively supported Elmer Benson, the Farmer-Laborite, and partially because he was an "indifferent reporter."

In April of 1940, "due to malnutrition, overwork, heartache," he entered a sanatorium for treatment for tuberculosis. Of this experience he later wrote:

> It saved me as an organism and helped make me a writer. It taught me how to live both as a natural animal and as musing human being. It drilled into me an early-to-rise, catnap-at-noon, early-to-bed kind of health discipline. It also gave me two 'free' years to think about where I had been, where I was, and where I might go. It gave me a chance to take a deep breath and a good look around before plunging into the battle again.[25]

In 1943 after a brief period as a writer for *Modern Medicine*, marriage to Maryanna Shorba, a University of Minnesota journalism graduate, and aiding Hubert Humphrey's Minneapolis mayoralty candidacy, he decided "it was now or never as a writer. . . . He felt that if he was to develop his own particular style as an American of Old Frisic-Anglo-Saxon descent, if he was to write his individual kind of prose, Manfredean . . . prose, he had to avoid Latinate vocabulary."[26]

With the help of a University of Minnesota writing fellowship (1944–45), a one thousand dollar grant-in-aid from the American Academy of Arts and Letters (1945, after the publication of *The Golden Bowl*), and writing fellowships from the Field Foundation, Inc., and the Andreas Foundation (1948–50), Manfred wrote four novels and a trilogy in the next seven years. Near the end of this productive period, "as part of the 1849–1949 Minnesota Territorial Centennial Celebration he was honored, along with the writers Sinclair Lewis and Robert Penn Warren as one of the state of Minnesota's 100 Living Great."[27] In more recent years, he has made his home near Luverne, Minnesota, where he continues to write.

Until 1951 Manfred wrote under the name of Feike Feikema; his books since 1951 have been written under the name Frederick [Feikema] Manfred. The change was made, he said, partially to anglicize the name, partially because of the difficulty many had in pronouncing the name:

---

25 Frederick Feikema Manfred, *Twentieth Century Authors*, first supplement, ed. Stanley J. Kunitz (New York: Wilson, 1955), pp. 633–35.
26 Manfred, *Twentieth Century Authors*, pp. 633–35.
27 Manfred, *Twentieth Century Authors*, pp. 633–35.

" 'Feikema' can be a sort of seen but silent insignia tying the old name with the new. . . . Both names . . . mean 'man of peace.' "[28]

Manfred, who likes to invent words, uses the terms "rume," "novel" and "romance" as categories for his works. To him, the "rume" is autobiographical, "made universal by exalting and transmuting personal agonies"; the novel is invented, written from the outside rather than the inside, and has an "artificially imposed consistency."[29] The term "romance" singles out a romantic story.

By his definitions, then, Manfred's "rumes" are: *Boy Almighty* (1945), *The Chokecherry Tree* (1948), *The Primitive* (1949), *The Giant* (1951) and *The Brother* (1962). When these last three were first published, they were intended to become part of a trilogy, *World's Wanderer*. In 1962, considerably revised and shortened, they were published in one volume as *Wanderlust*.

His novels are: *The Golden Bowl* (1944), *This is the Year* (1947), *The Man Who Looked Like the Prince of Wales* (1965), (published in paperback as *The Secret Place* 1967), and *Eden Prairie* (1968). Five of the novels which deal either with the Indian or the plains country have been labeled his "Buckskin Man" tales: *Lord Grizzly* (1954), *Riders of Judgment* (1957), *Conquering Horse* (1959), *Scarlet Plume* (1964), and *King of Spades* (1966).

Manfred has also written *Apples of Paradise* (1968), a collection of short stories; *Arrow of Love* (1961), an anthology of three novelettes—the title story (discussed in Chapter 2), "Lew and Luanne," and "Country Love"; and *Winter Count*, a volume of verse (1966). Not all of these constitute "Iowa literature" as it is defined for this history.

Winter Count, privately printed, contains a long autobiographical poem, and "The West Sends a Call," written at Calvin College in 1934; the latter could be said to express Manfred's literary credo:

> I know that learning and manners
> and books and sophisticated graces
> are little known on the dreaming prairies.
> Yet the whistle of the western meadowlark
> singing of its eggs in the grass,
> the sweep of the swallow in the yard
> diving through a cloud of flies,
> the bawl of the wetborn calf
> staggering in the crackling straw,

---

28 Frederick Feikema Manfred, "Feikema Explains Name Change," *Publishers' Weekly* 161 (May 3, 1952), p. 1834.
29 Feike Feikema (Frederick Feikema Manfred), "Postlude," *The Giant* (Garden City: Doubleday & Co., 1951), pp. 403.

all these,
have an appeal and a message that are pleasing
to the primitive nature in man.[30]

Boy Almighty, the first of Manfred's autobiographical "rumes," is set in a Minnesota sanatorium where Eric Frey, a charity patient, has been brought because he is dying of tuberculosis. The time of the story is the early 1940s, coinciding with the time when Manfred himself was in a sanatorium. Like Manfred, Frey is a writer, has no sisters, and hails from "Bonnie Doon, Iowa," Manfred's fictional name for his home town. The story tells of Frey's physical and spiritual recovery; the structure of the book pairs the day-to-day life and work of the hospital as it effects Frey's cure with a kind of subjective stream-of-conscious reporting of his mental states as he goes through the cure.

There are in the book a number of statements which seem to represent a kind of groping toward a theory of creation on the part of Manfred. In one of them, Frey refers to "Whitman, Rolland, Doughty, Gandhi, Marx, Jesus [and] Tolstoi" as "brothers of mine [who] are waiting for me, their younger brother, to report on what I think that wrestle is." In another, a janitor says that "a man must be strong to write about himself honestly." Other statements read as if they were anticipations of critical comments on the style of the book, or as if they were a process of self-education.[31]

Manfred said of *Boy Almighty* that it "was a personal and a vital truth, a testament of suffering and of faith in life, a tale with roots that went back to my private inner life, an odyssey created out of my very flesh and blood, as if the words were my cells and the phrases my tissues and the paragraphs my organs and the book my body."[32]

Professor Peter DeBoer thought that "*Boy Almighty* is not a notable book. It is instructive for what it says about Manfred's early yearnings as a writer, for it indicates something of the passion and even confusion which afflicted him." But he felt that the novel (along with *Morning Red*) was "less artistic than Manfred's country settings, be they Northwest Iowa and South Dakota, or farther west."[33]

Jennings Rice, noting that Manfred had "attempted a more difficult theme" than in the earlier *The Golden Bowl*, thought he had succeeded.

---

30 Frederick Manfred, *Winter Count: Poems 1934–1965* (Minneapolis: James D. Thueson, 1966), p. 11.
31 Feike Feikema (Frederick Feikema Manfred) *Boy Almighty* (Saint Paul: Itasca Press, Webb Publishing Co., 1945), pp. 71–72, 121, 181–82, 260, 314.
32 Feikema, "Postlude," *The Giant*, pp. 416–17.
33 Peter P. DeBoer, "Frederick Manfred: The Developing Art of the Novelist" (M.A. thesis, University of Iowa, 1961), p. 20.

But he wondered why "Eric, the college graduate, the poet, should be made to use such execrable grammar."[34]

The Chokecherry Tree is the story of young Elof Lofbloom, another of Manfred's "heroes." The tree, an obvious symbol for Elof, "cowers beneath thirteen massive cottonwoods" at Chokecherry Corner. Residents or travelers in northwest Iowa will recognize the T-junction of Highways 18 and 75 two miles west of Hull—called locally, Perkins' Corner.

Elof is a young man for whom, at first, fate seems to have much in store. He is sent to a seminary for two years but not sensing a "call," he is sent to the state university for two years. Failing there also, he has "bummed" around the country for two years. It is on his return home to Chokecherry Corner where his tight-fisted father operates one of the three filling stations, that the story begins. Elof's story is one of successes and failures—he works hard for his father but gets no pay, he helps the Hello (Hull) baseball team to a victory but he fails as a lover afterwards, he fails as a door-to-door salesman, and for a while he seems to be running second to his father in the contest for the hand of Gert, a cow-like country girl whom he eventually marries.

To Richard Sullivan, Elof is "the so-called 'little man'—the common person floundering through life with moderately good intentions" who "has been quite widely treated in the fiction of our time. Usually he has been posed against an industrialized background, and often he has turned out to be a rather grim and depressing figure. But in *The Chokecherry Tree* he is a warm and urgent, bumptious little man, surrounded by the wide flat prairies."

"Somewhere along the route of his little experiences," added Sullivan, "he has acquired a shocking but honest suspicion that he is never going to be a great public figure, a recognized name in the prairie world. Somewhere along the route he has gained a simple wisdom."[35]

Sullivan, like Paul Corey,[36] liked the book for its "antic humor" and "absolute sincerity," but Professor Peter DeBoer called it "one of Manfred's poorest attempts—a relatively low spot in the development of his art." He thought that there was "a lack of control in characterization"; that there was occasional "authorial intrusion"; and that the "language and detail" were often inappropriate, and, on one occasion at least, "sacrilegious" and in "exceedingly poor taste."[37] (DeBoer comes from the same Calvinistic background as Manfred.)

---

34 Jennings Rice, *New York Herald Tribune Books*, December 9, 1945, p. 6.
35 Richard Sullivan, "Little Man on a Big Prairie," *New York Times Book Review*, April 11, 1948, p. 7.
36 Paul Corey, "Small Time Boy," *New York Herald Tribune Books*, August 22, 1948, p. 9.
37 DeBoer, "Frederick Manfred: The Developing Art of the Novelist," p. 33.

Robert B. Heilman, perhaps the most prestigious of Manfred's critics, was also not happy: "the fare in [Manfred's] *The Chokecherry Tree* is strictly lean-year. . . . The manner is journalistic . . . short sentences and paragraphs predominate, and the diction is popular. . . . [The] preoccupation with little men . . . necessarily leads to triviality.[38]

The original three volumes, *The Primitive*, *The Brother*, and *The Giant*, had thirteen hundred pages, a circumstance which has not pleased his critics: "[Manfred] tends to overwhelm the reader by massiveness of design and by a tanklike rush of his writing. . . . [There is too much] mere piling up of profitless detail."[39]

The hero of this massive literary effort is six-feet-nine-inch Thurs Waldron who is first seen as a farm laborer at an orphanage near "Bonnie Doon." The home's female preceptress sends Thurs off to "Christian College" in Zion, Michigan. The time is September 1930, and Thurs' trek across Iowa, Illinois, and Michigan is made in a broken-down Model-T Ford with several of his future classmates. At college his size presents logistics problems, but it helps him become a star basketball player.

There are a number of standard scenes of college life—rushing, hazing, games, binges, pranks, chapel—which are fairly well reported. Thurs meets two fellow students to whom he is attracted—Huse Starring, a sensitive, keen-minded boy, and Hero Bernlef, "the elfin queen," and daughter of the head of the English Department, whom he saves from drowning.

In his four years at college, we see Thurs grow emotionally, intellectually, spiritually, and creatively. He almost flunks out of school the first semester but becomes a "B-plus" student by the end of his four-year term. From extreme difficulties with a freshman composition course, he moves to the presidency of the literary society. He also composes two promising musical scores.

But after crushing Hero's ribs in a sudden burst of emotions, and after his music teacher, Mr. Manfrid, is dropped from the faculty, Thurs resolves to go to New York City. "No music, no song, no poetry," he tells Huse, "I'm going to get in among . . . the common folk and toss my lot in with them."

George R. Stewart thought that *The Primitive* demonstrated that Manfred had "magnificent qualities as a novelist: a fine and basic honesty, tremendous powers of observation, considerable knowledge both of nature and of humanity by which to direct his observation, a Whitman-like

---

38 Robert B. Heilman, "Versions of Documentary, Arts and Letters," *Sewanee Review* 56 (Autumn 1948):678–79.
39 George R. Stewart, *New York Times Book Review*, September 18, 1949, p. 37.

enthusiasm for life. He displays an intense interest in the powers of language, and a willingness for linguistic experiment."[40]

Other critics, however, were put off by Manfred's neologisms and his attempts at parody. Paul Corey said that the book was "considerably weakened by [his] use of such words as 'lornsick' and 'stumbered' to get an effect of 'fine' writing. His trick of parodying contemporary writers' names and book titles [B. S. Idiom, "The Love Song of J. Freddie Petticoat"] is not really clever but an annoyance to the reader."[41]

Howard Nemerov reacted almost completely negatively: "*The Primitive* . . . makes no secret of its proposal to be the great American novel . . . [Manfred's] frequent protestations of heroic purpose sit particularly ill in a work whose most dramatically successful incidents follow, though in unexpurgated form, the conventions of the Rover Boys . . . ."[42]

In *The Brother*, we see Thurs in Passaic, New Jersey, where he labors in a rubber works, reads Marx, gets involved with the CIO organizers and a strike, and then, after meeting the daughter of the factory owner, finds himself in a society of intellectuals and aesthetes. This leads him to what Paul Corey called a "sudden preoccupation with sex" and affairs with an "uninhibited sculptress" and the "handsomely packaged" Bernadine Makepeace.[43] Confused by his love affairs and once again involved in an act of violence, Thurs solicits the advice of a psychiatrist. "Get the hell out of New York and go back to the midlands," the doctor tells him, and *The Brother* ends with Thurs once more back on the highway, hitchhiking.

By now Thurs has failed to find himself twice—in the midwestern parochial environment of a small sectarian college, and in the larger parochialism of the East, where he had been exposed to both the working classes and the intellectuals and rich people. In the first novel he had rejected Christ; in the second novel he rejects Marx; and in the third novel, *The Giant*, he comes to grips with Scire, the new science-god.

In this third book, Thurs meets a bright young physicist, Bruce Farrell, and a university librarian, Eva Nordling, "a writ-large Hero." Thinking about Eva's over-sized resemblance to the "elfin queen," Thurs comes to see Minneapolis as an enlarged Zion (the college town). Married to Eva, his fertile mind is soon producing musical compositions again. Then, as Paul Corey says, "in [Manfred's] Frisian-rooted, modern mythology,

---

40 Stewart, *New York Times Book Review*.
41 Paul Corey, "A Wanderer Sets Forth," *New York Herald Tribune Books*, September 18, 1949, p. 9.
42 Howard Nemerov, "Of Giants and Islands," *Sewanee Review* 58 (Summer 1950): 539–40.
43 Paul Corey, "A Midlander in Manhattan," *New York Herald Tribune Books*, November 26, 1950, p. 16.

" 'Old Man Reality' bumps up against the new God, Scire, of the Atomic Age. The latter's disciple, Bruce Farrell (who returns to the physics laboratory and helps create that destructive 'Thing') becomes the instrument that brings Thurs, symbol of the individual as creative artist, man of peace, to a violent end."[44]

Although Manfred had once called structuring "cross word puzzling," he showed in these three books (and others) an obvious delight in (or need for) structuring. The trilogy is itself divided into three parts, and each of the three parts is further divided into three parts, called (in each book), "The Chancing," "The Nexus" and "The Rending," thus indicating a logical relationship among the volumes.

Paul Corey questioned whether Manfred's "inward gusher" (Manfred's term) was a success;[45] Harrison Smith thought that *The Giant* was "the best of the three volumes, though it reveals all of the author's idiosyncrasies and his bewilderment at the astonishing brainchild he has conceived."[46] By far, the most negative criticism of Manfred's work came from Granville Hicks: "The trouble is that [Manfred] has been unable to communicate his passion and seriousness, principally because he cannot command the necessary resources of style. By no means a careless writer, in fact almost too self-conscious in his handling of words, he achieves an infelicity of language that is staggering in its consistency."[47]

Considering the trilogy as a whole, John R. Milton felt that Manfred had striven for a deeper meaning:

Thurs, then, becomes a gigantic symbol [of man's attempts to "learn for himself his place in life and the meaning of life"], an impressive although frequently comic figure moving about America, the promised land where traditional strains unite to form giants. . . . The hope which Manfred holds out lies in the old land-traditions, in nature, in the honesty and joy of living on or near the land. The end of the individual is his knowledge of his origins. Once Thurs discovers this truth, he dies. As a symbol he has fulfilled his function. As a man he has lived a full life, identified himself, made his contributions.[48]

One of Manfred's novelettes and one of his novels treat of the close relationships of young males, and the complications deriving from the

44   Paul Corey, "Mr. Feikema Concludes His Trilogy," *New York Herald Tribune Books,* December 30, 1951, p. 8.
45   Corey, "Mr. Feikema Concludes His Trilogy."
46   Harrison Smith, "World Wanderer," *Saturday Review* 35 (January 12, 1952):14.
47   Granville Hicks, "The End of Mighty Thurs," *New York Times Book Review,* December 30, 1951, p. 5.
48   John R. Milton, "Frederick Feikema Manfred," *Western Review* 22 (Spring 1958): 181–82, 186–87; "Voice From Siouxland: Frederick Feikema Manfred," *College English* 19 (December 1957):104–11. These articles are essentially the same.

advent of a girl on the scene. "Country Love," is a "pastoral," a tale of two boys who grow up on a northwest Iowa farm, forming a close relationship. Jute is blinded as the result of an automobile accident; Ray, taking the blame, becomes morose. Eventually, however, Ray marries Jute's girl, Doll; Jute in the meantime has become a drunkard. Finally, Jute is won over to an acceptance of his situation by one of Ray and Doll's sons.

In *Eden Prairie,* Manfred was apparently heeding the advice of those critics who had told him he wrote best when he was writing about his native Siouxland. For the setting, he returned to "Bonnie" (Doon)—a setting he had abandoned for his previous five "Buckskin Tales." The time of the novel is the 1920s. The protagonists are Karen Alfredson, Konstant (Kon) Harmer, and Kon's brother Brant. An incestuous homosexual relationship between the brothers prevents Kon's marriage to Karen until both are in their thirties. Ultimately, Brant's jealousy of the forthcoming birth of Kon and Karen's first child leads him to blow his head off. The ultimate end of this relationship is foreshadowed in a prologue in which two redwings destroy two butterflies. The point of Manfred's novel seems to be that such human butterflies as those shown in his novel are too delicate to live in our rapacious world. The difficulty with this theme is that Kon and Karen do survive—helped somewhat by a Methodist minister who reminds them that "it is good for the tongue to sometimes taste a bitter radish."

Professor Scott Donaldson saw in this novel Manfred's continuing concern as one of making his Siouxland "come alive," making it "stand for all places in all times," bringing to the task "a well-developed sense of history; an empathy with all manner of people, rich and poor, educated and ignorant; a keen ear for patterns of speech; a sharp eye for the natural world; and an awareness of tragic undertows running beneath the placid surface of rural life." Nevertheless, he added, "Manfred's latest novel sometimes seems contrived rather than created." And he concluded that Manfred "fails only to give his story the kind of universality that is the gift of genius."[49]

Stong and Manfred, then, have each set up a literary territory, one in southeast Iowa, the other in northwest Iowa and beyond. Each has developed the territory in his own way. Stong, a romantic naturalist, showed us the first settlers (*Buckskin Breeches*) and then presented the town and countryside from about 1900 on. He depicted farmers and villagers, blacks and whites, educated and noneducated, merchants, professional people and politicians, adults and children. Manfred, the naturalist and

---

49 Scott Donaldson, "Manfred Nets Human Butterflies," *Minneapolis Tribune,* December 1, 1968, Section E, p. 1.

sometimes symbolist, has attempted to establish a chronological line beginning with the Indians and western pioneers, but he has shown us the Iowa settlers in only brief detail. He has not done much with small town people. But he has gone into much more detail with country people, studied more types, even the county agent, as we shall see in the next chapter. Because he seems to have taken his work more seriously, he has attracted the attention of more serious critics, although they have not always been happy with his work.

Farmer in the Dell

WRITING in *The Midland* for May–June 1918, L. H. Bailey asked: "Can Agriculture Function in Literature?"

"Yes," he said, "the open country contains material in abundance for an elegant literature, delicate and brilliant and powerful . . . this literature will be of the essence of the open country, founded in its experiences":

> There are "characters" in abundance,—the country doctor, the lawyer, the teacher, the farm wife whose qualities slowly improve on acquaintance, the highway commissioner, sales agents of many breeds, the local politician, the horsetrader, the thresher, the blacksmith and other artisans, the farmer who has gone daily to the exacting school of experience.

And, Bailey concluded, "whether the imaginative poems and dramas and fiction of the open country are to be written by farmers themselves is of small consequence; but they must be the work of those who are born to the environment and driven by the motive."

At the time of the writing of this essay, there were in existence, according to Professor Roy Meyer, only fifteen or sixteen farm novels; of these Hamlin Garland had written six, five of which were about Iowa or Wisconsin.[1] In the next forty years, over a hundred novels and an uncounted number of short stories were to be written about the farm, along with poems and plays. What part Bailey's essay had in motivating any of these is not known; but John T. Frederick, the editor of *The Midland* (himself to be the author of two novels about the farm) was to play a predominant part in the education and training of persons who were to write about the farm in Iowa: Ruth Suckow, Walter Muilenburg, Roger L. Sergel, Ival McPeak, Phil Stong, James Hearst, and others. Phil Stong recalled that

> the man who first pointed out that there was literary gold in them thar cornfields was, without a doubt, John T. Frederick. . . . [*The Midland*] was

---

1 Roy Meyer, *The Middle Western Farm Novel in the Twentieth Century* (Lincoln: University of Nebraska Press, 1965), p. 178.

devoted to stories and verses showing what a horrid place the Iowa farmlands were. Farm gentlemen were butted by bulls and farm ladies drank sheep dip; scrawny farm children groveled with the pigs and little farm girls all made for the haymow where the hired man was waiting with lust in his eyes and manure on his overalls.[2]

John T. Frederick in later years made an investigation of the farm as a literary subject which took him back as far as Johnson Brigham's *Midland Monthly* of the 1890s. He found only three farm stories and he concluded that "it seems the result of a fortunate accident—that Hamlin Garland lived for a time on Iowa farms and went to school in Iowa— that 'the Iowa farm in fiction' is firmly established in the literary history of America."[3]

Of the Iowa writers who came of age after Garland ceased to write about the farm (ca. 1900), Susan Glaspell wrote a few farm stories, George Cram Cook, Harry Hansen, and Floyd Dell were perhaps too oriented toward city life and literary concerns; James Norman Hall was concentrating on England, the war, and the South Seas; Carl Van Vechten had gone to "the Left Bank of New York"; Ross Santee had gone "woolly west"; Ellis Parker Butler was writing humor; and Arthur Davison Ficke became an "exquisite."[4] "Many readers," said Caroline Sherman in 1930, "would probably find it difficult to realize how little was published about the farm or agriculture in the general and literary magazines, and in fiction and popular non-fiction, before [1920]."[5]

The rise of realism and naturalism in fiction probably contributed to the upsurge in farm fiction—rural themes and settings were "well calculated to meet the robust demands made by the exponents and the followers of realism" and naturalism:

. . . they fitted even more exactly the requirements brought about by that rather definite trend toward nationalism, or the embodiment of the national spirit, in the arts, as shaped and encouraged and exemplified by Stuart Sherman in criticism, Hamlin Garland . . . Harriet Monroe in poetry, Lorado Taft in sculpture, [Louis Sullivan in architecture], Jens Jensen in landscape architecture, and a few other adventurous spirits in the midlands and elsewhere.[6]

The experience and influence of Willa Cather of Nebraska contributed in part. Miss Cather had shown her first novel, *Alexander's Bridge* (1912),

2   Phil Stong, *Hawkeyes* (New York: Dodd, Mead & Co., 1940), pp. 48–50.
3   John T. Frederick, "The Farm in Iowa Fiction," *Palimpsest* 32 (March 1951):121–52.
4   Stong, *Hawkeyes*, pp. 48–50.
5   Caroline Sherman, "Farm Life Fiction Reaches Maturity," *Sewanee Review* 29 (October–December 1931):473.
6   Sherman, "Farm Life Fiction Reaches Maturity," p. 474.

a story about the East, Canada, and England, to Sarah Orne Jewett. Miss Jewett, who was writing sketches about her own state of Maine, advised Miss Cather that she would do better with the life, characters, and scenes she knew best—the farms of the Middle West. Miss Cather followed this advice, and her subsequent success with *O Pioneers* (1913), *The Song of the Lark* (1915), *My Antonia* (1918), and *One of Ours* (1922), undoubtedly influenced younger writers.[7]

Concentration on the development of writing and of young writers on the Middle West, particularly at the University of Iowa under the direction and encouragement of John T. Frederick, Frank Luther Mott, and Edwin Ford Piper, at Drake University under Lewis Worthington Smith, and at Cornell College under Clyde Tull, was an important factor in the development of farm fiction, for these students were encouraged to write about their home state, and subjects they knew about.

Caroline B. Sherman,[8] Ruth Suckow,[9] and John T. Frederick[10] at various times outlined the criteria for good rural fiction. It must at least suggest both sides of farm life—its limitations and advantages. It must show the essential differences in the attitudes of rural people toward both the land and farming; it must show in "diverse ways a kinship between the leading characters and the soil"; it must be "permeated with the sense of growth: growth of character, growth of living things, growth of farms or of community"; a "sense of interdependence of the country town and country, a deep realization of their profound relationship" is valuable; and it must delineate "the satisfactions of the truly rural characters" for these "are not the conventional satisfactions of most modern fiction."

Recurring themes in Iowa farm fiction are: the history of Iowa, the rebellion against complacency, provincialism and exploitation, the rise of technology and its concomitant impact on the community, the naturalistic documentation of special ways of life, the perennial problems of personal adjustment, the chronicle of a family or community, the indictment of the farm's dreariness and its suffocating effect on the individual, and the appearance of actual incidents and people.

The farm novel took many forms: the novel of pioneer life, the romantic novel, the novel of adventure, the political novel, the chronicle or saga, the psychological novel, the novel of social life, the idyl, the national novel, the regional novel, the historical novel, and the biographical or autobiographical novel.

A typical biographical novel is Eleanor Saltzman's *Ever Tomorrow*

---

7   Willa Cather, "Preface," to *Alexander's Bridge* (Boston: Houghton Mifflin, 1922).
8   Sherman, "Farm Life Fiction Reaches Maturity," p. 481.
9   Ruth Suckow, *New Hope* (New York: Farrar & Rinehart, 1942), pp. 93, 96.
10   Frederick, "The Farm in Iowa Fiction."

(1936), which covers the period from about 1870 to 1931 and shows how one man's life could bridge the time period from the construction of the first permanent farm buildings (after the log cabin or "soddy" had served its initial purpose) to the point where the man's sons have revolted against the farm and have moved to the city.

The novel is set in the country near Mt. Ayr, in south-central Iowa, where Kathryn Eleanor Saltzman was born in 1904. Her family was of French descent from the Alsace-Lorraine area. Miss Saltzman grew up on her parent's farm; at twelve she was stricken with polio and left partially crippled. She attended country schools and Mt. Ayr High School, then graduated from Drake University. After advanced work in the classical languages, she received a Master of Arts degree from the University of Iowa in 1928. For a time she served as a secretary in the Department of Classics, and then she took a position as an editorial assistant in the Child Welfare Research Station. From 1930 on her stories of farm life began to appear in *Prairie Schooner, The Midland, Frontier, American Prefaces,* and other magazines. Some of her stories were published in pamphlet form by the Child Welfare Research Station.

"Pastoral" recounts the preparations of a farm girl for her lover's evening visit. In "One Morning Early," a girl who might be the same girl a few months after marriage is seen—on a morning when she has perceived that her lover and husband is an "awkward, overgrown, not too brilliant boy," and that she, as her mother before her, is fated for a life of cream checks, egg checks, scrubbing and cooking. "In Memoriam" looks into the mind of another farm girl as she sits in church before the casket of her domineering father—an old maid with no past, no future.[11]

When reading these stories, which are no better or worse than other good undergraduate writing, it is difficult to conceive that Miss Saltzman had already written *Ever Tomorrow*, so great is the contrast in writing skills. In terms of maturity, style, grasp of subject matter, control of materials, development of characterization, structure and the like, the novel is far superior.

Ever Tomorrow is the story of Joe Mueller from the time he first begins to comprehend the world about him until he is about sixty. The action is always seen through Joe's eyes. The theme of the book is that Joe's life is a series of "tomorrows" which are never realized; he is "caught in a treadmill that would not let him go." A second theme is the revolt against farm life. Joe's brother and his son leave the farm, but Joe can't: "I wanted to get away, too, when I was a boy . . . I thought I

---

11   Eleanor Saltzman, "Pastoral," *American Prefaces* 3 (October 1937); "One Morning Early," *American Prefaces* 1 (May 1936); "In Memoriam," *American Prefaces* 4 (January 1939).

couldn't stand to stay here." And Carl says, "I haven't got anything against the farm. . . . Only I don't want to get myself stuck off down here in the sticks and never get out. You don't go anywhere on a farm. I want to go places and do something else besides plow corn."

Professor Roy Meyer says of *Ever Tomorrow* that it is "written in subdued tones, with no peaks of emotional tension . . . this novel displays a fine delicacy, especially in regard to its handling of the inner feelings of its characters."[12]

Miss Saltzman's other novel, *Stuart's Hill* (published in 1945, the year before her death) is a pastoral idyl set in a small rural community of devout Scotch. In biblical language, the novel recounts the building of a rural church and the forces which work against the church from both within its membership and without. John T. Frederick (who called *Ever Tomorrow* "a peculiarly warm and easy rendering of the texture of farm and community life") said that *Stuart's Hill* is a "fine example of a writer's recognition and realization of a significant theme in Iowa rural life . . . of a country church and . . . its slow disuse, its decay, and its final destruction."[13]

A more considerable author of farm fiction is Frederick Feikema Manfred, whose novels and stories of pioneer life are discussed in Chapter 2, and whose novels and stories of "Siouxland" have been discussed in Chapter 8. Manfred's stories and novels of farm and rural life are also set in his fictional countryside.

Manfred's first novel, *The Golden Bowl* (1944), is set in South Dakota during the "dust bowl" years of the 1930s. The protagonist is Maury Grant, a young farmer from Oklahoma who with his guitar, on the way to the Black Hills to look for work in the gold mines, stops at the farm of Iver Thor. Pa Thor's neighbors have moved on when the "golden bowl" turned into a dust bowl, but he has remained on the land with his wife Thelma and daughter Kirsten. Maury's youthful sense of hopelessness is set off against Pa's faith in the land:

"Son . . . I kin still see this land as it's been. They say it's a dustbowl now. . . . But I can close my eyes and see the golden bowl it's been. There's been gold corn an' wheat an' hay, an' buffalo grass in the fall, an' gold pheasants an' cows an' women, all gold. . . . This land ain't empty for me. . . . It's been full of gold before an' it'll be full of gold again. I know."

Maury leaves the Thors and goes on further west where he experiences many of the incidents and situations common to those faced by wander-

---

12 Meyer, *The Middle Western Farm Novel in the Twentieth Century*, p. 231.
13 Frederick, "The Farm in Iowa Fiction."

ing homeless men in the thirties. Manfred could write about these with authority because he too had wandered over the face of America in those years. Eventually Maury realizes that man's real strength lies in the land and the work it requires, and he returns to the Thor's farm.

Critics praised the novel and many compared it to Steinbeck's *Grapes of Wrath*, a novel with similar situations and themes. Rose Feld said that Manfred "excellently develop[ed] the portraits of a youth who has succumbed to the hopelessness of a fight against nature and an old man who lives with memories of the earth's bounties and is willing to suffer until it recovers from its fever." She added that Manfred was a "poet as well as a novelist. His prose has a deep lyric quality which he sustains throughout the book."[14]

Andrea Parke thought that Manfred wrote "of a life and a land that have real meaning for him. His genuine feeling for his subject shines in every page; his understanding goes deep to recreate an image of the tortured earth—and the miracle of its renewal."[15]

John R. Milton argued that "all of Manfred's work consistently operates on two levels, and the driving force behind the work is just as concerned with the long view of Man as it is with the shorter view of Maury the dust bowl victim, Pier the farmer, or Hugh the plainsman."[16]

Professor Peter DeBoer thought that the novel stands somewhere between Manfred's best work and his worst work, but for all that it still "has proved seaworthy."[17] And the American Academy of Arts and Letters gave the book its fiction award for 1944.

"Lew and Luanne" (one of the three novelettes in *Arrow of Love*, 1961) is set in the town of Bonnie, Manfred's fictional name for Doon, Iowa, his birthplace. The novelette furnishes a good picture, entertaining and not exaggerated, of northwest Iowa farm life. There is one very comic scene in which an attempt to load Barney the Bull into a truck ends with Barney in the haymow.

The Man Who Looked Like the Prince of Wales is also set in Bonnie, except for the final chapter which takes place in Bellflower, California—a suburb of Los Angeles to which many northwest Iowa farmers have moved. The protagonist, Garrett Engelking, supposedly looks like the "Prince of Wales"—which one is not made clear, although the story takes

14   Rose Feld, *New York Herald Tribune Books*, October 1, 1944, p. 10.
15   Andrea Parke, "Dustbowl People," *New York Times Book Review*, October 8, 1944, p. 14.
16   John R. Milton, "Frederick Feikema Manfred," *Western Review* 22 (Spring 1958): 181–82, 186–87; "Voice From Siouxland: Frederick Feikema Manfred," *College English* 19 (December 1957):104–11. The two essays are essentially the same.
17   Peter DeBoer, "Frederick Manfred: The Developing Art of the Novelist" (M.A. thesis, University of Iowa, 1961), p. 20.

place in Iowa's horse-and-buggy days. Through his Frisian lineage, Garrett is even said to be related to the Prince. Garrett's two love affairs lead to quite a bit of duplication of incidents for such a short novel, and his personal habits bring him to a tragic end. The duplication of incidents, incidentally, is a characteristic of Manfred's fiction.

"Footsteps in the Alfalfa" (from *Apples of Paradise*), one of Manfred's earliest short stories, seems to be "sodbusting" for the later *This is the Year*. Frank Bromsted is a renter; his wife, Laura, is barren; and the third person in the story is Jack Mattly, a sometime veterinarian. A long scene describing the "birthing" of a calf is echoed in the novel. Like the later Pier, Bromsted raises dairy cattle; like Pier, he dreams about "the Big year . . . the one we all lay back for." Laura is compared to the earth, and Frank speculates about the life of the farmer:

> Farming was the biggest gamble this side of heaven. In no other walk of life did a man put out so much in the form of sweat and money, and expect to get so little, with so slim a chance of getting it, as in farming. There was no two ways about it—farming was for the dumbheads.

Frank thinks that the best life is that of the small town: "What fools men were to live in the city."

Scott Donaldson said of this story that Manfred is at his best "when he ignores the modern urban America he obviously detests and sticks to the same prairie frontier that provides the time and place for [Willa] Cather's work." He finds that Manfred's moral position is on firmer ground when he writes of the Siouxland past.[18]

Manfred has said that the concept of Siouxland came to him when he was writing *This is the Year* (1947):

> . . . that that would be my core, my center, from which all other novels would gradually work out because I knew that country and the people best—and that somewhere in every book there would be someone related to Siouxland or who would live in Siouxland. And then I decided that some day I would write a series of books . . . so that when I got through I'd have something all the way from 1800 on to the day I die. . . . naming that country Siouxland helped . . . crystallize a lot of things in my mind . . . it's spiritual . . . it's a piece of four states; and that sort of lifts it even geographically even above one state . . . I use the word "Siouxland" because the Sioux lived there . . . the Indian is related too, closely and warmly related to the soil of this country.[19]

The setting of *This is the Year* is Pier Frixen's farm which adjoins the

---

18   Scott Donaldson, Review of *Apples of Paradise*, *Minneapolis Tribune*, May 5, 1968.
19   "West of the Mississippi: an Interview with Frederick Manfred," *Critique* 2 (Winter 1959):35–36.

Big Sioux River just southeast of the intersection of Iowa, Minnesota, and South Dakota. On this farm Pier lives with his father Alde who had dreamed of "establishing a new race of Free Frisians," a herd of Frisian Holsteins, and a "red velvet-covered placard with its silver letters GOD is the Head of this House." The novel begins on the day that Pier is to be married to Nertha Andringa, "earthy as the loess that lay on his prairie farm, with her green eyes and peach-round breasts, with limbs as slender as summer creeks and silver hair so long it reached below her waist. . . ." The nature imagery is deliberate; throughout the novel Manfred maintains a "symbolic parallelism between earth and woman."[20]

Pier marries Nertha despite last minute objections from his father: "Soan, dy faem is net goed genoch." Alde is disturbed because Nertha will introduce a Norwegian strain into the pure Frisian bloodline. An analogy between human and animal breeding is maintained throughout, both in imagery and in symbolism.

Other differences arise between father and son. Pier, "a strong and towering bull of a man" wearies of Alde Romke's Old World beliefs and superstitions, and he forces his parents off the farm. "By a river in Siouxland he stood weeping," the novel says of the old man as Manfred's uneven style becomes biblical for the moment.

The novel expands on the themes of Pier's conservatism, stubbornness, ignorance (his wife pleads with him to learn to read, and he can write only his name), frustrations, and his technique of bulling his way, whether he is farming, making love to his wife, dealing with his son or others—all except the animals, with whom he is gentle. He refuses to listen to the advice of the Old Dreamer on good farming methods: ". . . a farmer should farm according to his own ideas. Too many of them high monkey-monk ideas don't get y'u nowhere. . . . I'm agin anybody tellin' me what to do. I'm independent, I am. I run this farm myself. I don't ask nobody about nothin', do as I please, an' am my own boss."

As John R. Milton has said, "the defiance [sometimes expressed in song] brings tragic results to Pier, just as the same kind of outburst of self-reliance brought the vengeance of the gods down upon the old Greek heroes."[21]

Because Pier refuses to practice contour farming, his land erodes and eventually a corner of his house falls into a gully created by the erosion. Because he refuses to listen to advice about women, he loses his wife's love and affection, and ultimately his wife as well. Because he takes his frustrations out on his son, the boy hates him and leaves him.

---

20   Nelson Antrim Crawford, "The American Farmer in Fact and Fiction," *Literary Digest International Book Review* 4 (January 1926):25, 101.
21   Milton, "Frederick Feikema Manfred," pp. 181–99.

Yet Pier has another side. He is often a man of good spirits and good humor who finds pleasure in music, and sometimes hears music in the air around him. He is able to commune with nature and the land.

Pier's ultimate defeat is not altogether caused by his pride or conditions of his own doing. He overextends his financial situation by buying a second farm which he hopes his son will someday have; the financial distress of the early years of the depression cause him to lose it. Weather conditions are not always favorable, and his income suffers as farm prices are depressed. His son is injured by an accident with a cornpicker which the son persuaded his father to buy.

The time of the story is 1916 to 1934, and the conditions which affected the farmers of Iowa during those years affect Pier. In the latter pages the farmers' strikes at Sioux Center, Le Mars, and Sioux City, the "penny" farm foreclosures, and the dust storms and drought all become incidents. The range of other incidents is broad—the County Fair where the unsophisticated farmers are gulled by the sharp practices of the concessionaires, the "birthing" of pigs and calves, the wolf and coyote hunt which becomes a massacre, the search for wild grapes in the Big Sioux River bottoms, Pier's near-fatal falls from a barn roof and a windmill, his survival in a blizzard through his sacrifice of a cow, and the like.

Many of these incidents are reported in a style which, in Professor Roy Meyer's opinion, is a

. . . mixture of realism and mysticism, of coarseness and poetry, of bathos and beauty. Frankness in language and in the physical details of farm life has seldom if ever been carried farther than in this novel; every indelicate and repulsive feature of Pier's life is given sober treatment . . . terrifying experiences are reproduced with great fidelity . . . gory details are the author's specialty . . .[22]

Manfred's style also relies on a number of word inventions: telescoped words, onomatopoeic words, slang, and patois. His use of Frisian immigrants, representing a fresh theme in farm literature, permits him to use words of Frisian derivation as well as distinctive Frisian cultural features. A number of Frisian folk legends are related, and so much Frisian dialect that it was necessary to append a glossary of translations and explanations.

The use of Frisian material is one way of attempting to insinuate a sense of the past into the novel. A second is through the geographical features—the "Hills of the Lord," the Red Bluff which reminds Alde Romke of the old country, the Blood Run mounds where the old man has his biblical vision and where all kinds of Indian artifacts are found.

---

22   Roy Meyer, *The Middle Western Farm Novel in the Twentieth Century*, p. 123.

A third way is through the farm animals—the "cow is sacred to us Frisians." A fourth is through the earth-woman analogy.

Manfred has said that the structure of the novel was based on a concept of "the flowing seasons over the soil, rolling almost like a cycle again" which "happened to fit the most dramatic years that I remember my uncle's and my father's living." As for his style, he said that he tried to emulate "the rare ones like Chaucer and Shakespeare" who tried to "describe the entire [growth] process—soil, roots, stalk, leaves, petals, rain, sunlight." His goal was "truth" because "truth is beauty . . . the full truth."[23]

To this latter statement, John R. Milton responded that "it is perhaps the *full truth* which gets Manfred into technical difficulties . . . he frequently forgets that fullness may be conveyed by implication as well as by literal transcription."[24]

John T. Flanagan has said that "our farm novelists on the whole have not succeeded in individualizing their people," but this statement cannot be applied to Pier Frixen, who must be the most memorable character of all those created by Iowa writers.[25] In part, this comes about because almost the whole of this lengthy novel is seen through Pier's eyes—the exceptions being an occasional soliloquy on the part of one or the other of the major figures.

Professor Roy Meyer called *This is the Year* "one of the most significant farm novels in recent years."[26] Walter Havighurst said it was an "[over] long morality tale";[27] *Time* called it a "unique regional novel," and noted that both Van Wyck Brooks and Sinclair Lewis had seen the novel in manuscript, liked it, and permitted the publisher to say so;[28] the *Saturday Review of Literature* said it had the "vitality of an epic narrative."[29] But all the critics agreed in general with John R. Milton's opinion and with John T. Frederick's summary: ". . . in disregarding [selection and restraint, Manfred] has robbed his characters of much of their interest and convincingness, and *This is the Year* of its tragic significance."[30]

A major contribution to the Iowa farm literature has been the work of Paul Corey: *Three Miles Square* (1939), *The Road Returns* (1940), *County Seat* (1941), and *Acres of Antaeus* (1946). The first three novels

23   "West of the Mississippi: an Interview with Frederick Manfred."
24   Milton, "Frederick Feikema Manfred."
25   John T. Flanagan, "The Middle Western Farm Novel," *Minnesota History* 23 (June 1942):113–47.
26   Meyer, *The Middle Western Farm Novel in the Twentieth Century*, p. 211.
27   Walter Havighurst, *New York Herald Tribune Weekly Book Review*, March 23, 1947, p. 10.
28   *Time* 49 (March 31, 1947):105.
29   Harrison Smith, *Saturday Review of Literature* 30 (March 29, 1947):16.
30   Frederick, "The Farm in Iowa Fiction."

form a trilogy focused on the Widow Mantz and her children Andrew, Wolmar, Verney, and Otto, who at various times live near or in Elm in Moss County, Iowa. The fourth novel refers to the Mantzes briefly, but the protagonists are Jim Buckly and the Midwest Farms Company.

The descriptions of Moss County make it resemble Shelby County in southwestern Iowa where on July 8, 1903, Corey was born on a farm, the son of Edwin Olney and Margaret Morgan (Brown) Corey. He was the youngest in a family of five boys and two girls. His paternal grandfather had served in the Mexican War and then joined in the California gold rush—without, however, discovering gold. An even more distant ancestor was that Giles Corey who had attained distinction as the only male victim of the colonial witchcraft mania, pressed to death under layers of planks and stones laid upon his chest, and who achieved an immortality of sorts in Longfellow's *New England Tragedy*. When Paul was two, his father died, and his mother was faced with situations similar to those of the Widow Mantz as she struggled to keep her family together. The family moved to Atlantic, Iowa, in 1918 and Paul graduated from the Atlantic High School in 1921. He worked his way through the University of Iowa as a librarian for the geology library; in the summer of 1923 he worked in a lumber mill in the California redwood country. He received a B.A. at Iowa, his mother living just long enough to see him graduate.

At Iowa he met Ruth Lechlitner who was working for John T. Frederick's *The Midland* in Ruth Suckow's old job. In 1928 they were married in New York City where Corey was writing for the *Economist* and Miss Lechlitner, a poet, was working as a poetry critic for the New York *Herald Tribune Books*. The Coreys went to Europe on their honeymoon, traveling and writing in France, Spain, and England. In the spring of 1931, they took over a few acres of rocky New England hillside. Corey built a stone cottage and the couple terraced their land as was the custom in France. They began living on less than $1,000 a year (the whole experience is reported in the *Reader's Digest* for September, 1939). Later, Corey built a larger stone house on the hilltop above the cottage; when it was completed, the couple sold the cottage at a profit and moved into their new home.

When Corey moved to New York from Iowa he had with him manuscripts of a novel and several short stories, none of which he was able to get published. Several of his short stories were published in minor magazines in the thirties and one in *Scribner's* in 1936, but his first real publishing success was *Three Miles Square*.

The three novels cover the years from 1910, beginning on the day of Chris Mantz's funeral, to 1930, a few weeks after the death of the Widow Mantz and the reading of her will. The years are marked off in the novels, each year forming a section. Occasionally there are flashbacks or summaries, as at the beginning of the first and third books. Otherwise, the account progresses chronologically, Corey's method being to show us an incident in the affairs of one person or group, in the course of which some other incident is casually mentioned. Later the second incident is detailed, with a new character or group. Occasionally there is some cross-referencing.

These twenty years, in the words of a letter in the third book, addressed to "Paul Corey" and signed "Otto Mantz," "are probably the most vital in the history of the Middle West. The beginnings of all that has happened since 1930, chain farming, the Holiday, the AAA, soil conservation, can be found in that period."[31]

Although *Three Miles Square* and the other novels maintain their focus on the Mantz family, they are primarily novels of social relationships. In the first novel there *is* a dust storm when "the air's so thick with dust . . . that if it stood still you could farm it," and the slow cycle of the seasons with their patterns of rain, snow, and sunshine goes on. But the focus is on people: the constant petty tensions, dissensions, and bickerings within a family; the manipulations of greedy persons and of persons bent upon vengeance for some deed done to them; the constant boy-girl and man-woman relationships, some within the moral code of the community, more without—the kind of thing which Ruth Suckow had protested against. There is the barn dance, the meat ring, the threshing (with steam power rather than horse power as in Garland's and Quick's novels), the coming of the automobile and the airplane, ice-making, the baseball games between the town and country teams, the introduction of alfalfa by the more liberal farmers, the revival meeting, the incidence of hog cholera, the question of mule power versus horse power.

The farm life is set off against the intrusive outside world—the omnipresent banker with his changing attitudes about loans and mortgages as economic conditions change for better or for worse, Taft, Wilson, and the "Bullmoosers," the "*Tityanic's*" and the "*Lust-aynia's*" sinking. Debs, the war in Europe, the situation in Mexico—all matters scarcely mentioned in Manfred's *This is the Year*. And there is Womar's introduction to socialism—"getting rich is wrong and war is wrong."

The incidents and events in *Three Miles Square* are so interrelated and ordered as to present a logical sequence and pattern of cause and event and consequence; we never get the sense that any incident has been manipulated by Corey for the benefit of his tightly woven and carefully worked out story line. The sequence of events suggest a natural causation. The Mantzes attend church but they do not seem to feel any supernatural interference in their affairs. "If Chris had only changed his shoes and

---

31   Paul Corey, *County Seat* (Indianapolis: Bobbs-Merrill Co., 1941), p. 418.

socks that night," is Mrs. Mantz's reaction to her husband's death of "pew-money" [pneumonia]; "Guess we gotta take things as they come . . . the bad with the good," is Pete Thorne's response to his learning that his girl must always be a cripple. Pete, the good friend of the Mantzes, is always having hard luck; Sorrel Jensen, their enemy, who stoops to bribery and trickery whenever so inclined, succeeds.

"Move over, big boys, to make room for Iowa's Paul Corey," shouted the *Des Moines Register*. More quietly Grant Wood said that the book contained "realism of the best sort." Lewis Mumford said *Three Miles Square* was "one of the best novels of Agricultural America that anyone has produced in our generation."[32] James Gray felt that Corey was "compassionate, gifted in insight, and well equipped with detailed knowledge of his scene."[33] Richard Rovere called the book a "fine novel," though he deplored Corey's schematization—which everyone else has praised.[34]

Louis Bromfield, himself a writer of highly praised farm novels, and a 1927 Pulitzer Prize winner as well, called *Three Miles Square* "a notable novel which established a new and serious writer out of the Middle West."[35] John T. Frederick concluded that the novel "traverses the circle of the farm year and the full range of farm occupation and experience, with unfaltering accuracy and authority. . . . Events . . . are presented as matters of course, as part of the texture of farm living, properly subordinated to the more significant human experience to which they are peripheral and incidental."[36]

The Road Returns continues the various strands of the Mantz family life from April of 1917 through 1923—the war years and the boom-and-bust cycle of American agriculture. The family debate over the values of preparation for a non-farm life versus life on the farm continues.

But broader social issues are seen as well. The farm depression of the early 1920s—caused by the fact that American farmers, prosperous with their world grain markets during the war, had overextended their obligations and overproduced—hits Elm and Moss County hard. The Spanish influenza epidemic of 1918 closes schools and churches, and makes its deadly inroads on the farm and town families. An accident to a threshing rig creates a spy scare and a mob forms before the home of Hans Schwartz, a German neighbor. Otto Mantz attempts to do something about the farmer's plight by proposing a united action:

---

32 Comments by the *Des Moines Register*, Grant Wood, and Lewis Mumford are quoted from the biography of Paul Corey in *Twentieth Century Authors*.
33 James Gray, "Good Earth in Iowa," *Saturday Review of Literature* 20 (September 23, 1939):6.
34 Richard Rovere, *New Republic* 100 (October 18, 1939):316.
35 Louis Bromfield, "A Mid-Western Tale With a Pieter Brueghel Quality," *New York Herald Tribune Weekly Book Review*, October 20, 1940, p. 6.
36 Frederick, "The Farm in Iowa Fiction."

'Farmers produce all the country has to eat and if they all got together and said they wouldn't sell anything until prices came up—then prices would have to come up . . . it's the law of supply and demand. . . . When the demand's great prices come up—if the farmers refused to sell, then the demand would have to increase.'

. . . 'What'd you want farmers to do, strike?'

Otto hadn't thought of it that way and his idea being construed as a strike startled him.

This novel also deals with the theme of causation. Corey's people try to determine their own affairs, but their choice of direction is often influenced by forces and people over whom they have no control. "What is it that shapes a life," Andrew Mantz wonders, and then he glances at the model sailboat his father had carefully put together years before.

Critics had an even higher opinion of Corey's second novel than they had had of the first. "*The Road Returns* is an even better book," said Edith H. Walton, "its scope and implications are wider. . . . [It is] an honest and admirable novel which deals with living people, juxtaposed against a community. Not only is it one of the best Midwestern stories which we have had for some time but it re-creates superbly an era of the first importance."[37]

Louis Bromfield compared the novel to paintings by the medieval Flemish painter Pieter Brueghel with their many people and activities—"bitter, sad, comic and even ludicrous things." And he saw the Widow Mantz, with her ambitions for her children, as a typical American figure, akin to many of Ruth Suckow's mothers: "Almost every middle-class American mother over fifty is a Widow Mantz, and for this reason *Three Miles Square* and *The Road Returns* achieve an epic quality."[38]

County Seat, the third novel in the trilogy, is the story of the Mantz family, the townspeople of Elm, and the nearby farmers from the years 1924 to 1930, but it is also a story of widespread corruption and human degradation in those years. One feels as one reads that the novel is an indictment of the whole American populace, and not merely of an Iowa countryside:

'You ain't used to cheatin' people—that's the trouble with you [a worker tells Andrew Mantz], but I'm tellin' you, you've got to get used to it if you expect to get anywhere in this world. . . . The idea is, don't try to buck 'em. You'll end up the way I have. And don't worry about it—it ain't your fault that's the way things are done.'

---

37   Edith H. Walton, "Paul Corey's The Road Returns . . . ," *New York Times Book Review*, October 20, 1940, p. 6.
38   Bromfield, "A Mid-Western Tale With a Pieter Brueghel Quality."

A number of Iowa novels present the anti-German attitudes of the First World War (as *The Road Returns* does), but in this novel racism becomes a bitter issue as a Klan organizer comes to Elm and soon has the citizenry stirred up about the only Jew and the only Negro in the town. The novel makes the point that some small town people joined such movements because they wish to settle a personal grudge against some other member of the community.

In a small way, the novel also demonstrates how Prohibition and economic conditions led to the development of criminal operations such as that of the Dillinger gang or the Capone syndicate. In microcosmic form, the complaisance of the town leaders, the corruption of the county officials, and the greed of local business men creates a situation that leads to gangland-type murders.

One of the themes in the novel is anti-intellectualism:

> . . . 'Well, what did you learn down there?' [Wolmar asks Otto on Otto's return from the university.]
>
> 'Guess I'm beginnin' to learn how much I don't know,' replie[s] Otto with a grin.
>
> 'You don't need to waste a year at college to find that out,' [says] Wolmar. 'You can learn that right here.'

Another theme is the attitudes toward farming:

> . . . When they finished the twelve-acre piece in front of the house, [Otto] surveyed the regular clumps of bright corn patterning the black earth. 'That's beautiful,' he said and his eyes shone.
>
> Andrew . . . replied to his brother: 'It's just a cornfield. If it makes forty or forty-five bushels an acre, we'll be lucky.'

For all the concentration on social problems, Corey, by skillful control of his materials, keeps the Mantzes always in the forefront of his story. The trilogy concludes with Otto getting the university education the Widow Mantz had wanted for each of her sons in turn. But it is evident all along where Otto's real interests are, and it comes as no surprise to the reader when he takes over the operation of his father's farm. His decision represents no romantic dream on his part; his education and his interest in the farmers' problems have given him a realistic attitude toward farm life.

There are many resemblances between the books in this trilogy and Manfred's books. A major one is the use of the coyote hunt as subject matter for a chapter each in *This is the Year* and *The Road Returns*. In these hunts there is a mass effort on the part of farmers and townsmen to reduce the numbers of foxes, wolves, and coyotes by first forming a "ten mile circle" and then converging toward its center. Some idea of the variations in style and approach of the two men can be gained from a comparison of brief sections of these hunts:

(*This is the Year*) Drips and puddles of blood spread everywhere. Cornstalks were drenched red. The earth seemed to be bleeding out of myriads of pores. Bits of torn flesh, scraps of live fur, burned powder, dust, corn smut, weed seeds flying in the air made it hard to breathe. Men cursed. Guns rumbled. Dogs barked and snapped, became confused with the mass of animals, were called back, were shot at. More guns thundered. Ejectors ejaculated empty shells, yellow and blue and red.
(*The Road Returns*) The line of hunters had broken and they crowded around the kill, excited voices jerking: "Got one! Boy-oh-boy! One less!" Mel Wallace tried to extricate the animal from the pack but the dogs weren't through with it. Some of them withdrew a little, sniffing one another, hackles standing; they seemed to be discussing the run, boasting to one another. Now and again a dog would rush at the limp wolf with a furious growl and shake it violently as if to show what he had done, to re-enact for the others the part he'd played or prove to them that he'd done it all by himself.

Manfred, whose style can range from the colloquial to the biblical, is, in this case, primarily impressionistic and literary. Corey, on the other hand, maintains the dispassionate narrative tone of all three books. As one critic remarked, "the manner of the writing has none of that nervous brilliance which we have come to expect of young writers whose theme is struggle and exploitation. Mr. Corey seems never to gesticulate or raise his voice."[39]

Unlike Manfred, Corey coins no words; his is the language of the times. The natural language of the farmer is occasionally interlaced with the slang of the period: "tomcatting," "a fast jane," "peacherino," "spiffy," "pippin"; but that is all.

County Seat, like the two earlier novels, drew praise from the critics.[40] The reaction of Phil Stong who, like Corey, constructed an imaginary small Iowa town and studied it in several novels, perhaps tells us more about Stong than it tells about the book:

The word "pregnant" which is quite unjustifiably considered a mild obscenity, or at least a word in bad taste, runs through this book like a chorus from Aeschylus. Everything is always being that way, to the great satisfaction or discomfort of the ladies concerned. About page 150 one lady has had five

39   Gray, "Good Earth in Iowa."
40   Edith H. Walton, "Iowa Town," *New York Times Book Review*, September 7, 1941, p. 7; Rose Feld, "On the Good Flat Earth of Iowa," *New York Times Book Review*, September 24, 1939, p. 7.

children, another has had a homemade miscarriage, another has given birth in the distress of uremia, and everything is budding anew.

Iowa, the locale of this story really isn't that fruitful. . . . Nevertheless, this is an interesting story. . . . [Otto] is [his mother's] symbol of the family pride. This is very true and good for there is nearly always one in every farm family. This fellow is naturally the one who wants to farm and does farm, without benefit of Veblen or any of the other high falutin' folks he read at Iowa U.[41]

And, although *County Seat* is primarily a novel about a farm family, John T. Frederick noted that it "has integration as a portrayal of the town itself. Nowhere else in our fiction is there a study of an Iowa town so deliberately conclusive and representative, so accurate in observation, and so honestly put down."[42]

The three novels of the trilogy had been produced on a yearly basis, and readers and critics began to anticipate a Mantz family saga. But Corey's next five books (published during the years 1944 to 1946) were either factual texts or juvenile books, and *Acres of Antaeus* is primarily concerned with the question of the creation of an agricultural empire, based on commercial-business procedures, and social protest.

Acres of Antaeus is not as richly textured as the novels in the trilogy. Four strands are interwoven: the marital relationship of Jim Buckly, a supervisor for Midwest Farms, Inc., and his wife Emily, daughter of a farmer; the power struggle within the corporate structure of the farm organization; the 1932–33 farm protests; and the field work on several of Midwest's farms. Most of the fourth strand appeared as a long story in *The American Caravan* in 1936, ten years before the novel. Although in that story a number of the novel's characters appear (including Otto Mantz) the farm workmen are the central characters.

Acres of Antaeus is essentially a thesis novel—a discussion of the validity of the "agribusiness" concept (although that term is not used in the novel). But because the drive of the novel is along the four strands mentioned, the validity of the concept is never tested. At the novel's end the reader is still wondering if large-scale farming under the direction of a corporation and following corporation procedures, with farm workers on standardized hours and having the right to bargain collectively, will work.

Professor Roy Meyer in his *The Middle Western Farm Novel in the Twentieth Century* (1965) says that since 1930 "a dominant theme among farm novelists has been one of reconciliation to the soil." Some writers, including Corey, "have made explicit the contrast between rural

---

41 Phil Stong, "Corey . . . ," *Saturday Review of Literature* 24 (August 30, 1941):14.
42 Frederick, "The Farm in Iowa Fiction."

and urban life by taking their characters to the town, allowing them to be disillusioned, and then bringing them back to the farm." This course often produces conflicting attitudes toward rural life. Here, for instance, is Wolmar in *Three Miles Square:* "A guy got like a lump of dirt working on the farm—a lump of dirt. You picked corn day after day until you couldn't stand the sight of a cornfield. And what did it get you? Nothing, not a thing." In *County Seat*, his brother Otto voices the opposite point of view: "I spend all my days trying to chisel a few extra cents out of somebody so that stockholders of the company'll be paid for doing nothing. . . . There's a chance for honor and success and respectability in making [a farm] into a good farm. . . . I don't see why the production of food isn't as respectable as sitting in an office with my name on the door, producing nothin'."

Other farm writers, including Phil Stong whose farm novels we have seen in the previous chapter, "have assumed the question of relative superiority of town and farm to be settled and have contented themselves with depicting the wholesome life on the farm, without offering any overt contrast to city life." Professor Meyer concluded that "Corey's fiction represents the farm novel in its most highly developed form to date [1965]."[43]

J. Hyatt Downing's *The Harvest is Late* (1944) is set in the country a few miles west of Le Mars, Iowa, and has as its protagonist a middle-aged banker who is also a "gentleman farmer." Peter Oliver, starting from scratch like Ruth Suckow's August Kaetterhenry and operating in much the same fashion, is finally able to buy the coveted "Sundown, once the property of Captain, the Honorable H. W. Norton, youngest son of a wealthy British family and formerly a member of the English colony at Le Mars, . . . an estate of 1,280 acres" (p. 11).

Downing thus introduces into Iowa literature an unusual aspect of Iowa history, the colony which at one time covered up to half a million acres of land in and adjacent to Plymouth County, Iowa. The colony had been founded in the hopes that young Englishmen would learn "the methods of American agriculture which were being publicized in London newspapers as the sure and gentlemanly road to success." On the Iowa prairies, the colonists tried to reproduce their native England:

. . . there were plenty of horses to ride, there was excellent hunting, good whiskey and pretty women. What more could any young man of spirit demand? There was even a club, the Prairie, as exclusive in its membership as the best in London, where liveried servants brought stirrup cups to the gay young men who rode up on their long-tailed ponies. Two bars, the House of Lords

---

43 Meyer, *The Middle Western Farm Novel in the Twentieth Century*, p. 98.

and the House of Commons were open twenty-four hours a day, and there, by God, sir, bartenders were in service who knew how to mix a proper drink for a proper man. Polo teams were organized . . . Le Mars of that day was a small prairie town and the citizens learned to take cover when a troop of young Englishmen came roaring down the streets on their ponies.

The Harvest is Late focuses on a number of rural problems. There is the matter of "renters": are they hard workers for whom things just don't turn out right, or are they people who are easily satisfied "with just what they turned out to be?" Against the argument that renters ought to work harder, there is presented the point of view that not all people are "blessed" with the kind of personality, physique, and luck that leads to farming success.

Another theme is the exodus of young people from the small towns and farms. The loneliness of the prairie community is stressed; a student who has been off to college says she'll never return to such little "jay towns"; a Minneapolis waitress says of her former country town that it's "so dead it stinks." Small town gossiping is also offered as a reason for leaving home.

Other farm novels have dealt with the cycle of good and hard times on the farms in the 1920s. This novel, written from Downing's background in small town banks, offers an insight into the problem:

. . . Peter turned his head away from the lavish fecundity. For the first time in his life he looked with jaundiced eyes at cornfields where every stalk lifted up its burden of heavy ears. For the first time he saw still uncut, waving stalks of wheat and he wished that he had the courage to set a match to them. For, he knew, with every bushel of grain that poured from the snouts of threshing machines, the already glutted market would fall lower. Every hog and steer, stuffing themselves in the feed lots, would send the price of pork and beef further into steep decline. [P. 217]

"By the 1890's," said Professor Allan G. Bogue, "the work of the pioneers was done" in converting "prairie to cornbelt." Now, just thirty years later, the midwestern farmer, growing crops in a land "where each year the rains, the summer heat and productive soils produced the broad-leafed fields of green," had become a potent factor in the world economy.[44] His hard work and his broad fields had, during the years of World War I made up for the loss of crops normally grown on the vast farmlands of central Europe. With the close of the war the European farmers had gone back into their fields, armed with lessons learned from American

---

44 Allan G. Bogue, *From Prairie to Farm Belt* (Chicago: University of Chicago Press, 1963), p. 287.

technology. The depressed farm conditions, according to this novel, are due to "fear" and the "aftermath of war. We came out of the war just as stupidly as we went into it, with no machinery set up to absorb the shock of curtailed buying abroad."

The main asset, therefore, of *The Harvest is Late* lies in its presentation of the banker-farmer relationships during those post World War I days when so many country banks and so many farmers suffered the consequences of unwise economic practices and unsettled world conditions.

The novel also makes a point about absentee ownership of large farms, and quotes Henry Ford's opinion that "it's wrong for these big farms to be kept up just as a single place. They ought to be divided into smaller tracts where a great many families could live instead of just one or two" (p. 113).

The Harvest is Late is a skillfully written novel, but it does not have the power to hold the reader's attention that Downing's Sioux City novels have.

The problems of life on the farm versus life in town are discussed more thoroughly and expertly in John T. Frederick's *Druida* (1923) and *Green Bush* (1925) than in any other novel. In focusing on the lives and career decisions of Druida Horsfall and Frank Thompson, Frederick chose a favorable attitude toward the farmer. "There have been in the past two popular attitudes toward the farmer: 'God bless him' and 'devil take him,'" said Nelson Antrim Crawford of the U.S. Department of Agriculture and a friend of Frederick's; "On the one hand he was viewed as the romantic pastoral husband-man, on the other as an uncouth boor or a troublesome agitator against the economic and political status quo."[45] In Frederick's novels, although one farmer is shown as a drunken lout who drives his wife to suicide, there is never any question as to the value of life on the farm. However, for both Druida and Frank Thompson, life on the farm must be weighed against other choices.

Druida, who comes close to being a tragic figure, must choose between life with an English professor (who has lost his position because of vicious small town gossip) and with a country boy she has known for several years. Her choice is made during a mystical vision in which she senses "a symbol of the mystery of the earth" and perceives that "pitiless and unsure as life must be, it is beautiful because men dare to match their weakness against the unmeasured powers of earth and sky." She marries the farm boy, even though he is intellectually inferior to her, and goes with him to take up farming in the unknown lands of Montana.

For Frank Thompson there are several choices: operation of his father's newspaper in the small county seat town of Green Bush; operation of his

---

45   Crawford, "The American Farmer in Fact and Fiction."

father's farm in the sandy country nearby; or fulfillment of his mother's and his best friend's wish that he become a college professor. The real choice for Frank Thompson lies between farm and university, and the university has strong appeals, for Frank has a real interest in literature and literary criticism. Frank's problems parallel those of his creator; for several years, John T. Frederick published *The Midland*, taught in a number of colleges, and operated a farm (in the summers) at Glennie, Michigan. Several of the novel's scenes are obviously based on Frederick's first-hand experiences in and acquaintanceship with all three areas.

Frank's choice for the farm is made after a long argument with his friend over the merits of life on the farm versus life on the campus, and the intellectual life versus farm labor. This argument in the hands of the average novelist would be mere pretentious verbiage, but John T. Frederick knew what he was writing about, and he manages the conversation quite well:

> So far as interpretation of the deepest aspects of farm life is concerned, John T. Frederick's *Green Bush* reaches the high point in recent fiction. Here, as in no other American novel, implicit unity with the soil is given adequate and coherent expression.[46]

Paul Engle, better known as a poet and teacher than as a writer of fiction, has written three books about the Iowa farm. *Always the Land* (1941) is a novel set on a farm in the Squaw Creek and Indian Creek area northeast of Cedar Rapids. Although there is a great deal of talk in the book about such matters as farm electrification, participation in government corn-hog programs, the use of farm machinery, and other farm innovations of the times, the main burden of the book is Joe Meyer's interest in horses, and his rather conventional love affair with a girl who also likes horses. The novel introduces a Bohemian farm hand, reflecting the Czech background of the Cedar Rapids area; he is treated more realistically than Phil Stong's hyperbolic types. Although the novel is well-written, reflecting Engle's skill with language, it is too conventional to be thoroughly interesting.

Engle's two other books, *Prairie Christmas* (1960), and *An Old Fashioned Christmas* (1964), the latter superbly illustrated by Eleanor Pownall Simmons of Iowa City, are nostalgic melanges of fact and fiction about his memories of Christmas on an Iowa farm and in his Cedar Rapids home. Although the books are obviously gotten up to lie on the table at Christmas time, they still present two very interesting people, the somewhat alcoholic Uncle Ben, and his temperance-minded wife, Aunt Minnie, who

---

46 Crawford, "The American Farmer in Fact and Fiction."

could smell sin at ten or a hundred feet, and who said of her railroad husband's routine trips to Chicago that they came just often enough "to ruin the fool, not often enough to teach him anything."

Wallace Stegner's *Remembering Laughter* (1937), though set on an Iowa farm near Sac City, is primarily a novel about an illicit love between Elspeth MacLeod and her brother-in-law Alec Stuart, its consequences on the couple, Alec's wife, Margaret, whose discovery of the affair terminates it, and Malcolm, Elspeth's and Alec's illegitimate son. Unlike many of the farmers seen in Iowa farm novels, Alec Stuart is immensely well-to-do, and his several farms are operated by tenant farmers. Stylistically, this long short story (or shortened novel) is superior. Its account of the long period of expiation which follows the discovery of the lovers' guilt is uninteresting. Roy Meyer found the book to be "melodramatic and not entirely convincing,"[47] and John T. Frederick said that this early novel of Stegner's was "inferior in every way to his highly distinguished and substantial later books." He added, "Mr. Stegner's psychological insight and all his artistry—by no means inconsiderable even in this early work—scarcely avails to give it validity and importance in the reader's emotion." Moreover, Professor Frederick's own farm background led him to question some of Stegner's "admittedly . . . trivial" details—the formation of "ears plumed with green silk" on "waist high" corn, and the fact that "Mr. Stegner's pigeons lay speckled eggs."[48]

Wallace Stegner was born on his grandfather's farm near Lake Mills, Iowa, in 1909, but very little of his life has been spent in Iowa. He was, according to Francis Paluka, "one of the first students in this country to take a graduate degree in writing, his Iowa master's thesis (*Whitemud*, 1932) directed by Edwin Ford Piper, being a group of three short stories."[49] Stegner also received his doctorate at Iowa.

Curtis Harnack's *The Work of an Ancient Hand* (1960) is a first novel with an unusual structure—a *Spoon River Anthology* of prose, one critic called it.[50] The novel is set in a rural northwest Iowa community, and it features both town and country people. Most of the novel concentrates on analyses of the characters—in that respect it is typical of many of the novels of the 1960s. It focuses on a rural minister and his wife; gradually, through a number of sketches of incidents in the life of the rural community, and through a series of interpolated flashbacks, the reader learns of the son's past which tragically haunts the minister. Throughout the novel the minister's life is touched by the lives of the community's people, but

47 Meyer, *The Middle Western Farm Novel in the Twentieth Century*, p. 234.
48 Frederick, "The Farm in Iowa Fiction."
49 Frank Paluka, *Iowa Authors: A Bio-Bibliography of Sixty Native Writers* (Iowa City: Friends of The University of Iowa Libraries, 1967), pp. 217, 242.
50 *Chicago Sunday Tribune*, June 1, 1960, Section 17, p. 3.

they are rarely touched by his life—until the very end when his futile attempt to hang himself, using the rope in the church belfry, brings the townspeople together for a moment.

A number of interesting sidelights on rural and small town life are presented as background for the novel—corn detasseling (used here to emphasize the fertility aspects of the rural scene), the small town centennial celebration, the plight of the retired farmer, an accident in which a farm boy is maimed by a farm animal, the wedding dance in which the men who dance with the bride pin dollar bills to her dress, farm deferments during World War II—all events not found in other farm novels.

Critics thought that Harnack might have done better to have constructed the sketches as a series of short stories to illustrate his thesis that there is "an ancient hand" at work in the affairs of men. They noted that the "reader gets involved in a series of characters only to have them disappear."[51] There is very little sense of a close interrelationship among the novel's characters, such as there is in Corey's trilogy.

Harnack's second novel, *Love and Be Silent* (1962), has its center also in Kaleburg, and its time—from the early years of the depression until after World War II—is also approximately the same. Some of the characters seen briefly in the first novel become the central characters of this novel. In fact, this novel might be seen as a story which was too long for inclusion in the first book. In any case, this novel stands by itself, and has no relationship to the tragedy of the minister's family.

The farm plays only a minor role in this story; the novel is more of a novel of interpersonal relationships and their significances than it is about farm life. Like Paul Corey's novels, it is about mediocre people, but with this difference: the behavior of the characters is constantly analyzed in terms of the psychology of the individuals involved. When Otto Mantz had a sexual relationship with an Elm girl, he worried afterward about a possible pregnancy and the degree of his responsibility to the girl; when one of Harnack's characters makes love to his wife on one occasion, the author spends a page and a half in an analysis of the meaning and significance of their coming together.

The novel also bears some comparison to Ruth Suckow's *Country People* and to other of her fictions. Like Miss Suckow, Harnack reports details—but he is always looking for the significance in the details. A pony, for example, becomes a symbol:

Though other whims dissolved and no tangible evidence was left behind, this pony existed to haunt his life, to remind him of all the dreams that had once been theirs but which had curiously vanished, replaced by others that were

---

51 *Chicago Sunday Tribune*, June 1, 1960, Section 17, p. 3.

doomed to disappear too, until, perhaps, their lives became too cluttered with solid or ethereal ghosts for them to move, for them to believe in the efficacy of hope.

It is this kind of attempt to find profundity in every ordinary action which sets *Love and Be Silent* apart from other farm novels.

Curtis Harnack is a native of that northwest Iowa area in which the farm portions of this novel are set. He was born in Le Mars in 1927, and spent his boyhood on a farm south of Remsen—a town all too thinly disguised in the "Kaleburg" of his novels. He has a B.A. from Grinnell and an M.A. from Columbia. Much of his life he has been a teacher; he has also been an assistant fiction editor for *Esquire;* he has published articles and stories and, with Paul Engle, he edited the O. Henry *Prize Story* anthologies for 1958 and 1959.

Donald Dean Jackson's *Archer Pilgrim* is a novel of farm life set in that same southwest Iowa area used by Julie McDonald and Paul Corey. The book is divided into four time periods: 1920, 1927–28, 1929–37, and 1938. The novel focuses on Archer Pilgrim at nine, sixteen to seventeen, eighteen to twenty-six, and at twenty-seven, and his hesitancy in choosing between automobile mechanics or farm life as a career. At the end of the novel, learning that his father is about to lose the family farm, Archer makes his ultimate choice. His wife refuses to stay on the farm with him, but he knows he can be content out in the fresh green fields.

The farm has also been a subject for Iowa's writers of short stories and poetry. Susan Glaspell (whom we shall see in a later chapter) wrote two rather good stories about the farm. "Pollen" (1919) is the story of a man who learns a lesson about social relationships from his observations of the manner in which corn is pollinated. But her "A Jury of Her Peers" (1917) is a far better story, and marks a trend in short farm fiction which came to be known as "kitchen sink Realism." In this fictional version of her earlier one-act play, *Trifles,* Miss Glaspell shows the reader the ultimate in the direction a dreary farm life (such as that seen in Garland's "Lucretia Burns") can take. The story's two themes—male-female antagonism over the social status of women, and poetic justice—are excellently developed in this tightly written dramatic tale. The idea for the story, incidentally, came from a court trial which Miss Glaspell had reported for a Des Moines newspaper.

Perhaps the dreariest pictures of farm life were written by Jay G. Sigmund of Cedar Rapids and Waubeek and published in his *Wapsipinicon Tales* (1927). "Merged Blood" has a sense of warmness in its brief account of a northeast Iowa farmer who has married a woman from a nearby town, and who thereby becomes the father of a half-Negro child, the woman having been pregnant when he married her. "At Ten

O'Clock" is bitterly ironic; Otto Frank, awaiting the final rites of his wife Barbara, recalls how his wife has nagged him into long hours of hard work for the twenty years of their marriage, and how she has never let him fish or hunt as he had wished—then he slyly peeks at a mail order catalog, anticipating the pleasures he will have after her burial. "The Attic Chest" relates the circumstances of Ira Dahms's two affairs with women; the first, his "housekeeper" for some years, the second his wife after the housekeeper has become insane. On the day the housekeeper dies in an asylum, Ira hurries home to reveal his relationship with her to his wife—but she has learned his secret and has hanged herself in the attic.

Some of Sigmund's stories first appeared in *The Midland*. In his *Hawkeyes*, Phil Stong has given us his version of what happened:

. . . during my college years, 1915–19, all of us little farmhands were trying to make *The Midland*. The method was to summon up memories of the most miserable and feckless family we had ever heard of around the home town, adorn them with some tragic graces and see that one or all the outfit (1) went crazy, (2) murdered the others, (3) committed suicide, incest or arson before the end of the story. It was Eugene O'Neill gone mad in the pigpens: yet Frederick was such an excellent editor that he made the business seem plausible. . . . By and by there were countless little magazines which detailed the sordid facts of farm life and did not pay for contributions. . . . This could not go on for ever, of course, for too many of us had happy farm childhoods behind us, but it was great sport while it lasted.[52]

Others joined Stong in this protest, among them Herbert Quick in his *One Man's Life*, and Professor Sam Sloan of the University of Iowa Department of English. Perhaps the most effective stroke was this brief bit of parody by John Riddell (Corey Ford) which Wilbur Schramm quoted in *American Prefaces* (Autumn 1941):

Minnie Timkins stared out of the window across the desolate prairie, drab and flat and hopeless. A wet rain dripped from the eaves, like the cold water tap in the kitchen sink, piled high with last week's breakfast dishes, on which the grease had hardened in grey lumps. They had not eaten since last Thursday.

The door slammed. Eben shuffled to the clothes-closet to hang up his coat. She did not raise her eyes: "The baby died today, Eben."

He did not reply. He had hung himself in the coat closet, inside his coat.

There was a revolver in the top drawer, but she was too weary to cross the room to get it. Outside the window the rain dripped steadily over the dull, empty prairie. Drip, drip.

She broke her arm at the elbow, just to hear it snap.[53]

---

52 Stong, *Hawkeyes*, p. 45.
53 Wilbur Schramm, "The Thousand and One Tales of Edward O'Brien," *American Prefaces* 7 (Autumn 1941), p. 7. (No original source found.)

A few Iowa poets have gained distinction for their poetry about the farm. One is Jay Sigmund; another is Paul Engle, whose early ventures in the writing of poetry were encouraged by Sigmund.

The best of Iowa poets who have chosen the farm as their subject is James Hearst of "Maplehearst Farm" in Cedar Falls. He comes from a line of farmers reaching back to 1651 in New England. His paternal grandfather, after farming in Ohio and Illinois, established the farm three miles southwest of Cedar Falls where Hearst's father, Charles Ernest Hearst (1869–1936), his brother Charles, and James Hearst were born—the latter August 8, 1900, "under the sign of the threshing machine."[54] His mother was Anna Katherine Schell of Montezuma. The elder Charles Hearst was elected president of the Iowa Farm Bureau in 1923 and served in that position until 1936, and from 1932 to 1936 he was a vice-president of the American Farm Bureau.

James Hearst was educated in a rural school, graduated from the State College High School in Cedar Falls, and attended the Iowa State Teacher's College (University of Northern Iowa) for two years. Professor H. W. Reninger says that at the college

. . . under the critical guidance of Professor Brock Fagan [he] learned two very valuable lessons: that a writer could *learn* how to organize his ideas and sensations and communicate them to other people; and that a writer should write from his own experiences . . . writing about a silo or litter of young pigs is a thoroughly legitimate affair.[55]

A swimming accident when he was a young man left him partially paralyzed, but it did not keep him from partnership with his brother in the operation of the farm, nor has it interfered much with the production of his poetry which to date consists of five volumes.

His first poems were sent to Harriet Monroe at *Poetry;* although she did not immediately publish any of his verse, she did encourage him. John T. Frederick at *The Midland* was the first to publish his poems, along with a short story "Old Joe" in December of 1927. Soon his poetry was being published in *Wallace's Farmer, Poetry, Furioso, Prairie Schooner, The Bookman, The Independent,* and other magazines and literary periodicals.

His first volume of verse, *Country Men* (1937), was published by Car-

---

54 H. Willard Reninger, "James Hearst: A Country Man as Poet," in James Hearst, *Man and His Field* (Denver: Alan Swallow, 1951), p. 10. (This essay and *Paluka* are sources in this section.)
55 Reninger, "James Hearst: A Country Man as Poet."

roll Coleman at his Prairie Press, and carried an appreciative statement by Ruth Suckow: "[James Hearst's poems are] in content and expression, an outgrowth of prairie country: not merely descriptive, rural in the lesser sense of the term, but having their center in a prairie farm, and sharing in its homeliness and its broad horizons."[56]

The volume, says Professor Reninger, is "profuse with the growing-impulse of nature and man."[57] Reninger quoted James Hearst as saying that

. . . poetry, like many other human endeavors, is a thing, something made, complete in itself, like a house or a streetcar, or a crop of corn. You make it yourself out of your experiences [from which in turn] you shape and form a single experience by expression, words, language: these are your tools for making the poem. [For poetry] is an effort to capture through images the reality underlying illusion.'[58]

"I have tried," James Hearst wrote on another occasion, "to give a form, an attractive form if possible, to my experience and my environment. It seemed to me that farm-life had never been looked at honestly —either it was sentimentalized or brutalized. I was trying to find out the truth."[59]

James Hearst's other volumes are: *The Sun at Noon* (1943); *Man and His Field* (1951); *Limited View* (1962); and *A Single Focus* (1967). Hearst "is a rigorous critic of his own work," said John T. Frederick. In his poems, "readers who really know the farm life of the Middle West find its truest and most satisfying interpretation."[60]

Joseph Langland was born in Minnesota, but grew up on a farm in Iowa, and he was educated at the University of Iowa; he began publishing poetry while still in college. His *The Wheel of Summer* (New York, 1963) contains many excellent poems based on farm life. One of these, "Sacrifice of the Old Gentleman," uses a theme which Hamlin Garland had used in *Boy Life on the Prairie:*

> When our two great sires fought in the burroak grove
> Their bellows disturbed my sleep. I rolled in a heat
> Of black hooves stomping the bottom lands, woke in a sweat,
> Crying, "Mother, what is it?" . . .

---

56 Ruth Suckow, "Foreword," in James Hearst, *Country Men* (Muscatine: Prairie Press, 1937).
57 James Hearst, *Man and His Field* (Denver: Alan Swallow, 1951), p. 15.
58 *Man and His Field*, pp. 13–14, and fn. 4, p. 14.
59 *Man and His Field*, p. 9.
60 John T. Frederick, *Out of the Midwest* (New York: McGraw-Hill Book Co., 1944), p. 301.

> Our great Hereford bulls! Their fierce heads were as strong
> As the iron bars of their gates, their bodies as thickly
> Bound as the earth they stormed. . . .
>   Their deep growls broke
> And sank in a tunnel of throat.[61]

"There always was a relation between poet and place," said Archibald MacLeish, writing about this volume. "Placeless poetry, existing in the non-geography of ideas, is a modern invention and not a very fortunate one. [Langland's verse] is a bold step out on the old and long untraveled path, and we should be grateful for it. Langland's poems belong where they are, and where they are turns out to belong to poetry, thanks to him."[62]

Caroline B. Sherman, writing in *Agricultural History* (January 1938) said:

In the twenty or thirty years of its development, American rural fiction has weathered discouragement, obscurity, and neglect. . . . It has survived precocious prize-taking, popularity and praise. Years ago it reached the stage where its supporters demanded as much . . . as of any other school of fiction, not only in characterization and description but in insight, revelation and craftsmanship. It has brought the American past and ways of growth or deterioration clearly before us and interpreted them in everyday terms. [P. 76]

John T. Frederick, thirteen years later in the *Palimpsest* (March 1951), was able to look back at nearly all of the farm fiction that was to be written and say:

The portrayal of the Iowa farm in fiction, from Garland to [Manfred], has shown a faithful response to the major currents in our national literature. It has attained levels of high achievement in each successive phase. Sincerity has been the prevailing common denominator of the writers who have created this portrayal. Many have been moved by love of the life they portrayed, some by rebellious anger against its circumstances. But in general they have been clear sighted, blinded neither by anger nor by love; and they have tried to tell the truth. Almost without exception they have escaped the trap always baited for the unwary regionalist: the mistaking of the means for the end, the exploitation of regional peculiarity or idiosyncrasy as such, for its own sake. . . . no other state can show a portrayal of its rural life in fiction so rich, so varied, and so generally sound as can Iowa.[63]

---

61   Joseph Langland, "Sacrifice of the Old Gentleman," *The Wheel of Summer* (New York: Dial Press, 1963), pp. 10–11.
62   Archibald MacLeish, quoted on dust jacket of *The Wheel of Summer* (New York: Dial Press, 1963).
63   Frederick, "The Farm in Iowa Fiction."

Life on the Mississippi

THREE Iowa writers have attracted audiences far beyond the borders of Iowa primarily because they have made men laugh and smile. They are "Bob" Burdette of Burlington, Ellis Parker Butler of Muscatine, and Richard Bissell of Dubuque.

Robert Jones Burdette was born "where the Monongahela runs itself out of breath to catch up with the Ohio" in Greene County, Pennsylvania, on July 3, 1844.[1] When he was eight, the family moved to Peoria where Burdette got his public school education. "I was born in Pennsylvania, weaned in Ohio, kidnapped by Illinois, adopted by Iowa and married to California," he said in later life. From his days at Hinman School in Peoria came one of his most famous pieces, "The Strike at Hinman's," an account of a Burdette-led mutiny against the innovation of "speaking pieces" by boys at the school.

Burdette graduated from the Peoria High School at Christmas of 1861, and the following summer he enlisted in the Union Army. He described his wartime experiences many years later in *Drums of the Forty-Seventh* (1914).

In the fall of 1868, after a number of odd jobs, he enrolled in Cooper Union in New York City. There, he began sending humorous letters signed "Bob Burdette" to the Peoria *Weekly Transcript*. His subjects were the great names of the times (Ulysses S. Grant, the sermons of the Reverend Henry Ward Beecher, later to become a close friend, and the English poet Robert Browning were some), and his techniques were irreverence, parody, puns, and the *non sequitur*. He also wrote some serious critical reviews of art shows.

After a brief filibustering expedition to Cuba (which resulted in his being wounded by the Spanish), he returned to Peoria as a reporter for the *Transcript*. One of his first assignments was to interview the eminent Horace Greeley:

---

1 Clara B. Burdette, *Robert J. Burdette: His Message* (Philadelphia: John C. Winston Co., 1922). All Burdette biographical information is from this source.

I knocked on the door and Mr. Greeley called out: "Come in."

I went in and was so badly frightened that I could not think what to talk about, but finally I ventured:

"You have been lecturing, have you not, Mr. Greeley?"

Answer—"Yes."

Then it was so quiet that you could have heard the microbes gnaw if there had been a smallpox patient around.

I sat there for a minute or two and was getting more frightened every minute. At last I thought of another question:

"Have your lectures been successful, Mr. Greeley?"[2]

On March 4, 1870, Burdette married Carrie Garrett, a daughter of a pioneer Peoria family. She was an invalid and remained so until she died fifteen years later.

During the year he worked for the *Transcript* his irrepressible sense of the comic element in life found its way more and more into his columns, until one day the editor told him, "When I want anything funny in the paper, I'll write it myself." So Burdette went over to an afternoon paper, the *Review*, which soon folded and several of the employees began a new paper, the *Peoria Evening Injunction*. Newspapers around the country soon were praising its liveliness and the genius of Burdette. "I was writing up immortal dog fights and fadeless 'river news,' and undying 'real estate transfers,'" he said.

Among those who had noted "with increasing interest the liveliness of the *Review* columns" were the publishers of the Burlington *Hawk-Eye*, "a sober staid old paper, financially solid." In 1874, the paper offered Burdette a position as city editor and reporter. Burdette accepted and so an Iowa legend came into the making. He came to the *Hawk-Eye* in October 1874 and maintained a connection of sorts with the paper for about eleven years, but in that short span of time he became an internationally famous humorist, numbering among his friends Mark Twain and the Hoosier poet, James Whitcomb Riley. For five or six of those years, he lived in Burlington, writing for the *Hawk-Eye;* for a while, because of his wife's precarious health, he lived in Bryn Mawr, Pennsylvania. During this period he became a Baptist preacher, and he remained a preacher until his death, November 19, 1914, in Pasadena, California. During those years he remarried, and his preaching and lecturing took him all over the United States.

Burdette's humor is of several types: the rhyming prose paragraph, gentle satire, ridicule of our cultural myths, the epigram, local color, the humorous analogy—all stock in trade of the nineteenth century humorists. Two of his creations, Middlerib and Bilderback were known all over

---

2 Burdette, *Robert J. Burdette: His Message.*

the world. Because of his humor, the *Hawk-Eye* became a nationally known newspaper with a circulation which reached practically every state in the Union. The editor, Dr. Charles Beardsley, believed that the city editor ought to "tell all the doings of the town and refrain from all printed mirth as unseemly," but the business manager simply showed Beardsley the improving profit and loss statements, and the editor let Burdette have his way.

Burdette's essays and shorter bits were published in: *Before He is Twenty* (New York, 1894); *Hawkeyes* (New York, 1880); *Innach Garden and Other Comic Sketches* (New York, 1886); *Old Time and Young Tom* (Indianapolis, 1912); *Smiles Yoked With Sighs* (Indianapolis, 1900); *Chimes From a Jester's Bell* (Indianapolis, 1897); and *Rise and Fall of the Mustache* (Burlington, 1877). His biography, *Robert J. Burdette: His Message* (Philadelphia, 1922), was edited from his writings and compiled by his second wife, Clara B. Burdette.

Ellis Parker Butler was born at Muscatine, December 5, 1869, the son and grandson of two pork-packers. But the business failed, and Butler went to live with his Aunt Lizzie. "The three greatest influences in my work were my aunt Lizzie Butler and my high school English teacher, who gave me an admiration and appreciation of literature, and my father, who was an enthusiastic admirer of Mark Twain and the other humorists of that day. Mark Twain was close to us, having lived in Muscatine awhile, and Bob Burdette was but sixty miles down the river."[3]

After one year of high school, he worked for eleven years at odd jobs in Muscatine, at the same time writing verses and short humor for the *Midland Monthly*. On the advice of Tom Masson of the old *Life*, who had published some of his things, Butler went to New York to write humor. In 1899 with Thomas A. Cawthra he established the *Decorative Furnisher*. That same year he married Ida A. Zipser of Muscatine.[4]

In 1906, Butler was writing a series of humorous articles about one Mike Flannery for the *American Magazine*. Flannery was a semi-literate, literal-minded Irishman, "the Westcote agent of the Interurban Express Company," and a man who had a great deal of trouble with language, particularly the language of the directives and printed forms sent to him by the Company, and, as a consequence, with patrons and would-be patrons of the Company. One of these articles, "Pigs is Pigs," became an overnight sensation, and soon was being reprinted as a small paperback book. In 1930 Frank Luther Mott commented that "*The Golden Book,*

---

3 Stanley J. Kunitz, *Authors Today and Yesterday* (New York: H. W. Wilson Co., 1934), pp. 120–21.
4 Kunitz, *Authors Today and Yesterday*.

in reprinting the story a couple of years ago, said that something like a million copies of it had been sold in book form. Editions of it seemed to have caught the adding and multiplying contagion from the pigs themselves."[5] In 1945 the story was included in the Modern Library Edition of *The Best American Short Stories.* Its title has long since passed into the folk language, and is probably used by many people who never have seen the source.

Happy with the success of this venture into the world of comic literature, Butler made other attempts, but none quite succeeded in repeating the success of this one essay. Among his more popular works were *Perkins of Portland, That Pup of Murchison's,* and *The Great American Pie Works,* the latter set, according to Butler, in Cedar Rapids.

In *Kilo* (1907), Butler made his first attempt at a novel. Kilo is a country town, which like Ruth Suckow's New Hope, had replaced an older town when the railroad came through. The novel's burden is a love affair between a comic traveling book salesman and a Kilo girl. Although the novel has an excellent description of an Iowa small town of the turn of the century, it does not merit much attention today.

One of Butler's better efforts is the story "Bread" (1917), a moving account of the importance of bread in the life of one family.[6] Another, equally moving and equally simple, is "Interlude" (1927),[7] the narrative of the effects of a brief illness on a family. Of this story, Frank Luther Mott said, "the little story is filled with fine understanding of the boy heart. It is a gem."[8]

Butler was at his best writing about boys; his "Phil Gubb" and "Jibby Jones" stories are readable tales about boy life on the Mississippi in the last century. The boys seem like real boys, and the river is as vividly depicted as it is in Mark Twain's stories of the river. Some of the endings are artificial and contrived, but Butler's readers didn't seem to mind that.

His *Dominie Dean* (1917) is one of a half dozen novels by Iowa authors which have focused on the life of the small town minister. While it lacks the sense of an exuberant life in *One Foot in Heaven,* or the fresh spring idealism of *New Hope,* or the awareness of family life in *The Bonney Family,* or the sense of impending doom in *The Work of an Ancient Hand,* it provides in its history of the life and work of a small town minister a study of a man who is good, and who will not tamper with his

---

5 Frank Luther Mott, "Ellis Parker Butler," in *A Book of Iowa Authors by Iowa Authors* (Des Moines: Iowa State Teachers Assn., 1930), p. 34.
6 Ellis Parker Butler, "Bread," *Prairie Gold* (Chicago: Reilly and Britton Co., 1917), pp. 37–45.
7 Ellis Parker Butler, "Interlude," *The Behind Legs of the 'Orse* (Boston: Houghton Mifflin Co., 1927), pp. 175–98.
8 Mott, "Ellis Parker Butler."

own goodness for any vicissitude, whether it stems from his meager income, church politics, or small town evil doing. Unlike some of the other novels which show a minister moving from town to town and changing his circumstances with each move, *Dominie Dean* is the account of a man who takes his first charge at the age of twenty-one and retains it until he becomes an impoverished "pastor emeritus." Unlike *The Work of an Ancient Hand*, this novel shows a man who is constantly embroiled in the affairs of his parishioners and his own family, a man who effects changes in others (for better or for worse), a man who is affected by the wills of others.

The time of the novel is from 1860 until just after the turn of the century; the town is Riverbank, Iowa, a small town on the Mississippi, not too far from the larger city of Derlingport (Butler later said his models were Muscatine and Davenport). The novel embraces the whole social structure of these towns from the very poor to the well-to-do, from the professional baseball player to a "Copperhead," from the minister to the bartender. There is even an analysis of the economic structure of Iowa small towns of the period:

. . . [Dominie Dean] had made out a new schedule of his indebtedness, and had been shocked to see how it had grown since his trustees had made the last advance. . . . He still owed something on last winter's coal; he owed a goodly drug bill; his grocery bill was unpaid since the first of the year; he owed the butcher; the milkman had a bill against him; there were a dozen small accounts for shoes, drygoods, one thing and another.

In Riverbank at that time, business was nearly all credit business. Bills were rendered twice a year, or even once a year, and, when rendered, often remained unpaid for another six months. As accounts went David's accounts were satisfactory to the merchants; he was counted a "good" customer.

Dominie Dean has probably not had the attention it should have had, for as John T. Frederick says, the figure of David Dean is "something rare in fiction: a character who is wholly and consistently a good man, and yet both credible and interesting."

. . . the quality of this serious novel is so good as to make one wish that Ellis Parker Butler had written others, rather than devoting his powers to *Pigs is Pigs* and the other little books, pleasant as they are, that won him fame as a humorist.[9]

Aside from *Pigs is Pigs*, Butler made one other contribution to our folklore. Shortly after publication of the book, which sold for a quarter,

9 John T. Frederick, "Town and City in Iowa Fiction," *Palimpsest* 35 (February 1954):57–58.

Butler was asked by Edgar Harland, curator of the State Historical Department, to contribute a copy. Butler complied with the request, but he inscribed these lines on the flyleaf:

> O Iowa, state of my birth,
> Accept this book, a quarter's worth.
> O state of corn, take it from me,
> And ever let thy motto be:
> "Three millions yearly for manure,
> But not one cent for literature."

Butler died in 1937.

When Richard Bissell was born in Dubuque on June 27, 1913, Robert Burdette was near the end of his career, and Ellis Parker Butler had already made half of the fifty thousand dollars he was to make on *Pigs is Pigs*. Burdette and Butler were born in impoverished households; Bissell was born "in the old house on Fenelon Place . . . of poor but wealthy parents." His father was Frederick Ezekiel Bissell. ("My father is a frustrated journalist, himself," says Bissell. "He went to Harvard College, was editor of the Crimson.") His mother was Edith Mary (Pike) Bissell. Her family was Pennsylvania Dutch and French Canadian; his father's was English—in 1845 they had moved from Windsor, Connecticut, from where, according to Bissell, "all the Bissells in the U.S.A. come from."[10]

One must always be cautious with the statements of a professional humorist. Bissell says that in Dubuque "he attended the public schools as seldom as possible in order to have more time to hang around on the river. At the age of fourteen, he floated from Winona to Dubuque on a raft, bummed the freights to Hannibal, Missouri, to prostrate himself at the Mark Twain shrine, and flunked Latin for the first time."

He was, in his own words, then "sent off to Phillips Exeter Academy for three years, where he coxed the crew and flunked Latin three more times." At Exeter "English . . . was *The Mill on the Floss* and *Silas Marner*," but one teacher, Professor Joseph Barrell, managed to turn "Bissell's head a bit" with his enthusiasm for Hemingway.

After graduation from Exeter in 1932, Bissell was admitted to Harvard where, he says, he spent four years "perfecting his game of pool." But he was attracted to the teaching of Professor Earnest A. Hooton, the anthropologist. Following graduation from Harvard in 1936 with a B.S.

---

10 Sources for the Bissell biographical information in this chapter are: *Wilson Library Bulletin* 37 (January 1963):441; "The Way He Sees Business is Funny," and "Factory Laughs Give Broadway a Hit," *Business Week* (June 5, 1954), p. 68; the dust jacket of *You Can Always Tell a Harvard Man* (New York: McGraw-Hill Book Co., 1962); *Contemporary Authors*, vol. 4; and *Paluka*, pp. 230–31.

in anthropology, Bissell worked in a Venezuelan oil field, then shipped out "as an ordinary seaman on an American Export Lines freighter," and following that voyage, "worked as a licensed mate and pilot for the Central Barge Company on river boats on the Mississippi, Illinois, Ohio, Tennessee, and Monongahela rivers." The salty language which flavors the pages of his river stories is either honestly derived from this experience, or he has made it all up.

On February 15, 1938, he married Marian Van Patten Grilk, whom he had met at Exeter. That same year he became a vice-president of a family enterprise, the H. B. Glover Co. of Dubuque. The company had been founded by one of Bissell's great-grandfathers as a "job-lot outlet for Chicago notions," and it "went into pajama manufacture" after World War II.

Aside from time out for maritime service in the Second World War, Bissell spent most of the next fifteen years with the company, serving as superintendent, plant manager, and vice-president of production. Although he later complained that "business was dull," he said that he loved "the garment business . . . especially the salesmen. They are wonderful. Out west in Montana, they were selling pajamas to Indians. One spoke Indian —he'd been born near a reservation. Hell, those Indians never heard of pajamas."

Rejected by the navy because of his eyesight, Bissell spent World War II on the "inland waterways system . . . hauling coal on the Mississippi, Ohio, and Monongahela rivers." In three years, like an earlier river man whom he admires, Mark Twain, he got his pilot papers, but he never made captain: "I'd rather be a pilot—not so much responsibility."

"I have had a personal love affair with the Mississippi ever since I was a kid," Bissell said once. For a year after their marriage he and his wife lived on a river boat, and he is now an officer of the Bissell Towing and Transportation Company of Dubuque. Although his home is in Connecticut, Bissell spends his summers in Dubuque, looking after business matters and occasionally piloting a tugboat.

In 1949 "his wife egged him on to write about his experiences" on the rivers for the *Atlantic* "I Personally" contest, and so he wrote "The Coal Queen." After she rejected the first draft, he "quit trying to be literary and just set it down." The second draft won her approval and the thousand-dollars first prize. The story of life on the Monongahela had the *Atlantic* editors asking for more. Eventually he was to publish *The Monongahela* (1952) as part of the Rivers of America series.

But before that, in 1950, came *A Stretch on the River*, Bissell's novel about coal barges moving from St. Louis up to St. Paul. The story has its roots in his wartime experiences, and there are many similarities between incidents in the book and his real life experiences.

The novel begs for comparison with Mark Twain's *Life on the Mississippi*. Both books report an upriver cruise, both books report the learning process of a river man, both books report life on the river and ashore, both are first person narrations, and so on. (Both books ran serially, in part at least, in the *Atlantic*.) But Twain's book describes the heyday of steamboat traffic on the river, while Bissell's book describes diesel-powered boats after the river has been relatively tamed by dams and locks. Both books mix passages of comedy with more serious passages, but Bissell's book is much earthier, with its insistence on masculinity and virility, its salty language, its emphasis on drinking and on the pleasures of shore visits with women. Aesthetically, *A Stretch on the River* is inferior to the early part of *Life on the Mississippi*, equal to or superior to the latter part of the Twain work.

Bissell's stylistic techniques include the use of a number of literary devices which had their origins in the Greek epic and have been literary fare ever since: the catalog of names, the heroic (or mock-heroic) battle scene, the use of names based on physical characteristics of characters. Others of his devices include (as in some of Twain's books) the epigram at the head of the chapter, many of which form satirical comments on the chapter itself; some of these are taken from other writers, some are Bissell's own inventions. Sometimes he uses parody, as in one scene in the pilot house where the pilots are discussing their favorite detergent; the parody is both of a television commercial and a famous scene in *Life on the Mississippi*. He uses the pithy statement—"if you're not clever to start with, college won't cure the condition"; he quotes lines from other books but with a twist: " 'What do they call you?' 'Call me Ishmael.' . . . One thing about the old boy, he was a lightning pilot.' " He uses the wisecrack:

"The last time I was uptown there," Joe said, "I run hard aground in that bar acrost from the hotel. 'Do you wanna go upstairs, honey?' says this little bitty black-haired grinder. 'I might as well,' I says, 'I been here a hour and no celebrities come in yet.' "

Critics praised the "bawdy brawling novel of riverboat life"[11] though the *New Yorker* said that Bissell "almost spoils his book by the pose he strikes as a writer,"[12] and Bernard DeVoto complained that at times "a thin, slick smartness shows up, almost as if he were out to convince the *New Yorker* that the old lady in Dubuque brought up her family on the right magazine." But DeVoto, a chronicler of the river himself and a Mark

11 *Chicago Tribune,* July 16, 1950, p. 6.
12 *New Yorker* 26 (July 22, 1950):71.

Twain scholar and admirer, compared Bissell favorably to his predecessor.[13]

Bissell's next novel of life on the river was *High Water* (1954). Once again the scene is the Mississippi from St. Louis upward with the Twin Cities the intended destination, but this time the river is in a record flood, and the *Royal Prince* barely clears the CB&Q railroad bridge at Quincy before her doomed voyage comes to an end.

Carl Carmer, editor of the Rivers of America series, praised the book although he complained that the apparent decision to make the novel "racy, gay, amorous," kept it from being "a minor masterpiece outranking even his praiseworthy first novel."[14]

Bissell's third book about the Mississippi, *Goodbye Ava* (1960), is set in the Mississippi River town of Eagle Rock and its harbor, a place obviously modeled on Dubuque. The protagonists of *Goodbye Ava* are Frank Blanchard, the first-person narrator, who owns a factory in Eagle Rock but prefers life on a houseboat in the harbor to living up on Western Boulevard with its "lovely homes"; Clyde Valentine and his wife Jeri who live on a seventy-foot-long two-story houseboat next to Frank; Rip Ryan, a "sort of semi-professional son of a bitch" who wears "225-dollar suits," races up and down the river in his seventy-foot cruiser, and owns a great deal of property in Eagle Rock and elsewhere; and girls named Gladys, Billie, and Ava, the last of whom exists only in the narrator's dreams, though she is, in fact, Ava Gardner, the motion picture actress.

The story line has to do with Clyde Valentine's protest against the attempt of the Eagle Rock Dock Commission to move the river dwellers off the waterfront to make room for Rip Ryan's "Imperial Fertilizer Company," and Frank Blanchard's amours and drinking bouts. Although Frank makes love to at least two women, his heart belongs to Jeri Valentine (she's the mother of three small girls) and eventually he marries her, after Clyde's untimely death, caused by his effort to block traffic on Rip Ryan's toll bridge.

Goodbye Ava was the second of Bissell's novels to be set in a mythical Iowa town which is easily recognizable as Dubuque. The first was *7½ Cents* (1953), "a Rabelaisian approach to a Marxist situation," which is set in Junction City, Iowa, "a trap consisting of fifty-thousand dazed customers wondering what to do after five o'clock." (Bissell's heroes all feel that life in a metropolis is to be preferred to life in the boring small towns of the Middle West.) The hero is Sid Sorokin, an ambitious man

13 Bernard DeVoto, "A Fine New Talent on Ol' Man River," *New York Herald Tribune Books*, July 23, 1950, p. 7.
14 Carl Carmer, "Mississippi Odyssey," *New York Herald Tribune Books*, September 26, 1954, p. 4.

from Chicago, who has come to Junction City as "superintendent of the Sleep Tite pajama plant (*Sleep Tite, the Pajama for Men of Bedroom Discrimination*)." The plant is faced with a union-called strike because the workers want a seven-and-one-half cent per hour raise, and because "a sap called Mr. Myron Hasler who did all the dirty work" for the owner is opposed to the raise.

Sorokin is a practical man—he knows that the plant must be run efficiently if it is to make a profit, and for his own benefit he wants it to make one. But he also thinks that the workers deserve a share of the profits and favors the raise.

Sorokin's life is complicated by woman troubles as well as factory troubles, for he is attracted to Catherine "Babe" Williams, a production worker, and a member of the union grievance committee. She is cast in the same mold as Bissell's other "Big Girls." Moreover, Sorokin proves attractive to Celeste Watson, daughter of the pump king who lives in one of those gaudy houses on Western Avenue that Bissell's heroes dislike.

Even though Bissell is much more realistic and honest about the labor situation than Alice French was in *The Man of the Hour,* one must not take his novel too seriously. Bissell doesn't intend that, and his critics agree. Frederick Morton, for one, called the book "an opulent mess . . . a subtle, many-faceted, penetrating piece of nonsense," suitable for summer time, a hammock and a tall drink.[15] Amy Loveman was a bit more considerate, for though she agreed in part with Morton, she thought that "the book as a whole has the ring of truth, and its satire, despite its good nature, has bite enough to give point to the narrative." As for the author, she said that he belonged in "that small company of American writers who, like Sinclair Lewis, Jerome Weidman, and Arthur Kober, have a special aptitude for capturing turns of speech and whose ear for the vernacular is so accurate that they can bring a whole stratum of society to life by the talk of their characters."[16]

Up to this point in time, an Iowa subject, based on a book written by an Iowan, had never been used on the New York musical stage. Intrigued by the fact that 7½ *Cents* had been a Book-of-the-Month Club selection, and that its author had been praised as demonstrating "a gift for parody, an ear for absurd conversation, and an eye for the commonplace idiocies which generally slide by unnoticed . . . a couple of George Abbott's young executives . . . got Abbott's O.K. to produce it."[17] Bissell came to New York to help write the book, and liked the place so well he moved his home to Connecticut.

---

15 Frederick Morton, *New York Herald Tribune Books*, May 24, 1953, p. 6.
16 Amy Loveman, "Epic of a Pajama," *Saturday Review* 36 (May 23, 1953):17.
17 *Business Week* (June 5, 1954), p. 74.

Pajama Game opened at the St. James Theatre on Thursday, May 13, 1954, and at once became a popular and financial success. All of the New York drama critics praised it, all but one enthusiastically. Later, the play was made into a film with Doris Day as its star.

Bissell's next novel was *Say, Darling* (1957), a story of an author from Iowa who comes to New York City to help write and produce a musical comedy. Subsequently, this novel was also converted into a successful musical play.

Two later Bissell books, *You Can Always Tell a Harvard Man* (1962) and *How Many Miles to Galena* spoof two venerable American traditions, Harvard University and highway travel, but they are beyond the scope of this study. In a 1970 letter, Bissell said that he liked the travel book best of the things he has written, but *Goodbye Ava* and *A Stretch on the River* are superior to it.

Bissell's history cannot end here. His most recent publication, *Julia Harrington Winnebago Iowa 1913* (1969) is what might be called a "picture book," but the pictures are reprints of catalog pages and advertisements from magazines and newspapers for the most part—there are some reprints of picture postcards—all taken from the 1913 era (the year of Bissell's birth). Interpolated among and between the illustrations—which were furnished by Bissell—are pages of text which provide a sort of running account of the life of a "twelve-going-on-thirteen" year-old Iowa girl of that period.

In the mid-thirties in Dubuque, there sprang into existence an ephemeral literary periodical, the *Dubuque Dial*. Its editor was Karlton Kelm, then teaching creative writing in Dubuque; its sponsors included Mr. and Mrs. Frederick E. Bissell, Miss Bess G. Bissell (who was also the associate editor), Miss Marguerite Bissell—all relatives of Richard Bissell—several other Dubuque persons, and Ruth Suckow. In its brief existence the magazine published stories by a number of people, including Mildred Fowler Field (an Iowa poet of some repute), Meridel Le Seur (an Iowa writer who has spent most of her life away from the state), Josephine Herbst, Raymond Kresensky, and Kelm.

At the same time Kelm was also writing for the University of Iowa's *American Prefaces*. In 1936, he published two novels: *The Cherry Bed*, a novel of Wisconsin village life, and *Brother*, a novel set in "Ducaine," a mythical midwestern town somewhere west of Chicago. Neither is a major work, although the two novels and the short fiction indicated a promising future for the young writer. *Brother*'s major interest is in its theme of small-town provincialism, and the domination of personal affairs by religious beliefs. Unfortunately, whatever value these themes have in the novel is marred by the unlikely melodramatic ending the author used to resolve his character's dilemma.

Maquoketa, on the Maquoketa River in northeast Iowa, is not far from Karlton Kelm's and Richard Bissell's Dubuque—and John Scholl's "Omega" (an Iowa town about the size of Maquoketa) is not any farther from Sinclair Lewis's "Gopher Prairie" or Sherwood Anderson's "Winesburg, Ohio." The distance is greater in years than in miles (about four decades separate *Winesburg, Ohio* and *Main Street* from Scholl's *The Changing of the Guard*, 1963), but the chief distance between the earlier books and the later one is the greater permissiveness in the use of language and descriptions of such incidents as sexual relationships which Scholl allows himself. In his clinical descriptions of abortions, strabotomies, and canine operations, Scholl very much resembles Frederick Manfred.

The Changing of the Guard is the story of Guy Tallman from his birth in 1922 to 1959, the year in which his dreams of a hospital and membership as a Fellow of the American College of Surgeons are realized, along with a conclusion to his marital misadventures. It is also the story of Guy's home town of Omega, Iowa, a town which shared, along with many other Iowa and American small towns, a Chamber of Commerce dream of boom, expansion, and growth.

Scholl was born in Maquoketa on August 7, 1922, and from 1940 to 1960 had a great deal of journalistic experience. Since the publication of this novel, he has continued a career in Maquoketa as a free-lance writer.

Calvin Kentfield was born in Keokuk in 1924. He graduated from the Keokuk High School in 1942 and then became an art major at the University of Iowa. His education was interrupted by service in the merchant marine, and he, the son of a railroad man, began to feel an affinity for ships—"both [ships and trains] have whistles, and they both go from here to somewhere else."[18] He finished his degree at Iowa in 1949, his return to school having been prompted by lack of employment opportunities on the high seas, and by a growing desire to become a writer rather than a painter: "It was the sea that changed me."[19]

Kentfield had begun work on a first novel, supported by unemploy-

18 Calvin Kentfield, *All Men Are Mariners* (New York: McGraw-Hill Book Co., 1962), p. 251.
19 Frank Paluka, *Iowa Authors: A Bio-Bibliography of Sixty Native Writers* (Iowa City, Iowa: Friends of The University of Iowa Libraries, 1967), p. 240.

ment insurance. He was also contributing short stories to the *New Yorker*, *Harper's Bazaar*, and *Tomorrow*.

Most of his fiction has centered on the sea. However, six of the ten short stories in *The Angel and the Sailor* (1957) are set in southeast Iowa, either in Keokuk or at Brigham's Crossing, a settlement on the Mississippi where the Mormons crossed from Nauvoo on their way west. Two of the stories in *The Great Wandering Goony Bird* (1963) are also set in Iowa; one of them, "Windmills," is the account of an old man who repairs windmills. Kentfield's Iowa material is set in the 1930s in a lower-class milieu.

The narrator of his 1962 novel, *All Men Are Mariners*, is also from Brigham's Crossing, and *his* father is a railroad man.

In 1955 Kentfield returned to the University of Iowa for a year as a teacher in the Writers Workshop. In 1958 he became editor of *Contact*, a magazine published on the West Coast. He is presently living at Sausalito, California, with his wife whom he married in England in 1955.

Parnassus on the Prairie

IN the late nineteenth and early twentieth centuries, Davenport became an "extraordinarily literary and intellectual town." Alice French was there, and literary and discussion societies flourished—one of these, the Contemporary Club, was founded by members of her family and the father of Arthur Davison Ficke, among others.

"I had formerly felt that the goldenness of my years in Davenport was a special miracle performed by a suddenly kind universe for my especial benefit," said Floyd Dell in his autobiography. Later he

. . . thought of it as the result of definite social forces. Davenport was what it was because it was so largely German and Jewish, with an 1848 European revolutionary foundation, and a liberal and Socialist superstructure. There was also some native American mysticism in the picture, a mysticism of the sort which blossomed in the '30's and '40's, a curious religious expression of romantic libertarian ideas.[1]

A major reason for the atmosphere in Davenport in those years was the presence of five people and their relatives and friends—Dell, Susan Glaspell, George Cram Cook (and his mother, Ellen), Harry Hansen, and Arthur Davison Ficke, all of whom were born in Davenport (with the exception of Dell) in the 1870s or '80s, and all of whom knew each other (and Alice French as well).

Cook, the oldest, was born on October 7, 1873, the great-grandson of Ira and Rachel Cook who came to Iowa in 1836, and of Christopher Rowe and Elizabeth Looke Rowe who also crossed the Mississippi to Iowa on a ferry that same year. For the most part the families prospered in Davenport—"George Cram Cook grew up in a town that had a Cook Memorial Library, the Cook Home [for old ladies], and Cook Memorial

---

1 Floyd Dell, *Homecoming: An Autobiography* (New York: Farrar & Rinehart, 1933), p. 70. Most of the Dell biographical material comes from this source.

Church,"[2] the money for which, however, had come from an uncle—George's own grandfather had failed as a banker.

When George was eight years old, his mother—he called her "Ma-Mie" all her life—did something "Iowa people with money for new houses" were not doing in those years—she moved her family back to the log cabin home of her childhood at Buffalo, about seven miles downriver from Davenport. But this was no ordinary cabin—Plato and Ruskin were on the bookshelves, Greek urns on the tables, and one might find Hungarian refugees there with a touch of Old World culture, or hear Beethoven, or discussions on "the mysticism of India, old rites, the beginnings of art."

Cook attended the Griswold College military prep school in Davenport because "the public schools were too tough." He was valedictorian of his class and, in accordance with custom, read an essay of his own composition.

At the University of Iowa where he enrolled at sixteen and spent the next three years, he fell in love with Plotinus, Wordsworth, and his first girl—he was engaged to her for several years. He also played on the baseball team, and one afternoon he walked away from the game at the end of the sixth inning to catch a freight train to Davenport to see his girl. "Well, if you make love as well as you play ball you'll be all right," one of his teammates called after him.

At Iowa he set forth plans "for a culture that shall occupy the next fifty years: I want to understand the language of all great souls. . . . I would receive into myself all Germany, all Greece, all Palestine. In their art lies history. . . . I must know that I may enjoy the harmony in all things, mounting at last to Plato's absolute Beauty."

The Iowa teacher he remembered was Professor Melville B. Anderson, "the man who first awoke in me the love of letters and thereby shaped my life."

In the fall of 1892, he went to Harvard to take his senior year. There he studied with Barrett Wendell and Charles Eliot Norton. He worked his way deeper into the Greek language and Greek literature, preparing for university teaching, and was disappointed that the panic of 1893 was to keep him from an anticipated tour of Europe with John Alden, a friend with a "clean, incisive, definite" mind whom he had met at Harvard.

Back in Davenport, Cook became a friend of Robert French (the younger brother of Alice French) who was working in a Moline steel mill. Before long the death of French was to bring him "the deepest sorrow" he had known; French was "the strongest and tenderest man," and Cook was to remember him until the day of his own death.

---

2 Susan Glaspell, *The Road to the Temple* (New York: Frederick A. Stokes Co., 1927), p. 13. Most of the Cook biographical material comes from this source.

In 1894 Cook made his delayed tour of Europe, his aim being to prepare himself further for teaching. In the fall of 1895, he came back to the University of Iowa to teach English; often he played the violin in his classrooms, and devised means for working Dante into his lectures. He told his students about Dante's home town: "The Florentines changed the name of a section of their city to *Borge Allegro*, because the Cimabue Madonna had come to live there. Would the Board of Aldermen of Iowa City call the Fifth Ward 'The Joyous Quarter' because one of the citizens had painted a beautiful, happy picture?" (By 1972 the closest that Iowa City had come to this was to name a public school for Grant Wood!)

Although in one place he said that in Iowa City "a dismal Puritanism waged war with a dismal vice," elsewhere he wrote that Iowa City "feels the mystery of existence deeply" from Athens, and the river flows through "that strange little wooded river valley which has not yet lost its Indian character." For all his growing longing for Greece and things Greek, he loved his native state:

> I remember like heart-beats the beat of the
>   hoofs of our horses
> Over the roads in the night from the gas-lighted
>   town.
> The afternoon's rain in the ruts—minute watercourses
> Shimmering down.

In October of 1898, Cook wrote prophetically on his twenty-fifth birthday that half of life was gone and he had done nothing. He began work on a novel of Mexico in the time of Maximilian—*Roderick Taliaferro*—and another called "The Faggot and the Flame." In succession he married a Chicago girl "of beauty and charm," saw his novel published, taught at Leland Stanford University, and then returned to the Buffalo farm to work the land and write. He began *The Balm of Life*, a novel about whiskey and marriage; a publisher rejected it. At thirty-two he was becoming aware that the "infinite accomplishments" promised by youth were not so easily attained. People in Davenport were saying: "George Cook peddling vegetables! He goes to Harvard and Heidelberg, and then takes up truck farming!"

After three years his marriage failed. Despondent over the directions his life was taking, he contemplated suicide. Then he met Mollie Price (who was to become his second wife and the mother of his children), and Floyd Dell.

Dell was born on June 28, 1887, in Barry, Illinois, just east of Hannibal, Missouri. His father, Anthony Dell, was an impoverished butcher; his mother was Kate Crane Dell. Dell was the youngest of the family. Necessity brought him to Davenport in 1904; one of his first surprises was to learn that "Octave Thanet" was alive, and living in Davenport. (Alice French, who had once quarreled publicly with her bishop because of her opposition to socialism, never apparently got to know Dell very well—her only reference to him is that "young socialist poet . . . something Dell.")³ Davenport people soon discovered his interest in poetry and encouraged it. In due time he became a newspaper reporter, then the editor of the "Tri-City Worker's Magazine," a Socialist monthly. He began selling poems to *Harper's*, the *Century*, and *McClure's*.

When Cook and Dell first met, they did not take to each other; Cook found Dell "excessively bookish and rather 'inhuman.'" They were introduced by Marilla Freeman, Dell's "beautiful and adored librarian goddess," who had taken Dell under her wing. But Dell, "as a Socialist," could not approve Cook's "romantic-philosophical" ideas or his "reactionary Nietzschean-aristocratic conceptions of an ideal society founded upon a pseudo-Greek slavery."⁴

Before Cook and Dell did become friends some three years later, Dell met Harry Hansen, another young reporter. Hansen (born in 1884 in Davenport) and Dell found a common interest in plays and poetry, and they would meet in Davenport's Central Park (now Fejervary Park) to walk and talk:

. . . Floyd's Socialistic activity was largely due to a lad's hunger for new intellectual contacts, a reaching out for new friendships to replace the inadequacy of association with mere schoolboys. . . . I remember a walk with Floyd Dell . . . that yielded my first acquaintanceship with Hueneker, and through him with the dramatists who played so large a part in the early reading of Felix Fay [the hero of Dell's *Moon-Calf*]; a walk that brought me my first glimpse of *A Shropshire Lad*—quoted for the most part by Dell . . . .⁵

But they talked about Davenport as well:

We young and aspiring writers spoke with admiration of Susan Glaspell, who had won the huge prize of $500 for a short story. . . . We . . . wondered whether we could do as well. . . . One day Floyd Dell told me that McClure had bought a poem of his, and as we walked down the street Dell recited it. This

3 George McMichael, *Journey to Obscurity: The Life of Octave Thanet* (Lincoln: University of Nebraska Press, 1965), p. 181. The reference to Miss French's quarrel with her bishop is taken from Lydia Margaret Barrette's "Alice French (Octave Thanet)" in *A Book of Iowa Authors by Iowa Authors* (Des Moines: Iowa State Teachers Assn., 1930), p. 83.
4 Dell, *Homecoming: An Autobiography*, pp. 145–55.
5 Harry Hansen, *Midwest Portraits* (New York: Harcourt, Brace and Co., 1923), pp. 208–16.

was the nearest I had ever come to knowing a successful author, and I glowed by reflected light.[6]

Three years after their first meeting, Cook and Dell came together again to form "The Monists," a society of freethinkers. Dell soon found himself the mentor of a "miserable . . . non-producing 'man of genius.' " Under Dell's tutelage, Cook who "wanted to live in a world which put truth and beauty first," became a Socialist, and "began work on a Socialist novel, *The Chasm* . . . laid partly in Moline and partly in the revolutionary Russia of 1905." Cook was commuting to Davenport and keeping open house at the Buffalo farm for those intellectuals who could sympathize with his dreams. He believed that "a writer should not be economically dependent upon his writing, but should remain free to write what he chose." Then one day he discovered that his truck farm was operating at a loss, and he hadn't written much either.

Now Susan Glaspell came into the lives of Dell and Cook. She had been born in Davenport on July 1, 1882 (although her biographer notes some evidence for 1876), the daughter of Elmer S. and Alice Keating Glaspell; the Glaspells were also among some of Davenport's first settlers, having arrived in 1835. She attended the Davenport Public Schools and spent several summers on an aunt's farm near Davenport, thus gaining insights into rural life. Like Alice French she accepted the country as she found it; she never had the hostile attitudes toward rural life that Garland had. Professor Bartholow V. Crawford, himself a native Iowan, said of her that she remained "at heart a daughter of Iowa. . . . The Middle Western scene was for her not something to be lived down or forgotten, but one of her richest resources; and in every reference to the region of her birth, there is affectionate sympathy and understanding."[7] "I have never lost the feeling that this is my part of the country," she said years later.[8]

Miss Glaspell enrolled at Drake University in 1897; in 1899 she tried unsuccessfully to become editor of the *Delphic*, losing out to her lifelong friend, Lucy Huffaker. After graduation with a Ph.B. in 1899, she stayed on in Des Moines, taking a reporter's job with the Des Moines *Daily News* which claimed to be the first newspaper in Iowa to hire women as reporters. Lucy Huffaker was a fellow reporter; she was destined to become a prominent Chicago journalist and an important person in the growth of the Washington Square Players. Miss Glaspell covered the state house and murder trials, and out of her experiences came several

6 Harry Hansen, "A Davenport Boyhood," *Palimpsest* 37 (April 1956):215.
7 Bartholow V. Crawford, "Susan Glaspell," *Palimpsest* 11 (December 1930):517–21.
8 Florence Haxton Bullock, "Conflict in a Modern Midwest Family," *Chicago Sun Bookweek*, October 28, 1945, p. 1.

of her short stories, including "Jury of Her Peers" (discussed in Chapter 9).

One of her stories based on her state house experience is "The Preposterous Motive," a story about the attempt of a party machine to win a United States Senate appointment for its candidate. A second is "The Plea," a story about a legislature's consideration of a request for a pardon for a Johnson County boy who was sent to prison at eleven for murdering his father. A third, "How the Prince Saw America," deals with the subject of an attempted strike in the statehouse building. All three, and many others of the twenty-six she wrote about "Freeport" from 1904 to 1922, show influences of Alice French—the use of romanticized endings and the use of the name "Freeport" are only two.

In 1901 Miss Glaspell returned to Davenport to work as a writer. In 1903 she enrolled at the University of Chicago for graduate work in English. It was on her return to Davenport (about 1907) that she became close to George Cram Cook and Floyd Dell. Soon she was reading portions of her first novel to the two men. "Susan was a slight, gentle, sweet, whimsically humorous girl, a little ethereal in appearance, but evidently a person of great energy, and brimful of talent," said Floyd Dell; he and Cook "admired greatly" the "liveliness and humor" of the novel but Cook deplored "the lamentable conventionality of the author's views of life." She was, the men agreed, "too medieval-romantic in her views."[9]

Jig Cook (as his friends called him) began to persuade Miss Glaspell that "our fiction is juvenile—written for people who are no longer children but who have never grown up, men and women who have neither naïveté nor maturity. There is no hope for American writers until they can forget the existence of immature adults."

But the Davenport group was not fated to remain together or in Davenport. Still, there was one final burst of pyrotechnics to remind the Mississippi River city of what it was about to lose. George Cram Cook had accepted an invitation to a meeting of the Contemporary Club—an organization "supposed to contain the leading male intellectuals of the town." Arthur Davison Ficke, a "young lawyer and poet, whose somewhat Shelleyan poetic drama [Dell] had read and reviewed [a little snootily]" was to read a paper on certain aspects of labor cases. Cook invited Dell and another Socialist friend to go along:

The tall, slender, handsome young poet-lawyer read his paper. The Three Musketeers could scarcely credit the evidence of their ears. It was a recital—accurate, they took for granted, and a masterpiece of concision, for all they knew—of the ways in which the injunction had been used in labor cases. But

---

9 Dell, *Homecoming: An Autobiography*, p. 170.

not a word about the social significance of that class use of the courts. No criticism, no attack, no defense, no comment. An informative piece, no doubt; useful, perhaps. But as a "paper" read in a club for intellectual discussion? Was *this* the intellectual pablum of Davenport's brightest and best minds?

"The Three Musketeers" in turn got to their feet, and each offered his criticism. Cook, somewhat self-conscious of the presence of his solid-citizen father in the room, was mild; then Dell spoke, somewhat more violently; and finally the third of the trio exploded "in furious unintelligibility." Later Cook said of the evening, "We met the enemy and we are theirs."[10]

Dell moved to Chicago to take a job as literary critic for the *Friday Literary Review* of the Chicago *Evening Post*. A young Evanston Socialist, Margery Currey, was an additional attraction. When Dell became editor of the *Review* he hired Cook as his replacement. In 1911 Harry Hansen went to the *Chicago Daily News* as a reporter; in 1917, after experience as a war correspondent, he became its literary editor. In 1909, Susan Glaspell, using the royalties from her first novel (*The Glory of the Conquered*, 1909), spent a year abroad (in the Latin Quarter in Paris), and on her return to the United States went to a ranch in Idaho. In 1913, she married George Cram Cook and they went to Provincetown to live.

The story of those remarkable Davenport years has been preserved in two fine books, Susan Glaspell's *The Road to the Temple* (1927) and Floyd Dell's *Homecoming* (1933). Some of it is fictionized in Dell's *Moon-Calf* (1920), and in one of George Cram Cook's abortive unfinished novels. *Homecoming* contains a brief quote from this novel, and it contains many of Dell's and Ficke's poems as well.

Moon-Calf is one of Dell's two fictional autobiographies; *Briary Bush* (1921) is the second. *Moon-Calf* is a novel of the development of a poet and Socialist with agnostic ideas; Felix Fay's birth and early life in Maple, his removal to Vickley, and his coming to Port Royal follow closely details of Dell's life in Barry, Quincy, and Davenport, as recorded in Dell's autobiography, *Homecoming*. But the fictional study of an awkward genius who bumbles his way through life has a quality of its own unlike the quality of the factual account. This account of the growth of a poet's mind, while not as well documented with actual samples of Dell's verse as the autobiography, has a poetic and spiritual quality missing in the later book. Dell has an eminently readable prose style which holds up well a half-century later; there is nothing at all of a period quality in his novel.

The novel which Miss Glaspell had read to Dell and Cook is a romantic story whose subtitle "The Story of a Great Love" indicates its theme. It

---

10   Dell, *Homecoming: An Autobiography*, p. 151.

is set in a badly-realized Chicago. Despite Cook's and Dell's reactions, the book turned out to be a best seller. "Either 'Susan Glaspell' is a *nom de plume*," said one critic, "or else an entirely new writer of importance has emerged." And the *New York Times* said gravely: "It is not often that a new writer comes forward with a first book so worthy of serious attention as is Miss Glaspell's notable romance."[11]

The Visioning (1911), perhaps because of the comments and advice of two skilled critics (Cook and Dell) is a better novel. It is set on Rock Island in the Mississippi River opposite Davenport—a setting Alice French had used for one of her short stories. *The Visioning* is a novel about social classes and their differences—the girls who work in the Fairport candy factory at fifty cents and a dollar a day, and the young women who live in the big houses on the hill and plan garden parties for the factory girls at which it is hoped they will learn "better management"; the officers, secure in their world of the Arsenal, playing golf and cantering on their horses, and the enlisted men, doing the dirty work of the army, and wondering about their attitudes toward "their betters." There are also men in the Arsenal shops who cast dirty looks at their superiors, particularly when their superiors make no effort to understand them. Alice French had seen this world, but her Arsenal story had been about a golf match and the ladies and gentlemen taking part in it. She had also seen the shanties of the workers and she knew of Socialist philosophies. But Miss French had made no real effort to step down from her patrician viewpoint—she could discuss his working day with her brother Robert, but apparently she could not learn to sympathize with the ordinary worker or his viewpoint.

The novel, whose heroine changes just as Miss Glaspell must have been changing under the influence of Cook and Dell, is a much better novel than Miss Glaspell's first, but it is still not entirely successful. She still has the romantic urge to pair up her men and women at the end of the novel, and sometimes her style is ambiguous. But, as Professor Arthur E. Waterman says, *The Visioning* indicates that its author was beginning to realize that her art had to speak first to the present about the political and social ideas of the immediate scene.[12]

In Provincetown in 1913, the affairs of George Cram Cook and Susan Glaspell took a turn that was to make theatrical history. In 1911, in Maurice Brown's Chicago Little Theater, Cook had seen a performance of Euripides' *The Trojan Women*. He loved all things Greek, and he began to wonder about doing something similar elsewhere—in a theater such as Brown's. In New York, Cook and Miss Glaspell were bored by the

---

11   Bullock, "Conflict in a Modern Midwest Family."
12   Arthur E. Waterman, *Susan Glaspell* (New York: Twayne Publishers, 1966), p. 38.

Broadway productions—they didn't appeal to the imagination as Brown's play did. Moreover, Cook had been impressed by the Irish Players: "Quite possibly," Susan Glaspell said later, "there would have been no Provincetown Players had there been no Irish Players. What [Cook] saw done for Irish life he wanted for American life—on stage conventions in the way of projecting with the humility of true feeling."

When in 1914 the Washington Square Players made their inauspicious start they inspired Cook and Miss Glaspell to write the one-act play, *Suppressed Desires*. When the Washington Square Players (later to become the Theater Guild) would not perform the play, Cook and Miss Glaspell performed it on their own in an old fish-house at the end of a Provincetown wharf owned by a friend, Mary Heaton Vorse, calling themselves the Provincetown Players.

In 1916 the Provincetown Players and Eugene O'Neill discovered each other. That summer, the Players presented O'Neill's *Bound East for Cardiff* and Miss Glaspell's *Trifles* (which she converted later into the short story, "A Jury of Her Peers"). Professor Crawford has called *Suppressed Desires* and *Trifles* two of the best short plays in English.

After two successful seasons on the Wharf, Cook brought the Players to Greenwich Village. There, at Eugene O'Neill's suggestion the name was changed to the Playwright's Theatre.

Meanwhile Miss Glaspell was continuing to write short stories and her novel, *Fidelity* (1915). Many Iowa authors have written briefly about the effects of small town gossiping and rumor mongering—Corey, Kantor, Downing, to name three—but *Fidelity* is the first and only book-length fictional study of the effects of social and personal attitudes devolving out of a tightly knit small town social structure—the sort of attitudes of which gossip and rumors are symptomatic.

Fidelity is the story of the love affair of an unmarried woman with a married man and the consequences for the couple, their families, their friends, and their community because of their decision to live together, even though the man can not get a divorce from his wife. Miss Glaspell could write of such a situation at first hand, for she had loved a married man (Cook) and must have experienced first-hand the consequences of that love in a small midwestern community. *Fidelity* is a detailed study and a good one of small town manners and morals—of social relationships where all are of the same class and one member has betrayed the class by violating its code of morals and manners. In the novel the class members band together to present a united front against the betrayer.

In *The Visioning* Miss Glaspell had counter-pointed the opposing viewpoints of the two central feminine characters. In *Fidelity* she allowed each of the chief characters in the story to express his own attitudes by using each one in turn as the point of view. The result was a deliberate ambiguity about the issues at stake.

Taking each of her first three novels in sequence, one can see the improvements in technique, style, character development, and level of idea that Miss Glaspell was making. She was not only learning from Cook—she was also learning from O'Neill and the others she was meeting in The Players, and she was learning as well from the demands the writing of drama makes on an author.

"Finality in Freeport" (1916) is a story which also reflects small town attitudes. It is an outgrowth of an earlier incident in Davenport. A distinguished liberal theologian, George Burman Foster, had written a book, *The Finality of the Christian Religion*, which the Davenport Public Library had refused to buy. The Monist Society, George Cram Cook and Susan Glaspell had taken up the issue in an epistolary war directed at the newspapers; businessmen debated the issue on street corners; Dr. Foster came to Davenport to address a huge meeting; and a new mayor came into office on his pledge that he would appoint a Library Board which would buy the book.

The story is a satire on the "Midwestern pretentiousness and cultural aspirations" of Freeport. Miss Glaspell, living in Greenwich Village, looks back at her home town with a mocking tone. Her satire works because she knows the Midwest; she is aware that the frontier is just past: "Some of us were children of pioneers; some of us still drove Grandmother to the Old Settler's Picnic the middle of August."[13] But she is also aware of the town's "humorless pursuit of culture," its feeling that its people "are as good as anybody," the conflict between an "over-cautious morality" and "an insistence on freedom."[14] These themes were to appear again in her final novel.

Miss Glaspell and George Cram Cook were actively engaged in the Playwright's Theatre from 1915 to 1922. Cook wrote *The Athenian Women* (1918), produced and directed plays, and managed the playhouse and the acting companies. Miss Glaspell acted in plays and wrote both one-act and three-act plays: *The People* (1917), *Close the Book* (1917), *The Outside* (1917), *Woman's Honor* (1918), *Tickless Time* (1918) in collaboration with Cook, *Bernice* (1919), *Inheritors* (1921), *The Verge* (1921), *Chains of Dew* (1922) unpublished, *The Comic Artist* (1928) with Norman Matson, and *Alison's House* (1930). Her best short stories of this period are "The Busy Duck" (1918), "The Escape," (1919), "Government Goat," (1918), "The Hearing Ear," (1917), "Jury of Her

---

13 Glaspell, *The Road to the Temple,* p. 193.
14 Waterman, *Susan Glaspell,* p. 26.

Peers," (1917), and "Pollen" (1919). Not all of her plays or stories have Iowa as their subject.

Writing for the stage taught Miss Glaspell a number of skills which are reflected in the increasing quality of her fiction—the necessity of visualizing a scene, the necessity of developing well-realized characters, the values of conciseness and compactness, the technique of building to a climax, and the techniques of reporting speech.

Close the Book is the first of two of Miss Glaspell's plays to be set in a middle western university town, and to be focused on descendants of the founders of each school. Both deal with unconventionality of behavior and freedom of speech, and with the function of the university. (Both, incidentally, have many echoes of the dramatic style of George Bernard Shaw.)

Close the Book is a comedy whose themes are the "crevices in these walls of respectability" which people build up around their lives through reliance on such things as family trees, and the roles of teachers and students: "What business has a professor of English to say anything about society?" a character asks.

The *Inheritors* is set in a middle western farm house on the bank of the Mississippi River in 1879; in a corridor in the library of Morton College in October of 1920, on the occasion of the fortieth anniversary of the founding of the college; and a few weeks later, again at the farm house. In the 1879 scene the characters are Silas Morton, his mother, and Felix Fejevary; in 1920 they are Felix's son (also named Felix), and the younger Felix's son, Horace; Ira Morton, Silas Morton's son; Madeline Fejevary Morton, Silas's granddaughter; Professor Holden, and a state senator. A major theme of the play is the erosion of the principles on which the college was founded.

Inheritors is a play of ideas—so many that not all are resolved. "But that a dramatist of ideas has taken her place in the theater, of that there can be no doubt," said J. Ranken Towse, who like other critics noted that "history and literature were being made" in the "little, rather dingy, but proudly insurgent theatre" on MacDougal Street.[15] *Inheritors*, moreover, demonstrates the influence of life in Greenwich Village: "I like in memory the flavor of those days when one could turn down Greenwich Avenue to the office of the *Masses*," she said later, "argue with Max [Eastman] or Floyd [Dell, who with Eastman was to face a Federal Court because of the ideas expressed in the *Masses*] or Jack Reed; then after an encounter with some fanatic at the Liberal Club, or (better luck) tea with

---

15   J. Rankin Towse, "The Play," *New York Evening Post* (March 23, 1921), p. 9.

Henrietta Rodman, on to the Working Girl's Club (it's a saloon, not a charitable organization) or if the check had come, to the Brevoort."[16]

Inheritors begins with Silas Morton who "sets great store by learning—and freedom," and who decides to give the most attractive part of his pioneer farm (which had been taken from the Indians for a pittance) to establish a "college in the cornfields" because of his admiration for his friend, Felix Fejevary, a man of learning who had fought for freedom in Hungary in 1848: "There will one day be a college in these cornfields by the Mississippi because long ago a great dream was fought for in Hungary."

The scene shifts to the library of Silas Morton College. The younger Felix, chairman of the Board of Trustees, is pleading with Senator Lewis for a state appropriation which will aid the growth of the college. Lewis demurs—the campus has "a pretty radical man," Professor Holden. Outside, students led by Horace Fejevary are harassing two students from India who are protesting the deportation of a third Indian student for political reasons. Madeline Fejevary Morton joins the Indians' side and assaults a policeman with her tennis racket. Professor Holden is on her side, but he has a sick wife and needs an increase in salary—an increase which can come only if the state makes an appropriation. Madeline's father, Ira Morton, a breeder of championship corn, is so concerned with his personal problems he cannot see what is happening. Thus the issues are joined, to be worked out by the chauvinistic senator, the practical and conforming elder Fejevary, the idealistic Madeline, the tragic Ira, the vacillating Holden, and the hotheaded rightist Horace.

Although Alexander Wolcott was unhappy with the play, other critics were warm in their praise. Floyd Dell said that the "justification of the Provincetown Players' existence—aside from discovering Eugene O'Neill, a mixed blessing, . . . was in two plays":

. . . one was Susan Glaspell's *The Inheritors;* a beautiful, true, brave play of war-time. In this play Susan Glaspell brought to triumphant fruition something that was George Cook's, in a way that he never could—something earthy, sweet and beautiful that had not been in her work before. To much that was in her plays I was not responsive—*Bernice* was not for me. But to my mind *The Inheritors* was a high moment in American drama.[17]

And Ludwig Lewisohn said:

It is the first play of the American theatre in which a strong intellect and a ripe artistic nature have grasped and set forth in human terms the central tradi-

---

16   Glaspell, *The Road to the Temple*, p. 247.
17   Dell, *Homecoming: An Autobiography*, p. 267.

tion and most burning problem of our national life, quite justly and scrupulously, without acrimony and compromise.[18]

In March of 1922 Susan Glaspell and George Cram Cook went to Greece and took up residence on Mt. Parnassus, living the same life as the Greek peasants until Cook died in 1924, a Greek national hero. (Miss Glaspell has recorded these years in her biography of Cook.) From 1928 to 1931, she was married to Norman Matson. Until she died in July 1948, she made her home on Cape Cod.

Back in America, Miss Glaspell began writing novels once more (she wrote two more plays and the biography of Cook): *Brook Evans* (1928); *Fugitive's Return* (1929); *Ambrose Holt and Family* (1930); *The Morning is Near Us* (1939); *Norma Ashe* (1942); *Judd Rankin's Daughter* (1945). In 1925, she collected Cook's poetry in *Greek Coins;* to the collection she added an essay of her own and one each by Floyd Dell and Edna Kenton which help illuminate Cook's life.

Brook Evans is a novel of three generations: Naomi Kellogg, her daughter Brook Evans, and Brook's son, Evans Leonard. The story ranges in time from 1890 to 1920, in setting from the Middle West to Colorado and Paris, and back to the Middle West where Evans Leonard comes to an understanding of himself. In 1930 Paramount Pictures made the film *The Right to Love* from the book. It starred Ann Harding in her second Glaspell role; the first had been as Madeline Fejevary Morton in *Inheritors* on the Playwright's stage.

Fugitive's Return uses Miss Glaspell's personal experience of childhood in Davenport and life in Greece as a basis for a novel of a middle western woman who becomes an exiled recluse in Greece. Portions of the Greek section are an accurate account of persons and places she and Cook had known in Greece.

The novel is divided into three parts—an initial section which describes the protagonist's attempted suicide and her arrival in Greece, a center section which (using the device of the flashback, a favorite Glaspell technique) describes how, in her small town middle western childhood, she became the sort of woman she is, and a final section which describes her return to a normal life.

Critics noted the dichotomy in the book between Christianity and classic paganism deriving from Miss Glaspell's attempt to equate her understanding of Cook's idealism and passion for things Greek with her own sense

---

18 Ludwig Lewisohn, *Nation* 112 (April 6, 1921). See also Lewisohn's *Expression in America* (New York: Harper & Bros., 1932), p. 395. Pp. 391–99 contain an essay on Glaspell's contribution to the theater.

of values growing out of her roots in the Midwest.[19] Professor Waterman concluded:

> In its treatment of an American who finds his native moral and ethical values strengthened through the influence of a foreign culture, *Fugitive's Return* is like Henry James's *The Ambassadors*. . . . The enormous differences, however, between these two international novels—differences in style, characterization, range, control, and complexity of theme—indicate the kind of artistic problems that Miss Glaspell had to solve for each new novel.[20]

For *Alison's House*, Miss Glaspell turned her attention to the American poet, Emily Dickinson. She had been reading Genevieve Taggard's *The Life and Mind of Emily Dickinson*, and wanted to use the poet as the subject of a play which would have as its theme the artist's conflict with the world. But Miss Dickinson's family—perhaps much like the Stanhope family in the play—would not let her use Emily's name or her poetry. So Miss Glaspell set her play near a "small midwestern city" on the Mississippi and used Emerson's poems. But Alison Stanhope looks a lot like Emily Dickinson. The burden of the play is the family's division over releasing information about the dead poet and some of her unpublished poems to the public for fear of unwelcome publicity.

Two of the elements that give the play its power are its compactness—it is confined to Alison's house and a few hours of time—and its focus on an off-stage personality who is never seen. Miss Glaspell's best work—this play, *Trifles*, "A Jury of Her Peers," *Bernice*—as well as *Brook Evans* (where the dead Naomi continues to dominate the novel in spirit) use this device effectively. The reader or playgoer is able to let his imagination play over the character of the unseen woman.

Perhaps because of the success of the Civic Repertory Theatre's production of the play, with Eva Le Gallienne playing the part of Elsa Stanhope (a character quite reminiscent of Ruth Holland in *Fidelity*), as much as for the qualities of the play itself, *Alison's House* won the 1931 Pulitzer Prize for drama. Many critics, however, thought that Philip Barry's *Tomorrow and Tomorrow* or Lynn Rigg's *Green Grow the Lilacs* (the basis ten years later for the musical play *Oklahoma!*) were better possibilities.

Miss Glaspell was at the half-century point in her life, but her three best novels were yet to be written. "The future of this distinguished daughter of Iowa intrigues the imagination," said a close friend in 1930 just before the production of *Alison's House*. "Just now at her prime as writers go,

19   Myron Brynig, *New York Times*, April 12, 1931, p. 4.
20   Waterman, *Susan Glaspell*, p. 98.

with her rare mental and spiritual gifts, with a record of much fine work done, the high adventure of Provincetown and Greenwich Village behind her—the high tragedy of Greece among her memories—how may she not write now?"[21]

Ambrose Holt and Family is, like some other themes of Miss Glaspell's, a theme considered twice. When she went to Greece with Cook, she left behind a play, *Chains of Dew* which, as it turned out, was the last play performed by the Players. *Chains of Dew* was acted but never published and no manuscript of it has been found. But we know that the play was about a middle western poet whose radical friends felt that he would be a greater poet if only he could be freed from the chains that bound him— his home, his wife, his mother, and his position of prominence in his small midwestern home town. Ultimately the friends learn that the poet is a prig, that the wife is the real liberal in the family. At the end of the play, however, the wife sacrifices her own individuality "and becomes once more a wife and mother, in order to provide the proper atmosphere of oppression which her husband needs in order to write poetry."[22]

The theme of the novel is much the same, though the details are different—the poet's father (Ambrose Holt) plays a strong part in the novel. And, perhaps, the novel ends on a happier note with the poet treating his wife as the woman she is. "It is almost a sentimental book," said John Chamberlain, "but Miss Glaspell's humor—a delicately pervasive humor, akin to that of the Emily Dickinson who could forgive God his duplicity —acts as the perpetual astringent that more than cuts the glycerine."

Chamberlain provides a perceptive insight into Miss Glaspell's larger purpose in her work:

Miss Glaspell is all for uncovering the idealist and letting him live in his glory. But most idealists, and most idolators of idealists, seem a little alien, and books about them a little too self-consciously noble. Idealists are like ghosts; they can't rest, and they are forever clanking chains that disturb the neighbors in their sleep. They are seemingly menaces in a world in which the norm lies across the doldrums. But under the skin, of course, they are lovable, and Miss Glaspell knows it. And because she treats them with the amused tolerance, mingled with protective compassion, that one would accord a household pet, she is the best person in the world to act as mediator between the idealist and the rest of humanity. Her husband, George Cram Cook . . . needed just such a mediator, and in *The Road to the Temple*, a biography of that husband which is a great American document, Miss Glaspell shows how he got it. In *Brook Evans* . . . she acted as the interpreter for another idealist who was unduly bruised by the impact of all that was worst in the "genteel tradition" of the

21 Gladys Denny Shultz, "Susan Glaspell," in *A Book of Iowa Authors*, pp. 121–22.
22 Heywood Broun, *New York World*, April 29, 1922, p. 11.

American '80s. . . . *Alison's House* . . . does its best . . . to mediate between the world and a poet [Emily Dickinson] who is only now beginning to be understood. . . . In [*Ambrose Holt*] Miss Glaspell tackles other idealists. It is difficult to see how she could write of anything else, for her life and art are all of a piece, and she believes in cultivating her garden.[23]

The Morning is Near Us sets the theme of the conflicting values of the small town with those of more exotic places against a riddle—what dark events have taken place in the Chippman house and family which cloud the past and present of Lydian, the heroine? Many critics thought that the "mystery of Lydian's past [was] a trick to raise suspense," but Professor Waterman thinks otherwise:

. . . it is a symbol of the fear and chaos that the past contains along with its beauty and meaning. . . . *The Morning is Near Us* is Susan Glaspell's most successful presentation of the meaning of the Midwestern heritage for the individual seeking a complete life.[24]

Norma Ashe considers the problem of idealism and idealists in the twentieth century materialistic world. The novel focuses on the careers of five people who, in a small South Dakota college, have been taught by a professor to live their lives so as to produce a better world. Professor Waterman says that the novel "continues the condemnation of postwar America found in *Inheritors,* and it shows us that both Madeline Morton's insistence on the worth of her idealism and Norma Ashe's inability to come to terms with her world symbolize the failure of the midwestern idealist to adjust to present day reality."[25]

Judd Rankin's Daughter, Miss Glaspell's last and perhaps best novel, is a "clarion call" directed against the provincialism of the Midwest—"not its too-tough, too-tender hide (though [perhaps] she is after that too!) but to get its warm heart: to coax and challenge it to action in the directions its loyal daughter thinks it ought to go."[26] Through its focus on a small town midwestern newspaper editor (who may have been modeled after William Allen White, the Kansas journalist), the novel debates the "Bible Belt's" smugness, self-satisfaction, and narrow-mindedness—as Miss Glaspell saw it.

As a writer of short stories Miss Glaspell produced one good story which demonstrated, before Hemingway, the values in a compact dramat-

23   John Chamberlain, "A Tragi-Comedy of Realism in Miss Glaspell's Novel," *New York Times,* April 12, 1931, p. 4.
24   Waterman, *Susan Glaspell,* pp. 106, 107.
25   Waterman, *Susan Glaspell,* p. 111.
26   Bullock, "Conflict in a Modern Midwest Family."

ically written tale. As a novelist she did nothing new. She began as a local colorist, using many of the devices of romantic fiction, then became a regionalist and realist, though her novels retained romantic elements. Theatrical influences, such as the use of the flashback and extensive passages of dialogue with very little action, colored the structure of her later best novels. Although as a novelist she never attained the stature of a Willa Cather, among Iowa novelists she must rank with Ruth Suckow. She did attain a popular success—*The Morning is Near Us* was a 1940 Literary Guild Selection—but perhaps not as great as Phil Stong's.

It is as a dramatist that Miss Glaspell's reputation reached its peak. With Eugene O'Neill she gave the American theater direction and the beginnings of a tradition which it never had before. Rejecting previous theatrical models, she experimented, and it is perhaps as an experimenter rather than as a systematic dramatist that she will be remembered. Her plays still hold the stage—*Inheritors*, for example, is as timely today as when it was written.

As a final note the remarks of two theatrical historians should be repeated:

She was one of the finest actresses in the [Provincetown Players]; she played Henrietta Brewster in *Suppressed Desires*, the Woman from Idaho in *The People*, Mrs. Root in *Close the Book*, and The Cheated One in *Woman's Honor*. Years later . . . Jacques Copeau . . . came to the Provincetown to see her *Inheritors*. It happened that Ann Harding, who was playing the leading role, was ill that evening and Susan stepped into the part. The following day Copeau devoted the greater part of a lecture to a eulogy of her performance. He called her "a truly great actress."[27]

The first part of Harry Hansen's novel, *Your Life Lies Before You* (1935), is set in the Davenport of his early newspaper reporting days. The novel is the story of a Davenport newspaper reporter who has to make a choice between his newspaper career and a career as a concert violinist for which he has some possibilities. There are some good things in the novel: the description of the Davenport waterfront at the turn of the century, the life in the newspaper editorial rooms of the time, the picture of the small town musical scene—the concert, the music teachers, the musical groups, and the like. As a music critic, Hansen came to know this scene very well, and he has preserved it for us.[28]

---

27 Helen Deutsch and Stella Hanau, *The Provincetown: A Story of the Theatre* (New York: Farrar & Rinehart, 1931), pp. 24–25.
28 In the *Palimpsest* of April 1956, Harry Hansen has described the composition of *Your Life Lies Before You* (New York: Harcourt, Brace and Co., 1935).

Arthur Davison Ficke was born at Davenport, November 10, 1883, the son of German emigrants, Fannie Davison and Charles August Ficke. The Fickes were friends of the family of Alice French; George W. French, Alice's brother and Charles August Ficke were two of the founders of the Contemporary Club.

The history of the Ficke family is in Charles August Ficke's *Memories of Fourscore Years* (Davenport, 1930). The Ficke family traveled exten- sively—to Mexico, to the Middle East, to the Orient—and Mr. Ficke pur- chased rare books, artifacts such as mummies and mummy cases, paintings and prints, manuscripts, and the like. Most, if not all of this material now forms the core of the collections in the Davenport Public Museum and the Davenport Municipal Art Gallery.

Arthur Davison Ficke attended public schools in Davenport and then matriculated at Harvard University where he studied under William James and George Santayana, and where two of his classmates were Franklin Delano Roosevelt and Witter Bynner. Bynner was also to become a poet and a lifelong friend of Ficke's as well.

Ficke graduated from Harvard in 1904 and that summer began a ten- month long trip around the world with his father, mother, and two sis- ters. Some of the poems he published in his first volumes of verse, *From the Isles* (1907), and *The Happy Princess* (1907), are based on observa- tions he made on the trip.

From 1906 to 1907 he was at the University of Iowa where he taught a course on the Arthurian Legend and completed work on a law degree. He was in partnership with his father until 1918, at which time a gift from his father made it possible for him to give up law for a career as a poet. During the ten years of his law practice, he found time to write eight books of poetry, a poetic drama on the problems of labor and management, and two studies of Japanese painters and prints.

One of his poems was "An Outrageous Person to Floyd Dell":

> God forgive you, O my friend!
> For, to be sure men never will.
> Their most righteous wrath shall bend
>   Toward you all the strokes of ill.
>
> You are outcast—Who could bear,
> Laboring dully, to behold
> That glad carelessness you wear,
>   Dancing down the sunlight's gold? . . .[29]

---

29 Dell, *Homecoming,* pp. 235–36, reprints the whole poem. With two minor varia- tions, it is also found in Arthur Davison Ficke's *Selected Poems* (New York: George H. Doran Co., 1926), p. 177.

In 1912 the magazine *Poetry* was founded in Chicago. The first two poems in the first issue were sonnets by Arthur Ficke. Two years later his 1914 volume, *Sonnets of a Portrait Painter,* served notice on the American literary public that a "distinguished poet and one of America's most expert sonneteers" had arrived on the scene.

The Man on the Hilltop (1915) followed, and then one day in the autumn of 1916, "magazine editors and reviewers of poetry found on their desks a new and quite unobtrusive-looking volume of verse of some sixty-odd pages," *Spectra.* The volume of "New Poems" was the work of co-authors Emanuel Morgan and Anne Knish; the preface by Miss (Mrs.?) Knish announced that the volume was "the first compilation of the recent experiments in Spectra. It is the aim of the Spectric group to push the possibilities of poetic expression into a new region . . . ."

In a day when "schools" of poetry were springing up in every garret in the land, critics turned to the "Spectric" group joyously. Two years later, these same critics had an opportunity to recant when it was revealed that *Spectra* had been a hoax, planned by Witter Bynner ("Morgan") and Arthur Ficke ("Knish") in February 1916, in Davenport. Put out of the Ficke home when Mrs. Ficke had found the process of recitation and composition too much for her, the men had gone across the river to a Moline, Illinois, hotel where "from ten quarts of scotch in ten days they extracted the whole of Spectric philosophy."[30]

After the entrance of the United States into the First World War, Ficke was commissioned a captain and served overseas until July 1919 when he was discharged as a lieutenant colonel. One of his poems expresses his mood at one point in the war:

> . . . We shall not live to see the day of peace
> That men will make sometime, somewhere, somehow—
> See ignorant mobs bring their new hates to birth
> And celebrate them with the conqueror's drum.
> Their secret madness will possess the earth
> When the frank madness of the guns is dumb. . . .
> If we return, be it with savage mirth
> To loathe the thing we fought for, and called home.[31]

Some of Ficke's poetry was topical (one poem to his father showed "how profoundly [he] longed to be released from the law so that he might turn to literature"); a great deal of it was romantic, about the far-

---

30 William Jay Smith, *The Spectra Hoax* (Middletown, Conn.: Wesleyan University Press, 1961) is my source for this incident.
31 Arthur Davison Ficke, "October First, 1918," *Selected Poems* (New York: George H. Doran Co., 1926), p. 61.

away places he had seen and visited. But some of his poetry showed a concern for social ills:

> And one of my friends was battered into a pulp by the police
> Because he dared to say in Indiana
> That it is indecent to starve men and women and children
> Who work in factories. . . .
>   I, like you, my friend, see much—and am powerless.
> I see the desperate houses of coal-miners in Pennsylvania.
> And the bleak homesteads of farmers in Iowa.
> I see the faces of hopeless men in the streets of New York
> And the faces of lazy men everywhere who are fattening on
>   the nation, like tent-worms.
> The politicians run about making noises like hollow gourds that
>   have gall-stones inside them,
> And the wisdom of today is the manifest folly of tomorrow. . . .[32]

In 1922 he published this tribute to Alice French in *Scribner's* (but he did not admit that his "princess" was Alice):

"My Princess"

I

> I have known but one princess in my day. . . .
> I always knew that princesses would wear
> Long strings of pearls wound through their golden hair,—
> That they were young and delicate as some fay
> Caught in mid-forest, and that smiles must live
> Like sunlight in the swift blue of their eyes.
> A princess, though a hunted fugitive,
> Surely trails her cloud of mysteries!
> But this my princess was distressed and tired,
> Her eyes were puffy and her hands were old;
> She had forgotten all she once desired;
> Eternal grayness held her in its fold:—
> A sick old woman, shuffling down the way.
> That leads to where the story's end is told.

II

> And yet a princess is a princess still,
> Though she remembers 40 years behind,

---

32 Arthur Davison Ficke, *The Secret and Other Poems* (New York: Doubleday, Doran & Co., 1936), pp. 8–10.

The days when lovers to the Hollow Hill
Came for her sake, and lonely, bitter, blind,
My princess was my princess as she said—
"I will deny while I have living breath,
All that is lonely, bitter, blind," she said:
"I will allege life though I look on death.
All things are nothing. Happiness is a dream.
Yet, now that I am honored with the old
I will contest everything but that gleam
Which makes, a little while, the days of gold.
Spare me your kindness:—For my pennon shall stream,
Down to the place where the story's end is told.[33]

No biography or critical estimate of Ficke has yet been written. He was a man of many talents and many friends, and something more needs to be said about him.

---

33 Arthur Davison Ficke, "My Princess," *Scribner's Magazine* 72 (December 1922), p. 666.

A New Athens?

"THE last time I saw him," said Floyd Dell of George Cram Cook, "he said half in jest, half in earnest, 'Floyd, let's gather the old Davenport crowd together, and go back there and make it a new Athens!'"[1] The affairs of their lives took Dell, Glaspell, Ficke, Hansen, and Cook along other routes, but in the nineteen-twenties and -thirties, an Athens of sorts was created among the pigs and cornfields of Iowa. Its heart was the University of Iowa with its School of Letters under the guidance of Wilbur Schramm, Norman Foerster, and Edwin Ford Piper offering new programs which led to Master of Fine Arts and Doctor of Philosophy degrees for creative theses.

This spirit of creativity was not to be limited to Iowa City alone; it was to overflow into Des Moines at Drake University (under the direction of Professor and Mrs. Lewis Worthington Smith), into Cedar Rapids at Coe College (under the leadership of Vernon Lichtenstein), into Mt. Vernon at Cornell College (under the genius of "Toppy" and Jewel Tull), and, as we have seen, into Dubuque, under the tutelage of Karlton Kelm.

Nor was this spirit of creativity to be limited to literature alone. A new theater and a new art building came into being at Iowa City, an art colony sprang into existence at Stone City, and art galleries were opened in several Iowa towns. Community symphony orchestras flourished.

The names that came into view in those two decades—Paul Engle, Grant Wood, Tom Duncan, MacKinlay Kantor, Hartzell Spence, Verlin Cassill, Carl Van Vechten, Winifred Mayne Van Etten, James Stevens, Wallace Stegner, Jay Sigmund, James Hearst, Phil Stong, Margaret Wilson, Josephine Donovan, Ruth Suckow, Josephine Herbst, James Norman Hall—were to attract the eyes of the cultured world to the Hawkeye State. Iowa books and paintings were reviewed in New York and the East, and translated into foreign tongues; the *New Yorker* could make its

---

1 Floyd Dell, "A Seer in Iowa," in George Cram Cook, *Greek Coins* (New York: George H. Doran Co., 1925), p. 16. The same remark is quoted in Susan Glaspell's *The Road to the Temple* and Floyd Dell's *Homecoming*.

jokes about the "little old lady from Dubuque," but *New Yorker* critics were commenting seriously about Iowa creations.

Carl Van Vechten was not directly a part of this scene, but because he flourished during the twenties he seemed to be—especially because the people of Iowa of that decade and the next took a warm interest in the artistic achievements of native sons and daughters, wherever they were. It was a natural consequence when citizens of Cedar Rapids were talking about what Grant Wood was up to at No. 5 Turner Alley, and what young Paul Engle and Robert Downing were doing at Washington High School, and what Jay Sigmund's most recent poem had been about, to turn the conversation to a man who was writing flamboyant novels about New York and Paris and Hollywood—a man who was a close friend of Gertrude Stein and Alice B. Toklas and F. Scott Fitzgerald—a man whose books were being published by Alfred A. Knopf who was also publishing Ruth Suckow and John T. Frederick.

Carl Van Vechten was born in Cedar Rapids on June 17, 1880, the son of Carl Duane and Ada Amanda Fitch Van Vechten. He was a graduate of Columbia Law School; she was a graduate of Kalamazoo College. There was an older brother, Ralph (born 1862), and an older sister, Emma (born 1864).

Writing in *The Borzoi* in 1920, Carl Van Vechten said of his birthday that it was the "one day in . . . the year which is every way worthy of being a birthday . . . a day on which charming people are born. . . . Nothing can be expected of [them] and everything!"[2]

Carl was educated in the Cedar Rapids public schools; there were magazines, books and music in his home, and he attended plays and operettas at Greene's Opera House in downtown Cedar Rapids. One of his friends was Mahala Dutton Benedict Douglas, whose family was associated with the Quaker Oats Company and the Douglas Starch Works. Many people in Cedar Rapids considered her too "emancipated." One day Carl said to her, "I'm so damn bored with this town, I'd like to put on a bath towel and run through the streets naked." Mrs. Douglas went into the house without a word; a few moments later she was back with a towel. "Go ahead, Carl," she said. And that, Van Vechten said years later, put him in his place. The Douglas home at that time was the one which later became the site of the Turner Funeral Home; it was the carriage house in the rear which the Turners made available to Grant Wood as the site for his studio.

---

2 Quoted from Bruce Kellner, *Carl Van Vechten and the Irreverent Decades* (Norman: University of Oklahoma Press, 1968), p. 6, who in turn is quoting from Carl Van Vechten, "On the Advantages of Being Born on the Seventeenth of June," *The Borzoi 1920* (New York: Alfred A. Knopf, 1920), pp. 49–51.

But Cedar Rapidians like Mahala Douglas were rare, and perhaps more than once, Carl Van Vechten said what Gareth Johns was to say in his *The Tattooed Countess:*

I want to know everything, *everything* . . . and . . . I'm going to. . . . I want to get away from this town. . . . I want to visit the theatre and the art galleries. I want to meet people. I want to learn. Somewhere there must be more people like me.

The words were almost identical to those uttered just a few years later by the young Felix Fay of Floyd Dell's *Moon-Calf*. A half-century before many young men in the East had turned their eyes westward to lands of new opportunities—now at the turn of the twentieth century the eyes of many young western men looked back toward the East.

In 1899 Carl Van Vechten left Cedar Rapids to go to the University of Chicago. He was there until 1903, majoring in English, and then worked for two years for the *Chicago American*. George Cram Cook had told young Floyd Dell that working on a newspaper was good experience for a budding poet. But Van Vechten said: "I think it's the worst thing in the world for anybody to do who wants to be in writing, but I wanted to go on a paper."[3]

From 1906 on he was in New York, working as a music critic for the *New York Times* (he had been fired in Chicago because he had "lowered the tone of the Hearst newspapers").[4] In 1907 he married Anna Elizabeth Snyder, whom he had met while playing golf in Cedar Rapids. They were wed in London on a trip financed by the elder Van Vechten, whose estate was eventually to make his son a rather wealthy man.

For the next several years Van Vechten worked as a Paris correspondent for the *New York Times*, wrote symphony program notes and musical biographies, was a dramatic critic for the *New York Post*, and, beginning in 1915, wrote several books about music and cats—two of his life-long loves. He was divorced from Anna Snyder in 1912; in 1914 he married Fania Marinoff, an actress; the marriage was to last a half century until Carl's death.

In 1922 Van Vechten turned to the writing of novels and in the next six years he turned out one novel a year—at which point he stopped writing novels. Four of the novels are set in New York: *Peter Whiffle* (1922), *The Blind Bow-Boy* (1923), *Firecrackers* (1925), and *Nigger Heaven* (1926). One, *Spider Boy* (1928) is set in Hollywood and the southwest.

The scene of *Nigger Heaven* is primarily the Negro Harlem of the

---

3 Edward Lueders, *Carl Van Vechten* (New York: Twayne Publishers, 1965), p. 23.
4 Lueders, p. 24.

nineteen-twenties, a world which Van Vechten had come to know intimately. It is one of the earliest studies of the Negro scene by a white who knew what he was writing about; moreover it is honest and sympathetic, as Van Vechten's literary Negro friends knew—James Weldon Johnson, Countee Cullen, Langston Hughes, and others. Although there were those who complained about the title, the title was authentic for its times; moreover it is a symbol of the situation of the Harlem Negro, then and now:

Nigger Heaven! Byron moaned. Nigger Heaven! That's what Harlem is. We sit in our places in the gallery of this New York theatre and watch the white world sitting down below in the good seats in the orchestra. Occasionally they turn their faces up toward us, their hard, cruel faces, to laugh or sneer, but they never beckon. It never seems to occur to them that Nigger Heaven is crowded, that there isn't another seat, that something has to be done. It doesn't seem to occur to them either . . . that we sit above them, that we can drop things down on them and crush them, that we can swoop down from this Nigger Heaven and take their seats. No, they have no fear of that. Harlem! The Mecca of the New Negro! My God![5]

The term, as this quotation implies, comes from the theatrical world; for years American theaters permitted Negroes to sit only in the back seats of the balcony, or in a special gallery above the balcony and just under the ceiling at the rear of the auditorium. Greene's Opera House in Cedar Rapids, the model for the "Hall's Opera House" of *The Tattooed Countess*, had a "nigger heaven."

The Tattooed Countess is set in "Maple Valley," Iowa, in 1897. Cedar Rapids readers had no trouble at all identifying Maple Valley sites with Cedar Rapids sites, and many insisted that the novel's characters were for the most part all too thinly disguised Cedar Rapidians of the late eighteen-nineties; all this despite a "red herring" mention in the novel of Cedar Rapids as being a nearby town.

Six years before (1918) in an essay "The Folksongs of Iowa," Van Vechten had hinted of his possible interest in writing about his home state:

The Iowa scene has been infrequently described in literature and no writer, I think, has as yet done justice to it. There is indeed a feeling abroad that the Iowa scene is unworthy of description, as Iowa is usually imagined as a fecund but unbeautiful state laid out in flat squares. The contrary is the case. This fair land is unusually personal in its appeal and its beauty, which may not be immediately appreciated by those who glance at it casually from the back of an observation car on the Overland Limited, in the end proves to be haunting.

---

5   Carl Van Vechten, *Nigger Heaven* (New York: Alfred A. Knopf, 1926), p. 149.

Indeed, to me the Iowa scene boasts a peculiar picturesqueness which I do not find elsewhere in the United States. I might explain this prejudice by recalling how often Pennsylvania or Connecticut suggests England, while Iowa remains essentially American.[6]

The Tattooed Countess relates the return of the Countess Nattatorrini (born Ella Poore) to her home town of Maple Valley after an absence of thirty years, her subsequent romance with Gareth Johns, a high school boy (who as a writer of some reputation appears in *Nigger Heaven* and elsewhere), and her departure with young Johns.

The Countess is a very worldly woman who smokes cigarettes in public, uses facial makeup, and reads French novels; there is high comedy in the novel's accounts of the tattooed lady's introduction to the middle-western world of "receptions and kettle-drums and euchre-and-cinch-parties."

The dual structure of the novel results in a focus on the Countess and the Town in the first half, with strong overtones of *Main Street,* and on the Countess and Johns in the second half. The first half may be seen as a quest of sorts by the Countess, with the second half representing an ironic fulfillment of the quest. The novel begins with the arrival of the Countess and ends with her departure. Near the beginning and at the end, two chapters focus on the "Parcae" and their gossip, which concentrates on characters and incidents in the book, and serves as a commentary on what is about to happen and what has happened.

A feature of the book is Van Vechten's style; he likes the recherché word: pinguid, fastuous, passerine, internecine, carious, kerb (for "curb"), morigeration, sciapodous; he quotes French epigrams. This language is set off against the vulgarisms of the "Parcae" (two Cedar Rapids ladies of the working class), contemporary terms such as "scorching" (speeding on a bicycle) and even commonplaces—"The oak box which contained all that was left of his mother."

Van Vechten called the novel, "a romantic novel with a happy ending," but it is clear that that is not the case. Edward Lueders has said that *The Tattooed Countess* is "almost an elaboration" of Oscar Wilde's aphorism "that there are two tragedies: not getting what you want and getting it."[7]

"Get ready for a shock or a pleasant surprise," the *Cedar Rapids Gazette* of August 13, 1924, said on its editorial page. "What Edgar Lee Masters did for Spoon River and Sherwood Anderson for Winesburg,

---

6 Carl Van Vechten, "The Folk-Songs of Iowa," *In the Garrett* (New York: Alfred A. Knopf, 1920), p. 30.
7 Lueders, p. 83.

Ohio, Carl Van Vechten has done in a measure for Cedar Rapids. . . . he writes the town into real modern 'literchoor,' adds romance to our Main Street and advertises us beyond the confines of the valley. His mirror may be warped but it is a mirror."

How accurate was this opinion, Cedar Rapidians wondered. When Van Vechten came to Cedar Rapids in October of that year, he was asked if it was true that "Maple Valley" was Cedar Rapids. "Certainly," he is quoted as having said, "you see I have never lived anywhere else. I had to draw on my own experiences, as any writer does, for the material for his book. . . . But why assume that the book reflects my own point of view?"[8]

One of the novel's readers wrote to Van Vechten:

What is the use of writing such filth? Your crime is the greatest crime of all . . . poisoning the mind of *youth*. There is certainly enough rottenness in this world—without writing romances about it. . . .
You dedicate it to Hugh Walpole. Poor Walpole! He must feel honored using *his name* betwixt the covers of such gutter slime.[9]

But Walpole admired the book, along with Gertrude Stein, M. P. Shiel, F. Scott Fitzgerald, Eleanor Wylie, Sinclair Lewis, and Somerset Maugham. The latter wrote that *The Tattooed Countess* was "a triumph in [its] difficult genre"—the "light book."[10]

Two months after his fiftieth wedding anniversary, Carl Van Vechten died in his sleep. On the eighty-sixth anniversary of his birth, his ashes were scattered in the Shakespeare Gardens in Central Park in New York City.

Jay G. Sigmund, another of the group identified with Cedar Rapids, was born on December 11, 1885, in Waubeek, a town northeast of Cedar Rapids on the Wapsipinicon River settled by New England whalers in the eighteen-fifties and -sixties. His parents were Herman R. and Sarah Jane Bruce Sigmund. Jay Sigmund attended the Central City schools (a few miles upriver from Waubeek), then at nineteen he came to Cedar Rapids to live. In 1907 he entered the insurance business in Cedar Rapids, eventually becoming a vice-president of the Cedar Rapids Life Insurance Company. On August 9, 1910, he married Louise B. Heins of Cedar Rapids.

He continued to maintain a summer home in Waubeek, and many of his poems and stories are about country people and people living along the Wapsipinicon. Paul Engle once said:

---

8 *Cedar Rapids Gazette*, October 24, 1924, p. 1.
9 Kellner, p. 155.
10 Kellner, p. 156.

He knew every buffalo-wallow and Indian village site in this area, the little cast-away towns in the valley of the Maquoketa, the Tetes des Mort, the Mississippi, and all the many kinds of people who lived in them, the trapper, the hog buyer, the shell button cutter. More than any man I have met, he recognized the great variety of life in the middle west.[11]

He wrote poetry about these people:

> It's hard to pen Bill's name
> Without a tear;
> I couldn't write of him
> Without a sigh;
> For underneath his barkeep's
> White duck coat
> There beat a heart as
> Mellow as old rye:
> You don't get scouts like Bill
> Since it's gone dry![12]

He wrote about the land also, as in this selection from a poem which he called his "favorite":

> There was a ghostly lane wound by his house.
>   He had the sort of porch a screech owl seeks;
>   Within his plastered walls were high-pitched squeaks,
> Almost too loud for any cat or mouse.
>
> Old buildings, where the grizzled sides of Death
>   Have planned and plotted in each mildewed room,
>   Hold something sinister within their gloom,
> Which sends one to his couch with bated breath.[13]

His first book of poetry was published in 1922. About that time he was frequenting a neighborhood drug store in Cedar Rapids, and one evening he discovered that a young man who was working there also shared his love for poetry. The young man was Paul Engle, then attending Washington High School in Cedar Rapids and publishing verse occasionally on the once-a-week school page of the *Gazette*. Sigmund encouraged Engle's interest in poetry, as George Cram Cook had encouraged the young Floyd Dell.

---

11 Paul Engle, "The Man and the Poet," *American Prefaces* 5 (December 1939):39.
12 Jay G. Sigmund, "Bill M'Kellum," *Land O'Maize Folk* (New York: James T. White & Co., 1924), p. 69.
13 Jay G. Sigmund, "River Road Wedlock," *A First Book of Iowa Poets* (Des Moines: Maizeland Press, 1928), pp. 47–51.

One of Sigmund's last poems spoke (prophetically in view of the nature of his death) of his feeling for the woods and river:

> The tracks I see by the river here
> Are deep-etched, dog-like, many and clear,
> And a red fox brush has scattered the snow—
> He barked at the grouse as he watched it go.
> These other tracks saw light of the moon;
> The prints of the shy ring-tailed raccoon.
> These tracks so wobbly, crazy, drunk.
> Were made by my silent neighbor, skunk.
> Tiny scribblings by the bittersweet
> Are left by a mouse's four white feet.[14]

On Tuesday October 19, 1937, he was accidentally wounded by a blast from his own shotgun as he hunted near his home by the river. He died that evening.

Charles J. Finger, in commenting on Sigmund's stories, noted a circumstance which could also apply to Sigmund's poems: "He writes of common things . . . but he distinguishes sharply between the merely ephemeral and that which endures, and rejects the former."[15]

And John T. Frederick said:

Sigmund's stories seem without art. They are utterly simple and natural in their response to the demands of his material. They are marked by unerring choice of the revealing detail, by profound sympathy. Sigmund had a keen eye for the eccentric, the comic, and a warm sense of humor. He had also a deep sense of the tragic reality which often underlies a surface seemingly dull and prosaic. Sigmund's poems, often fictional in effect and actually highly condensed short stories, possessed the same quality. His interpretation of Iowa farm people and experience in poetry has been surpassed only by the work of James Hearst.[16]

Sigmund's poems with their sharp etchings of river and village types are much better poems that those of James Cloyd Bowman in his *On the Des Moines* (Boston: Cornhill Company, 1921). Bowman's poems derive from the poet's hiatus as a fisherman. In the course of his time on the river, he meets a retired farmer, a farm boy, a farm girl, a suffragist, a river rat, another poet, and several other characters. Each of these is the subject of a poem. But Bowman's types are too generally realized, and his

---

14   Jay G. Sigmund, "Tracks," *American Prefaces* 3 (October 1937):1.
15   Charles J. Finger, "Preface" to *Wapsipinicon Tales* by Jay G. Sigmund (Cedar Rapids: Prairie Publishing Co., 1927).
16   John T. Frederick, "The New Realism," *Palimpsest* 32 (March 1951):134–35.

language too much that of the schoolbook. Bowman's types are merely words and phrases on a page, but Sigmund's people are people we have known.

Paul Hamilton Engle was born in Cedar Rapids on October 12, 1908, and attended the public schools there. His ancestors had come to the prairie long before; Engle remembers that his "grandfather rode with the Fifth Iowa Cavalry in the 60's [chasing] the Sioux in Dakota Territory, but never caught up with him," and that others spoke these words of grace before partaking of their simple fare:

> Mush is rough,
> Mush is tough,
> Thank Thee, Lord,
> We've got enough.[17]

He worked his way through Washington High School, soda-jerking at an east-side drug store and delivering the *Cedar Rapids Gazette*. He played football and one day "an opposing lineman stepped on [his] face and changed its topography permanently."[18] As class poet he "read the class poem, which was buried in a new-planted class tree in the school yard. The tree died."[19]

He went on to Coe College with some notion of studying for the ministry and preaching at the Stumptown Church on the Cedar River bottoms downstream from Cedar Rapids, "but heard no call." His English honors essay at Coe, where he graduated in 1931, was on "The Relation of John Keats and Leigh Hunt"; this may have been influenced by the presence in Cedar Rapids of the Luther A. Brewer collection of items pertaining to the life and career of Hunt.

That same year he went to the University of Iowa where the new programs in the arts were just being set up. His master's thesis, *One Slim Feather* (1932), a volume of poems, was one of the first creative theses ever accepted by an American university in what has since come to be a common practice. With some additions and omissions, the thesis was published that same year in the Yale Series of Younger Poets as *Worn Earth*, and dedicated to Engle's parents and Mr. and Mrs. Luther A. Brewer.

Worn Earth is divided into four sections, "Elegies," "Men With Dirty Hands," "For a Girl," and "Wind-weathered." Half of the poems are

17   Paul Engle, "Iowa," *Holiday* 20 (October 1956):42, 90.
18   Earl Wilson, "Blue Monday," *Des Moines Register*, December 23, 1968.
19   April Daien, "The Quality of Writing is Wanting," *Arizona Republic*, November 28, 1969, Section E, p. 1.

sonnets; half are longer poems. One of the poems in the last section was written on the occasion of his graduation from Coe.

The sonnets in the "Men With Dirty Hands" section are grouped around a common interest in the industrial part of a city and the people who live there:

> "God but it's hot these summer nights,
> With ironing to be done and clothes to soak."
> She flung a window up and heard the cars
> Shunted across the yards, and saw the lights
> Of switchmen's lanterns dancing in the smoke,
> And watched the street lamps calling to the stars.

"A poet cannot repudiate his age," said Engle in 1937, outlining a poetic theory about poems such as this one. "Certainly poetry will as a whole become more 'social-minded.' It will react instinctively to social movements as it once did to the moving wind. . . . One result of this awareness will be the desire to use common speech and contemporary images, and new verse forms and cadences to fit them."[20]

The section "For a Girl" initiates an often-recurring theme in Engle's poetry. Here, for example, is the first of his poems for "Mary":

> Your hand in mine, our fingers interlaced,
> We wandered through the moonlight night and heard
> The crunch of leaves beneath our feet and traced
> The loops of wind behind a startled bird . . .

Reactions to this first volume of verse were encouraging. William Rose Benét said that "the work of Paul Engle, in its own beginnings [was] sound."[21] And Harriet Monroe, long-time editor of *Poetry* said that "a young poet of unusual talent flies his flag in this book":

The book is manifestly a beginning, the work of dreaming youth not yet muscular with developed manhood. But there is promise of strength in it; one finds not only a trained technique capable of the closely chosen word, the winged phrase, the grace of fine music, but also, in certain poems, the hint of more solid qualities, which may prove, let us hope, the beginning of power.[22]

For the next few years, Engle was a student at Columbia University, and, after winning a Rhodes Scholarship, at Merton College, Oxford.

---

20   Paul Engle, "Poetry in a Machine Age," *English Journal* 26 (June 1937):436.
21   William Rose Benét, *Saturday Review of Literature* 9 (December 24, 1932):344.
22   Harriet Monroe, "Paul Engle's First Book," *Poetry* 42 (July 1933):222.

There he studied English literature under the English poet Edmund Blunden, and "then broke all precedent by insisting on studying in the newest Oxford school, doing 'modern Greats,' consisting of philosophy, politics and economics."[23] He was an energetic young man, rowing for three years on Merton's rowing team, playing on the University championship water-polo team, and, oddest of all, playing on Merton's cricket team. He was also editor of *The New Oxford Outlook*. During the "long vacations" he toured in Europe, where he wrote a great deal of poetry.

His next volume of verse, *American Song* (1934) included a poem "America Remembers" which won *Poetry*'s Century of Progress prize in June 1933—a topical poem inspired by the Century of Progress Exposition at Chicago—and an elegy to Luther A. Brewer:

> Give him the praise
> Only of silence. Let the filled-up land
> For which he labored quietly, accept him
> Quietly back again. His was the dignity
> Of life worked humbly out. O let him have
> Now the dignity of simple earth.

The time of the writing of *American Song* was a time of great internal dissent in the United States, a time when all of the old, long-accepted standards and values were being questioned, and it was natural that a book of poetry dealing with the themes of *American Song* should find its foes and advocates. Malcolm Cowley said that "technically Engle has two accomplishments, both of them rare in young poets: he knows how to build a poem in big square solid chunks and he is able to keep it moving. But his verse is inferior in metrical texture; it alternates between the two extremes of awkwardness and monotony."[24]

John Gould Fletcher offered a considered attitude:

His *America Remembers* . . . is neither a masterpiece nor a journeyman's piece of botching. It is an extremely competent job.[25]

Engle's next volume of poems, *Break the Heart's Anger* (1936), speaks with the voice of "a newer Lazarus from the living," and asks,

> Do you think, America, you can forever
> Walk the thin and tight-rope edge of time
> With the umbrella of a silver dollar?

---

23 Paul Engle, *Break the Heart's Anger* (Garden City, N.Y.: Doubleday, Doran & Co., 1936). Dust jacket.
24 Malcolm Cowley, "Eagle Orator," *New Republic* 80 (August 29, 1934):79.
25 John Gould Fletcher, "The American Dream," *Poetry* 45 (February 1935):285–88.

giving the impression that Engle had listened to some of the voices of criticism and had taken a new look at his country. Curiously, the poems are addressed from various European places—Kitzbühel, Tyrol; Chiemsee, Bavaria; Eze, France, are a few—and all are critical of the poet's homeland:

> Yet now I see
> In Alabama cotton burned, in Iowa
> Hogs slaughtered and buried, in Montana
> Wheat plowed under. While ten million men
> Shiver and hunger. This is not your way
> America . . .

In 1937 Engle returned to the University of Iowa to begin that long and fruitful tenure which has done so much for Iowa, the University, young writers from all over the world, and literature. He joined with Edwin Ford Piper and Wilbur Schramm in continuing the publication of *American Prefaces,* a literary magazine begun two years earlier at the University under the auspices of the School of Letters. He also took part in the founding of the Poetry and Fiction Workshops which he was to direct for the next quarter-century or so.

His next volume of poetry, *Corn* (1939), had this poem on "February":

> Now when the briefest darkest day
> And white snow meet,
> Comes the month of blow-your-hands
> And stamp-your-feet.
>
> A man, watching cold earth follow
> Its snow-shoe track,
> Knows it will never end in fire
> But freeze and crack.

Noticeably in the works to this point there had been a cycle through which Engle had gone; he had begun with tight lyrical forms in his first volume, then had moved on to long stanzas of Whitmanesque blank verse, and he was now returning to the tighter lyrical forms again—with a noticeable improvement in the quality of his verse.

West of Midnight (1941) had some very good examples of the sonnet:

> Twenty below I said and closed the door,
> A drop of five degrees and going down.
> It makes a tautened drum-hide of the floor,
> Brittle as leaves each building in the town.
> I wonder what could happen to us here
> If that hard winter ever stopped,

No man again could watch the night grow clear,
The blue thermometer forever dropped.

I hope, you answered, for so cruel a storm
To freeze remoteness from our lives too cold.
Then we could learn, huddled all close, how warm
The hearts of men who live alone too much,
And once, before our death, admit the old
Need of a human nearness, need of touch.[26]

Engle's next book was *American Child, Sonnets for My Daughters* (1945, 1956). It is dedicated to the poet's daughters who "lived this book." First published privately as a volume of eleven sonnets, the book was subsequently published and republished in two editions; one with sixty-three sonnets and a thirteen-line lyric, and one with thirty-six additional sonnets for a total of ninety-nine. In general these sonnets follow an octave-sestet pattern (as in the sonnet just above), but the rhyme scheme varies. Moreover, some sonnets use an iambic trimeter line.[27]

The Word of Love (1951) has only twenty-three poems. Of these, in the words of Robert Hillyer, the Pulitzer Prize winning poet, there are six lyrics and two sonnets in Engle's "finest vein." But he felt that some other lyrics "abandon good taste, dignity, and elevation in favor of raucous violence and frustration."

For the Iowa Dead (1956) "was written for a Service of Dedication (on March 25, 1956) at the University of Iowa—a service dedicating the Memorial Honor Roll of students and alumni of the university who have given their lives in the armed forces of the nation."[28]

There are twenty-two sonnets in the book. Four of the sonnets have been set to music as a "Requiem for the Iowa Dead" by Professor Philip Bezanson of the Department of Music of the University, a long-time friend of Engle's, and a collaborator with him on other occasions. The first eight lines of the second sonnet were cast in bronze and placed in the Iowa Memorial Union at Iowa City, alongside similar tablets bearing the names of servicemen who died in World Wars I and II and the Korean conflict:

Morning Sun, Stone City, Boone, What Cheer:
In the hysteria of history

---

26 Paul Engle, *West of Midnight* (New York: Random House, 1941), p. 46.
27 A complete discussion of the technical aspects of Engle's sonnets is in Richard B. Weber's "The Sonnets of Paul Engle" (M.A. thesis, University of Iowa, 1958). See also *Haselmayer* in the bibliography for this chapter.
28 Paul Engle, *For the Iowa Dead* (Iowa City: University of Iowa, 1956), introductory statement, n.p.n.

These names for home rang in the homesick ear,
With the warm sound of friend and family,
Of Iowa, where winter cracks your skull,
Where summer floats on fields, green river flowing,
Where autumn stains your hand with walnut hull,
Spring shakes the land with a loud gust of growing.

American Prefaces ceased to publish in the war years. After the war, Ray West came to Iowa bringing with him the *Western Review*, so Engle no longer had the direct responsibility of publication. Now the Workshop flourished. Among them, Arthur Davison Ficke, Carl Van Vechten, and Paul Engle knew every American and British writer of any accomplishment in the last sixty years, and Engle brought a great many of these to the Iowa campus, either as teachers for a period, as lecturers, or as students. Volumes of verse and short stories, and novel after novel flowed from the pens of Workshop writers. Awards followed, including the Pulitzer Prize for Poetry (Dee Snodgrass, 1960) and the Lamont Prize (Donald Justice, 1960). Some of the writers who were in Iowa for more than a brief visit: Robert Penn Warren, Paul Horgan, Eric Knight, Josephine Johnston, Hansford Martin, Walter Van Tilburg Clark, Robie McCauley, Herbert Gold, Harvey Swados, Joseph Langland, James B. Hall, Oakley Hall, Thomas Williams, Vance Bourjaily, Philip Roth, George P. Elliott, Henri Coulette, Hortense Calisher, Curt Harnack, Calvin Kentfield, Philip Levine, Herbert Wilner, Walter Sullivan, Wirt Williams, Robert Lowell, Karl Shapiro, William Stafford, and Andrew Lytle. It is safe to say that only a man of Engle's stature and energy could have persuaded these writers and many others to share their talents with the Workshop.

In 1959 Engle published *Poems in Praise*, a volume which contains a number of poems "in praise of people," "in praise of children," "in praise of the war dead," in "praise of places," and simply "in praise." Engle's critics found much to praise and much to blame in this volume of work by a mature poet. The *Saturday Review* said that Engle's "good qualities . . . his affirmative and manly tone, his clear passionate statements of Americana, a quick and agile mind skipping over a wide variety of subjects" were displayed in the book. But it deplored his failures: "Iowa produce crowds out the Grecian asphodel," acknowledging, however, that this kind of criticism was unfair: "Paul Engle writes the kind of poetry he admires, and it has its own place in the multiple American scene."[29]

---

29 *Saturday Review* 43 (February 6, 1960):22.

William Meredith was critical of some of the poems, but in others he saw that Engle's "more modest and attentive attitude toward the world . . . shows in some fine lines and [more] successful poems."[30] Josephine Jacobson, writing in *Poetry* said that much in the book shows "grasp and vigor, but a hard and honest fact remains in all its blunt factness: praising everything, it is difficult to praise anything."[31]

Golden Child (1962), a book belonging in the Christmas tradition which from time to time has occupied Engle's attention, is a story of pioneer days in California. It was also performed on television with music by Philip Bezanson.

A Woman Unashamed (1965) contains a series of poems inspired by a visit to Japan and Asia on a round-the-world-trip which led to the founding of the International Writing Program which Engle now heads at Iowa; a tribute to Edmund Blunden, the Oxford teacher; three poems on a favorite Engle theme, "Love"; "poems on art," and some Christmas verse.

Two stanzas from "The Word and the Poet" in the volume enunciate a poetic credo:

> Verse is not written, it is bled
> Out of the poet's abstract head.
> Words drip the poem on the page
> Out of his grief, delight and rage.
>
> Words hold his life, as window glass
> Holds sunlight it allows to pass.
> The word becomes the poem where
> His pencil's point becomes the air.
>
> The word which only tries to sing
> A lived-through act, becomes live thing,
> As if a mirror, black with night,
> Turned the astonished air to light.
>
> . . . .
>
> Man is the metaphor of is.
> Verse is the metaphor of his
> Abandonment of self, live man
> Transformed to poem's formal plan.
> Through brain and gut and furious heart
> The artist dies into his art.

Of this volume the *Saturday Review* commented that Engle was

---

30 William Meredith, *New York Times Book Review*, December 27, 1959, p. 6.
31 Josephine Jacobson, "Comment," *Poetry* 96 (July 1960):231.

"apparently too nice a man to write very good poems."[32] But Professor John Willingham said that Engle was a "generously gifted poet," and he praised especially "The Word and the Poet," and Engle's tribute to Edmund Blunden.[33]

For several years from about 1950 on, Engle edited with various associate editors the O. Henry Prize Stories. In 1960, he published *Midland*, a collection of poems and short fiction, presenting a generous sample of the best efforts of members of the Writers Workshop from its inception to that date. Neither the O. Henry annuals or the *Midland* contain much written by Iowa writers—for too many years the Workshop had been national and international in its scope, and, if anything, has tended to discourage writing about Iowa.

Engle's final volume, to date, is *Embrace* (1969), a volume of "love poems," of which only four are labeled "new poems." Most of these had appeared in earlier volumes; one might assume, therefore, that this is Engle's judgment, at age sixty, on his own work. This being the case, one notes that some of the poems included in the collection are among those harshly criticized earlier. But it must be recognized that the work of Engle discussed in this history and the quotations used do not represent the directions of the poet's latest work. The citations represent works which "are back in the Urzeit" of his writing, as Engle has phrased it. The omission of his latest writing is deliberate because Paul Engle's poetry has moved beyond what is defined in this book as "Iowa" poetry, and the reader must search out these new directions for a full consideration of Engle's contribution and career.

In a sympathetic study of Engle's poetry, "Three Contemporary Poets in Iowa," Professor Louis A. Haselmayer in 1959 summarized Engle's poetry as falling into "successive periods"—*Worn Earth* contains short poems, mostly sonnets, "with nature or love poems and personality sketches predominant." In *American Song*, Haselmayer says that "Engle developed that distinctive content and style which has ever since been associated with his work . . . a vigorous, if not blatant, Midwestern patriotism, a glorification of America as a land of opportunity, an exaltation of the soil, the force of nature as an *élan vital*." Poetry of the late nineteen-thirties "draws upon [the poet's] foreign experiences," and contrasts American materialism with "the simplicity of the past." In the nineteen-forties, Engle shifts his subject matter to "childhood and love." Haselmayer sees Engle's achievement as lying in "the craftsmanship of

32 *Saturday Review* 48 (July 3, 1965):32.
33 J. R. Willingham, *Library Journal* 90 (March 1, 1965):1123.

phrases, the firmness of the single line, the splendor of the individual poem rather than in a creation of a great poetic structure."[34]

However, the last word on Engle is yet to be written, awaiting any further publication and his eventual retirement from the writing scene. In the long run it will probably be seen that Engle's greatest contribution to the cause of Iowa and American literature was his long-time direction of the Iowa Writers Workshop to which he gave unstintingly of his time, energies, love and affection, and money, surely at the sacrifice to some extent of his own career and reputation. Currently Paul Engle is the Director of the International Writing Program in the School of Letters at the University of Iowa and is the general editor of the Iowa Translations Series published by the University of Iowa Press.

Among the Iowa writers developed (in part, at least) by the workshop (in addition to those discussed elsewhere in this history) are Betty Sunwall of Waterloo, Wallace Stegner, and Harry Duncan. The last-named is best known for his Cummington Press, but he is the author of one book of poetry, *Poems and Translations* (1954), one of Scribner's "Poets of Today" Series, and of numerous individual poems and translations. Other writers, both of poetry and the short story, who have been encouraged by the Iowa English staff since about 1935 include Milford E. Wence, Marion Louise Bliss, Thomas Duncan, Zatha Pilson Weems, Raymond Kresensky, John Noble Campbell, and R[obert] V[erlin] Cassill.

Cassill was born in Cedar Falls, Iowa, in 1919, the son of schoolteachers who taught in several small Iowa towns, so that Cassill's education was always conducted under his parents' eyes in a variety of places. "That I was born in Iowa seemed to me once a highly fortuitous circumstance," he once said, "but in my middle age [when he was forty] it looks more like a fatality, an originally neutral event which comes more to have the force and color of choice." He graduated from the Blakesburg High School and enrolled in the University of Iowa. "When I first went to the University of Iowa, I had no good reasons for registering there, but the good reasons emerged—as if they had been the basis for my prior decision —in the course of time."[35]

At Iowa one of his inspirational teachers was Edwin Ford Piper—who is immortalized as Orin Corrigan in his story "And In My Heart." In June 1939 *American Prefaces* published his short story "To the Clear Mountains." In that issue, Cassill, who had just received his B.A. *magna cum laude* from Iowa, was described as being "equally skillful as painter

---

34 Louis A. Haselmayer, "Three Contemporary Poets in Iowa," *Iowa English Yearbook* No. 4 (Fall 1959):2–4.
35 Paul Engle, ed., *Midland* (New York: Random House, 1961), p. 583.

and writer" and also as "one of the youngest graduate students at the University."

Cassill served in the Army Medical Administrative Corps in the South Pacific during World War II, an experience which forms the basis for his story "The Conditions of Justice." After the war he returned to the University; in 1947 he was awarded an M.F.A. degree on the basis of *New Mexican Sun and Other Stories*. His thesis directors were Wilbur Schramm and Paul Engle. He continued to teach at the Workshop with Engle, Hansford Martin, Ray West, and Warren Carrier until 1952 when he received a Fulbright Fellowship; he spent the following year in France.

In 1950 he published his first novel, *Eagle on the Coin*. The fictional setting of the novel, Riverton, is rather easily identified as Quincy, Illinois. Riverton is "a bustling Mid-Western town that believed in keeping Negroes in their places," publicly parades its spirit of pretended tolerance in the form of a "monument to its indigenous hero, Ezekiel Mountwood," who in pre-Civil War days had published an Abolitionist newspaper in Riverton until "pro-slavers from across the river" in Missouri had raided his shop, smashed his press, and lynched him. The novel, set in post-World War II days, focuses on the attempt of some idealists to further the career of a Negro who is running for the Riverton School Board. The novel skillfully mixes overtones of idealism, of scrupulous and unscrupulous justice, of homosexualism, of attitudes toward young people and blacks, toward Socialism and the labor movement, as it moves to its somewhat predictable end. Mary Ross thought that the novel was "not wholly successful" but that it was "nevertheless an honest and interesting novel . . . [written] with perception."[36]

From 1950 to 1960 Cassill (who married one of his former students during this period) was writing short stories of considerable skill and quality, and at the same time supporting himself and his growing family by writing a series of novels characterized by such titles as *Left Bank of Desire, Taste of Sin*, and *Lustful Summer*. Later he taught at several colleges and universities—Monticello College, the University of Washington, the New School for Social Research, Columbia University, the University of Iowa, Brown University, and Purdue. Five of his short stories were first collected in *Fifteen by Three* (1957); the other two authors were former Workshop teachers, Herbert Gold and James B. Hall. Two other collections followed: *The Father and Other Stories* (1965), and *The Happy Marriage and other stories* (1966). Many of these stories have specifically named Iowa settings; others are easily identified as having midwestern settings and characters. These stories establish Cassill as

---

36 Mary Ross, "Probing a Hide-bound Town," *New York Herald Tribune Books*, September 24, 1950, p. 15.

not only an Iowa writer of eminence—they establish him as an American writer of eminence.

Cassill's "And In My Heart" is a story set within a college English department and its writing classes—a scene which Cassill, who has only rarely been away from the academic world, knows very well. The chief characters are Orin Corrigan, an older professor who writes poetry about Nebraska, Moore Tyburn a younger professor and poet, Steve Forest, a writing student who dreams of becoming a second Dostoievski, and his wife, Elaine Biddle Forest, a sorority girl and nymphomaniac. The story plays off the infighting and academic snobbery which takes place within university departments against the writing efforts of Forest and his marital problems—a situation which leads Corrigan to become involved in the lives of the young couple, both actually through encounter and vicariously as he reads Steve Forest's thinly disguised *roman à clef*. The story's title is a pun on the emotional involvements which ensue and Corrigan's heart failure at the end.

The story has a peripheral comment on the kind of regionalism which is the basis for much of Iowa fiction:

. . . there are still those highly emotional sodbusters who go on trying to extend the Whitman catalogue of American goodies, busters who feel that coming from west of Chicago is, in itself, qualification as a poet. . . . The smell of horse dung does not automatically make it literature. . . ."

"The Father" is the story of the guilt complex of an Iowa farmer who blames himself for the accidental loss of his son's hand, and who seeks punishment for his imagined crime by a deliberate crime against his grandson.

Cassill's first volume, *Fifteen by Three*, contains an introduction by Cassill which says some useful things about his method of composition and ought to be read before reading Cassill's short stories. The general introduction to the volume, by James Laughlin, is valuable for its attempt to place Cassill's stories in their time, and for its comparison between Cassill's work and short stories of the type published in the *New Yorker*.

In the next decade three major novels by Cassill appeared: *Clem Anderson* (1961), a study of the corruption and downfall of a writer; *Pretty Leslie* (1963), a novel based on a sensational murder case in Cedar Rapids a decade and a half earlier, and *The President* (1964), a novel about a college administrator which presciently outlines the campus conditions which led to the situations the college campuses experienced in the late nineteen-sixties.

Cassill has at one time or another experimented with innovations in literary techniques on his way to developing a style which is deceptively simple. Some of these techniques may be seen in *Clem Anderson* which intermixes flash-backs and "flash-forwards," passages with editorial commentary from Clem's unpublished novel, narrative based on personal experience, narrative based on events reconstructed from hearsay, and omniscience. If there is any flaw in his work, it probably is due to a circumstance noted by Bernard Bergzorn in commenting on Cassill's short stories:

> It's a pleasure to see language used with such precision, even though the stories carry with them a certain air of the creative writing class; even if they weren't produced in one, I can readily imagine these well-made pieces being put on the seminar table and opened up for examination.[37]

Criticism of Cassill's novels varies. David Dempsey, himself a novelist, thought that if Cassill never "entirely succeed[ed] in explaining why Clem [Anderson] fail[ed], he is a master at showing us how; and it is this fascinating how that makes *Clem Anderson* a major novel."[38] Granville Hicks, although he thought that *Clem Anderson* had some "admirable scenes" and some "splendid moments," concluded that the novel was "a book in which talent and consecration and tremendous labor come to nothing."[39]

Professor Robert Alter thought that *Pretty Leslie* was a "moving novel, honest in its conception and skillful in its execution." He thought that Cassill had achieved his goal "with a surprising degree of success."[40] Professor David Boroff said that Cassill was a "writer of the first rank," and *Pretty Leslie* was "a novel of unusual power . . . a jolting, disturbing book [whose] revelations of the darkness within will make some readers cringe."[41]

In *The President*, said Professor Boroff, Cassill was "a writer of commanding mind and stylistic power—but he has not yet learned to harness those gifts to the demands of an audience, to dramatize his people and his

---

37 Bernard Bergzorn, *The New York Review of Books*, April 22, 1965, p. 16. Other valuable criticism of Cassill's stories is found in: Jonathan Baumbach, "The Prizes of False Prophets," *Saturday Review* 48 (April 24, 1965):36; Ivan Gold, "Amid Confusions, a Stunning Vision," *New York Times Book Review*, April 4, 1965, p. 5.
38 David Dempsey, "Bigger Than Life, Yet Not Quite Real," *New York Times Book Review*, June 4, 1961, p. 4.
39 Granville Hicks, "Midway to Destruction," *Saturday Review* 44 (June 3, 1961):15.
40 Robert Alter, "Madame Bovary in a Mid-West Milieu," *New York Herald Tribune Books*, May 19, 1963, p. 3.
41 David Boroff, "Lady's Lust for Drama," *New York Times Book Review*, May 26, 1963, pp. 26–27.

situations in ways which will reach the emotions as well as the mind."[42] Robert M. Adams said of the same book that for "all its merits, the book has not worked out quite as richly as [one] expected it to; it's been a spectacle, a drama, an entertainment, but not a fully authentic moral study."[43]

Final judgments must be withheld on Cassill, but sooner or later serious criticism will focus on him, and in time the judgment of history. It will be interesting to see what literary historians a half-century or so hence make of this generation of writers (including Cassill, Harnack, Stegner, Kentfield) who have identified so strongly with the academic way of life and its highly literate, intellectual audiences, as contrasted with writers like Stong, Kantor, and Bissell who have deliberately turned their back on the academic world and sought other audiences. In some ways the criticism reported in this history demonstrates that some lines are already beginning to form.

A minor figure on the Iowa City scene whose name has been mentioned in other connections was Roger L. Sergel. Sergel's one novel, *Arlie Gelston* (1923), is a study of a lower-class small-town Iowa girl through five or six years of her life from her nineteenth year on—from about 1912 until just after the end of World War I. Arlie is an independent girl, tormented by her self-consciousness of her inadequacies, and also subject to unidentifiable fears and uncertainties.

The novel plays on the contrasts between the lower-class life of the Gelstons and the middle-class life of the "cultured" well-to-do farmers, the Shumans, and the attitudes of the latter toward the former:

The more you read, the more "cultured" you were, the more you thought about people in the back of your mind, even while you talked with them, ... [P. 244] People's thoughts were important in that life. She had left Bright Valley because of what Gloria and Mrs. Shuman thought. At home in Coon Falls what you thought and what you saw were far less important than what you had to do, and had to do with. [Pp. 318–19]

The immediate background of Arlie's life is the newly-begun motion picture business. Arlie sells tickets and cleans at the Coon Falls *Bijou* for a dollar a day. Later, she helps Ed Sommers build and develop the *Isis* in Grand Forks, another Iowa town. There are only glimpses of the films and the reader learns little about them, but in the character of Ed Som-

---

42 David Boroff, "Academic Smart Set," *New York Times Book Review*, June 21, 1964, p. 33.
43 Robert M. Adams, "Saturday Night and Sunday Morning," *New York Review of Books*, July 9, 1964, p. 15.

mers and his promotional ideas, the reader sees the beginning of the years when the old neighborhood nickelodeons became the cinema "palaces."

John T. Frederick said that "a well balanced realism" marks *Arlie Gelston:*

The major values in *Arlie Gelston,* however, arise from universal human situations, the regional specification of which, though authentic and emotionally valid, is not of itself of primary importance. They are values of character and conduct which, in their complexity and in the sympathetic comprehension with which they are viewed, give the novel a continuing claim on serious attention.[44]

Elsewhere, Frederick said that the novel "has been perhaps more violently condemned for its picturing of Iowa than any other novel," but he did not censor Sergel—Sergel was not "one who writes hatred in contempt. . . . In so far as he does present the Iowa landscape and the Iowa small town his work is brilliant and accurate. *Arlie Gelston* is a novel of great insight."[45]

One of Clyde Tull's students at Cornell College came from Emmetsburg, Iowa, where her father had been a newspaper man. (Emmetsburg's literary reputation was also to be enhanced by Dwight McCarthy, a tolerably good poet and writer, by Bruce Bliven who served as editor of the *New Republic,* and by Beatrice Blackmar Gould, who was to serve as a long-time co-editor of the *Ladies Home Journal.*)

Winifred Mayne (1902–), after graduation from the Emmetsburg High School, worked as a stenographer in her home town and helped "a county nurse gather statistics on bathing habits of rural Iowans."[46] When she came to Cornell College, determined to work her way through college with her stenographic skills, she had in mind a career as a court reporter. Then she enrolled in Professor Tull's English classes, and began writing short stories for the *Husk,* the Cornell College literary magazine.

She graduated from Cornell in 1926 and went back to Emmetsburg to teach for two years in the high school. A Lydia Roberts fellowship from Columbia enabled her to earn an M.A. degree there in 1928, and she then returned to Cornell to teach in the English department. At Tull's urging, she continued to submit stories to the *Husk,* but because she was antipathetic about people reading her stories, she published under the name of her grandmother, Janet McBroom.

---

44   John T. Frederick, "Town and City in Iowa Fiction," *Palimpsest* 33 (March 1951):67.
45   John T. Frederick, "The Younger School," *Palimpsest* 11 (February 1930):79.
46   "Winner of $10,000 Prize Shudders at Thought of Public Reading Her Novel," *Cedar Rapids Gazette,* May 18, 1936, p. 3.

In 1934 she married Bernard Van Etten, a contractor whose hobby was fox hunting. Mrs. Van Etten disliked this hobby: ". . . there's not an iota of sportsmanship in fox hunting, the odds being all stacked up against one poor defenseless animal."[47] She retired from teaching after her marriage, and gleaning a theme from her controversy with her husband, she began writing her novel *I Am the Fox* (1936). The six weeks of blizzard, cold, and accumulated snow which struck Iowa in 1935–36 and gave the state one of its worst winters in history, provided the opportunity for finishing the novel in a storm-isolated farmhouse near Independence.

I Am the Fox is the story of Selma Temple and her visit with her suitor, Gardner Heath, to his parents' farm. At the farm, Gardner, who employs Selma as a stenographer and secretary, proposes marriage. At this point, a fox hunt, in full holler, comes over a nearby hill and Selma watches with horror as the hounds tear the trapped animal apart (his den has been blocked to prevent his escape into it). Now Selma sees Gardner as hunter and herself as his prey. "I am the fox," she says.

The novel is actually a series of short stories, each one representing flashbacks in Selma's mind, and each of which illustrates a projection of the novel's metaphor. One chapter, "Saga of the Bible Belt," comments on *that* aspect of Iowa culture: "Cross section of Iowa life . . . the richest agricultural state in the Union. This was the Bible Belt, where all the rural virtues still resided, godliness, the sanctity of the hearth, thrift, and bucolic content. This was the Bible Belt, where a man had, not a wife, but a woman; where Selma daily heard language that would make a dock rat blush. . . . Profanity seemed to be the way of establishing [oneself] as [a man] of the world; it proved them sophisticated—no backwoodsmen, but masters of nonchalance" (p. 145).

Although Mrs. Van Etten had no real confidence in her book, she did mail it off to the *Atlantic Monthly*—Little, Brown 1936 literary contest, and at once began to write a second novel. She had barely finished the first chapter of the new work when she got a call from Boston that she had won a ten-thousand dollar prize "for the most interesting and distinctive contribution" to the contest. She never finished the second novel, and indeed has published only one short story since ("The Judas Goose," *Atlantic*, 1938). There was entirely "too much fuss made over the first novel. . . . Another reason is that I don't like persons reading and criticizing my work."[48]

Some of the "fuss" apparently came from persons living near the Cor-

---

47 "Winner of $10,000 Prize Shudders at Thought of Public Reading Her Novel," *Cedar Rapids Gazette*, May 18, 1936, p. 3.
48 "Mrs. Van Etten's Goal is Simple: To Be Happy," *Cedar Rapids Gazette*, May 31, 1953, Section 3, p. 5.

nell campus who thought they recognized themselves in the "Batterston" college scenes. And perhaps some of Mrs. Van Etten's reactions were to the criticisms of her novel, not all of which were happy ones.

Although Lorine Pruette liked the novel, calling it a "remarkable first novel," and Elmer Davis called it "not only a very creditable piece of writing but good reading," Bernard De Voto said that it was a "women's magazine serial with a touch of suavity," and Louis Kronenberger said it was "just facile and plausible enough to be inordinately bad. . . . it reads . . . like one of those many novels which Phil Stong, prior to publishing *State Fair*, is reported to have torn up."[49]

Most critics agreed, however, with Lucy Thompkins' comment that "the one particularly Iowan piece, 'Saga of the Bible Belt,' gives a glimpse, little more than a glimpse, of Corn Belt despair, of depression and drought ridden Iowa farms, of down at the heel Iowa towns. It is quite enough of a glimpse, however, to be moving and memorable."[50]

Mrs. Van Etten returned to teaching at Cornell, became a professor of English and retired in 1969. During those years she and her husband lived in a home built with the prize money. On one occasion she said that she wrote poetry "but only when she was mad," and whatever writing she was doing was "only for her own entertainment." Only one piece of her work has been made public since her 1938 *Atlantic* story. It was "the narrative covering the last twenty-five year period of Cornell College's centennial pageant" in 1953.[51]

A somewhat older resident of Mount Vernon was Mrs. Andrew W. (Elizabeth Smith) Ford. Elizabeth Ford was graduated from Cornell College in 1915 and went to Columbia University where she received an M.A. degree. She returned to Cedar Rapids to work on the old *Republican* for a time, then in 1918 she moved to New York City to work for the *New York Evening Telegram*. There, in 1944 at age fifty-one, she died, the year of the publication of her second novel, *Amy Ferraby's Husband*.

Although Mrs. Ford's first novel, *No Hour of History* (1940), ostensibly covers three hundred years of history (1630–1927) most of the novel is set in Hillview, the seat of Crollon College. Crollon College, like

49 Lorine Pruette, "Husband as Huntsman and Wife as Quarry," *New York Herald Tribune Books*, August 23, 1936, p. 3; Elmer Davis, "Fear of the Chase," *Saturday Review of Literature* 14 (August 29, 1936):6; Bernard DeVoto, "Prize Novels," *Saturday Review of Literature* 14 (September 26, 1936):8; Louis Kronenberger, "Booby Prize," *Nation* 143 (August 29, 1936):247; Dawn Powell, "O Genteel Lady," *New Republic* 88 (September 16, 1936):163–64.
50 Lucy Thompkins, "Sharp Pictures of This Predatory World," *New York Times Book Review*, August 23, 1936, p. 7.
51 *Cedar Rapids Gazette*, May 31, 1953, Section 3, p. 5.

Cornell, is situated on a "thickly wooded knoll a hundred feet above the valley and looking over forest and prairie stretching in all directions for ten or twelve miles." Of her fictional Hillview, Mrs. Ford said that in the town, "where servants were unknown there was a caste system as rigid as that of India."

No Hour of History is primarily the story of the life of Victoria Ashe who was born in Hillview just before the Civil War and died there in 1927. The scope of the novel is somewhat larger than a fictional biography, for the events of Victoria's life are set off against well-known national events—"a kind of minor American Cavalcade," as one critic noted.

Amy Ferraby's Husband is a smaller canvas set in "Prairie Grove . . . in the Middle Mississippi Valley . . . among the fertile Iowa cornfields" near the "thriving little city of Comanche Falls." The difference between Prairie Grove and other Iowa towns is that it has been "settled" by "settlers," not "pioneers"—people who came by train rather than by covered wagon: "the day of the covered wagon and the log cabin had been brief. The railroads had cut it short. With them had come necessities, comforts, occasional luxuries. The railroads had even brought oysters."

The novel is the story of Amy Ferraby who is unhappy because her husband has bought the mill in Prairie Grove, and it is also the story of Amy's daughter Caroline who loves the family man of all work but can't marry him because of the difference in their social status. For in this novel also, Mrs. Ford insists on the matter of social demarcations in a small Iowa town. When the Ferraby's came to Prairie Grove, for example, people just knew they would live on the "right side" of the Northwestern tracks.

The problem with both of Mrs. Ford's books is that, as one critic said, they are "less appealing as novels than as lively genre pictures of a century of change."[52]

Martin Flavin's *Journey in the Dark*, the Harper Prize novel for 1943, covers the period from the 1880s to World War II—some six decades. The first and last parts of this novel are set in "Wyattville," a little town on the Mississippi a few miles below Muscatine; the middle part is set in Chicago where Sam Braden, the central character, goes to make money and to marry, unhappily and briefly, the aristocratic and unfaithful Eileen Wyatt, daughter of Wyattville's eccentric rich man.

---

52 Edith H. Walton, "American Cavalcade," *New York Times Book Review*, October 6, 1940, p. 6. See also review in *New York Herald Tribune Books*, October 13, 1940, p. 12, and John T. Frederick's comments in "Town and City in Iowa Fiction," *Palimpsest* 32 (March 1951):87 ff. Frederick's quote about the caste system in Prairie Grove is, I believe, an error; the statement is made about Hillview on page 88 of *No Hour of History*.

The best portions of the novel deal with Sam's boyhood as the son of the lazy and stupid town marshall. Sam's mother is of aristocratic birth and breeding (although she is not at all like Elizabeth Ford's Amy Ferraby).

John Frederick said that *Journey in the Dark*'s theme "closely parallels" that of J. Hyatt Downing's story of Anthony Trant:

The "Dark" of the title is a confusion of ideals, a wrong direction in the journey of life; and it results from the equation of happiness with wealth. The motivation of the book is different from that of Downing's, however, and superficially viewed it is more adequate.[53]

Dow Mossman's *The Stones of Summer* (1971), published by Bobbs-Merrill, was in galley proof as this history went to press, and the only criticism available was Professor William Murray's opinion that the book is the best thing of its kind since *Young Studs Lonigan*. The theme of the novel might well be Barbara Tuchman's statement that "our time is one of disillusion in our species and a resulting lack of self-confidence." The obviously autobiographical novel is an account of young Dawes Williams growing disillusion with his world, his early confidence and then his loss of it, and his final defeat.

The three parts of the novel are set in Dawes City (Dow City, Iowa, Mossman says), Rapid Cedar (Cedar Rapids), and Mexico. Dow Mossman has his roots in these places (in the 1920s and 1930s, an uncle was Iowa's undeniable horseshoe pitching champion!), and he uses them successfully as the background for the adolescence of his protagonist. Through a series of flash-backs (based on Mossman family history) and the use of an older woman as a confidante in the earlier parts of the novel, Mossman is able to give Dawes Williams an historical context which places him, in somewhat Faulknerian fashion, against the background of the white man's coming to Iowa, his take-over of the land, and his development of farms and towns. Dawes Williams, like his creator, is also a writer, and the third part of the novel contains generous chunks of a novel which Dawes is writing about himself. Unhappily the publishers have chosen to set these large blocks in a small type which is difficult to read.

In Van Vechten's *The Tattooed Countess*, the townspeople of Maple Valley (Cedar Rapids) were described as "stupid, provincial and narrow," and the town is called "a God-forsaken hole full of stupid fools." In *The Stones of Summer*, Dawes Williams, although attacking his father, manages to include the whole country:

---

53   John T. Frederick, "Town and City in Iowa Fiction," *Palimpsest* 32 (March 1951): 92–93.

"You know," Dawes said, "if this baron of the earth, this cog that is six percent by population and thirty-five percent by consumption of the world, doesn't get his muddy foot off the population of the world, if he thinks he can just keep dealing himself from the top—while my whole generation, created in his own image to serve him, is just somehow meant to be rationalizers to his thought, and janitors to his pollution, sweeping the mess up behind him—he is just nuts."

Mossman's novel will undoubtedly make the people of Cedar Rapids as unhappy as *The Tattooed Countess* did.

Mona Van Duyn was born in Waterloo in 1921 and grew up in Eldora, an experience which she recalls in "A Day in Late October":

> The helpless tribe in Iowa
> could neither beat nor conjure
> its little savage into line.
> The child would scream at beasts,
> at cows who lifted gaunt faces
> to feast their bulged, hallucinating eyes
> on her. When the corn grew over her head,
> Reform School boys broke out
> and hid in the cornrows till dark.
> She hid with them . . .
> but she didn't hop the freight.[54]

Miss Van Duyn got her B.A. at the University of Northern Iowa where she studied with James Hearst. "She tried some traditional forms and free verse, and she soon learned to cut and strip words down to the core," says Hearst. Later she spent two years in the Iowa Writers Workshop, earning her master's degree, and marrying Jarvis Thurston who, with her, now edits *Perspective*, a quarterly journal of literature.

Miss Van Duyn has published three volumes: *Valentines to the Wide World* (1959), *A Time of Bees* (1964), and *To See, To Take* (1971) which won the 1971 National Book Award in Poetry despite Allen Ginsberg's evaluation that the poetry was "ignominious, insensitive and mediocre." To this Miss Van Duyn responded: "I notice the obscenities but write about the heart and lovers. Ginsberg notices the heart but writes about the obscenities. Both are there and both are valid subjects for poetry."[55]

---

54 Mona Van Duyn, *To See, To Take* (New York: Atheneum, 1971), p. 21. The biographical information is from Barbara Severin Lounsberry's "Poetry Winner," *The Iowan* 19 (Fall 1971), pp. 50–51. The Dickey quotation is from the cover of *To See, To Take*. Miss Van Duyn shared the 1969–70 Bollingen Prize with another Iowa Workshop poet, Richard Wilbur.

55 *The Iowan* 19 (Fall 1971):50–51.

Of *A Time of Bees*, James Dickey has said that the poems "are good poems, indeed," and "Mona Van Duyn is one the best women poets around."

An interesting sidelight on literature in the eastern area of Iowa was contributed in 1965 by Professor Harry Oster of the University of Iowa's Department of English with his recording of *Folk Voices of Iowa* (University of Iowa Press), and the publication of an accompanying explanatory and useful bibliography. Professor Oster, both scholar and talented performer, accumulated his materials in on-the-site visits to the Czechoslovakian community in Cedar Rapids (which Carl Van Vechten had thought was superior to the middle-class culture of his home town), the Norwegian community at Decorah, the Amana community, and the Mennonite and Amish communities near Iowa City, the Dutch community at Pella, and the Mesquakie ("Fox") community near Tama. Other folk materials are also presented in a musical demonstration of the wealth of this kind of literature in the state.

You Gotta Know the Territory

MOST people think of Meredith Willson as a composer of marches ("Mail Call March," 1944), college songs ("Iowa Fight Song," 1951), popular lyrics ("Till I Met You," 1950), or as the composer and lyricist of musical comedies (*The Music Man,* 1958, *The Unsinkable Molly Brown,* 1960, *Here's Love,* 1963), or as an instrumentalist, orchestra leader, radio and television performer. Not many people would think of him as an author in the terms of this book.

In this last sense, Willson first became an author (though not of *belles-lettres*) in 1948 when he published his autobiography, *And There I Stood With My Piccolo,* a title which predicts the humor found in the book. Willson was born in Mason City in 1902; his father was a lawyer and his mother was a pianist, an amateur actress, and the superintendent of the Sunday School.

Early in life, he learned to play musical instruments—the piano (although he said that, like other boys, he preferred playing circus to playing piano), the piccolo, and the flute. On the record jacket of *The Music Man,* he also claims he tried to learn to play "bones," the jew's-harp, and the harmonica.

After graduation from Mason City High School in 1919, he attended the Damrosch Institute of Musical Art. Two years later he was first flutist for John Philip Sousa's band. From that point on his life is one of one musical success after another. Many of these are detailed in the autobiography noted above, and in the later *Eggs I Have Laid* (1955).

In 1952 Willson became a novelist with *Who Did What to Fedalia?* The novel is the story of a Fort Madison newspaperman's daughter whose slight musical talent is encouraged by her family. In New York City she manages to preserve her innocence and virtue against a number of potential threats, including a sadistic uncle. But the real point of the novel is the lesson Fedalia learns—that she has no real talent, for only one person in a million has that; what she does have is a "kind of determination . . . a kind of one-track courage." Back in Fort Madison she decides to marry Charlie Landry who once ran his heart out in a six-mile race to show that, while he had no talent either, he also had that "one-track determination." The lesson that Fedalia has learned is very much like the lesson Elof Lofbom (of Manfred's *The Chokecherry Tree*) also learned.

In *Eggs I Have Laid*, two of the many anecdotes relate incidents about the writing of *Fedalia*. There is also a letter which accuses Willson of having written the book in a "monumental hangover": "I do not mean delirium tremens—I discovered no indication in your work of any imagination whatever."

Willson's next accomplishment was *The Music Man* which exists in three forms—the book for the Broadway musical (1958), the script for the film version (1962), and a novel based on the film script, *The Music Man* (1962). In *But He Doesn't Know the Territory* (1959), Willson has described the writing of the original Broadway play. Unlike Richard Bissell's *Say, Darling*, this very similar book will probably not become a musical comedy.

The setting for *The Music Man* is River City in 1912. (Willson has said that "River City" and Mason City are the same place.) "Professor" Harold Hill (the term "professor" was a broader term in those days than it is now) comes to River City determined to sell a set of band instruments and uniforms to a gullible populace, collect his money and flee. But in River City he meets Marcellus Washburn who knows him for the sharper he is; he also meets Mayor Shinn, owner of the pool hall, the Board of Education, and Marian Paroo, the town librarian and her "lisping" brother, Winthrop. The rest is predictable, but nevertheless it is also what Willson has called "theater magic." ("You don't know what makes it, you only know when you've got it.")[1]

Writing in the Sunday *New York Herald Tribune* just before the Broadway opening of *The Music Man*, Willson said that he "remember[ed his] own childhood so well that each character in the show is not one, but a composite of three or four people."

One of the best things in *The Music Man* is the song "Iowa Stubborn" which summarizes that "Iowa kind of special chip-on-the-shoulder attitude" in a way no other work of Iowa literature has. The combination of Iowa friendliness—"you're welcome[,] join us at the picnic," neighborliness—"we'll give you our shirt," with Iowa conservatism—"we're so by God stubborn we can stand touchin' noses . . . and never see eye-to-eye" is a quality every Iowan knows.[2]

Martin Yoseloff also grew up in Mason City, although he was born

---

1 Meredith Willson, *But He Doesn't Know the Territory* (New York: G. P. Putnam's Sons, 1959), p. 184.

2 Meredith Willson, "Iowa Stubborn," *The Music Man* (New York: Pyramid Publications, 1962), pp. 148–49.

in Sioux City (in 1919), and in his autobiographical novel, *No Greener Meadows* (1946), he speaks (through the narrator, Martin) of living in the small town of "Silver Lake," Iowa. *No Greener Meadows* is the story of a boy's life from the age of six until he is ready for college; any one familiar with Mason City will easily recognize the "Stone City" of the novel—the cement plant, the packing plant, the "Bijou" theater, the street cars, the schools. They will also recognize Carleton Stewart, the music teacher; "Gilly" Gilmore, the long-time YMCA secretary; the high school English staff; the church building across from the "Y," built by the evangelist who later had to leave town.

Although "Martin's" family is intimately described–it includes an older brother, Thomas, just as the author's does—one never has any sense of what it might be like to be a Jewish person in a small Iowa town. "Martin's" family is Jewish, but very little is made of it, and if Martin Yoseloff, himself, ever was aware of any discrimination, he has kept it carefully concealed in his novel. The only discrimination practiced against the story's narrator comes about because he is small.

No Greener Meadows is a quiet book, moving slowly along the years, incident by incident, letting us know what it was like to very poor in a small midwestern town. There is no story line as such, no plot—merely the slow unfolding of the years, the attempts of a boy to get along with his fellows, going to the movies (with no discussion of the morality of the films such as appears in *One Foot In Heaven*), attending school, collecting stamps, trying to learn to play a musical instrument, and working on the school newspaper.

Martin Yoseloff was editor of *The Masonian*, the Mason City high school yearbook, and president (1936–37) of the Iowa High School Press Association. People who lived in Mason City in those years were talking about young Martin Yoseloff's literary abilities just as ten years before residents of Cedar Rapids had talked about young Paul Engle.

At the University of Iowa, from which he graduated in 1941, Yoseloff was a feature writer for the *Daily Iowan*. He left Iowa City to work in New York, then, like many others of his age, he went into the Armed Forces where he served from 1943 to 1946. *No Greener Meadows* was written during those years.

In *The Family Members* (1948) Yoseloff treated a theme which Ruth Suckow was to use four years later in *The John Wood Case*—the problem of a fall from a state of grace in a "good" family. In this case the family is that of F. M. Hollenbeck, the general secretary of the YMCA, and a rural minister typical of the Middle West's "Bible Belt" with his notions of patriarchy and sin. The setting is "Rock Centre,"—a town in Iowa very much like the "Stone City" of the earlier book. A feature of the novel is the gallery of characters with which Yoseloff has peopled his novel—including a number of "grotesques" in the Sherwood Anderson sense of the word.

John T. Frederick said of Yoseloff's novels that "more than in any other works . . . except Paul Corey's, an Iowa community as such is fully realized and is dramatically functional in these two books [particularly in] the texture of social relationships through which Yoseloff reveals his community."[3]

The Girl in the Spike-Heeled Shoes (1949) is a novel about a girl who becomes, in the parlance of the town of Kenyon, Iowa, "a hard ticket," "fast," "tough," "a girl with a reputation." Marybelle Reardon's immorality and "low" behavior are symbolized by the pair of patent leather spike-heeled shoes she buys at fifteen.

Marybelle exists at almost the bottom of the Kenyon social ladder—only her friend Myrna Sears who becomes a prostitute falls any lower:

The sophomore girls, the ones who wore the expensive clothes, the girls whose fathers held "position" in Kenyon, Iowa, position in the gas and electric company, position in the bottling works, position in the packing plant, position in the eyes of Kenyon citizens, maintained their own society. They created an aristocracy, an aristocracy at fifteen. . . . These were not girls from wealthy families.

These girls were, in other words, members of the same aristocracy to which Ruth Suckow's "nice girl" belonged in another Kenyon, Iowa. It is to the credit of Martin Yoseloff that he has chosen to explore the "inferior" Iowa world and has done it so well. *The Girl in the Spike-Heeled Shoes* is, as is Miss Suckow's *Odyssey*, much more than a case study; it is a rich mixture of human relationships, a fine novel about an Iowa social stratum too rarely sympathetically treated.

In his most recent novel, *A Time To Be Young* (1966), Yoseloff explores the life of a young Jewish boy on the East coast. The middle portion of the novel is set in Lincoln, Iowa, a town much like Yoseloff's other midwestern towns.

Yoseloff's older brother, Thomas, is also an author and the head of his own publishing company.

Hartzell Spence's two Iowa-based books, *One Foot in Heaven* (1940) and *Get Thee Behind Me* (1942), are autobiographical in intent, but the treatment of both is fictional. *One Foot in Heaven*, subtitled "The Life of a Practical Parson," is the story of a Methodist minister and his family at their "charges" in a number of Iowa towns—Clarion, Lake Mills, Sioux

---

3   John T. Frederick, "Town and City in Iowa Fiction," *Palimpsest* 35 (February 1954):93 ff.

City, Fort Dodge, Mason City, and Burlington. (The latter, by intent, remains "nameless" in the book, although Spence named it "Riverton . . . for convenience.") A charge in Denver, Colorado, is also described. The several chapters in the text each report an anecdotal type of experience, and there is often very little transition from one chapter to the next.

Get Thee Behind Me, subtitled "My Life as a Preacher's Son," seems to have been intended to capitalize on the success and fame of the first book; it focuses on Spence's own life, particularly his years at the University of Iowa.

Hartzell Spence was born in Clarion in 1908. Early he began to show more interest in a career as a journalist rather than as a minister; at Burlington, while only a high school sophomore, he served as a cub reporter for the newspaper which had once employed "Bob" Burdette. At the University of Iowa he majored in journalism and English, and served as a staffer on the *Daily Iowan* with Harry Boyd (later to become publisher of the *Cedar Rapids Gazette*). Spence had hoped to become editor of the student newspaper but lost out in a political scuffle to a rival. He was elected to Phi Beta Kappa and AFI, another honorary fraternity, and in 1962 was elected by the Iowa chapter of Kappa Tau Alpha, national journalism honorary fraternity, to its Hall of Fame.

From his graduation in 1930 until the beginning of World War II, Spence worked for the Associated Press, except for one brief period when he was with the Gallup Poll. During these years he wrote a dozen novels, none of which were published. He began to feel an aimlessness in life, and then he met George Reynolds, a printer of New Bedford, Massachusetts. Reynolds was able to change his attitude, and

. . . in a mood of self-psychiatry, I sat down one night to crystallize on paper just exactly what my father's teachings had meant to me—or should have. That evening's meditation became the opening chapter of *One Foot in Heaven,* which enabled me to realize an ambition cherished from childhood, to make a career of writing.[4]

One Foot in Heaven was an immediate popular success; it went through a number of editions and was translated into several foreign languages. It was dramatized, and then made into a very popular film (1941), starring Martha Scott and Frederick March.

In World War II, as Captain Hartzell Spence, he was one of the founders of *Yank,* the military magazine. Since the war he has written a great many articles and books, none of which are about Iowa.

---

4 Hartzell Spence, "The Most Unforgettable Character I've Met," *Reader's Digest* 66 (April 1955):155.

Bess Streeter Aldrich (whose novels of pioneer life are discussed in Chapter 2) got five dollars for her first story when she was seventeen and just out of high school. Although she had been writing poetry and stories since childhood, this first sale did not immediately lead to a career as an author. Rather she turned to teaching, and after graduation from Iowa State Teachers College in her home town, she taught for six years in Cedar Falls, then at Boone, Salt Lake City, and Marshalltown. There she met and married Charles S. Aldrich, and after the birth of a daughter, Mary Eleanor, the couple moved in 1909 to Elmwood, Nebraska, where "Cap" Aldrich had purchased an interest in a bank. In 1911, Mrs. Aldrich, who never lost the "writing bug," won a one hundred seventy-five dollar prize in a magazine contest. However, writing fame did not come her way until in 1918 she sold the first of her "Mother Mason" stories. The popularity of this story with American soldiers led to demands for more, and the Cutter family stories followed later.

The death of her husband in 1925 was the final turning point in Mrs. Aldrich's life, for it forced her to turn what had been a hobby into a career.

The year before had seen the publication of *Mother Mason*, an anthology of the stories which the *American* magazine had published. In this book, the common theme of family life unites all the stories. In the stories there appears a maid of all help, Tillie, whose personality and treatment remind us very much of Phil Stong's farm hands—except that in point of time Tillie came first. Although the Mother Mason stories place some emphasis on the notion that one ought to remain in one's station, Tillie is both servant and friend.

The point of *Mother Mason* is the good conservative small town life of a middle-aged couple and their family. There are references to World War I (some of the stories had been written as early as 1916), but the War seems far away. Each story presents a problem which is happily resolved within that story. There is not so much reference to social climbing as in the later *The Cutters*—Mother Mason and her husband are at the top of the social order in their small town because Mr. Mason owns the bank. One character, Grandpa Warner, anticipates the later Abbie Deal, but in a less solid way.

The Cutters (1925) is set in Meadows, Iowa, not far from Dale Center: "It was a small town in one of the Mid-West states where there are almost as many hogs as automobiles. It had some pleasant homes, a good school, five churches, and a few blocks of stores." The Cutters are supposedly "typical of many thousands of American families of the times." There are the young mother, Nell Cutter, her husband Ed Cutter, Grandmother Cutter, and the Cutter children. Other characters enter the stories—the well-to-do Mrs. Ramsey, Dr. Rhodes, Barbara Cutter. The unifying theme of family life is presented from a woman's point of view. A second theme is dissatisfaction, usually related to some attempt of Nell Cutter's to rise in the social order, either because she is dissatisfied with her lot or because of some desire to improve herself. In every story, the original social and economic status is upheld and accepted at the end. The small town world of the Cutters is the best of all possible worlds—and in that world it is best to remain as one is. The big-city folks who come to Meadows seem at first worthy of emulation, but they usually turn out to be unhappy, or small-town folks at heart, or even slightly fraudulent.

Oddly enough, in implying that the small town woman ought to be happy with the situation as she finds it, Mrs. Aldrich was contradicting her own drives and goals.

Both *The Cutters* and *Mother Mason* contain a great deal of intrusive moralizing, and both have a great many quotations from other authors—two characteristics of all of Mrs. Aldrich's fiction. The books avoid mentioning life's uglier aspects—there is one "h——," and only an oblique reference to the pregnancy of a *married* woman.

Miss Bishop (1933) was inspired by the razing of "Old Central" on the Cedar Falls campus; Mrs. Aldrich, reading an account, decided to relate the career of a schoolteacher—"one who saw the opening of the college and lived through its growth—who will be there at the end of the old building as she was at the beginning."[5] The setting of *Miss Bishop* is Oak River, a town much like Cedar Falls. And Midwestern College, the fictional site of the novel (which runs from 1876 to about 1932) resembles the University of Northern Iowa as it was when it was Iowa State Teachers College:

> It stands at the edge of town in a lovely, rolling campus, sweet-smelling in the springtime from its newly-cropped blue-grass and white-clover, colorful in the autumn from the scarlet and russet and gold of its massive trees,—a dozen or more pompous buildings arranged in stately formation, a campanile lifting its faces high to the four winds, a huge stadium proudly gloating over its place in the athletic sun. Concrete driveways and sidewalks curve through the green of elms and maples, and young people walk or drive over them continually,—a part of that great concourse of Youth forever crossing the campuses of the world.

Miss Bishop "went on the best seller lists," in the words of its author. In 1941 it was made into a film, *Cheers for Miss Bishop*, which featured Martha Scott. But it is not nearly as accurate or good an account of college life of the times as Ruth Suckow's "A Part of the Institution." Miss

---

5   Bess Streeter Aldrich, "The Story Germ," *The Writer* 54 (December 1941):356–57.

Suckow told the truth of college life as she saw it. But Mrs. Aldrich felt that stories must be written with "an eye to business . . . something must happen to hold the interest or stir the blood, to bring that laughter or that tear."[6]

The best of Mrs. Aldrich's other short stories have been collected in *Journey into Christmas and Other Stories* (1949), *The Man Who Caught the Weather and Other Stories* (1936), and *A Bess Streeter Aldrich Treasury* (1959). Two of the stories, "How Far Is It to Hollywood?" and "Juno's Swans," feature two girls, Emma-Jo Thomas and Angie Bryson, perhaps two of Mrs. Aldrich's finest characterizations. "The Man Who Caught the Weather" is equally good, partially because it is not a formula story, partially because it lacks the moralizing and forced sentimentality of too many of Mrs. Aldrich's stories. "Youth Is All of an Up-and-Coming" uses a plot which another Iowa writer also used. An elderly couple return to their former home, ostensibly to rehearse their wedding ceremony on its anniversary. After the marriage, it is discovered that they have lived together all the years as common-law man and wife.

The comment which best places Mrs. Aldrich's stories and novels in context is this:

There was a curious dichotomy in the American fiction of the 1920's, well illustrated in the treatment of Iowa cities and towns. On the one hand there was the hostile attitude toward American life which Quick strongly indicted. On the other hand there was the discovery of excellence in American life, the celebration of heroism and of dramatic achievement, chiefly in the record of the American past as exemplified in specific communities. This second attitude, less striking than the first, was nonetheless an important and characteristic aspect of the fiction following the First World War, in all regions of the nation. In the Middle West it is illustrated by O. E. Rölvaag's *Giants in the Earth*, by Quick's *Vandemark's Folly*, and by the best work of Margaret Wilson and Bess Streeter Aldrich.[7]

Unfortunately, MacKinlay Kantor has not chosen to focus more on the Iowa scene in his novels and short stories. He was born on February 4, 1904, in his grandparents' home in Webster City. His mother was Effie Kantor and his father (who was not present) was John Kantor, whom she had met at Drake University. The five years following their marriage in 1899 had been years of

lost jobs, new jobs, American Beauty roses never paid for, scrofulous hotel

6 Aldrich, "The Story Germ."
7 John T. Frederick, "Town and City in Iowa Fiction," *Palimpsest* 35 (February 1954):62–63.

rooms, jail doors opening and closing and opening again, baffled tearful trips back home to Webster City, furniture dumped out on sidewalks, letters, telegrams—and always check after check written by my grandfather, checks written with a crabbed hand.[8]

His mother's father, Adam David MacKinlay, came to Webster City in the eighteen-sixties—his family had come from Scotland. In Webster City he married the daughter of Lt. Joseph Bone. On his father's side, as Kantor once said, "No generation has been born in the same country for the last four generations: my grandfather in Russia, my father in Sweden, myself in the United States, and my daughter in Canada." On his father's side, his male ancestors were all cantors for sixteen generations.[9]

Kantor, who seems first to have been named for his father (John MacKinlay Kantor), then several days later for a biblical character (Benjamin MacKinlay Kantor), long ago dropped the Benjamin, and prefers to be called "Mack." His autobiography *But Look the Morn* (1947) recalls the years of his childhood in Webster City; *The Day I Met a Lion* (1968) and *Author's Choice* (1944) contain autobiographical material; and much of the early part of *The Jaybird* (1932) is autobiographical.

Kantor's writing career had its inception when his mother took a reporter's job with the Webster City *Freeman-Tribune*. Kantor began helping her in one way or another, and was persuaded to enter a short story contest sponsored by the *Des Moines Register* in 1922. His story, "Purple," submitted under a pseudonym, was about a farm family who buy a reproduction of a painting of a farm without realizing that their farm is the subject. One of the contest editors was Herbert Quick, and one day, while reading the *Register*, Kantor discovered that his story had won the fifty-dollar first prize.

He began writing stories and poems "for all [he] was worth," and while he had some success with his poems, his stories were rejected by editors. In 1924, a poem on the plight of Floyd Collins, a Kentuckian trapped in a cave, got a lot of attention, but a novel went unpublished. In Chicago for a time, he worked at two political jobs, married Irene Layne, a commercial artist, and got the material for *Diversey* (1928), a "story of millionaire gunmen, bootleggers, and gangsters."[10]

Kantor has outlined his development as a writer of short fiction in *Author's Choice*, an anthology of forty of his short stories, together with "copious notes, explanations, digressions, and elucidations; the author

8 MacKinlay Kantor, *But Look the Morn* (New York: Coward-McCann, 1947), p. 8.
9 "MacKinlay Kantor," *Wilson [Library] Bulletin* 7 (September 1932):82.
10 *Wilson [Library] Bulletin* 7 (September 1932):82–86.

telling frankly why he selected these stories, why they were written, how much money he received for them, and of his thrilling adventures with wild editors in their native haunts." (Title page.)

Kantor's media through the years, in addition to his verse and one long poetic novel *Glory For Me* (1945), from which was made the award-winning film *The Best Years of Our Lives*, have ranged from the "short short" story to the long historical novels named in an earlier chapter. Three of his "short novels" are set in Iowa: *Valedictory* (1939), *Happy Land* (1943), and *God and My Country* (1954). (Other short novels, such as *The Voice of Bugle Ann* (1935), *The Romance of Rosy Ridge* (1937), and *The Daughter of Bugle Ann* (1953), have their settings outside Iowa.)

Valedictory, which John T. Frederick saw as "a story marked by warmth and kindliness as well as by a vivid sense of the place and event"[11] is a story of the last night on duty of Tyler Morley, 76, a GAR veteran who is retiring as the janitor of the Shelldrake, Iowa, high school after twenty-one years of service. The story is seen through the eyes of the janitor, primarily through flashbacks and a recollection of incidents. *God and My Country* uses the same formula. In this story the viewpoint is that of a sixty-four-year-old Scoutmaster recalling his forty years of service in that capacity. In *Happy Land* we are in "Hartfield, Iowa," on the day when Mr. and Mrs. Marsh, who operate the Marsh Drug Co., learn that their only son has been killed in battle—an incident which Kantor was to repeat in *God and My Country*.

The Jaybird is novel length. The first third of the book, "Village Quickstep," takes place in Clay City, Iowa, in the early summer of 1916, just preceding and on Memorial Day. There are three central characters —"Grampa" or "Red" Feather, a Civil War veteran who subsists on alcohol and his memories of the War; Elva Feather, his daughter-in-law, whose decision to flee Clay City precipitates "Red's" own flight; and Kenny Feather, her son, who accompanies his grandfather. Elva and "Red" both leave Clay City for the same reason:

The rumors run like water in a black, crashing September rain storm—they pour across the uneven bricks, they dam themselves up with fallen leaves on sunken street corners—they break through and go splashing ahead all day and all night, and run all over town before they empty themselves down the sewers. . . . That's Clay City, Iowa; it is rancid.

And "Red" Feather adds: "This town. Never have liked it. Never did like it. Don't know why I came back here after the war."

<hr />

11   John T. Frederick, "Town and City in Iowa Fiction," *Palimpsest* 35 (February 1954):80–81.

In the second and third parts of the novel we find Kenny and "Red" making their way across Iowa, sometimes hiking, sometimes catching a ride with a motorist, and having an adventure with a sadistic sheriff in a small Kansas town. At the end of the novel, Kenny and "Red" have given up their goal of reaching Dodge City, but they have no intention of returning to Iowa.

John T. Frederick has said that *The Jaybird*, "alone among our works of fiction . . . does justice to what [he] knew as a truly distinctive aspect of small town life fifty years ago: Decoration Day . . . ."[12]

Kantor is one of Iowa's most prolific and successful writers. *Long Remember* was a Grosset & Dunlap "novel of distinction"; *The Voice of Bugle Ann*, *Gentle Annie*, and *The Romance of Rosy Ridge* have been filmed; *Andersonville* won the 1956 Pulitzer Prize; and Kantor has been awarded a number of honorary degrees. For the last few years he has lived in a hundred-thousand dollar home on Siesta Key, off the Florida coast, not far from Sarasota. The population growth of this island has led him to comment that what "Siesta Key needs are two hungry bears"; his further displeasure has led him to compose "The Tourist Song," all of whose several hundred verses about the supposed virtues of the countryside are unfortunately unquotable.[13]

The Kantors have a son Tim who cooperated with his father on his most recent book—a picture-prose text about Hamilton County—and a daughter, Layne, who is also a writer.

Raymond Kresensky was born at Algona, Iowa, on December 28, 1897, the son of a German mother and a Polish stonemason who was both a singer and a lover of music. He graduated from the Algona schools and then worked his way through Coe College by teaching dancing in a downtown studio and "hashing" at a fraternity house of which he was also president. Following work at McCormack Seminary in Chicago, he was ordained in the Presbyterian Church in 1929. In 1931 he published *Emmaus*, a volume of religious verse. Not long after he gave up the ministry because, "as his friends expressed it he was an honest man,"[14] and during the remainder of his life worked either as a teacher in several Iowa high schools or as a salesman in the sporting goods department of a Des Moines store.

Both Dr. John Westburg and Professor E. L. Mayo have commented on the influence of the music in his home on his later verse, on his con-

---

12   Frederick, "Town and City in Iowa Fiction," pp. 80–81.
13   Stan Windhorn, "The Author," *Saturday Review* 44 (October 21, 1961):23–24.
14   John Edward Westburg, "The Life and Poetry of Raymond Kresensky," in *The North American Mentor Anthology of Poems* (Conesville, Iowa: John Westburg & Associates, 1965), pp. 11–12.

sciousness of his "Polish forbears" and pride in the Polish "cultural and historical tradition—rebellious, colorful, and aristocratic—of his grand-father's native land," and on his childhood "impish sense of humor and a wild dramatic imagination"—perhaps akin to that of MacKinlay Kantor who, standing in his Boy Scout uniform, told Webster City people he was a Civil War veteran![15]

Kresensky was active in writing programs in Iowa. He supervised and edited *Iowa, A Guide to the Hawkeye State* (Viking Press, 1938); from 1936 on he edited and helped publish *Hinterland*, a regional literary magazine which Dale Kramer of Sigourney had founded in 1934. In 1953, with Grace Hunter of Grinnell College, he helped compile *A List of Iowa Poets*, and he had a part in publishing *Lyrical Iowa* until his death, September 26, 1955, in Des Moines.

After his death, his sister and brother-in-law, Mr. and Mrs. Don K. Allen of Des Moines published a *Memorial Edition of Selected Poems* (Francestown, N.H.: Golden Quill Press, 1956).

Kresensky's poems testify to his interest in and abiding sympathy with the unfortunate in stanzas such as "Nigger Greens," and "The Bull." Some of his poems are "portrait" poems: "My Father's Coat," or "Widow-hood." On occasion he is a nature poet, sometimes in a realistic vein, sometimes in a mythical vein, as in "The Panorama of the Prairie." Some-times he is a lyrical poet, his range running from the light-hearted to the sorrowful or even bitter:

> I learned
> Two things while autumn turned
> Ahead: Nothing is lost
> By worm, and wind, and frost;
> And earth's complete design
> Is a tough and ancient vine.

MacKinlay Kantor who knew him "first thirty-one years ago [1925] when he came often to my little Cambridge Avenue kitchenette in Chicago, 'walking alone in wind and rain,'" said that "I believe several poems by Raymond Kresensky may rank with the finest lyric verse given to our heritage in our time." Paul Engle said that "there are two qualities in Raymond Kresensky's poetry which recur as readily as heartbeats: the warm human feeling, and the quick lyrical expression." Dale Kramer, author of *The Wild Jackasses, Ross of the New Yorker*, and other books said: "Iowa has produced few men as gay and charming as Ray Kresen-

---

15 E. L. Mayo, "Introduction," *Selected Poems by Raymond Kresensky* (Francestown, N.H.: Golden Quill Press, 1956), pp. 11–12.

sky. [The Memorial Edition] established his high place in the ranks of contemporary poets." Clark Mollenhof, himself an Iowa poet, and a Pulitzer Prize winner for investigative reporting, said that "Ray has captured the lonely searching that is at least periodically a part of all men." Frederick Bock, an editor of *Poetry: A Magazine of Contemporary Verse*, said: "Humbly and richly concerned with the fundamental experiences of living, Raymond Kresensky sought a poetry free from the preciosity that sometimes troubles the flow of song."[16]

In the year 1940, Carroll Coleman at the Prairie Press in Muscatine published a slender volume, *Oh Millersville!* by Fern Gravel, who, according to a prefatory note, had written the volume's poems "in the first half-decade of the present century" when she was a "little girl," of nine, ten, and eleven years. Both Millersville and Fern Gravel, it was said, were fictitious names for a real Iowa town and a real Iowa girl who, now grown, had given her consent to publication of her childhood poems.

One of her poems was "Iowa":

> Of all the different states in our country so grand
> Iowa is the best, and that is my land.
> It raises more corn than any other state
> And we ship thousands of hogs and cattle to Chicago by freight.
> We have only one poet so far as I know,
> Mr. Beyers, who wrote some songs a long time ago.
> He was very famous in the Civil War.
> "Marching Through Georgia" was one. He wrote many more.
> I am writing another kind of poetry,
> And some of my poems are beautiful to me.
> I hope, some day, people will travel
> To see the home of the poetess, Fern Gravel,
> Like they go to Longfellow's home, and Whittier's;
> And then I'll remember the day I wrote this verse.[17]

Reviewers were enthusiastic about *Oh Millersville!* "We have found the lost Sappho of Iowa!" said the *New York Times*. The *Washington Post* critic thought the poetry was "so good that it hurts. Fern Gravel never dreamed that she was writing social history." *Time*, in its issue of January 13, 1941, said:

Every so often some precocity in pigtails mesmerizes a U.S. publisher into

---

16 Quotations by Kantor, Engle, Kramer, Mollenhoff, and Bock are from an announcement of *Selected Poems* by Raymond Kresensky.
17 Fern Gravel (pseud. of James Norman Hall) *Oh Millersville!* (Muscatine: Prairie Press, 1940), "Note." Also pp. 13, 49.

printing her verse creations. The resultant rash on the nation's poetic body generally passes away as soon as the publisher's advertising appropriation has been spent. *Oh Millersville!* is a collection of juvenalia that no American will want to see pass away. [These poems are] as good examples of dead-pan lyricism as have ever been printed.

The *Philadelphia Inquirer* remarked, "It's rather early to be saying a book will be one of the most unusual and charming of the year, but here we are, out on a limb and unafraid." And it added prophetically, "Long after 1942, we think, you'll remember this book with a good warm feeling and smile."

And Paul Engle is quoted in *The Spectra Hoax* as having said, "There is so warm a feeling of validity about these verses and so accurate a sense of individual character that their impact is far stronger than a simple amusement at childish simplicity."

Six years passed—and then readers of the September 1946 issue of the *Atlantic Monthly* came across an article, "Fern Gravel: A Hoax and a Confession," written by the well known Iowa and American author, James Norman Hall, who with Charles Nordhoff wrote *Mutiny on the Bounty* (1932).

Hall, who had been living in Tahiti since 1920, said that as a boy in Colfax, Iowa (where he was born in 1887), he had danced a ring dance with other children to this song:

> Green gravel, green gravel, the grass is so green!
> The fairest young lady that ever was seen.
> I'll wash you in milk, and clothe you in silk
> And write down your name with a gold pen and ink.

In 1938 this song was recalled to him by a book; a dream a few nights later led to the names "Fern Gravel" and "Millersville,"—a name not unlike the name of the town of Mitchellville a few miles from Colfax. A girl in the dream was small, "plain and slightly freckled, and her hair was braided in two tight pigtails . . . a solemn little thing with large dark eyes, and she had a decisive way of stepping as though she knew at all times exactly where she was going and why, even in a singing game where she wasn't going anywhere."[18]

Hall graduated from Grinnell in 1906, and in 1914, while on a walking tour through England, he joined the British army, an experience which was the basis for his first book, *Kitchener's Mob* (1916). In May of 1918 he was reported (erroneously) as dead by the *New York Times*. Two books, *On the Stream of Travel* (1926) and *My Island Home* (1952), the

---

18   William Jay Smith, *The Spectra Hoax* (Middletown, Conn.: Wesleyan University Press, 1961), pp. 56–57.

latter reprinting "some material from books written earlier and long out of print," contain Iowa material. Most of Hall's books (some written in collaboration with Charles Nordhoff) are set in the South Pacific.

Thomas Duncan was born in Casey, Iowa, on August 15, 1905, "the son and grandson of doctors, and the grandnephew of a whole raft of doctors." (A doctor is the central character in *The Labyrinth*, and a town somewhat like Casey is the model for the "Litchfield" of the novel.) His "maternal grandfather was alive then, a huge, handsome man with the appearance but not the morals of Warren G. Harding. He had migrated to Iowa from Ohio back in the Sixties and as a youth he had freighted by mule team between Council Bluffs and Denver." Duncan used this grandfather as a model for Edward Thorne and George Cockfoster, fictional characters in two of his novels.

At fourteen, Duncan learned to set type for his uncle's newspaper, the *Casey Vindicator*. He began to form an ambition to be a writer, and at fifteen began sending things to magazines. At sixteen he sold his first story. Attracted by the "dramatic companies, magicians, circuses, carnivals, medicine shows," he also formed a desire to be an actor. But he did not let this desire interfere with his writing.

Despite his two dreams, when he enrolled at Drake in 1922, he was intent on becoming a lawyer. But under the influence of a dramatic arts teacher, "a blazing, colorful man" who "taught Shakespeare as Shakespeare should be taught," he renewed his dream of becoming an actor, and during the summers of 1924 and 1925 he toured the Midwest as an actor in a chautauqua troupe. Toward the end of his second season, he decided that law was out and that he "didn't like the theater well enough to starve for it."

In his second year at Drake, Duncan met the three Stong brothers from Keosauqua: Benton J. who was to become an editor for Scripps-Howard and then of *The National Farmer's Union;* Jo, who became a lawyer back in Keosauqua, and Phil Stong, the eldest, "a blond, powerfully-brained, sleepy-eyed young man, built like a bull moose." Phil Stong and B. J. became close friends of Duncan.[19]

"It was my youngest brother and I who saved [Duncan] from a career of writs and torts," said Phil. Under the influence of the Stongs, "it was not long before he sniffed printer's ink, that dangerous opiate against unadorned reality." He remembered Duncan as a young man who could "distort his face into solemnity for as much as seven and four-tenths seconds before it returned to his natural mould of a kind of mock-

---

19 Thomas Duncan, "An Autobiography of Thomas Duncan," probably published by J. B. Lippincott Co., Philadelphia, 1947, attendant on the publication of *Gus the Great* by the same firm that year. Pages are unnumbered.

ing geniality; . . . he looked something like Voltaire modelled as a cherub."[20]

In the spring of his sophomore year, Duncan was elected editor of the Drake student newspaper. Benton J. Stong was the managing editor and Phil Stong contributed a column, "Philler." Donald Thompson, later to become a Hollywood writer, also had a column; Mark Reno, later the advocate of liberal programs for Iowa farmers, was the business manager. Like the "John Nearing" of *We Pluck This Flower*, Duncan set out to reform the university; unlike him, he survived numerous sessions in which "the president had me on the carpet . . . always teetering precariously on the edge of expulsion." The next year Duncan went to Harvard—which admitted him on the basis that "four years of Drake were worth two years of Harvard." Until 1929, when he took his Harvard degree *cum laude*, he combined newspaper work for the *Register*, overwork at Harvard, a year of convalescence, and the writing of his first novel, "a literary catastrophe." The year of his graduation he "wrote a long poem, under the intense intellectual stimulation of such men as George Lyman Kittredge and John Livingston Lowes, and it won the Lloyd McKim Garrison prize at Harvard: $125 and a silver medal."[21]

From the summer of 1929, he worked as a reporter for the *Des Moines Tribune* and wrote fiction "on the side: working nights, Sundays, sometimes arising at 4 a. m. to write a couple of hours before going to the paper." The next year he quit the paper and went back to Drake, at the same time continuing to free-lance short stories and poetry.

Duncan has described the "literary revival" which was taking place in and around Des Moines in those days; MacKinlay Kantor was on the *Tribune*, Ruth Suckow lived in Des Moines for a time, and Grant Wood often came over from Cedar Rapids. Harvey Ingham, a brave old editor "fighting out his heart for world peace and economic justice," was piloting the *Register* and *Tribune*: W. W. Waymack, later a Pulitzer Prize winner, was an editor; Forest Seymour, also later a Pulitzer Prize winner, was state editor. J. N. Darling was drawing cartoons, Harlan Miller was writing his column, Richard Wilson was covering politics, and Mike Cowles (later to found *Look*) was an executive. Vernon Pope, later of *Pageant*, was picture editor; Victor Shultz, a liberal lawyer and collector of first editions, contributed editorials, and his wife, Gladys Denny Shultz, wrote serials for the *Register* syndicate. For a time Shultz also directed the Maizeland Press.

---

20 Thomas Duncan, "How I Wrote the Novel," *Book-of-the-Month-Club-News* (August 1947), pp. 4–5. Material is identical with that of fn. 19. Also see Phil Stong, "Thomas Duncan," pp. 6–7.
21 Duncan, "An Autobiography of Thomas Duncan."

Duncan recalled that "Frank Luther Mott and John T. Frederick would come up from Iowa City, where [Frederick] edited a rather gloomy "little" magazine . . . (They weren't gloomy themselves, but they certainly loved stories wherein the hero drank rat poison and the heroine jumped off the silo.)"[22]

And there were luncheons with the famous who visited Des Moines —Æ or Carl Sandburg or Carl Van Doren—drawn there occasionally by the luminaries of the town, or an invitation to lecture.

Some of Duncan's poetry was published by *The Midland*, and some in *Poetry: A Magazine of Contemporary Verse*. In 1935, Carroll Coleman at the Prairie Press in Muscatine put some of these together in *Elephants at War and Other Poems*. One of the poems is a "portrait" of a favorite fox-hound, "Chaucer H. Duncan." Another, "Unemployment Conference," looks at Iowa's depression years, ironically contrasting factory managers who smoke fifty-cent cigars and praise efficiency, while in the streets "lean girls sold love" to keep alive. "The Ballad of Jesse James" celebrates the world's first train robbery near Duncan's birthplace:

> Brave Jesse James galloped up from the south,
> His horse dripping lather, hot foam at its mouth,
> Galloped up from Missouri with all of his gang—
> Under thundering hoof-beats the baked prairie sang.
>
> .   .   .   .
>
> In a valley the village of Casey lay sprawled
> Where the shining steel rails of the Rock Island crawled.
>
> .   .   .   .
>
> Oh, you know the rest. How the pride of the line
> Was held up that day—the old Three-sixty-nine.

One poem is "A Good-Bye to Vic (Victor Shultz, 1896–1931)" the lawyer, poet, and editor:

> Let the blue heron cry across a thousand red sunsets
>   And it will be the same.
> Let the snow sift through a million windowsills
>   On a million nights of winter,
> And we will remember that the snow covers.

In 1935 Duncan's first novel, *O, Chautauqua,* based on his chautauqua experience, was published. *O, Chautauqua* looks back at days already past, as much of Duncan's writing does; it is set in northern Wisconsin in

---

22   Duncan, "An Autobiography of Thomas Duncan."

the paper-mill country, but all of the main characters are from Duncan's literary town of "Tamarack"—surely a projection of Des Moines, and not of Cedar Rapids as John Frederick once believed. The chautauqua is in this novel—its Swiss Bell Ringers, its dramatic productions, its "world famed speakers" presented in lieu of William Jennings Bryan, the "Junior Lady" and her enclave of children, the jockeying for "contracts" which will ensure next year's return of the chautauqua under the aegis of the local merchants.

But the "Nonpareil Chautauqua"—"a world by itself—transient as summer"—is only the setting—as all of Duncan's towns and cities and circuses are—for the rich gallery of rogues, sinners, and infrequent angels who pass before the reader's eyes: Bob Caliver, the dramatics professor from the "University of Tamarack," his deceitful wife, Effie, and his young amour, Karla Matchet, who dreamed of being the belle of the Tamarack sororities and fraternities; of Lee Blackthorn, the truck driver who hauled canvas through the black nights of Wisconsin to keep the chautauqua going, and who, with Charley Barnes, dreamed of "hog-killing"; and finally, of Dr. Herman Lingfish, the fat, fiftyish dean of men at Tamarack who in the summer served as a circuit manager for Nonpareil Chautauqua. Much of the activity in the novel concerns various kinds of sexual relationships; hardly a summer night or a chapter passes without some new confrontation, or the repetition of an old one.

O, Chautauqua had some success, but not enough to guarantee Duncan's full-time role as a writer. So he continued sandwiching in other activities with work on short stories and his second novel; he taught, wrote book reviews for the *Register*, performed as a magician, and managed political campaigns for a friend.

We Pluck This Flower appeared in 1937. The novel has two parts, but both concentrate on "The Girl From Sioux Creek," Ella Corkhill. The setting of the first part is the University of Tamarack where Ella and Johnny Nearing are students. After Johnny is expelled for an editorial in the student newspaper criticizing the college, Ella is also expelled for no reason; she is used as a scapegoat or smokescreen to protect the college.

The setting of the second part of the novel is a traveling tent show in which Ella becomes an actress. Although Duncan's second novel is not very successful, its picture of the traveling repertory company is a valid one, recalling an aspect of Iowa's cultural past that has all but disappeared. In 1972, only Don Davidson's continuation of the Neil and Caroline Schaffner "Toby" show, still showing in a tent in a number of smaller Iowa towns, maintains the tradition once upheld by J. Doug Morgan's shows, the Don and Maisie Dixon players, the Grand and Majestic theaters in Cedar Rapids, the Princess in Des Moines, and houses in almost every county-seat town and other towns of over two or three thousand population. Neil Schaffner has depicted something of that world in *The Fabulous Toby and Me* (1968), but the definitive history of the Iowa repertory company and the "Toby" shows (Iowa's only "folk art" form) remains to be written.

Duncan's next novel, *Ring Horse* (1940), is the slightest of his books in bulk, and is really only a long short story. Unlike the complex plots of his other novels, the story line of *Ring Horse* is simple: A clown bareback rider is stranded in Sioux Creek with his horse, Silver Fire. An attorney, John Canfield, tries to chase Danny out of town; a livery-stable owner covets the horse. The story is narrated by Paul Reese, another attorney, who doesn't like horses. Canfield's young daughter, Betty, who loves horses, completes the cast.

The story of *Ring Horse* came out of the research Duncan was doing for his best known work, *Gus the Great* (1947). Duncan had been inspired to write the book by his discovery, one November afternoon in 1936 of what had once been a circus farm; "the winter quarters of a circus, long dead" near Granger, Iowa. His interest in circuses suddenly renewed, he quickly discovered that

Iowa had been a circus state. The Ringling boys had been born in McGregor, and many other circus owners and performers had their origins in Iowa. . . . Circuses needed to headquarter in a land where there was plenty of hay and corn and oats for the stock, and Iowa was such a land.

As Duncan thought about his discoveries he began to sense a theme for his book: "there were philosophical implications in a ruined and abandoned circus. For a circus is a microcosm, traveling through the world as the earth travels through space; and I thought there was a hint of the ruin of civilization in this rotting circus." He began writing his novel that winter, and soon he saw that it "was not going to be a circus novel; it was to be a novel about a man who happened to own a circus." Duncan could see this circus owner: "huge and prosperous . . . a ruined man, tramping back to the farm." For Duncan, this first sight of "Gus" was "love at first sight."[23]

It took Duncan over ten years and 1,386 pages of manuscript to finish the novel. (He discarded over 200,000 words at one time, and rewrote the first chapter "about thirty times.") *Gus the Great* is the story of Tamarack and Clayton Junction (Valley Junction, now West Des Moines?), two adjoining Iowa towns, of the Sebastians who swing on rings at the very top of the big top, of their daughter Eloise, of the lion tamer Captain Philip Latcher, and Willie Krummer, the captain's cage-

---

23   Duncan, "An Autobiography of Thomas Duncan."

boy who does the captain in because he covets the captain's wife. It is the story of Ive Pawpacker, a small town banker who loves horses and who finances the circus. Above all, it is the story of the meretricious but ebullient Gus Burgoyne, the spawn of an illegitimate relationship between a railroad tycoon and the sister-in-law of a saloon keeper. Gus is, in John P. Marquand's words, a "shoddy but at the same time occasionally magnificent parody of a Mr. America, a product as purely American as plug tobacco. He is Gus the Great only out of courtesy, because of his dreams rather than his actions."[24]

Gus the Great was a Book-of-the-Month selection and sold three-fourths of a million copies. For the first time Duncan, who had exhausted his financial resources in writing the book, began to feel some financial security. He had sold the film rights to *Ring Horse;* he now sold the film rights to *Gus the Great*.

One wonders as he reads Duncan's novels if the author does not believe that all the world is corrupt. (Even when a newspaper is taking a collection for the legless Willie Krummer, we are told that a reporter pilfers five dollars from the fund and gives it to his bootlegger!) John T. Frederick has commented on this aspect of Duncan's work:

Duncan's writing has a good deal of the force and pungency of Stong's; but there is a fundamental difference in the attitudes of the two men toward their material. At bottom . . . Stong is fond of his characters and the places where they live. He likes people—he has relish even for bad people; and he likes Iowa even when he laughs at something Iowan. It is otherwise with Duncan. The reader shares throughout [Duncan's novels] what appears to be the author's controlled dislike for . . . nearly all the characters.[25]

One of the characters treated sympathetically is Alex Kerry, an artist, who first appears late in the novel:

At this late date, everybody knows that an artist of great talent and perhaps genius was working in the Middle West during the 1920's. But [at first] few persons knew Alex Kerry, and of those who did, almost nobody thought he was working. He spent his time painting. Not houses or barns. No. He painted pictures . . . Alex was of medium height with a tendency toward plumpness. He had reddish blond hair, a wide mouth, a funny little upturned nose, and he wore steel-rimmed glasses. His blue eyes were usually amused, and he laughed a lot.

---

24 John P. Marquand, "Gus the Great," *Book-of-the-Month-Club-News* (August 1947), pp. 1–2.
25 John T. Frederick, "Town and City in Iowa Fiction," *Palimpsest* 35 (February 1954):82–83.

The model for Alex Kerry is Grant Wood; on the ensuing pages of *Gus the Great* he is seen as a young painter, as a developing artist, and in his studio at No. 5 Turner Alley in Cedar Rapids.

Duncan's literary style in *Gus the Great* depends on the flashback and the principle of retardation. He begins his novel at a point near the end of his story, then hints of things to come, and then flashes back to a point in the earlier life of his hero. That treatment is repeated throughout the novel. Moreover, as the tale is narrated, a name of a person or place is introduced frequently, usually at a moment of suspense, and the story is stopped to supply the reader with details on the new subject. The danger that a writer faces in the use of these two devices—especially in novels as complex as *Gus the Great* or Duncan's later *The Labyrinth*—is mere garrulity. Duncan manages to avoid the worst faults of these devices and at times is successful with them. The Labyrinth devised by Paul Farber in the later novel is, apparently, an attempt at a symbol for Duncan's literary technique; if the reader can trace his way through the labyrinth of the novels, he comes close to the dead center of understanding.

Duncan's next novel, *Virgo Descending* (1961), is a story of the relationships between a twenty-nine year old writer living in Santa Fe, New Mexico, and a mysterious young Danish poetess who comes from the Virgin Islands. The tale is one of Duncan's brighter and frothier efforts; its main interest to an Iowa reader is that Pete McCabe, the narrator, grew up in Litchfield, Iowa, went to school at Drake, and worked as a newspaperman in Des Moines.

Duncan's 1967 novel, *The Labyrinth*, is a story which attempts to unravel the complex social patterns and personal interrelationships of the small town of Litchfield, sixty miles west of Des Moines. (Like all of Duncan's small towns, it is modeled on Casey.) The catalyst which sets off the unraveling is a disastrous train wreck on the afternoon of July 4, 1897, and the changes which take place in some of Litchfield's citizens as a result of the looting of the wrecked train and its cargo of whiskey.

James Stevens (1892–1972) was born on the farm of his maternal grandmother near Albia and lived there for a few years, an experience described in "A Prairie Town" (*American Mercury*, September 1925). After the age of ten, he lived away from Iowa, and most of his writing was about Paul Bunyan. But two of his *American Mercury* stories about his boyhood days in Moravia, Iowa, are classic stories of small-town life. "The Downfall of Elder Barton" (December 1931) concerns a horse-trading elder of the Hardshell Baptist faith who eventually meets his come-uppance because he consents to be a good Samaritan to an elderly Moravian lady with Roman Catholic leanings. The story's scenes of horse-trading and of the rural Methodist attitudes toward Catholicism are especially vivid.

In "Medicine Men" some of the same characters appear again. Again there is a feud, but this time it is between Dr. Benjamin Bearpaw, concocter of "Prairie Root for Kidney Trouble," and the Reverend Pearl Yates, the man who on other occasions "lit into rum and Rome." A high point of the story is the visit to Moravia of the old-time "medicine show," as seen through the eyes of the ten-year-old Moravia boy who narrates both stories:

The crowd was properly primed with sentiment when Dr. Bearpaw himself strode forth soberly in his Indian regalia. Indian war drums sounded from the gloom of the covered wagon, and with them shivery yells. I was deeply stirred. Dr. Bearpaw was a mighty sight there, in his beaded buckskin uniform, his head plumed with colored eagle feathers, his face streaked with war paint, a tomahawk in one hand and a bottle of Prairie Root for Kidney Trouble in the other. He set the bottle on the table, stuck the tomahawk in his belt, then stood and stared over the crowd. The drums beat on, but softer now, and the yells whined away.[26]

Iowans can only regret that James Stevens didn't mine this vein more extensively.

Josephine Herbst was born in Sioux City on March 5, 1897, of parents who came to Iowa from Emmaus, Pennsylvania, where the family had lived for a hundred years prior to the late 1880s. As a child she read omnivorously; her first book of her own was Bunyan's *Pilgrim's Progress*. In reading family diaries and letters, kept "for generations," she derived her "first inkling . . . of the complexity and significance of people in relation to each other and the world. . . . Living seemed constantly fertilized and damned by the tragic burden one generation passed to the next."[27]

Miss Herbst was "never satisfied" with her home town, and she found life at four different colleges—Morningside, the University of Iowa, the University of Washington, and the University of California—equally unsatisfactory. In the years after graduation from California, she began to earn her own way, typing, teaching, working in a print shop, a department store, for a charity organization, for H. L. Mencken as an editorial reader. In 1922 she went to Europe where she lived for three years in Germany, Italy, and France. "The beautiful Iowa land never came alive for me until years in Europe taught me to see it," she said.

In Paris she met many of the so-called "lost generation," but managed

---

26 James Stevens, "Medicine Men," *American Mercury* 28 (April 1933):487–97.
27 Stanley J. Kunitz, ed., "Josephine Herbst," *Twentieth Century Authors* (New York: H. W. Wilson Co., 1965), pp. 641–42. All Herbst biographical material in this chapter comes from this source.

to maintain her philosophical distance from them, although it is possible that she was influenced by Hemingway's literary style: "I have always considered myself to be in a constant state of new discovery," she once said. In 1925 she married John Herrman, also a writer.

During the next few years she traveled extensively: "I . . . visited the Soviet Union in 1930, returned to Germany to report the effect of Hitler's regime for the New York *Post* and the *Nation* in 1935, was in Cuba during the general strike of 1935, in my own state, Iowa, for the farm strike of 1932, in Flint, Mich., during the automobile strike of 1937, and in that same year I was in Madrid during its bombardment. In 1939 I went to South America."[28]

Miss Herbst's first novel, *Nothing is Sacred* (1928), like Ruth Suckow's much later *The John Wood Case*, is a fictional study of the discovery of a case of embezzlement, this time in a small Iowa city. Harry Winter, whose family accuses him of "high living," has taken eight hundred dollars from his lodge (of which he is secretary), and his mother must mortgage her home to keep him out of serious trouble. The tight respectable social balance of the family is so concerned with money that this defalcation represents near tragedy, and the novel shows the previously-hidden conflict within the family as it tries and fails to resolve its problems. Like Miss Suckow's characters, Miss Herbst's are ordinary people whom most novelists would have passed by as being too insignificant or too uninteresting.

Katherine Anne Porter was impressed with this first novel, saying: "The old mother is superb. The story of her life, struggles and death is told with touching gravity and tenderness. I know only one other old woman in a novel who compares with her for pure reality—Mrs. Moore in *A Passage to India*."[29] Critics admired the "simplicity of her idiom, the economy of her method and the unemotionalized detachment of her point of view." In comparing her style with Hemingway's, one reviewer thought that she had "extended the possibilities of his method."[30]

Miss Herbst's next novel is not on an Iowa subject, but critics complained that her attempt to deal with the commonplace in *Money For Love* (1929) had produced a commonplace novel (in the best sense of the word), "on a dead level of drab phrases, free of exaltation or elevation of any sort whatever."[31]

---

28 "Josephine Herbst," *Twentieth Century Authors.*
29 Katherine Anne Porter, "The Family," *New York Herald Tribune Books*, October 7, 1928, p. 2.
30 *New York Times Review of Books*, October 21, 1928, p. 6.
31 Clifton P. Fadiman, "Small Ways of Small People," *Nation* 129 (November 20, 1929):592; Florence Haxton, "Up in Harriet's Room," *New York Herald Tribune Books*, October 6, 1929, pp. 5–6.

Miss Herbst now set out to write a trilogy of "collective novels" in which the hero would be "not a man but a people."[32] Her goal, she said, was to "cover not only the decay of capitalistic society but also the upthrust of a new group society. To write historical stuff not in the romantic method or as history, but as living, breathing language and life. . . ."[33]

The three novels, *Pity Is Not Enough* (1933), *The Executioner Awaits* (1934), and *Rope of Gold* (1939) compose "an extraordinary history of America" from 1870 to 1939—"history written in terms of 'men's feelings . . . the hidden springs of men's actions . . . .' "[34] Of these only the last novel has an Iowa setting. The time is the depression years of 1933 to 1936. Part of the novel's setting is in the Dust Bowl around Mitchell, South Dakota, part is in and around Sioux City during the farm strikes there. The farmers who are beset with mortgages, dust storms, and farm organization movements are set off against auto factory workers who are unemployed, on relief or on strike. Miss Herbst made good use of her travel experiences in these three novels. Richard Cordell found *Rope of Gold* to be a powerful, original novel . . . better written than any of [John] Dos Passos's novels.[35] And Alfred Kazin said that

her books are the latest in that long line of Mid-West chronicles of failures which have joylessly hacked the Valley of Democracy. That line began with the passing of the frontier and is being toughened on the passing of the American dream; but the material is the same, the same hungry flies buzz around the kitchen linoleum, and the Iowa or Kansas farmer droops as helplessly in Miss Herbst's novels as he drooped for Hamlin Garland or Ed Howe.[36]

Miss Herbst's other novels are *Satan's Sergeants* (1941) and *Somewhere the Tempest Fell* (1947). In 1936 she received the Guggenheim Award in the field of the novel; she may well be the best novelist Iowa has turned out. But the "collective" novel, as a genre, did not survive the nineteen-thirties, and there is little interest in her books today.

Charles Tenney Jackson's *The Midlanders* (1912) is set in two southeastern Iowa towns, "Rome" and "Earlville" in the Sinsinawa (Skunk) River valley. The novel has some interesting scenes of Iowa small town life in the first decade of the twentieth century. We see the same class distinctions which Mrs. Ford presented in her two novels based on Mount

32   Alfred Kazin, "Flies in the Mid-West Kitchen," *New York Herald Tribune Books*, March 5, 1939, p. 7.
33   "Josephine Herbst," *Twentieth Century Authors*.
34   Rebecca Pitts, "The Trexler Trilogy," *New Republic* 98 (March 22, 1939):202.
35   Richard Cordell, "After the Gilded Age," *Saturday Review of Literature* 19 (March 4, 1929):7.
36   Kazin, "Flies in the Mid-West Kitchen."

Vernon life of the same period, and the anti-Catholicism we have seen elsewhere. The story line features a fight against corrupt county politics (one character, anticipating Quick's "Raws" Upright, runs "the county board—soaking us on bridge contracts") and the adventures of the heroine as an actress. But when the author asks his readers to believe that his heroine, kidnapped as a small child during the Mardi Gras and, after living in the Cajun country for several years, by chance makes her way to the same small Iowa town where her father lives (neither knowing of the existence of the other), he is beginning to ask too much. And when the relatively uneducated girl survives a pitched gun battle and marries the richest boy in town, a Harvard law graduate whose parents oppose the marriage, he has surely demanded more of his reader's sentiments than one is obliged to supply.

Charles Tenney Jackson was a native of Knoxville. According to the only available information about *The Midlanders*, it "is set in Knoxville, and a number of characters are based on Knoxville residents."[37]

Henry G. Felsen is not an Iowan by birth but he has lived in Iowa for over thirty years, and since 1946 all of his books have had an Iowa setting. Among these are the best-selling *Hot Rod* and other books about teen-agers and their automobiles. These so-called "teen-car" books have sold more than five million copies, thus making Felsen one of the leaders among Iowa authors in reaching vast audiences. Some of his books have been published pseudonymously. Among these is *Fever Heat* (by "Angus Vicker"); a movie of this book was made in Iowa.

In a letter to the author, Felsen said that he was not thought of as an Iowan (he lives in West Des Moines) because he was not "calved on sacred soil [Iowa soil]." And he concluded: " 'Real' Iowans are people who are born [in Iowa], move to California at the age of ten days and never return."

Other than the poets mentioned in this history in some detail, there have been many Iowans who have written verse about their state—too many for inclusion in this history. This study therefore has limited itself to those poets who have achieved critical status in the eyes of recognized critics of poetry.

There are several who might have achieved fame had they written more of the kind of verse of which they were capable. One is John Noble Campbell whose "Fox Hunt-Midland" and "Murals of a County Courthouse" were well received. Another is Edward Rowan whose poetic tribute to Jay G. Sigmund was reluctantly left out of this volume. A

---

37 Alice Marple, *Iowa Authors and Their Works* (Des Moines, Iowa: Historical Department of Iowa, 1918). The comment is found under Jackson's name in the "Literature" section following p. 347.

third is Oneita Fisher of West Chester, who writes often about Iowa, and whose slim volume, "To My First Martini," has been a source of pleasure. As this history goes to press a new novel, *The Last Fair Deal Going Down* by David Rhodes, a native Iowan, has just been favorably reviewed (*Saturday Review*, September 9, 1972, pp. 73–74). The novel is set in a symbolic "inner City" or "lower City" of Des Moines.

In expiation for whatever of worth has not been mentioned in this history, either through ignorance, the limitations of space, or (perhaps) the cavalier attitude of the author, there is attached to this chapter (pp. 263–64) a list of all the books and pamphlets on the subject of Iowa poetry which were discoverable.

Historians, Editors, and Publishers

ALTHOUGH the State Historical Society of Iowa had been established by law in 1857, the first recognition that there was a body of Iowa literature seems not to have been made until April 10, 1890, when Theodore S. Parvin, Grand Librarian of the Iowa Masonic Library at Cedar Rapids, compiled a "List of Iowa Authors." More than three hundred names appeared in the list, including several M.D.'s, several D.D.'s, S. L. Clemens (Mark Twain), Alice French, Ferris Jerome (Alice Ilgenfritz Jones), and Parvin's own name. Hiram Alvin Reid and Hamlin Garland were not listed. It was noted that some of the authors had published "from two to 10 distinct volumes," and that Parvin was attempting to collect all of the volumes for his library.[1]

Parvin's interest may have been encouraged by Johnson Brigham who had come to Cedar Rapids on March 1, 1882, to become editor and part owner of the Cedar Rapids *Republican*. Brigham (born DeWitt Clinton Johnson Brigham on March 11, 1846, in Cherry Valley, New York) was a man interested in both literature and history. His second wife, Lucy Hitchcock of Cedar Rapids, was the daughter of William Williams Walker, an influential man in the history of railroad building in Iowa, and sister-in-law of A. W. Lee of the *Ottumwa Courier*, who was to found the Lee Syndicate of newspapers, radio and television stations.

Brigham began to have an idea for "a magazine which would embody the spirit of the Middle West."[2] In 1893, after a short term as American Consul at Aix-la-Chapelle, he sold his interest in the *Republican* to William R. Boyd and Luther A. Brewer for twenty thousand dollars, and with this sum of money, moved to Des Moines (because of its central Iowa location, and also because of its superior printing and binding facilities) to begin the *Midland Monthly*. The magazine (its name was chosen

1 T. S. Parvin, "List of Iowa Authors," (Cedar Rapids: Iowa Masonic Library, April 10, 1890). This list refers to an earlier list "published early in March," and suggests the possibility of further information in "Annual Reports."
2 Luella M. Wright, "The Midland Monthly," *Iowa Journal of History and Politics* 45 (January 1947):3.

at a family conference) was to be "distinctively a magazine of the Middle-West and the Northwest . . . the historian and the prophet of this wide new land which is so rapidly reaching out toward art and the finer things of life and the greater things of human achievement."[3]

The magazine's beginnings coincided with three other efforts which were to focus attention on literature in the state and middle border country. One was the founding of the federation of the women's literary and study groups in Iowa; a second was the first Carnegie endowment of libraries in the state (soon these two programs were to be directed toward the establishment of traveling libraries, an activity in which Brigham was to play an important part); and the third was the publication of Hamlin Garland's *Crumbling Idols*, the clarion call for a literature of the middle border. Although Brigham was to praise the book, because "it aims to weaken the hold of conventionalism upon the public mind, and to strengthen the individualism of the artist mind,"[4] he published the opposite point of view, George Merriam Hyde's "Grumbling Realists and Great Story-Tellers" with its thesis that Garland "subordinates writing to geography . . . . Are all Western painters to confine themselves to golden grain and purple shadows because they happen to live in the West?"[5] Forty years later this quarrel was to rise anew in Iowa.

Brigham published a chapter of Garland's *Boy Life on the Prairie*, and also some of Garland's *Prairie Songs*, printing the "Massasauga" poem in a facsimile of the manuscript. He praised these poems, saying that they "came fresh and strong from the heart of a man who, reared on prairie soil . . . feels whereof he sings . . . ."[6] He also published Alice French, Alice Ilgenfritz Jones, Cyrenus Cole (later an editor of the *Republican*), S. H. M. Byers, Bertha M. Horak (later Mrs. Benjamin F. Shambaugh and author of *Amana That Was and Amana That Is* (1932), Barthinius L. Wick, Samuel Calvin, L. J. Palda, B. F. Tillinghast, Benjamin F. Gue, Abigail Gardner Sharp (survivor of the Spirit Lake massacre) and many others. Mary J. Reid, a former editor of the *Literary Northwest* at Minneapolis, submitted an essay on "Western Literature" and two articles on Alice French; another essay on the Davenport author came from a distinguished Frenchwoman, Madame Blanc (Th. Bentzon). Other authors included Ellis Parker Butler, Tacitus Hussey, Barton O. Aylesworth, then

---

3 Johnson Brigham, "Iowa's Strategic Position. A Talk with Broad-Gauge Advertisers," *Midland Monthly* 4 (July 1895).
4 Johnson Brigham, "The Midland Book Table," *Midland Monthly* 2 (November 1894):431–32.
5 George Merriam Hyde, "Grumbling Realists and Great Story-Tellers," *Midland Monthly* 5 (April 1896):327–30.
6 Johnson Brigham, "Editorial Comment," *Midland Monthly* 1 (January–June 1894): 95–96.

president of Drake University and later president of the National Broadcasting Company, Professor Selden L. Whitcomb of Grinnell, Frank Burlingame Harris, Emerson Hough, and Frank W. Calkins. There were many stories of pioneer life and many "local color" tales, most of which featured some form of dialect. Brigham's personal contributions to the magazine consisted of two features, "Editorial Comment" and "Publisher's Notes." In the former he "reviewed current books on politics, history, and literature and expressed his views . . . ." According to Professor Luella M. Wright, Brigham was "in the vanguard of the current movements of realism and regionalism" in his criticism.[7]

In the course of its existence, the magazine acquired four other midwestern magazines and assimilated them; still Brigham, who always paid his writers and sold advertising, had difficulties in maintaining his high standards and keeping his magazine going. When in 1898, he was offered the post of State Librarian by Governor Leslie M. Shaw, he took it, and shortly thereafter turned his magazine over to his printers. The printers sold the magazine to two men who moved it to St. Louis where, after five more numbers, the magazine ceased publication. Brigham remained as State Librarian until October 8, 1936, a vigorous, alert, and active man almost to the day of his death at age ninety.

Although in its lifetime the *Midland Monthly* drew national attention and had a distinct influence upon the literature of the middle border, perhaps its most significant contribution was that it prepared the way for John T. Frederick's *Midland* less than two decades later.[8]

One of the possible consequences of the magazine may have been at Iowa (Grinnell) College, where in 1898, the junior class, under the direction of Professor Selden L. Whitcomb, passed over its usual "annual" and issued a volume of short stories, *On A Western Campus* (Buffalo: Charles Wells Moulton), "with the view of presenting mainly in the spirit of realistic interpretation . . . varied scenes in the 'human comedy' of a co-educational college between the Missouri and the Mississippi."[9] The *Midland Monthly* praised the volume as a "radical, significant, and . . . altogether gratifying departure" from the usual practice.[10]

The next stage in the process of producing an Iowa literature came in 1902, although its ultimate fruition took a dozen years. That year Josiah Royce journeyed to Iowa City to deliver an address to Alpha of Iowa chapter of Phi Beta Kappa and its guests, warning against the dangers of

---

7 Wright, "The Midland Monthly," pp. 45–48.
8 Wright, "The Midland Monthly," pp. 45–48.
9 "Prefatory Note," *On a Western Campus* (Buffalo: Charles Wells Moulton, 1897), pp. xi-xii.
10 "The Midland Book Table," *Midland Monthly* 8 (October 1897):384.

industrial standardization. The subject of his talk was provincialism and Hamlin Garland would have been comfortable listening. Royce called for a "higher Provincialism," and warned that America "because of new social forces, lay in danger of losing 'its conscience, its spiritual dignity, its organic life'; that the country skirted the peril of becoming robotized in its thinking." The solution to this peril, said Royce, was to encourage the "individualities" of the provinces.[11]

The impact of Royce's address remained on the campus. The address itself, under the title of "Provincialism" was incorporated in *Race Questions, Provincialism, and Other American Problems* (New York, 1908) which became a standard text; "his effect as teacher and writer was profound," said one critic.[12]

Meanwhile, the literary atmosphere of the country was leaning toward romance and sentimentalism as we have seen in the careers of Alice French and Hamlin Garland from 1900 onwards. Rupert Hughes, Emerson Hough, Herbert Quick, and Susan Glaspell, among the few Iowans writing at the time, were writing sentimental romances for the most part.

From the century's turn to 1915 there were but a scant half dozen who were not revelling in the stickiness of lollypopism. Dreiser, David Graham Phillips, Stephen Crane, Edith Wharton, Willa Cather, and Frank Norris—these were almost the only ones to ride out of the mire of vapidity. It was an era when Eleanor Porters splashed unabashedly in their warm milk, gushing forth reams of Pollyannas. . . . The silliness is partly explained by the authors who had lost contact with the life which they legitimately should have explored.[13]

In 1910, a young native of Corning, Iowa, a man who had grown up on a southwest Iowa farm amidst fourth generation Iowans, came to the University of Iowa. There he came under the influence of C. F. Ansley, then head of Iowa's English department and later editor of the Columbia University Press, and Edwin Ford Piper, who had begun his teaching career in a Nebraska university at the turn of the century and who had come to Iowa a few years later. These men impressed John Towner Frederick (born 1892) with ideas which it was easy for him, with his Iowa farm background, to accept: that Americans should be reminded that they should stick to the subject matter of their native soil, that it was desirable, even necessary, for a writer to seek his materials in familiar, understood, environments. In later years Frederick recalled some of those classroom days:

---

11   Charles Allen, "The Midland," *American Prefaces* 3 (June 1938):136–40.
12   *Encyclopaedia Britannica* (1960), s.v. "Josiah Royce."
13   Allen, "The Midland," pp. 136–40.

Pictures fill my memory whenever I see or hear the name of Edwin Ford Piper—pictures that are good to hold and turn over in the mind. I am a member of a class studying English ballads—sitting in a stiff classroom chair and listening to a reading of "Sir Patrick Spens." I carry away from the classroom not only the music and feeling of the ballad itself, but some sense of contact with the people who first made and sang it. I am a member of another class—an informal one this time. Attendance is optional, but there are few of us who fail to find our way in the late afternoon to Mr. Piper's basement office, where we sit in nooks between bookcases or even share a table with heaps of papers and magazines, and read the stories and poems and essays we have written for the comments of one another and our leader.[14]

In these conversations, conversations in which later Roger L. Sergel, Ival McPeak, and Raymond Durboraw joined, there began to be a sense of the need for a literary magazine which would give these young writers and other young midwesterners a chance for publication. There was a recognition that

eastern commercial periodicals were not giving the best of the young Midwest writers an opportunity to be read. *Harper's, Atlantic, Scribner's,* and others were at that time more concerned with name writers than with the sincerity of the fiction they fed their readers. . . . Most seaboard editors were determined on one of two things from a trans-Allegheny writer. Either he must mold the middlewest outlook to conform with that of the East, or the midwest soul must be burlesqued for the amusement of the East. In either case, the writer could not honestly explore the spirit of his native people.[15]

The first issue of *The Midland: A Magazine of the Middlewest* was planned for January 1915. Edwin Ford Piper helped secure guarantors, the Economy Advertising Company of Iowa City was hired to publish it, and the magazine was in business.

The first issue contained an editorial by John T. Frederick which showed how much Royce's thinking and Frederick's were alike: "Possibly the region between the mountains would gain in variety at least if it retained more of its makers of literature, music, pictures, and more of its other expressions of civilization. And possibly civilization itself might be with us a somewhat swifter process if expressions of its spirit were more frequent."

Meanwhile other efforts were being made outside the University to develop pride in Iowa literature. In 1913, the office of Edgar R. Harlan, curator of the Historical Department of Iowa, directed Miss Alice Mar-

---

14 John T. Frederick, "A Maker of Songs," *American Prefaces* 2 (March 1937):83.
15 Allen, "The Midland," pp. 136–40.

ple, the assistant curator, to formulate "some scheme for disclosing whether there was any substance in the meaning of the phrase, then gaining currency, 'Iowa Authors and their works.'"[16] Miss Marple consequently began to assemble a set of library cards representing literature (in the broadest sense of the word). She worked from Parvin's list, from a list produced by Professor Selden L. Whitcomb, a list prepared by the Iowa Press and Author's Club, an essay "Some Recent Publications by Iowa Authors" in the *Iowa Journal of History and Politics*, "A List of Books by Iowa Authors," which had been published in 1904 by the Iowa Library Commission, and books and newspaper clippings in the Historical Library. A tentative list of names was published in the *Annals of Iowa* from October 1914 through October 1915. The complete volume, *Iowa Authors and Their Works*, was published in 1918.

On October 5, 6, and 7, 1914, an "Iowa Authors' Homecoming" was held in Des Moines in an "effort to restore the balance of emphasis in the life of the state," and to demonstrate to other states that "Iowa ears were attuned" to something more than "the sounds of the dinnerbell," and that she had books other than "a bulging pocket book and an agricultural report."[17] Gardner Cowles and Edwin Meredith were two of the hosts; Harvey Ingham, Hamlin Garland, Arthur Davison Ficke, Major S. H. M. Byers, Lewis Worthington Smith, and Alice French were speakers. Rupert Hughes and Emerson Hough were there; among those who sent notes of regret were Edna Ferber (who lived in Ottumwa when she was a child), Herbert Quick, and Susan Glaspell.

The first issue of *The Midland* contained a letter from Johnson Brigham noting that it had been just twenty-one years before that he had been planning the first issue of the old *Midland*. He was pleased with the new venture and saw it as "reviving [his] hope that a substantial medium for the best thought of the Middle West is about to be established at Iowa's educational center." But the letter also contained a friendly warning about economics and the necessity to sell advertising. Frederick, who was never to pay for any contributions, was to take in very little cash for advertising; moreover, the publication of the magazine was to cost him personally two hundred sixty-three dollars in the first year and as much as a thousand dollars a year near the end of publication.

The Midland's first year saw it win prestige: Mrs. B. F. Shambaugh, Nelson Antrim Crawford, Arthur Davison Ficke, Walter J. Muilenburg, Mahlon Leonard Fisher, Howard Mumford Jones, John G. Neihardt,

---

16   Alice Marple, *Iowa Authors and Their Works* (Des Moines: Historical Department of Iowa, 1918), pp. iii–iv.
17   James B. Weaver, "The Authors' Homecoming of 1914," *The Midland* 1 (January 1915):22–25.

William Ellery Leonard, Selden L. Whitcomb, Thomas D. Murphy (whose "Sunset Highways" was one of a long series on the new fad of motor travel), Edward A. Steiner, Robert J. Burdette, Lewis Worthington Smith, Roger L. Sergel, Ival McPeak, and Walter L. Myers were some of its writers. Not all of its material was *belles-lettres*. Some of the first year writers were destined for international fame in one way or another.

Part of the magazine's prestige came from another publishing innovation for that year, Edward J. O'Brien's *The Best Short Stories of 1915*. O'Brien reprinted Muilenburg's "Heart of Youth" (passing over "Prairie" with a word of high praise) and added this comment:

A year ago a slender little monthly magazine . . . was first issued in Iowa City. It attracted very little attention, and in the course of the year published but ten short stories. It has been my pleasure and wonder to find in those ten stories [O'Brien had read 2,200 stories before making the selections for his annual] the most vital interpretation in fiction of our national life that many years have been able to show. Since the most brilliant days of the New England men of letters, no such group of writers has defined its position with such assurance and modesty.[18]

Despite his financial problems and other matters (his moving to Minnesota to teach and to Michigan to farm, and the deaths of close friends), Frederick and *The Midland* persevered, with first Edwin Ford Piper and later Frank Luther Mott as coeditors. The magazine had its good days also; there was that day when Mott's "brilliant, mystically turned" and widely admired "The Man With the Good Face" came across Frederick's desk, and then there was another in 1916 when as "dusk came on in the narrow book-filled office, [he] read the partially completed manuscript of *Barbed Wire* offered [him] by Mr. Piper with some hesitation and with a characteristically genuine deference to the judgment of the young editor." Frederick said, "I felt sure then—as I have ever since—that in the opportunity for publication of these poems, if in no other way *The Midland* found a reason for being."[19]

In 1918 a poem of four lines, "Song in October," heralded the arrival of Ruth Suckow as a writer of stature, and in 1920 her story "Uprooted" (one of her best) marked the beginning of a long and cordial relationship between Suckow and Frederick.

In 1924, at the end of ten years, Frederick was able to say with his usual modesty and unpretentiousness:

---

18   Edward J. O'Brien, *The Best Short Stories of 1915* . . . (Boston: Small Maynard & Co., 1916), p. 9. See also "The Honor Roll" in this and subsequent volumes.
19   Frederick, "A Maker of Songs," p. 83.

It is still to me a joint adventure of readers, contributors, and editor—laborious and difficult, but joyous, slightly irresponsible, and devoted most of all to the cause of good fellowship. We are seeking, to be sure, some such things as truth and beauty. But I do not want to be too rigidly convinced that I know what these things are or where to find them.[20]

Meanwhile, in 1917, "as the first co-operative work done by Iowa writers," the Iowa Press and Author's Club published *Prairie Gold*, a volume of relatively undistinguished work by a group of fairly distinguished writers: Arthur Davison Ficke, S. H. M. Byers, Helen Cowles LeCron, Alice French, Jessie Welborn Smith, Hamlin Garland, Rupert Hughes, Lewis Worthington Smith, Henry C. Wallace, Tacitus Hussey, Verne Marshall, Frank Luther Mott, Bertha M. Shambaugh, Olney Fred Sweet, Helen Sherman Griffith, Emerson Hough, Honoré Willsie, and Randall Parish. There are three good things in the volume: Ellis Parker Butler's "Bread," James Norman Hall's "Kitchener's Mob," and Johnson Brigham's "Iowa as a Literary Field," the latter a resumé of the history of Iowa literature written by one who had lived it.

In 1923, Frank Luther Mott delivered an address, "Literature of Pioneer Life in Iowa," before the Iowa Academy of Science and Letters in Sioux City. The address, together with "a partially annotated bibliography" was published the same year by the State Historical Society. Mott discussed both fiction and non-fiction; his authors included Garland, Quick, Calkins, Piper, Byers, John Carl Parish, Willard Barrows, Warren P. Isham, Edward Bonney and many others. This book, coinciding with the publication of Quick's trilogy and Garland's autobiographical books of "the middle border" did much to publicize the value of Iowa's historical background as a source for *belles-lettres*. The awards of Pulitzer Prizes about this time to both Garland and Margaret Wilson also helped to give status to Iowa literature. The founding in 1920 of *Palimpsest*, a popular monthly historical periodical with its subsequent publication of articles about Iowa writers and their work, as well as about other aspects of Iowa history, contributed a great deal more to the rising spirit.

Although Frederick himself "never formulated a positive literary regionalism, . . . in seeking for honest stories interpreting the Middle West, [he] was advancing the same argument as his latter day descendants—the literary regionalists."[21] Moreover, the first volume of *The Midland* had carried an essay by Johnson Brigham advocating "Literature Local and General," and the title of the publication itself implied a built-in regionalism.

---

20 *The Midland* 10 (January, 1924).
21 Allen, "The Midland," pp. 136–40.

Frederick was seeking out and publishing Iowa writers—MacKinlay Kantor, Ruth Suckow, Paul Engle, Phil Stong, James Hearst, and Marquis Childs. Nevertheless, in the mid-1920s, the magazine was attracting more and more writers from outside the state—writers who, incidentally, were to acquire solid reputations: Tupper Greenwald, Warren L. Van Dine, William March, Raymond Weeks, James Farrell, David Cornel De Jong, Albert Halper, and Clifford Bragdon. With some of these men and with others, Frederick spent "hours and days . . . criticizing, encouraging"; the kind of teaching that the Iowa Writers Workshop was to do upon its inception a decade later. For a while the magazine prospered; its circulation was up to twelve hundred (although as many as two thousand copies were printed). Frank Luther Mott became coeditor in 1925, and his strong sense for journalism helped. Frederick and Mott began to dream "of a time when their magazine could become a more potent national influence."[22]

In its eighteen years of existence, *The Midland* published three hundred and thirty-seven stories. Edward J. O'Brien judged three hundred and twenty four of these to be of high merit when compared to stories being published in other magazines, and one hundred and five of the stories received his highest rating. Almost every volume of O'Brien's annual *Best Stories* had a story which had first been published in *The Midland*.

In 1930, Edward J. O'Brien, expressing the opinion that the quality periodicals were dying on their feet because they persisted in publishing second-rate stories whose only recommendation was the canonized names of the writers, called for "a new national monthly" which might pool the contents of several small magazines, and be centered in Iowa City. To O'Brien, "the geographical centre of American literary life" had shifted from the northeast to the Iowa town.

But Frederick had decided to move his magazine to Chicago "because of its energy, position, printing facilities, and *Poetry*." Late in 1930 he left Iowa City "with a box of subscription cards and a sheaf of manuscripts—alike slender, sole impedimenta of the [Iowa City] editorial office." In Chicago, his editorial offices faced "black roofs and the utilitarian facade of a twelve-story garage." But *The Midland* prospered for a while with Frederick as sole editor. But then the depression caught up with the magazine; for eighteen months, Frederick fought a losing battle, and then one day in 1933, he combined four months' issues into one and sent them out with an "Editorial" which announced the end:

For nearly twenty years I have given to [*The Midland*] money taken from my work as teacher and farmer, from my reading, from my family life; and

---

22 Allen, "The Midland," pp. 136–40.

though the money and time have been alike sometimes needed and hard to spare, my personal rewards have been great.[23]

It is unfortunate that *The Midland* could not have continued, for it had achieved a place alongside our best literary quarterlies. Moreover, said Wallace Stegner in the *Saturday Review of Literature,* "John Frederick and his friends on *The Midland* did for fiction, through the little magazine, what Susan Glaspell and George Cram Cook had done for drama through the little theater." And Stegner concluded that "the regional flavor not only of Frederick's magazine but of his own novels, and the fact that his work had been done in and for Iowa and the Middle West, have made this unselfish and helpful critic and editor the greatest single force in Iowa letters in the past twenty-five years."[24]

In 1930, the Iowa State Teachers Association published *A Book of Iowa Authors by Iowa Authors.* "Iowa is beginning to live in literature," said the preface. "We have our Garland, Quick and Suckow who may mean as much to us as Hardy means to Wessex. . . . If there is any reason why anyone anywhere should read the product of Iowa literary people, their poetry, their drama and their stories, surely it is Iowans themselves." The book is valuable for its descriptions of living Iowa writers written by their peers and critics: Brigham, Aldrich, Butler, Byers, Ficke, Frederick, French, Garland, Glaspell, Hall, Hough, Piper, Quick, L. W. Smith, Suckow, Sigmund, Muilenburg, Roger L. Sergel, Walter L. Myers, Nelson Antrim Crawford, and a number of others. The authors of the essays were Mott, Frederick, L. W. Smith, Brigham, Thomas Duncan, Gladys Denny Shultz, Helen Cowles LeCron, and others. "There are in Iowa dozens of young writers each seeing the life here in a different way," the book concluded. "Gradually will be born a literary Iowa."

". . . What a remarkable, what a decisive, literary transformation has taken place in a single generation," said Professor Sam B. Sloan in *Palimpsest* in 1931. "Within our own time, we have seen the literary grip of the eastern States and the southern States loosen, and the place they once proudly held has been passed on to the Middle West—the Middle West that used to be thought of as the home of hogs and hominy, and only hogs and hominy. . . . Most of what is original in American fiction, penetrating in American fiction, and significant in American fiction the last fourteen or fifteen years has emanated from Iowa and the surrounding States."[25]

23 John T. Frederick, "Editorial," *The Midland* 20 (March–June 1933): following p. 54.
24 Wallace Stegner, "The Trail of the Hawkeye," *Saturday Review of Literature* 18 (July 30, 1938):4, 16.
25 Sam Sloan, "Misrepresentative Fiction," *Palimpsest* 12 (February 1931):42–44.

But it was not easy to persuade those outside the state that Iowa had become a literary and aesthetic center; in New York, for instance (from whose literary critics Iowa writers have constantly had to take their lumps, as we have seen) the attitude was more likely to be this:

What is Iowa? One of the purest landholding communities on the face of the globe; a State of 200,000 farms; a region settled by Southerners, Yankees, and Germans, now merged into a uniform mass; a land of high literacy, diffused comfort, narrow vision, and drab plodding life; where nobody is poor, but the young aspire to cities far away and the retired farmers yearn for California; a State of mortgages, of movies, of lodges, of pervasive evangelism, of Fords, of mail-order catalogues, of prohibition, of Cummins and Brookhart. It has more telephones and eggs and autos and purebred hogs per capita than any other commonwealth; but a gibe by one of its sons, Ellis Parker Butler, about the comparative expenditures for manure and for literature indicates what many think of its spiritual expressions. Its largest centre, Des Moines, is a town of placid attractiveness, and it is full of idyllic nooks and picturesque streams; but it is one of the last States we associate with beauty.[26]

But ten years later, in 1938, Wallace Stegner could report that this older attitude was changing, and Iowa's reputation as a literary and aesthetic center was becoming established.[27]

Sam Sloan's essay was one of the first in a long *Palimpsest* series on Iowa literature and writers. The magazine looked at Susan Glaspell, S. H. M. Byers, Emerson Hough, Orion Clemens, Robert J. Burdette, Bertha M. Shambaugh, Harriet Connor Brown (author of *Grandmother Brown's Hundred Years 1827–1927*), Herbert Quick, Johnson Brigham, and many others. An especially fine contribution to this series was made by John T. Frederick in the early nineteen-fifties.[28]

An equally important contribution to Iowa literature was made in 1930 with the establishment of the School of Letters under the direction of Norman Foerster. It had already been possible for students at the University of Iowa to obtain advanced degrees with imaginative theses, but now there came into being a formal program.

About this time the long-smouldering quarrel over "local color" and "regionalism" in art and letters burst out anew. It was not localized in Iowa, but the novels of Ruth Suckow and the paintings of Grant Wood (and their aesthetic theories as well) played a prominent part.

---

26 Allan Nevins, "A Painter of Iowa," *Saturday Review of Literature* 18 (March 10, 1928):666.
27 Stegner, "The Trail of the Hawkeye," pp. 3–4, 16.
28 William J. Petersen, *Iowa History Reference Guide* (State Historical Society of Iowa, 1952). Pages 126–31 list many of these essays but not all. Also consult annual indexes to the *Palimpsest*.

The quarrel over regionalism was economic, political, social, and aesthetic. In economic terms it represented an attack by those outside New York City against monopolies, "chains," trusts, and the vested interests of those symbolized by Wall Street and the stock market. Politically, it was the quarrel between "collectivists," those arguing that our governmental structure had broken down and needed replacement by another system, one which resembled communism or socialism, and those arguing for the retention of the democratic system. Socially, it was in Grant Wood's phrase, "a revolt against the city," a return to agrarianism, to emphasis on the values of rural living, the qualities of farm life and small town life. Aesthetically, it was a quarrel over the focus in art on regions —the Middle West, the South, the Southwest, the Indians, the poor white, the Iowa farmer, and the like.

Grant Wood's statement summarized the situation:

Regionalism seeks to direct preponderating attention to the natural landscape, human geography, and cultural life of particular areas of the country, in the belief that writers who draw their materials from their own experience and the life they know best are more likely to attain universal values than those who do not.

And Wood added:

In this country, Regionalism has taken the form of a revolt against the cultural domination of the city (particularly New York) and the tendency of metropolitan cliques to lay more emphasis on artificial precepts than on more vital human experience. It is not, to my knowledge, a revolt against industrial civilization (in the William Morris sense), though it has reemphasized the fact that America is agrarian as well as industrial. It has been a revolt against cultural nationalism—that is, the tendency of artists to ignore or deny the fact that there are important differences, psychologically and otherwise, between the various regions of America.[29]

In *Palimpsest* for February 1930, John Frederick called attention to the work of "the younger school" of Iowa writers "in the whole movement of Middle Western realism, which in turn is a part of that nation-wide literary movement called 'regionalism'—certainly the most important development in American literature in the past generation."[30] As members of this younger school, he enumerated Sergel, Muilenburg, Sigmund, Clarence Sundermeyer of Mallard, Iowa, and later of the Department of

---

29   Grant Wood, "A Definition of Regionalism," *Books at Iowa* 3 (November 1965): 3. See also Wood's *Revolt Against the City* (Iowa City, Iowa: Clio Press, 1935).
30   John Frederick, "The Younger School," *Palimpsest* 11 (February 1930):78–86.

English at the university at Ames, Vernon Lichtenstein of Coe College, Grace Hunter of Grinnell, James Hearst, J. G. Neumann, Thomas Duncan, and Ruth Suckow.

The emphasis on Iowa literature was producing some interesting side-effects. At Des Moines the Maizeland Press, established for the production of Iowa literature flourished briefly in the late twenties. At Grinnell College, the *Tanager*, a journal primarily literary, was published on a bi-monthly basis after 1926, and carried articles by James Norman Hall, Ruth Suckow, Carl Sandburg, Gamaliel Bradford, and Hamilton Holt, as well as many less distinguished contributors. At Cornell the *Husk* and *Chapbooks* flourished; at Dubuque, the *Dial* survived for four numbers in 1934 and 1935; in Iowa City, the Clio Press projected a Whirling World series.

Disappointed by the removal from Iowa City of *The Midland* and its subsequent cessation of publication, the University of Iowa's School of Letters proposed a new literary magazine as a "place where young American writers could write the 'prefaces' to their careers, where they could try their wings and speak their minds without the necessity of 'slanting' their work toward one of the commercial magazines." With a glance at the University of Iowa theater, the magazine said that its opportunities would be similar to those of "the experimental theatre which gives the playwright a chance to produce work not necessarily salable on Broadway."[31]

Within its first year of publication, Wilbur L. Schramm, the editor of *American Prefaces* (begun in October 1935, with seven subscribers), was able to report that O'Brien's *Best Stories of 1936* had selected one of its stories (by Robert Whitehand) for inclusion and moreover had dedicated the volume to Mr. Whitehand, that Harry Hansen had selected Elsie Katterjohn's "Teachers" for the *O. Henry Memorial* volume, and that Milford Wence's "The Good Bed" had been anthologized. Five years later the magazine reported that it had survived the depression and had published Paul Engle, Eleanor Saltzman, Karleton Kelm, Sigmund, Piper, Verlin Cassill, Zatha Pilson Weems, Marion Louise Bliss, Hearst, Hall, Joseph Langland, Grant Wood (essays and reproductions of paintings), Sadie Seagrave, Kresensky, and Ferner Nuhn, among a host which also included T. S. Eliot and Ole Rölvaag.

In 1940, Paul Engle became associate editor, and the magazine changed to a smaller, better-bound format with more pages. The magazine continued successfully, but with an emphasis on the national scene, until the summer of 1943 when the editors announced suspension of publication

---

31 "One Year of *American Prefaces*," *American Prefaces* 2 (October 1936):15.

because of the war. After the war, Ray B. West came to the University of Iowa with his *Western Review*. This monthly publication continued until Mr. West's departure from the campus some fifteen years later. For several years there was no continuous literary publication at the University. Then in the winter of 1970 the first issue of a vigorous new quarterly—the *Iowa Review*—was published.

In that same year of 1935 in which *American Prefaces* began, Carroll Coleman founded his Prairie Press at Muscatine. Three and a half decades later, it was still a prosperous operation, although it moved to Iowa City in 1945. Coleman expressed his purposes for beginning the Press:

> I had given ear to the preachings of my friend, Grant Wood . . . and I was convinced that I could do no better than to follow, in publishing, the regionalism which he advocated in painting. I envisioned writers, artists and printers working together to produce beautiful books which would embody the life and thought of the heart of this great Mississippi valley region. Here on the rolling prairies, on the hills among the rivers, in the endless fields of corn that bend before the summer wind in green waves, in the soft little cities hardening under the growth of industrialism, these writers, artists and printers might record and preserve, for all to see, the form and direction of life here in the Middlewest.[32]

In his three and a half decades, Coleman has published over a hundred and fifty books. Two matters interest him—"the content of the books he publishes is always of the first importance; the typography is a secondary matter, but a very important one." His goal is to bring type (representing the subject matter and appearance as well) together with paper to produce fine books, and in that he has succeeded.[33]

Coleman's first published book was an anthology of *Contemporary Iowa Poets*, printed in an edition of two hundred twenty copies. Since then he has published volumes by Sigmund, Don Farran, Thomas Duncan, Hearst, Stegner, Hall, Engle, L. O. Cheever, Ruth Lechlitner (Mrs. Paul Corey), and Mott.

The net result of all this effort (and much else) in the nineteen-thirties led to a great feeling of optimism both within and outside of Iowa over its literature and art. In the late nineteen-thirties, Tremaine McDowell looked enviously at Iowa from its northern neighbor, Minnesota, and said:

> The state which is at the moment [1939] most articulate in literature is one for which few observers in the early century would have predicted such

---

32   L. O. Cheever, "The Prairie Press: A Thirty-Year Record," *Books at Iowa* 3 (November 1965):16.
33   Cheever, "The Prairie Press: A Thirty-Year Record," p. 16.

achievement, the state which, according to one of its native sons, Ellis Parker Butler, spends twelve dollars for fertilizer every time it spends one dollar for literature—Iowa.[34]

"Iowa," said Wallace Stegner, "has definitely come of age."[35]

But time and those drums of war which were to drown out *American Prefaces* came and passed—and took with them the hope for an Iowa literature which we have seen developing. After World War II, Paul Engle looked further and further afield for new talent, and the Iowa Writers Workshop became national and international in its scope. At present it has one Iowan on its staff, and young Robert Coover (born in Charles City) does not regard himself as an Iowa writer. Of those Iowans who are still writing, Verlin Cassill, Joseph Langland, Martin Yoseloff, and Richard Bissell live in the northeastern United States; MacKinlay Kantor lives in Florida; Calvin Kentfield, Thomas Duncan, and Paul Corey live in California. Frederick Manfred lives only a few miles from the place of his birth—but on the Minnesota side of the line! Only Paul Engle and James Hearst remain in their native state. Other than these two—and as this is written, Julie McDonald and Dow Mossman—only the Iowans who write annually for *Lyrical Iowa* now seem to deserve the title of Iowa authors.

But interest in Iowa literature is not dead. In 1945, the University of Iowa began its Iowa Authors Collection with the goal of building as complete a collection as possible of books by Iowa authors (those who have been born or have written in the state). In 1964, the Friends of the University of Iowa Libraries began publication of *Books at Iowa*, a biennial which often looks at Iowa authors, and in 1967 the same group published Frank Paluka's *Iowa Authors: A Bio-Bibliography of Sixty Native Writers*. Somewhere about that time the Correspondence Bureau of the University of Iowa initiated a course in "The Literature of Iowa." And libraries all over the state have built and are building collections of Iowa and local material.

At the same time, book publishers, in-state and out, are continuing to take a backward look at Iowa writers. In the last few years biographies and critical studies have appeared for Glaspell, Garland, Hough, Quick, Van Vechten, Alice French, Ruth Suckow, and others; Dorothy Dondore's *The Prairie and the Making of Middle America* and the entire run of *The Midland* have been reprinted; James Hearst and his associates at Cedar Falls are planning a volume of verse by Iowa poets; and *Vande-*

---

34 Tremaine McDowell, "Regionalism in American Literature," *Minnesota History* 20 (June 1939):114–15.
35 Wallace Stegner, "The Trail of the Hawkeye," p. 3.

mark's Folly, The Covered Wagon, Boy Life on the Prairie, Pigs is Pigs, a Ruth Suckow anthology, and other volumes by Iowa authors are being reissued.

But for creative writers—writers of short stories, novels, plays, and poetry—the job is not complete, as John T. Frederick has said:

The unused materials and unrecognized opportunities in the field far exceed those that have been utilized. Whole regions of the state have been neglected. Where are the novels which capture the immensely rich life of the great rivers which border the state, in their intimate relationship to the life of the people of the farms and towns beside them? Where is the novel which pictures the landscape of the northeastern corner of the state and its effect? We lack authoritative revelation of the dynamic relationship between farm and town in Iowa—especially in terms of the lives of business and professional men, merchants, doctors, and lawyers. We lack adequate portrayals of success in farming as opposed to failure—of the lives of the relatively prosperous and happy. In recent years the nation as a whole has been aroused to a new concern for the land itself, a questioning as to what we have done with our land and what we are to do with it. The American people are beginning to see, with rapidly increasing sharpness and clearness, the basic importance for the very preservation of our national life and the race itself of that essentially religious feeling for the land—that sense of stewardship—which has always been the mark of the true farmer. The writer can always find fresh terms for that ancient and ageless theme, men in relation to the earth.[36]

Iowa, what is there to sing? As the nation faces its bicentennial, beset with fear and plagued with doubt, perhaps a new generation of writers and artists, raised in the lush green of an Iowa farm or the streets of an Iowa small town, or even in one of the state's larger cities, will find answers to the first and, at the same time, solutions to the latter—and a new Iowa literature will arise.

------

36 John T. Frederick, "Town and City in Iowa Fiction," *Palimpsest* 35 (February 1954):151–52.

Bibliography

CHAPTER 1:

A Checklist of Iowa Imprints. Chicago: WPA Historical Records Survey Project, 1940. Catalog of early Iowa printed items.

Moffit, Alexander. "A Check List of Iowa Imprints: 1837–1860." *Iowa Journal of History and Politics* 36 (January and April 1938):3–95, 152–205. Catalog of early Iowa printed items.

Petersen, William J. *Iowa History Reference Guide.* Iowa City: State Historical Society of Iowa, 1952. An excellent bibliography of books about the history of Iowa and other subjects.

Tanselle, G. Thomas. *Guide to the Study of United States Imprints.* 2 vols. Cambridge: Harvard University Press, Belknap Press, 1971. Contains a listing of all known bibliographies of Iowa authors to date, and a listing of bibliographical information about Iowa private and public presses.

Wright, Luella M. "Verse in the Newspapers." *Palimpsest* 19 (May 1938): 173–84; "Journalistic Literature." *Palimpsest* 19 (December 1938):503–14. In these two essays, a former member of the Department of English at the University of Iowa has fully discussed the very early publication of fiction and verse in the territorial newspapers. She notes a heavy dependency on English and eastern American writers, and the publication of considerable overly sentimental verse and fiction. Much of the material had been lifted (probably without prearrangement) from books, magazines, and periodicals. *Palimpsest* is a monthly publication of the State Historical Society of Iowa, Iowa City. Since its inception in August 1920, it has published many articles about the Iowa literary scene.

CHAPTER 2:

Dondore, Dorothy Anne. *The Prairie and the Making of Middle America: Four Centuries of Description.* Cedar Rapids, Iowa: Torch Press, 1926. Reprinted. This book was "the first serious attempt to show the influence of the American Frontier on Literature." Professor Dondore traced out in detail the descriptions of the Mississippi Valley by explorers, missionaries, officials and travelers, revealing the glamor of the land and the chief factors in its settlement. The dust jacket of the book remarked: "In the later chapters [Professor Dondore] discusses the imaginative treatments of the middle western frontier, the portrayal of the distinctive characters and phases of its life in American and foreign novels, plays and short stories, in border ballads, campaign and minstrel songs, narrative poems, and free verse. The development of the territory and the resultant realistic interpretations [are] also depicted." Serious students of the literature west of the Alleghanies and east of the Rockies are forever in Professor Dondore's debt.

Mott, Frank Luther. *Literature of Pioneer Life in Iowa.* Iowa City: State Historical Society of Iowa, 1923. This volume contains an essay on the title subject, and a partially annotated bibliography. For the literature of pioneer Iowa consult this book and William J. Petersen's *Iowa History Reference Guide.*

Willard, P. E. "Franklin Wells Calkins: A Biographical Sketch." *The Midland Monthly* 6 (June 1895):569–71. Has information about Calkins, some of whose stories appear in 5:145–53 and 7:439–42. See also "Editorial Comment," 6:574.

CHAPTER 3:

Dougherty, Charles T. "Novels of the Middle-Border: A Critical Bibliography for Historians." *Historical Bulletin* 25 (May 1947). Not entirely accurate in its comments.

Paluka, Frank. *Iowa Authors: A Bio-Bibliography of Sixty Native Writers.* Iowa City, Iowa: Friends of The University of Iowa Libraries, 1967. Contains complete publication records of Aldrich, Kantor, Wilson, Hough, and Downing.

CHAPTER 4:

McMichael, George. *Journey to Obscurity: The Life of Octave Thanet.* Lincoln: University of Nebraska Press, 1965. A definitive and excellent record of the time in which Alice French lived. The bibliography of her writings and of secondary sources is comprehensive. My own chapter owes a considerable debt to Dean McMichael; it appeared in a different version in *The Iowan* (Winter 1969). The Newberry Library in Chicago is the repository of many of Alice French's papers and photographs. There may be additional materials in the Davenport Public Library and in the Davenport Public Museum. As of 1969, the manuscripts, documents, and books in the latter were uncatalogued.

CHAPTER 5:

Other relevant works by Garland not mentioned in this chapter:

Garland, Hamlin. *A Member of the Third House*. Chicago: F. J. Scholte & Co., 1892.

——. *The Long Trail*. New York: Harper and Brothers, 1907.

——. *The Trail of the Goldseekers*. New York: Macmillan Co., 1899.

——. *Wayside Courtships*. New York: D. Appleton and Co., 1897.

——. *Roadside Meetings*. New York: Macmillan Co., 1930. Illustrated by Constance Garland.

——. *Companions on the Trail*. New York: Macmillan Co., 1931.

——. *My Friendly Contemporaries*. New York: Macmillan Co., 1932. Decorated by Constance Garland.

——. *Afternoon Neighbors*. New York: Macmillan Co., 1934.

Andrews, Clarence A. "Hamlin Garland the Prairie Realist." *The Iowan* (Summer 1970). Another version of the present chapter and additional information.

Holloway, Jean. *Hamlin Garland: A Biography*. Austin: University of Texas Press, 1960. List of Garland's publications and bibliography.

Meyer, Roy W. *The Middle Western Farm Novel in the Twentieth Century*. Lincoln: University of Nebraska Press, 1965.

CHAPTER 6:

Andrews, Clarence A. "Prose Poet of the Prairie." *The Iowan* (Winter 1970). Another version of the present chapter and additional information.

Meyer, Roy W. *The Middle Western Farm Novel in the Twentieth Century*. Lincoln: University of Nebraska Press, 1965.

Paluka, Frank. *Iowa Authors: A Bio-Bibliography of Sixty Native Writers*. Iowa City, Iowa: Friends of The University of Iowa Libraries, 1967.

CHAPTER 7:

Books at Iowa. Iowa City, Iowa: Friends of The University of Iowa Libraries. Numbers 1 and 2 (October 1964 and April 1965) have information about Ruth Suckow manuscripts in the library.

Brigham, Johnson, ed. *A Book of Iowa Authors by Iowa Authors*. Des

Moines, Iowa: Iowa State Teachers Association, 1930. See Frank Luther Mott's estimate of Ruth Suckow.

Kissane, Leedice McAnnelly. *Ruth Suckow*. New York: Twayne Publishers, 1969. Contains a bibliography.

Mohr, Martin. "Ruth Suckow—Regionalism and Beyond." Master's thesis, University of Iowa, 1955.

Paluka, Frank. *Iowa Authors: A Bio-Bibliography of Sixty Native Writers*. Iowa City, Iowa: Friends of The University of Iowa Libraries, 1967.

Stewart, Margaret O'Brien. "A Critical Study of Ruth Suckow's Fiction." Ph.D. dissertation, University of Illinois, 1960.

The Iowan. Shenandoah, Iowa. The October–November 1960 issue has an "unpublished diary," and the periodical has published other Suckow material.

"Ruth Suckow Memorial Issue." *Midwest* (Spring 1960). Publication of Iowa State Teachers College [University of Northern Iowa].

CHAPTER 8:

DeBoer, Peter P. "Frederick Manfred: The Developing Art of the Novelist." Master's thesis, University of Iowa, 1961.

Heilman, Robert B. "Versions of Documentary, Arts and Letters." *Sewanee Review* 56:678–79.

Kellogg, George. *Frederick Manfred: A Bibliography*. Swallow Pamphlets, No. 17. Almost complete through 1965.

Milton, John R. "Frederick Feikema Manfred." *Western Review* 22:181–87.

Nemerov, Howard. "Of Giants and Islands." *Sewanee Review* 58:539–40.

Paluka, Frank. *Iowa Authors: A Bio-Bibliography of Sixty Native Writers*. Iowa City, Iowa: Friends of The University of Iowa Libraries, 1967.

Stong, Phil. *Hawkeyes*. New York: Dodd, Mead & Co., 1940.

———. *If School Keeps*. New York: Frederick A. Stokes Co., 1940.

CHAPTER 9:

Kramer, Dale. *The Wild Jackasses: The American Farmer in Revolt*. New York: Hastings House, 1956.

Kellogg, George. *Frederick Manfred: A Bibliography*. Swallow Pamphlets, No. 17.

Meyer, Roy W. *The Middle Western Farm Novel in the Twentieth Century*. Lincoln: University of Nebraska Press, 1965.

Paluka, Frank. *Iowa Authors: A Bio-Bibliography of Sixty Native Writers*. Iowa City, Iowa: The Friends of The University of Iowa Libraries, 1967.

Petersen, William J. *Iowa History Reference Guide*. Iowa City, Iowa: State Historical Society of Iowa, 1952. A bibliography of Iowa articles and books which supplements Paluka and Meyer. See also listings under "Agriculture."

Reninger, H. Willard. Essay in James Hearst. *Man and His Field: Selected Poems*. Denver: Alan Swallow, 1951.

———. "Afterword" in James Hearst. *Limited View*. Denver: Alan Swallow, 1963.

Sherman, Caroline. "Farm Life Fiction Reaches Maturity." *Sewanee Review* 29:472–83.

CHAPTER 10:

Brigham, Johnson, ed. *A Book of Iowa Authors by Iowa Authors*. Des Moines, Iowa: State Teachers Association, 1930. See Frank Luther Mott's essay on Ellis Parker Butler.

Burdette, Clara B. *Robert J. Burdette: His Message*. Philadelphia: John C. Winston Co., 1922.

Frederick, John T. "Town and City in Iowa Fiction." *Palimpsest* 35:57–58.

Paluka, Frank. *Iowa Authors: A Bio-Bibliography of Sixty Native Writers*. Iowa City, Iowa: Friends of The University of Iowa Libraries, 1967.

CHAPTER 11:

Brigham, Johnson, ed. *A Book of Iowa Authors by Iowa Authors*. Des Moines, Iowa: Iowa State Teachers Association, 1930.

Cook, George Cram. *Greek Coins*. New York: George H. Doran Co., 1925. In addition to the poems there are essays by Floyd Dell, Edna Kenton, and Susan Glaspell illuminating the life and art of Cook and the Davenport group.

Dell, Floyd. *Homecoming: An Autobiography*. New York: Farrar & Rinehart, 1933. Account of the interrelationships of the Davenport group, and many poems. The Newberry Library has a collection of Floyd Dell's manuscripts and books.

———. *Moon-Calf*. New York: Alfred A. Knopf, 1920. Includes a fictional account of Dell's life in Davenport.

Ficke, Charles August. *Memories of Fourscore Years.* Davenport, Iowa: 1930. Davenport pioneer record, with many incidents in the life of Arthur Davison Ficke.

Glaspell, Susan. *The Road to the Temple.* New York: Frederick A. Stokes Co., 1927. A biography of George Cram Cook with four illustrations.

Hansen, Harry. *Midwest Portraits.* New York: Harcourt, Brace & Co., 1923.

———. "A Davenport Boyhood." *Palimpsest* 37:215.

Hart, John E. *Floyd Dell.* New York: Twayne Publishers, 1971. Critical and biographical material. Also see Hart's 1962 essay in *Western Humanities Review.*

McDonald, Julie. "A Bohemian Ahead of His Time." *The Iowan* (Summer 1970). Account of Floyd Dell.

McMichael, George. *Journey to Obscurity: The Life of Octave Thanet.* Lincoln: University of Nebraska Press, 1965. The life of Alice French (Octave Thanet) and an excellent account of Davenport in the years 1875–1920.

Paluka, Frank. *Iowa Authors: A Bio-Bibliography of Sixty Native Writers.* Iowa City, Iowa: Friends of The University of Iowa Libraries, 1967.

Smith, William Jay. *The Spectra Hoax.* Middletown, Conn.: Wesleyan University Press, 1961. Insights into the life of Arthur Davison Ficke. All of his contributions to the original *Spectra* are included.

Tanselle, G. Thomas. "Faun at the Barricades." Ph.D. dissertation, Northwestern University, 1959. A study of Floyd Dell with an extensive bibliography.

Waterman, Arthur E. *Susan Glaspell.* New York: Twayne Publishers, 1966. A typical Twayne treatment with a useful bibliography.

CHAPTER 12:

Cassill, R. V. "Introduction" to *Fifteen by Three.* New York: New Directions, 1957. R. V. Cassill, James B. Hall, and Herbert Gold contributed to this volume.

Clements, Ralph. *Tales of the Town: Little-known Anecdotes of Life in Cedar Rapids.* Cedar Rapids, Iowa: Stamats Publishing Co., 1967. Photographs and anecdotes of Engle, Van Vechten, Sigmund, and Grant Wood and their times.

Cornell College *Husk.* March 1922 to May 1967. Fiction, poetry, essays. Single issues concentrate on writers such as Jay G. Sigmund.

Cornell College *Chapbooks*. Numbers 1–30. Since 1935. Much material with an Iowa orientation.

Engle, Paul, ed. *Midland*. New York: Random House, 1961. Collection of poetry and stories drawn from twenty-five years of the Iowa Writers Workshop. Introduction and brief biographies.

Haselmayer, Louis A. "Three Contemporary Poets in Iowa." *Iowa English Yearbook* (Fall 1959), pp. 2–4. Sympathetic study of Paul Engle's poetry.

Kellner, Bruce. *Carl Van Vechten and the Irreverent Decades*. Norman: University of Oklahoma Press, 1968. Definitive life of Van Vechten. Lueders reports some additional details.

Lueders, Edward. *Carl Van Vechten*. New York: Twayne Publishers, 1965.

Paluka, Frank. *Iowa Authors: A Bio-Bibliography of Sixty Native Writers*. Iowa City, Iowa: Friends of The University of Iowa Libraries, 1967.

Tull, Clyde, and Plummer, Anya, eds. *Stories From the Husk*. Mount Vernon, Iowa: English Club of Cornell College, 1940. Commemorates the twentieth anniversary of the founding of the *Husk*.

CHAPTER 13:

Aldrich, Robert Streeter. "Introduction" *A Bess Streeter Aldrich Treasury*. New York: Appleton-Century-Crofts, 1959.

Brigham, Johnson, ed. *A Book of Iowa Authors by Iowa Authors*. Des Moines, Iowa: Iowa State Teachers Association, 1930.

Contemporary Iowa Poets. Muscatine, Iowa: The Prairie Press, 1935. Carroll Coleman's first book at The Prairie Press. Only 220 copies printed.

A First Book of Iowa Poets. Des Moines, Iowa: The Maizeland Press, 1928. Poems of twenty-nine poets then living in Iowa. The editor was probably Victor Schultz.

Flannery, Agnes V. *Iowa Centennial 1846–1946 Poetry Anthology*. Lake Mills, Iowa: 1946. Contains an essay on Iowa poets by Margaret Hoffman Graper.

Haselmayer, Louis A. "Three Contemporary Poets in Iowa." *Iowa English Yearbook* (Fall 1959), pp. 6–7. Critique of the work of Raymond Kresensky.

Herringshaw, Thomas, ed. *Poets and Poetry of Iowa*. Chicago: American Publishers Association, 1894. Contains biographies of the poets represented.

Hunter, Grace, and Kresensky, Raymond, eds. *A List of Iowa Poets*. Iowa Poetry Association, 1953. Biographical data on more than one hundred Iowa poets.

Iowa Poets: An Anthology of 69 Contemporaries. New York: Henry Harrison, Publisher, 1935. Foreword by Jay G. Sigmund. Cartoon frontispiece by Grant Wood. Literary map of Iowa on the endpapers by Harriet Macy. Valuable for its record of poets of some stature in Iowa about 1935.

Iowa Poetry Association. *Iowa Poems.* 1946.

————. *Lyrical Iowa.* 1947 to date. Best of submitted poems to the Association in annual volumes.

Kantor, MacKinlay. *But Look the Morn.* New York: Coward-McCann, 1947. Kantor's story of his life in Webster City, Iowa.

Kresensky, Raymond. *Selected Poems.* Francestown, N.H.: Golden Quill Press, 1956. Edward L. Mayo's introduction is very good.

Luke, Lou Mallory. *Who's Who Among Prairie Poets.* Des Moines, Iowa: E. L. Kuhne, 1938. Inventory of Iowa poets by well-known Iowa poet of the time.

Paluka, Frank. *Iowa Authors: A Bio-Bibliography of Sixty Native Writers.* Iowa City, Iowa: Friends of The University of Iowa Libraries, 1967.

Smith, Mrs. Lewis Worthington (Jessica Welborn). *What of the Iowa Poets?* New York: Henry Harrison, Poetry Publisher, 1941. Lewis Worthington Smith, Drake University English professor, taught Phil Stong and Thomas Duncan, among others. Mrs. Smith considers nineteenth century Iowa poets as well as those of this century. She also mentions Iowans who have become poets laureate in other states.

Smith, Mrs. L. Worthington, ed. *Silk of the Corn.* New York: Henry Harrison, 1932. This record of poets writing in Iowa in 1932 was published by the Iowa Federation of Women's Clubs.

Smith, William Jay. *The Spectra Hoax.* Middletown, Conn.: Wesleyan University Press, 1961. Contains an account of the *Oh Millersville!* hoax. See also "Fern Gravel: A Hoax and a Confession." *Atlantic Monthly* (September 1946).

Westburg, John Edward. "The Life and Poetry of Raymond Kresensky." *The North American Mentor Anthology of Poems.* Conesville, Iowa: John Westburg & Associates, 1965. A special Raymond Kresensky edition.

CHAPTER 14:

Allen, Charles. "American Little Magazines—IV. *The Midland.*" *American Prefaces* 3:136–40. This 1938 history of *The Midland* was approved by its founder and editor John T. Frederick.

American Prefaces 2 (1937):81–96. The March issue is entirely by or about Edwin Ford Piper.

Books at Iowa. Friends of The University of Iowa Libraries, Iowa City: Iowa, 1964 to date. Many articles on Iowa writers and literature.

Brigham, Johnson. "Iowa as a Literary Field." *Prairie Gold.* Chicago: Reilly & Britton Co., 1917. Contains an excellent survey of Iowa writers (pp. 318 ff.).

————, ed. *A Book of Iowa Authors by Iowa Authors.* Des Moines, Iowa: Iowa State Teachers Association, 1930.

Cao, Myra. "Some Children's Books by Iowa Authors." *Books at Iowa* 9 (1968):3–21. Partial to complete bibliographies of sixteen children's authors and descriptions of books by types.

Earley, Jane F. "Iowa Authors: A Bibliography of Published Works 1917–1940." Honors thesis, Coe College, Cedar Rapids, Iowa, 1961. Supplements Marple's *Iowa Authors and Their Works* (1918).

The Iowan. Shenandoah, Iowa, 1952 to date. First a monthly, now a quarterly. Many articles about Iowa authors.

Marple, Alice. *Iowa Authors and Their Works: A Contribution Toward a Bibliography.* Des Moines, Iowa: Historical Department of Iowa, 1918. Comprehensive listing of writers who were "of Iowa birth or worked in Iowa," and who published substantially.

Mott, Frank Luther. *Literature of Pioneer Life in Iowa.* Iowa City, Iowa: State Historical Society of Iowa, 1923. Definitive, partially annotated bibliography included.

Odum, Howard W., and Moore, Harry E. *American Regionalism: A Cultural-Historical Approach to National Integration.* New York: Henry Holt and Co., 1938.

Schaffner, Neil E., with Johnson, Vance. *The Fabulous Toby & Me.* Englewood Cliffs, N.J.: Prentice-Hall, 1968. Non-definitive account of "tent repertoire" theater in the Middle West, especially Iowa. Focus is on the "Toby" character and the "Toby" play, a folk art which originated in Iowa.

Wright, Luella M. "The Midland Monthly." *Iowa Journal of History and Politics* 45 (1947):3–61. Definitive study of Iowa's first literary magazine.

Index